Harvard Historical Studies · 135

Published under the auspices
of the Department of History
from the income of the
Paul Revere Frothingham Bequest
Robert Louis Stroock Fund
Henry Warren Torrey Fund

The Invention of the Restaurant

Paris and Modern Gastronomic Culture

Rebecca L. Spang

HARVARD UNIVERSITY PRESS

Cambridge, Massachusetts, and London, England | 2000

First Harvard University Press paperback edition, 2001

Library of Congress Cataloging-in-Publication Data

Spang, Rebecca L., 1961–
    The invention of the restaurant : Paris and modern gastronomic culture /
Rebecca L. Spang.
      p. cm. — (Harvard historical studies ; 135)
    Includes bibliographical references and index.
    ISBN 0-674-00064-1 (cloth)
    ISBN 0-674-00685-2 (pbk.)
    1. Restaurants—France—Paris—History—18th century.
    2. Restaurants—France—Paris—History—19th century.
    3. Food habits—France—Paris—History—18th century.
    4. Food habits—France—Paris—History—19th century.
    5. Paris (France)—Social life and customs.
    I. Title.   II. Harvard historical studies ; v. 135.

TX910.F8 S667 2000
647.95443'61'09033—dc21   99-053378

Contents

Illustrations

RESTAURANT: Food or remedy that has the property of restoring lost strength to a sickly or tired individual. Consommé and extract of partridge are excellent restaurants. Wine, brandy, and cordials are all good restaurants for those whose spirits are drained. Some restaurants are distilled from the juices of light, flavorful meats combined with soft white bread, stimulating waters and powders, conserves, electuaries, and other good and sweet-smelling ingredients. Aspic is a sort of restaurant, but it is more nourishing and of a firmer consistency than a restaurant, which is liquid.

FURETIÈRE, *DICTIONNAIRE UNIVERSEL* (1708)

Recipe for Quintessence or Restaurant: Place several slices of onion, a little beef marrow, and some nice, white veal in a well-tinned and very clean casserole; on top of the veal place several clean and defatted ham rinds and then some slices of carrot and parsnip. Take a healthy chicken, very recently killed, and clean it thoroughly inside and out; cut it into pieces and then crush them; place them, still warm, in your kettle, and then put a few more strips of veal and ham rind. Note that for two *pintes* [approximately two quarts] of this quintessence, you will need only about four or five pounds of veal and perhaps four ounces of ham, in addition to the chicken. All being well arranged in your casserole, add a glass of bouillon; seal the kettle tightly, and put it on a high flame. If you place it first over low heat the meat yields its juices but does not brown, so then the liquid sticks and clots to the meat such that it hardens during the cooking process and does not fall to the bottom of the pan to form the restaurant.

When the meat has browned, place it over a moderate flame to sweat for three-quarters of an hour. Be careful that nothing sticks to the pan, and occasionally moisten it with a bit of bouillon, just enough so that the restaurant is neither too bitter nor too strong, but sweet, creamy, and proper for a variety of sauces, which ordinarily are made with ingredients that have their own taste and scent. Many cooks might put strongly flavored items in this quintessence, such as garlic, cloves, basil, mushrooms, etcetera, but I prefer the simpler fashion as I believe it to be the best both for taste and for health.

MARIN, *LES DONS DE COMUS* (1739)

RESTAURATEURS: Restaurateurs are those who have the skill of making true consommés, called restaurants or the prince's bouillons, and who have the right to sell all sorts of creams, rice and vermicelli soups, fresh eggs, macaroni, stewed capons, confitures, compotes, and other delicate and salutary dishes.

These new establishments, which from the beginning have been called Restaurants or Houses of Health, owe their 1766 institution in this capital to Messieurs Roze and Pontaillé.

The first of these Restaurants, which in no way cedes anything to the most beautiful cafés, was opened on the rue des Poulies; but not being in a favorable enough locale, it was transferred to the rue Saint Honoré, hôtel d'Aligre, where it is run with the same success, and on the same principles of cleanliness, decency, and honesty that must always form the base of this type of business.

The price of each item is specific and fixed; one may be served at any hour. Ladies are admitted and may have their catered dinners prepared for a set and moderate price. This establishment has for its slogan this charming couplet:

Hic sapidè titillunt juscula blanda palatum,
Hic datur effaetis pectoribusque salus.
[Here are tasty sauces to titillate your bland palate,
Here the effete find healthy chests.]

[MATHURIN ROZE DE CHANTOISEAU], *TABLETTES DE
RENOMMÉE OU ALMANACH GÉNÉRAL D'INDICATION* (1773)

RESTAURANT, adj., that which restores or repairs strength. *restorative remedy. restorative potion. restorative food.*

It is more generally used as a substantive. *Wine and bouillon are good restaurants.*

It is particularly said of a very tasty consommé, or a meat extract.

By extension, the establishment of a restaurateur. *A new restaurant just opened on this street. He runs a restaurant.*

RESTAURATEUR, noun, he or she who repairs or re-establishes. It is rarely used, except for cities and public monuments. *This city had been ruined, and the prince rebuilt it. He is its restaurateur.*

It is more often used in the moral sense. *This prince is the restaurateur of literature and the arts. That abbé was the restaurateur of the prior discipline to his order. Restaurateur of liberty, commerce, of law and order, etc.* . . .

Restaurateur is also used for a cook-caterer who provides foods at all hours, the type and price of which are indicated on a sort of placard, and which are served by the portion. *to have dinner at a restaurateur's; the menu of a restaurateur.*

DICTIONNAIRE DE L'ACADÉMIE FRANÇAISE (SIXTH EDITION, 1835)

Introduction:
To Make a Restaurant

Centuries before a restaurant was a place to eat (and even several decades after), a *restaurant* was a thing to eat, a restorative broth. This book traces the emergence of the restaurant (as we know it) from a tiny cup of bouillon.

In the fifteenth century, a recipe for a *restaurant* began by instructing that a freshly killed capon be cooked in an alchemist's glass kettle with sixty gold ducats, and noted that the cook might supplement the gold pieces with diamonds, rubies, sapphires, jaspers, or "any other good and virtuous precious stones the doctor may order."[1] The seventeenth- and eighteenth-century dictionaries of Furetière and Trévoux omitted the gems from the recipe but still defined a *restaurant* as a semi-medicinal preparation, while Diderot and D'Alembert's massive *Encyclopédie* (1751–1772) listed "Restaurant" as a "medical term," and offered brandy, chickpeas, and chocolate as examples of "restorative" substances.[2] Many French cookbooks of the eighteenth century included lengthy recipes for bouillon-based preparations called *restaurants,* which they promised would restore health to suffering invalids and flavor to otherwise insipid sauces.[3]

Restaurants of this period differed from all other bouillons by their highly condensed nature, since, unlike the more plebeian sorts of consommés, *restaurants* were often prepared without the addition of any liquid. The final product, after a cooking procedure of alchemical exactitude, was then a broth of pure meat essences. Recipes called for a variety of meats—usually ham, veal, and some fowl (chicken, partridge, or pheasant)—to be sweated and cooked for many hours in a tightly sealed kettle or *bain marie* (hot water bath). According to experts, the prolonged cooking began the process of breaking down the flesh and allowed the meat to reach the eater already partially digested. In the appetizing words of one recipe, a *restaurant* had the benefit of being solid food converted

1

into "a sort of artificial chyle."[4] *Restaurants*, it was thought, thereby provided the necessary blood-heating nutrition of meat, without taxing an invalid's weakened digestive system.

The restaurant as a space of urban sociability emerged from the consommé. In the beginning, in the last twenty years of the Old Regime, one went to a restaurant (or, as they were more commonly called, a "restaurateur's room") to drink restorative bouillons, as one went to a café to drink coffee. The first restaurateurs sold little solid food and advertised their establishments as especially suited to all those too frail to eat an evening meal. In its initial form, then, the restaurant was specifically a place one went *not* to eat, but to sit and weakly sip one's *restaurant*. Distinguished from inns, taverns, or cookshops by their individual tables, salutary consommés, and unfixed mealtimes, these first *restaurant* emporia had little in common with the picture today conjured by the words "Paris restaurant." By the 1820s, however, the restaurants of the French capital—with their four-column menus, confused eaters, and waiters of variable politeness—closely resembled those with which we are familiar today. The restaurant had become a true cultural institution, among the most familiar and distinctive of Parisian landmarks.[5]

Until well after the middle of the nineteenth century, restaurants were to remain an almost exclusively Parisian phenomenon, one rarely encountered outside the French capital. American and English travelers to Paris marveled at its restaurants, terming them among the city's "most peculiar" and "most remarkable" features.[6] In 1844 John Durbin, president of Dickinson College, wrote of restaurant dining that it was "in many respects peculiar to Paris," unlike anything he had experienced or witnessed in New York, Philadelphia, or London; a decade later, the children's book *Rollo in Paris* carefully explained that in Paris one did not stay at a boarding house but took rooms in a hotel and dined wherever one pleased.[7]

Foreign visitors were not alone in their conviction that its restaurants made Paris unique: as late as 1851, local officials in nearly two-thirds of France's provincial departments reported that their jurisdictions had no restaurants.[8] Yet when the prefect of the Var informed the Minister of the Interior that his department was without restaurants, he did not mean that all the food consumed there was prepared at home; inns, after all, had catered to travelers for centuries, and wineshops often provided some sort of fare to soak up the wine and brandy. Rather, the prefect was simply stating that the mere serving of food in public was not sufficient in his mind for a business to qualify as "a restaurant." As his rather muddled colleague in the Sarthe similarly reported, "Since all innkeepers here serve meals to non-residents, and since all restaurateurs rent rooms, we have no real restaurants."[9] Though he had used the term "restaurateur" to refer to purveyors of prepared food, the prefect was loath to call an establishment where rooms were rented and horses, as well as people, fed, "a restaurant." For an aura of urban sophistication, novelty, and mystery still clung to the term and the space, and something very specific was meant when people talked about "restaurants."

From eighteenth-century bouillon to nineteenth-century business, from miniature soup-cup to Rabelaisian excess, from sensibility to politics: these are the transitions that defined the term "restaurant." As we know it today, the restaurant represents the translation of an eighteenth-century cult of sensibility into a nineteenth-century sense of taste: the mutation of one era's social value into another's cultural flourish. The shift from bouillon to bounty was hardly inevitable; instead, there is a complicated story to be told here, one in which subjects that are often considered unrelated—restaurant reviews and political banquets, fashionable innovation and Enlightenment science, revolutionary zeal and aesthetic hierarchies, adulterous dalliances and medicinal concoctions—overlap and intertwine. In the past 230 years, the restaurant has changed from a sort of urban spa into a "political" public forum, and then into an explicitly and actively depoliticized refuge. Throughout, these transformations have been not so much a progression through a series of clearly defined stages as an ongoing and contestatory process in which every new understanding of the restaurant's place in Paris life has opened up the possibility of yet further re-evaluations and creative departures. The patterns explored in this book are not linear, but emergent.

Departing from the received wisdom and established chronology that have long insisted that restaurants were illegal until after the French Revolution, I begin this book in the mid-eighteenth century. The flourishing restaurants of the early nineteenth century have often been traced to the Revolution's abolition of rigid Old-Regime guilds and its bringing to Paris of kitchenless provincial revolutionaries (as well as its role in putting the chefs of beheaded or émigré aristocrats out of work), but this treatment of the restaurant as a revolutionary epiphenomenon has provided only the most limited insights into its Old-Regime antecedents. Purported analyses of the restaurant's place in Paris life, buttressed by the yawning divide of the Revolution, have merely evoked common themes and tropes: in the beginning there were no restaurants, but then there was the Revolution, after which there were restaurants that looked very much like the ones we know today. Yet as the image of resting one's argument on a chasm may make clear, there is something problematic, rather incompletely historical, about tracing a cultural institution to a moment of mythical originary rupture. While this perspective is, in its own way, highly revelatory, it has shrouded the restaurant (like the Revolution's other supposed by-products) in what has been aptly named "genesis amnesia": the widespread malaise that attributes the specific and contingent outcome of history to an ill-defined revolutionary "modernity."[10]

Belief in the restaurant's simple "modernity" has constrained its history to a sort of gastro-hagiography, in which anecdotal description of lavish meals and scrumptious dishes takes the place of more nuanced analysis.[11] Delimited to its iconographic, nineteenth-century form, the restaurant has been emptied of its history and, in a sense, naturalized—made into a perfectly predictable and unremarkable response to biological appetites. So naturalized, restaurant going has also been nationalized: treated as a mere offshoot of presupposed French culinary superiority. Nineteenth-century English and American tourists in Paris were among the first to assume that local "national character" revealed itself in restaurant dining rooms, but they came to this decision after investing considerable emotional energy in finding differences between their homes and the land "across the water." For even the most Francophile and enthusiastic of these visitors, each episode of French restaurant ostentation made homey English domesticity all the more desirable, and every incidence of flimsy Parisian finery made New York all the more self-evidently "substantial."[12] While such attitudes are hardly surprising, or even specific to the nineteenth century, it is somewhat strange that historians have accepted them so wholeheartedly and reinscribed them so zealously. What is perhaps even odder, twentieth-century French scholars and politicians have integrated the restaurant into almost every account of French exceptionalism, describing it, for example, as "a profoundly French institution, unlike any other establishment on the planet."[13] Such claims have helped to establish the restaurant as an icon of French life and hence, in a way, have made this book's project possible, but they have depended on a generally uncritical attitude toward the historical and textual processes by means of which the restaurant became so very emblematic. By considering restaurants as little but the incidental sites of "French" culinary extravaganza, previous studies have unquestioningly accepted gastronomic literature's own, initially quite polemical, claims for its remove from the realms of history and social analysis (as a matter of literal "taste" alone). My book picks up this theme and culminates with the nineteenth century's apotheosis of the culinary, but it is my hope that readers will see the cult of the gourmet neither as telos nor as rousing finale. Rather, it was a highly specific historical development, once utterly peculiar, now become largely banal.

Beginning with a moment in which restaurants were conceived as a potential site for social, as well as individual, regeneration, and continuing to a time when such an understanding of them is almost unfathomable, this book outlines historical developments responsible for the definition of the restaurant as a subject of analysis for gourmets and guidebook writers (but not for historians or literature scholars). It explores how the gastro-culinary became its own realm of expertise; how "taste" became distinct from "Taste"; how the myth structure called "gastronomy" came to be a predominant part of the picture of modern "Paris." By attending to the significance of the restaurant's general omission from prior scholarship, we confront gastronomy's success in defining a realm of "taste" widely accepted as autonomous and unsusceptible to external comment. (*De gustibus*, after all, *non disputandum est.*)[14] In this book I scrutinize the development of practices specific to restaurants and to gastronomic sensibility, rather than simply accepting the gourmet's self-perpetuating claim that "the table is a country like any other, with its own usages and customs."[15]

Throughout, I often have recourse to the unsatisfyingly abstract locution "the restaurant," as if there were but one restaurant, or as if all restaurants were identical and interchangeable. While such abstraction can sometimes be frustratingly vague or imprecise, it has the advantage of highlighting what is common to all (or, at least, to many) restaurant experiences and of emphasizing the peculiarities specific to restaurant culture. I began this project with two intentionally naive and deceptively simple questions: "What is a restaurant? What do people do there?" These have not always been easy questions to keep in focus, for we are all familiar with present-day restaurants and largely assume that a restaurant is, in Merriam-Webster's words: "an establishment where refreshments or food may be procured by the public; a public eating house."[16] In everyday life, we do not ask "Why do people go to restaurants?" but "What kind of food does such-and-such a restaurant serve? Where is it? How much does dinner cost? Is the fish fresh? Is the wine list good?" These latter questions, helpful as they may be in distinguishing one restaurant from another, are all internal to restaurant culture—that is, they make sense to us because we know what a restaurant is, but they cannot tell us how these came to be the "logical" questions to ask about a restaurant (but not about a library, or even a café). In this book I have moved away from these customary questions in order to ask what made going to a restaurant, any restaurant, a distinctive experience in Paris of the late eighteenth and early nineteenth centuries. How did people think about "going out" to eat (or to not eat, as the case may have been)? What new possibilities for, and anxieties about, social interaction did the development of the restaurant—as distinct from the inn, the tavern, or the café—introduce into urban life? While thinking and writing about "the restaurant" in this abstract way has meant sacrificing some valuable and fascinating specificity, it has also made it possible to address the far broader constellation of actions and meanings peculiar to this new kind of semi-private, semi-public space. For this book is concerned primarily with the practices and institutions specific to the whole category "restaurants," and only peripherally with the rise and fall of specific restaurants.

Whenever feasible, I have balanced generalizations with analyses focused on individual restaurants, restaurateurs, or restaurant customers, but I have not tried to write either a study of the life and times of the Véry family (whose members and in-laws ran a famous Palais-Royal restaurant for much of the period covered), or a tribute to the enduring attractions of the Grand Véfour or the Tour d'Argent, or even a chronicle of Rousseau's or Balzac's dinner habits. Past histories of French dining have often offered such perspectives, treating the restaurant largely as an icon of French gastronomic genius or as a major factor in the consolidation of the nation's "culinary patrimony."[17] Such studies, rich with anecdote and suggestion, have remained largely descriptive and antiquarian; basically part of restaurant culture itself, they have been content to offer so-called "walking tours" of gastronomy's former palaces, and to dispense a tour guide's "stars" or "bonnets" with rigorous eyes and discerning palates. Even the methodologically astute philosopher-historian Jean-Paul Aron so fully accepted these conventions that his 1973 *Art of Eating in the Nineteenth Century* awarded Michelin-type stars to long vanished restaurants, begrudgingly giving three to the 1850s Café Anglais while commenting, "But I, who have frequented Robert's and the Rocher de Cancale [two restaurants that closed at least eighty years before Aron's birth], find it disgusting."[18] In all such studies, the role of restaurants in eighteenth- and nineteenth-century life has been reduced to a frame around intrinsically valuable works of culinary art; small wonder then that histories of public and private life, and even of table-based sociability, have rarely mentioned restaurants.[19]

This book departs from that pattern. Rather than being a restaurant guide, it tells the far more complicated story of how such guides—and a public gastronomic sensibility, more broadly defined—came to be among the distinctive features of modern life. What is truly odd about the world we inhabit today is not that one restaurant should earn two stars and another none, but that someone should think to assign such rankings in the first place. To understand how the restaurant's logic of personal choice and specialist evaluation became generalized models (consider today's expanded use of the word and concept "menu"), we need to see where those models came from and what was dropped or cut from them along the way.

Eating Out in the Old Regime

When he went to Paris in the early eighteenth century, Joachim Nemeitz quickly discovered what was wrong with the French capital: the food. While the German erudite found the conversation in Paris cafés stimulating, and thought the capital's architecture magnificent, he was singularly disappointed by the cooking. "Nearly everyone believes that you eat well in France, and especially in Paris," he wrote, "but they are mistaken."[20] Though he cautioned his readers to be always alert in the crowded and potentially dangerous city, he concluded that the one substantive improvement he hoped to see in the capital concerned neither the lighting of its streets nor the policing of its pickpockets, but the quality of its cuisine. "For the sake of travelers, this is the only thing I wish to see changed," he sighed. "One happily pays a little bit more, to eat something good and occasionally varied."[21]

In his analysis of the city's fare, Nemeitz carefully distinguished public inns from private residences. Concerning the latter, he confidently asserted that "wealthy people of quality feast deliciously, for they all have their own cooks"—but he asked his readers to pity the ordinary voyager traveling without personal kitchen staff or extensive letters of introduction. Forced to eat at an innkeeper's or *traiteur's* (cook-caterer's) table d'hôte, the simple visitor to Paris would quickly discover that he "does not fare well at all, either because the meat is not properly cooked, or because they serve the same thing every day and rarely offer any variety."[22] Yet if the food was appallingly similar at these tables, the company was just as alarmingly varied, and the new arrival at a public table needed to be suspicious "since one cannot always tell who is sitting there."[23] As far as Nemeitz could tell, an unbridgeable chasm separated the private table, where "people of quality" enjoyed wonderfully varied and innovative meals in each other's company, from the inn—where variety and inventiveness characterized not the cuisine but the diner's wily companions.

Throughout the eighteenth century, many a traveler would have cause for similar complaints: in 1763, the English novelist Tobias Smollett, on his way to take the waters at an Italian health resort, fretted that the food served by French innkeepers and cook-caterers, though inexpensive, would further ruin his health; in the late 1780s, his countryman, the agronomist Arthur Young, bemoaned the rudeness of greedy table companions in hostelries throughout France; in 1790, Helen Maria Williams, though otherwise an enthusiastic Francophile, commented that conditions in French inns were so miserable that they could move most English people to suicide.[24] Philip Thicknesse perhaps explained everyone's fixation on the inns when he noted that it was "extremely difficult" for even the most important foreigners to gain invitations to the best French homes.[25] Like Nemeitz, these British visitors were effectively trapped between two largely insular institutions: on one side, the private, affluent home and, on the other, the equally forbidding world of the daily table d'hôte. For while the latter was ostensibly a hospitable institution—literally, "the host's table," open to all those without tables of their own—it was, in the reality of the eighteenth century, often more like a sort of pension, as forbidding in its own way as the closed gates of any *hôtel particulier.* A meal set at one large table, always at the same specified time, and at which the eaters had little opportunity to order or request particular dishes, the table d'hôte was frequently a regular midday meeting spot for local artisans and workers, old friends and long-time residents of a neighborhood. An urban tradition, the table d'hôte offered dependable gossip for those interested in neighborhood nourishment, but it could be a less than pleasant environment for recently arrived strangers.

For centuries before the first restaurants opened their doors, travelers and Parisians without their own kitchens had depended on the inns, cookshops, and wineshops so scorned by Nemeitz and Smollett. Early eighteenth-century Paris was, in fact, home to thousands of retail food and drink merchants, all organized by monarchial decrees into twenty-five different guilds.[26] As defined in their statutes, the retail food trades were characterized by extreme divisiveness and exaggerated compartmentalization: the *charcutiers,* for example, monopolized trade in sausages, ham, and other pork products; the butchers slaughtered and sold all other raw domestic meat; the *rôtisseurs* were purveyors of game and other "prepared meats, either furred or feathered, larded or roasted or ready to eat."[27] The gingerbread-sellers, the vinegar-makers, the pastrycooks: all had their governing, and mutually exclusive, bylaws. What a master of one trade had the right to do (such as making and selling gingerbread), everybody else was legally prohibited from doing. Thanks to the uncompromising nature of guild regulation, the man who made stews technically could not sell mustard, and the preparer of pâtés was prohibited from selling coffee. Master cook-caterers held the right to serve full meals to large parties, and master winesellers could sell liquid refreshments to groups and individuals, but no tradesman was allowed to combine those functions (and others) in order to operate what we today would define as "a restaurant."

That, at least, is the picture that is outlined by the letter of Old-Regime law, and that has long underpinned historians' assumptions about the role of those laws in preventing the development of anything resembling restaurants during the eighteenth century. Nearly every discussion of restaurant history briefly tells the tale of how a few early restaurateurs in the 1760s and 1770s—maverick, unregulated purveyors of the "restorative" bouillons known as *restaurants*—encroached on the rights of the established catering guild.[28] The cook-caterers (*traiteurs*), it is said, quickly brought legal charges against one particularly aggrandizing restaurateur named Boulanger who dared to sell a dish (sheeps' feet in white sauce) that was not a *restaurant* but a *ragoût* (anything composed of several different ingredients cooked in a sauce). After a series of appeals, we are told, the courts eventually decided in favor of the cook-caterers, and restricted the "restaurateurs" to selling bouillons. In our contemporary context, there is definitely something amusing about this image of the berobed and bewigged magistrates of the Paris Parlement, the highest court in France, learnedly debating the status of sauced sheeps' feet. Few stories more effectively evoke an Old Regime suffocated by arcane rules, or fit more neatly with the late twentieth-century sense of France primarily as an exporter of savory luxury goods and tightly argued, hair-splitting *explications de texte*. However, this account is, to all appearances, largely unfounded. True enough, "restaurateurs," per se, never formed a legal guild; their statutes did not exist, they had no patron saint and no meeting hall. But no evidence in the judicial, police, or corporate archives substantiates the story of Boulanger's defeat at the hands of the litigious caterers.

This tale has survived because it is ideal for the purposes of the corporate system's critics, whether those critics are Marxist historians of the French Revolution or Physiocratic liberalizers of trade. According to received wisdom, only with the French Revolution's abolition of the guilds were would-be restaurateurs "finally freed of directed gastronomy" and allowed to "give a personal touch to all their preparations."[29] Later scholarship has, however, questioned this once widely accepted notion of unyielding and resolutely backward-looking trade guilds. The historian Jacques Revel has argued that the guilds' inflexibility was as much a rhetorical construction used by their free-trade-advocating critics as it was a condition of daily existence; though this language was important in fueling the anti-corporatism of the Revolution, it must not be mistaken for an analysis of the real workings of each guild.[30] In fact, no single grand unified model suffices to describe the day-to-day functioning of the guild system.[31]

The retail food trades were notoriously difficult to delimit. The futility of enforcing divisions among the food trades derived in part from the combinative nature of the work itself: as one clever lawyer pointed out, the wheel on a carriage was made by a wheelwright because even when the decrepit and useless carriage had fallen to pieces, the wheel was still a wheel—but the same could hardly be said for the strip of bacon used to line a pâté. Bacon, in such an example, was not a finished product, the manufacture of which might be limited to one group of people, but a raw material, available to all who needed it.[32] Given the complications of a system in which the crust of a meat pie would technically have to be made by a pastrycook, and its filling prepared by a meatcook, it is hardly surprising that the accumulation of multiple and overlapping masterships was, in the retail food trades of the mid-1700s, more nearly the rule than the exception. Already in 1704, almost three-quarters of the master *traiteurs* were also cabaret-keepers; in 1748 the *traiteurs'* guild noted that "most of our masters" also had the privileges of pastrycooks or roast-meat-sellers.[33] Professional delineations, though firmly stated and neatly outlined in dictionaries and lawbooks, proved far more flexible in daily life.[34] A 1760 decision of Parlement instructed that, in order to prevent monopolies, the Paris caterers should henceforth elect their four "syndics in charge" from a group of fifty masters, of whom twelve should be *marchands de vin-traiteurs,* twelve *traiteurs-pâtissiers,* twelve *traiteurs-rôtisseurs,* and fourteen simple master caterers. In other words, of fifty elder masters in the guild, fewer than one-third were expected to be master *traiteurs* alone.[35] The combination of titles, while fairly common in all the retail food trades, was particularly prevalent among the *traiteurs.*[36]

It is evident that the cook-caterers of Paris had long had their fingers in numerous pies, and that by far the majority of them would have been well within their legal rights had they run businesses that sold a variety of foods and a wide range of potables. Such an accumulation of tasks was easily possible, but it did not distinguish the first restaurateurs from the established cook-caterers. Indeed, many of the first restaurateurs were also master *traiteurs* with close business and family ties to many of the other established Paris food and drink trades. Jacques Minet, who opened one of the first "salles du restaurateur" in 1767 on the rue des Poulies, was elected to a position in charge of the cook-caterers' guild in August of that same year (and held the post for the standard two-year term).[37] Far from being an antagonist of the *traiteurs* (as we might guess from the old story of restaurateur-*traiteur* contestation), he was among their leading lights. So, rather than following the master *traiteurs* on their monthly rounds through the *gargotes* (cheap cabarets) and *guinguettes* (popular dancehalls) of the outlying districts (where no restoratives were ever served), we need to shift the focus from corporate contestation to cultural innovation. For while the first restaurants were, in the words of a lawyer writing in 1786, "the product of our modern way of life,"[38] they were also the specific brainchild of one of the eighteenth century's lesser geniuses: the self-styled "Author" of the restaurant, Mathurin Roze de Chantoiseau.

1

The Friend of All the World

The following material would require more extensive treatment, but the nature of this work does not allow it. I would like to float on a peaceful river but I am dragged along in a torrent.

Commerce cures destructive prejudices, and it is nearly a general rule that everywhere manners are gentle, there is commerce and everywhere there is commerce, there are gentle manners.

MONTESQUIEU, *ESPRIT DES LOIS* (1748)

If Mathurin Roze de Chantoiseau's scheme to reduce the French national debt had been as successful as his bouillon-selling establishments, he might have prevented the French Revolution. Instead, he invented the restaurant. Certainly, his life story suggests that he had little doubt as to which was the greater accomplishment, which invention the most likely to endear him to future generations.

On a cloudy afternoon in late April of 1789, Roze de Chantoiseau, known to at least a few of his contemporaries as "the creator of the restaurant," journeyed from Paris to Versailles.[1] There, however, he presented the king and gathered deputies with neither a caterer's bill nor a proposed menu. Instead, now in his late fifties, the first restaurateur was (or so it seemed) finally about to be recognized for his numerous ingenious efforts on behalf of the French people.[2] "The Friend of All the World," as he signed himself, had already struggled valiantly for twenty years to bring his grand plan to fruition. Now to King Louis XVI and the few delegates already assembled for the first meeting of the Estates-General in 175 years, he offered his wondrous invention: a fiscal reform scheme, aimed at reducing the monstrous French national debt by replacing the "fruitless and imaginary idea of credit" with "Letters of Credit" of real value.[3]

Twenty years earlier, Roze de Chantoiseau had had copies of a similar proposal printed. Lovingly describing his system in a letter to Intendant Général des Finances de Boullongne (an important agent of the Crown), he had concluded with the admission that some would think his plan mere fantasy: "but they said the same about Christopher Columbus."[4] During the autumn of 1769, as the pamphlet outlining his system began to circulate in Paris, Roze de Chantoiseau had no doubt expected to receive the financier's grateful acknowledgment for his discovery of a means to increase the money supply without causing runaway inflation or levying new taxes. Roze's plan did, in fact, generate considerable interest: Président à Mortier of the Paris Parlement, Jean Omer Joly de Fleury, wrote to the Lieutenant General of Police that it had occasioned "much discussion." Yet these conversations overheard by the high-ranking magistrate did not exactly fuel a rush of public acclaim toward the "Christopher Columbus" of the French debt problem, and Chantoiseau soon found himself not thanked but arrested, and held for months in Fort l'Evêque prison on charges of printing and disseminating an incendiary text.[5]

In the atmosphere of reform-minded optimism characteristic of the spring of 1789, and with other major, Crown-backed business successes now to his name, Roze may have felt the time was propitious for the revival of his marvelous plan. All the evidence suggests, however, that the Estates-General received his proposal politely, and then hastily discarded it. Undaunted, Roze de Chantoiseau offered a similar scheme to the Paris city government in summer 1790, and later dedicated other versions to the "republican citizens" of the National Convention and the Thermidorean Committee of Public Safety.[6] Revolutionary governments, alas, seemed no more inclined than the monarchy had been to recognize the value of his scheme. So in spring 1799, Roze de Chantoiseau and a business partner abandoned the public sphere and proposed to implement their new credit system, which Chantoiseau had patented, by founding a private bank.[7] The "United Departmental Bank of Commerce and the Arts," as he called it, was hardly the smashing success Roze de Chantoiseau had foretold, and he died nearly penniless in March 1806.[8]

As the preceding brief outline suggests, the restaurant's "Author" (as he often called himself) pursued a wide range of business ventures: the restaurant did not develop in isolation, nor was it immediately a gastronomic haven, emerging fully formed from the cooking steam and heated imaginations of some bustling kitchen. Nor did it evolve from the inns and wineshops that had long served travelers and others in need of sustenance, for those institutions continued to exist and nobody ever claimed to be their author. For Roze de Chantoiseau, however, selling restorative bouillons to individuals was less like running a tavern than it was like peddling credit schemes to the monarchy—both of his life's tasks seemed equally viable, compelling, and innovative activities. The "invention" of the restaurant, the creation of a new market sphere of hospitality and taste, was but one component in Roze's plan to fix the economy, repair commerce, and restore health to the body politic.

Mathurin Roze de Chantoiseau was neither the most famous nor the most successful of eighteenth-century restaurateurs; in fact, his stint in the restaurant business was quite brief and largely anonymous. Nor was his a particularly powerful name with which to reckon in the retail food trades of eighteenth-century Paris: families such as the Gaugés and the Trianons, who had been cook-caterers, pastrycooks, and roast-meat-sellers for generations, were far better known and far more influential in the guild-regulated food trades. He was not even the era's most ingenious gustatorial entrepreneur: the mustard manufacturer Maille established a dynasty whose name endures to this day, and the boulevard entertainer Comus (named for the Greek god of cookery) made a fortune with his display of electrical entertainments.[9] Nevertheless, Roze's role in the invention of the restaurant is especially significant, for he epitomizes (if only by the variety of his projects) the restaurant's place in intricate networks of market expansion and commercial growth. Like others of his era, the first restaurateur saw the long-stigmatized mechanisms of trade (the circulation of goods and the stimulation of desires) as potential conduits of social benefit and national improvement.

Roze de Chantoiseau, who invented the restaurant while running an information office, attempting to abolish the national debt, and editing a commercial directory, was hardly unique in the range of his interests. In 1766, when this first restaurateur opened his door, culinary issues were often integrated into a wide range of discussions. Conservatives and radicals alike included diet and cookery in their numerous descriptions of what ailed France, and in their innumerable suggestions for cures. The *Gazetin de comestible,* a sort of mail-order catalogue of fine foods, appropriated the medieval idea of civic religious abstinence to suggest that if each of its readers would simply fast one day a month and donate the money saved on that day's food to the state, the national debt would be quickly under control.[10] The academician Etienne Laureault de Foncemagne wrote both scholarly prefaces to cookbooks, in which he praised the eighteenth-century's controversial nouvelle cuisine, and equally learned polemics in which he disputed with Voltaire over the authorship of *Le Testament politique du Cardinal Richelieu;* the abbé Claude Fleury commented on the varied cuisines of ancient peoples and authored a series of wildly successful catechisms.[11] While the chevalier de Jaucourt, who wrote many of the articles on food, dining, and physiology for the *Encyclopédie,* explored

diet and cuisine in his moralizing critique of "modern" luxury, other writers addressed the same topics as part of their optimistic celebration of nature's sensibility.[12] Thémiseul de Saint-Hyacinthe, the widely read editor
of the Hague's *Journal littéraire,* made the comparison of ancient and
modern cookeries one of the high points in his satire of the famous Homer
scholar, Madame Dacier (who herself had gone to considerable lengths to
prepare a properly Homeric meal); the aesthetician DuBos scattered references to food and cuisine throughout his *Réflexions critiques sur la poésie et
la peinture (Critical Reflections on Poetry and Painting),* thereby providing his readers with a series of pleasantly quotidian comparisons; Voltaire
went so far as to claim that in "every known language," the word "taste"
was used both literally, for the physical, gustatory sensation, and meta-
phorically, for the awareness of beauty.[13] If certain authors, such as the
academician Foncemagne, used their expertise in philosophy or aesthetics
in order to discuss cookery as an art, others dismissed as crude sensualists
any who described culinary endeavors in such a lofty fashion. In literal
heteroglossia, some tongues spoke while others savored.

In all of the above cases, interest in food was not a distinctive or peculiar
preoccupation, but simply a part of being involved in general social, cultural, and political life. In cookbooks and artistic treatises, personal letters
and medical books, eaters, doctors, cooks, and philosophers used often
identical vocabularies in order to discuss a variety of questions, ranging
from what cookery could tell them about the proper positioning of the
arts in society to the moral and medical implications of a fondness for ornamentation. While much of this discussion was in a bantering or jesting
tone, science seemed perpetually poised on the brink of proving even the
most extraordinary claims: if blood circulated through the body, and electrical currents moved through the atmosphere, who was to say that spices
had not caused the fall of Rome, or that a change in national diet might
not do much to revive French poetry? Diet and cookery, as subjects of
wide relevance, fascinated many of the era's most prominent thinkers, and
were located, if not always at the center, then at least on the margins (like
mesmerism, clandestine literature, and much else that mobilized public
opinion) of the major intellectual and artistic debates of the day.[14]

Like any number of these enterprising authors and would-be reformers,
Roze de Chantoiseau frequented the aristocratic and administrative circles
of Paris. Like Cerutti, Mirabeau, and a horde of fellow Physiocrats, he
wrote tracts about the money supply; like the patent medicine vendor
Ray, he accumulated royal endorsements and advertised his accomplish-

ments widely; like the journalist Pahin de La Blancherie or the playwright Beaumarchais, he proved incredibly resilient, reappearing time and again in the least expected contexts.[15] Roze de Chantoiseau's genius lay in his realization that the expanding discourse of cuisine that surrounded him— the curious product of mechanistic physiology, physiocratic emphasis on agriculture, and *mondaine* belief in the beneficial effects of luxury—called for and could support a new institution. With the restaurant, he transposed the era's widespread interest in dietary change—indicated by everything from the popularity of the so-called nouvelle cuisine and the huge boom in cookbook production, to the growing tendency to build houses in which one room was specifically for dining—from affluent households and the realm of print into the market.[16] Roze de Chantoiseau's life, in all likelihood, was full of people like the salonnière Marie-Thérèse Geoffrin, who attributed her good health (and, by extension, her place in the capital's intellectual life) to a careful and parsimonious diet.[17] Connected, by dint of ingenuity, tenacity, and reasonably comfortable family background, to this world of fussy eaters; related by business dealings to the many commercial innovators who swarmed through Paris in the final decades of the Old Regime; and linked by marriage to the Henneveu family whose cabaret-turned-restaurant, the Cadran Bleu, would remain a fixture in descriptions of the Paris restaurant world until the mid-nineteenth century, Roze de Chantoiseau was ideally positioned to be the restaurant's first theorist.[18] (We might call him "over-determined": if he did not exist, the historian of the restaurant would have to invent him.) Though a more rigorous or puritanical mind might have felt uneasy with the combination of worldly comfort, agricultural encouragement, and homely retail acumen on which the creation of the restaurant depended, Mathurin Roze de Chantoiseau happily borrowed bits and pieces from a variety of competing viewpoints, in the optimistic, or perhaps merely naive, belief that the most positive components of each could be combined to create the best of all possible worlds. Like the editors of the *Gazetin de comestible,* who argued that the importation into Paris of Italian pastas and provincial pâtés would stimulate agriculture and bolster commerce, the inventor of the restaurant heralded a world in which public utility and private pleasure could be simultaneously and mutually satisfied.[19]

Mathurin Roze de Chantoiseau, that "fertile genius,"[20] was one of three sons of Armand Roze, a landowner and merchant in the tiny hamlet of Chantoiseau, located roughly four kilometers southeast of Fontainebleau

Palace.[21] At his death in 1774, Armand Roze owned three houses in or near Chantoiseau, and his sons were well-positioned and prosperous. Two sons had remained in Chantoiseau as important figures in the community: Antoine Armand held the prestigious office of "Inspector of the King's buildings," while Louis Emery earned a comfortable living as a wholesale grocer and china merchant (*fayencier*).[22] Mathurin, the third son, grandly added the aristocratic-sounding "de Chantoiseau" to his name and moved to Paris in the early 1760s, where he busied himself with an endless series of reform projects and entrepreneurial schemes.

Loosely related both to one another and to the major intellectual themes of his era, Roze de Chantoiseau's many business ventures—including the first restaurants—shared a preoccupation with circulation, communication, and commerce. His attitude toward these issues can best be seen in the many versions of his precious debt-reduction scheme. Though his plan was unique, he was hardly alone in seeing the debt as France's greatest stumbling block: pamphlets suggesting fiscal reform to deal with the problem were printed and dispersed, usually illegally, throughout the mid-eighteenth century, to such a degree that the chronicler Petit de Bachaumont declared the urge to write on financial matters a veritable "epidemic."[23] Unlike many of the other planners, however, Roze directed his efforts to the fiscally conservative, long-term question of actually paying off the debt, rather than the short-term problem of finding sufficient stop-gap funds for the next year's operating expenses. His was to be the plan to end all plans, and to restore France to never-ending fiscal health.

Roze's plan, which changed little over the years, apart from the title, hinged on a cascade of diminishing value. In the basic formulation, the state, burdened by debt and unable to pay its creditors in hard currency (a situation in which France often found itself in the eighteenth century), would pay a few select purveyors by means of a new kind of "credit." Merchants and tradesmen would eagerly accept this letter of credit (a sort of disguised bond), and even seek it out, thanks to its rarity and because "the King had granted it, as a special favor to keep his creditors from lawsuits."[24] The letter of credit would pass from hand to hand, a kind of supplemental currency grounded in nothing except faith in the government and a desire to avoid legal costs. Yet in the long run, Chantoiseau assured his readers, these letters of credit would not have the catastrophic inflationary effect of John Law's System, which had caused such havoc during the Regency.[25] Instead, he claimed to have designed a scheme whereby the notes would eventually leave circulation completely: every time they were passed along, they would lose one percent of their value, until they finally "disappeared completely."[26]

Credit in Roze's plan would derive its value neither from the issuing authority's holdings of gold and silver, as in traditional paper-money ventures, nor even from colonial lands, as Law had proposed. Rather, the system's credibility would depend on trust in the monarchy and faith in the value of anything rare. Roze believed that the mere difficulty of obtaining one of these letters of credit—paid by the Crown only as a special privilege to fortunate purveyors—would make them desirable, and the simple fact of their movement would stimulate the economy. (One imagines he expected merchants, eager to pay off longstanding debts, to pass them along like hot potatoes.) Roze here perhaps missed the point, which had, in fact, been clear to the much-maligned Law, that value generally derives from a relation between availability and demand: scarcity alone does not ensure value, nor could rareness guarantee the desirability of this new paper money.[27] Indeed, given that Roze expected the letters of credit eventually to use up their own worth, it is curious that he imagined them likely to inspire much confidence whatsoever.[28]

Even though Roze's scheme was perhaps not the most feasible means of resolving France's debt problem, it remains of interest to us, for the understanding of value expressed there was not unique: it is actually much like that which drives any trade in novelty goods. "Nouveautés"—be they the Italian wines and cheeses imported by the publishers of the *Gazetin de comestible*, the bonbons à la Figaro sold by a famous sweet shop, or a dressmaker's latest innovation in skirt decorations—did all apparently derive their value simply from being new and different. While eighteenth-century critics of luxurious living condemned those who desired such frivolous trinkets, merchants of novelty and import items were thriving in Paris as Roze was writing.[29] Roze de Chantoiseau's real talents and sympathy—as demonstrated by both the restaurant and the commercial almanac, perhaps by his decision to marry a woman who had made a name for herself as a manufacturer and merchant of cosmetics,[30] and certainly by his quirky understanding of the basis of value—lay in the marketing of the apparently superfluous essentials of modern urban life. His ill-fated plan to abolish the debt would simply have applied the logic of rouge, ribbons, and truffles to the vexed problem of specie. Though perhaps not the most subtle theorist of economic modernity, he was nonetheless an astute observer of one of its key mechanisms.

When, in 1769, he so unwisely had this scheme published in pamphlet form, Roze de Chantoiseau signed it "L'Ami de tout le monde" ("Everybody's Friend" or, literally, "The Friend of All the World")—no doubt intending to evoke the Marquis de Mirabeau's 1757 *L'Ami des hommes (The Friend of Men)*, a proto-Physiocratic celebration of agriculture and attack on luxury. Mirabeau's book had enjoyed great success for a brief period, going through several editions in the four years after its publication and making the wealthy and rakish Provençal nobleman into one of the best-known figures of his day. The *Journal encyclopédique* had called his work the intersection of Montaigne's writing with Montesquieu's thinking; Paris merchants had had their signs repainted to indicate that they, too, were friends of mankind.[31] Roze de Chantoiseau's invocation of Mirabeau served largely the same function as a freshly refashioned shop sign, for there were few concrete ways in which Roze's brief pamphlet paralleled or expanded upon Mirabeau's voluminous work.[32] Instead, the title was an advertising slogan, a promise to surpass the elder Mirabeau, both in popularity and efficacy.

While Roze shared Mirabeau's concern with the question of "circulation," the difference in their goals (the former wanted to liquidate the national deficit, the latter hoped to encourage population growth) entailed disagreement on the manner in which "circulation" benefited society.[33] Far more abbreviated than Mirabeau's several hundred pages of rambling prose, Roze's ten-page plan addressed little but the perceived crisis of circulation. He proposed no critique of luxury, and fell prey to no Physiocratic obsession with the grain trade. Unlike Mirabeau, he privileged no single branch of commerce. Seeing the shortage of currency as the root cause of problems in the French economy (because without money chasing after them, goods did not circulate as quickly and as freely as they otherwise might), Roze outlined what seemed a viable new alternative, a way of increasing circulation without producing inflation. Each recipient of one of his "credit notes" would admittedly lose one percent of its value, but what was that compared to the inestimable advantage of "easier access to one's own wealth"?[34] As the *billets de crédit* and the beneficial effects of commerce spread across France, the "hard currency" would return to the center, guaranteeing confidence in the state and economic well-being. Roze's scheme would have, in effect, exacerbated the concentration of gold in Paris that Mirabeau had so decried.

The banking plan was not Roze de Chantoiseau's only contribution to the problem of sluggish circulation. If the shortage of specie limited the movement of commodities, so too, he thought, did the scarcity of reliable information about those goods. He proposed to remedy this dearth of knowledge by the creation of an *Almanach général d'indication d'adresse personnelle et domicile fixe des Six Corps, Arts et Métiers* (1769).[35] In this distant cousin of other encyclopedic ventures, Roze de Chantoiseau promised to list and describe

> by *alphabetical* order, the names, surnames, titles, and current addresses of all the most famous and important Wholesalers, Merchants, Bankers, Courtiers, Artists, and artisans in the country; serving as an *Inventory* of all those who have received royal *privilege* and *gratitude* for their *distinguished* accomplishments, *extraordinary* cures, innovative *businesses,* and other inventions *useful* to the *common good,* and of those who have made their reputations on *great* talents alone.[36]

Based on the model of the *Almanach royal* (which for decades had provided the names and addresses of venal office holders), and with many of the aspirations of an information bureau, Roze de Chantoiseau's almanac catalogued thousands of Paris merchants and businessmen. While the *Almanach royal* sufficed for those who came to Paris on legal or state business, he wrote, a new directory was needed for the "infinitely greater number" who arrived in Paris "because of their love of the Arts, or for business reasons."[37] Organized by alphabetical order, but with certain noteworthy individuals singled out for special commendation, the *Almanach* combined encyclopedic and meritocratic principles.[38] No trade or business was too lowly or too exalted for the *Almanach:* teachers of the deaf, the grocers of Paris, and the "gentleman from Nancy" who had invented a tool for fattening chickens—all were neatly categorized by the "kind of work each has chosen."[39] Roze's directory specified clockmakers who excelled in the creation of the mechanical works, and those who specialized in making wooden or porcelain cases; engravers who concentrated on music, and those who preferred to do portraits. Like the Encyclopedists, he provided a system of cross-references, in order to give his readers a sense of the relations between different trades. Aware not only of variations within the diverse fields but also of the possibility of further inventions, Roze wrote eagerly of the potential expansion of his directory. In order to serve his fellow citizens further, he asked that all manufacturers or merchants not listed in the first edition ensure their insertion in the improved second edition by simply leaving at his office a card with their name, address, and area of specialization.[40] For later editions of the *Almanach,* Roze depended further on the collaboration of a wide range of experts, again much as

Diderot and d'Alembert did for their *Encyclopédie*.[41] The Encyclopedists, however, wished their readers to become more virtuous, as well as wiser, while the almanac would simply allow them to be happier and to live more comfortably. And while the philosophes endeavored to create an enduring repository of knowledge for future generations, Roze's almanac, like any yearly publication, depended for its future success on its own forthcoming obsolescence. In short, it enacted the logic of his credit notes: desirable because it enabled access to rare items, but planned to disappear.

The almanac proved a considerable success (compared to the debt-reduction plan, at least), appearing regularly throughout the 1770s and 1780s.[42] In 1772 Roze de Chantoiseau, having recovered from the humiliation of his time in Fort l'Evêque Prison, presented a copy to the Dauphin (the future Louis XVI), earning it the subtitle *Almanach dauphin*.[43] As a business directory, the *Almanach* provided would-be purchasers with names and addresses; as a catalogue of achievements, it was also intended to promote further competition and accomplishments "by providing a model for business and the arts."[44] In the *Almanach*'s stated goals, as in the nearly identical work of running the General Information Bureau, Roze de Chantoiseau's position on the question of "luxury" more closely resembled that of the Dutch-born English physician Bernard Mandeville (author of the scandalous *Fable of the Bees*, in which private vices were shown to fuel public prosperity) than that of the Marquis de Mirabeau.[45] The production and sale of any item, Roze thought, regardless of the number of people who could afford to purchase it or would want to use it, would eventually result in everybody's gain. Like the credit notes of his banking scheme, which were desirable because few in number and issued by the king, the *Almanach*'s praises (often heaped on the bearers of royal privileges) were meant to encourage the circulation of goods and wealth. Innovations lauded in its pages—from economical and efficient soup kettles to new methods of embossing ornate patterns into fabric, from smelling salts to restaurants—would be desired and copied across France, thereby stimulating trade and manufacture.

Roze de Chantoiseau's banking and almanac endeavors both demonstrated a concern for facilitating circulation, for creating and confirming a nationwide economic network. In this, he shared the vocabulary and interests of many of his contemporaries.[46] The restaurant, too, promised to improve circulation—on the level not of national trade, but of the individual body, where the restaurateur's menu of healthful consommés would restore the proper balanced flow of chyle, blood, and other fluids. Serving "exclusively those foods that either maintain or re-establish health," the restaurant, sanctioned in the pages of the *Almanach dauphin,* would improve Paris life by freeing the fastidious traveler of the need to depend on an unknown, and potentially unreliable, innkeeper or cook-caterer. (In this respect the *Almanach,* which also indicated a hotel's range of room prices, was a distant ancestor of guides such as the Michelin—a star-giving mentality being not only contemporary with, but part and parcel of, the development of restaurants.) As goods traveled across France and through the central clearinghouse of Paris, merchants, of course, had to accompany them. And where could those forward-thinking and prosperous entrepreneurs be sure to find the salutary bouillons, soothing stewed chickens, and pure Burgundies necessary for clear thought and regular digestion? Where were they guaranteed prompt, courteous, and reliable service? Surely not in the ordinary run of inns and cookshops on which journeymen artisans depended. Where else indeed, but in Roze de Chantoiseau's recently opened "salle de restaurateur"?

The *Almanach général,* in keeping with its stated goal of aiding all commercial travelers to Paris by listing any "innovative establishment," in fact devoted numerous entries to the first restaurants. In the 1769 first edition, the category "Caterers, Innkeepers, and Hoteliers" extended for many pages, listing approximately 700 establishments. Roughly halfway through the list (alphabetized with the other "L"s), the reader found "Le Restaurateur," commended for his delicate and healthful bouillons by the almanac's nameless author. This was not the only mention, for the supplemental listing of further caterers told the reader that "Roze, rue Saint Honoré, Hôtel d'Aligre, the first Restaurateur, offers fine and delicate meals for 3–6 livres per head, in addition to the items expected of a restaurateur."[47] Should the reader somehow have missed this indication as well, he or she had not lost all chance of being restored, for the special section entitled "Secrets of the Arts and Sciences" further directed him or her to the always helpful "Roze, the king's restaurateur . . . founder of the first *maison de santé,*" as, in fact, did the heading "Varied Achievements and New Discoveries." Almost any reader of the *Almanach,* it seems, would eventually have come to know the Paris restaurateur who served healthful bouillons and delicious meals in a manner both scientific and delightful.

Only with difficulty might a reader have failed to learn of Paris's reliance on its "restaurateur"; only with equal effort would that reader have realized that "Chantoiseau" the compiler-publicist and "Roze, the first Restaurateur" were one and the same person.[48] In his anonymous business directory, Roze de Chantoiseau always credited a "M. Roze" with inventing the restaurant. On those few occasions when he put his name to anything concerning the almanac, however, he used the name "Chantoiseau," thus establishing two distinct identities for himself and allowing the almanac's author to write with impunity about the genius and munificence of the restaurant's creator. Roze de Chantoiseau's multiple contributions to modern life, which permitted him to create characters for himself as easily as he delineated market niches, allowed personal identities to circulate much as he hoped goods or services would. Several years later, in a famous bit of decentering dialogic prose, "Rousseau" promised to judge "Jean-Jacques," but that stylistic innovation had already been used by "Chantoiseau" to publicly sing "Roze's" praises.[49] In the later, better-known, case, the Genevan author's multiple literary personae provided a format in which the man called "Rousseau" could, in dialogue with "the Frenchman" (another emanation of the writer), review and put on trial the life and works of the public character called "Jean-Jacques." Having thus tried himself and "objectively" established his own innocence, Jean-Jacques Rousseau—the man, the author, and the self-made martyr—was left to conclude that the pain and anguish he so often felt were in fact caused by others' routine malevolence.[50] Rousseau's division of his own personality characteristically resulted in his blaming the outside world; Roze de Chantoiseau's had permitted him to entice it.

Nonetheless, the almanac was far more than an elaborate device for self-promotion. For if "the restaurateur" appeared under the greatest number of headings, Chantoiseau congratulated other inventors, artists, and merchants almost as enthusiastically: Despreville, the fireworks artist who busied himself with subjecting explosions to the "strictest rules"; Bathenay, the archivist who could render even nearly effaced documents readable; Robin and Leguai, craftsmen particularly distinguished by the quality of their wicker animals. Of these, many (like Jean-Baptiste Raux, enamel-artist to the King, commended in the *Almanach* for his Monday-afternoon donations of glass eyes to the poor) held royal privileges that conferred special status and exemption from the Paris corporate system.[51] The *Almanach général* both emphasized royal privilege as a form of endorsement and mark of excellence, and made it clear that the "king's merchants" were available to serve all the king's people—or at least an admixture of those who could pay, and those deserving poor who merited charity. Like the purveyors of "the king's water" who went into business in 1767, or the Comtesse d'Artois's gentleman-in-waiting who marketed his "Plusqueparfaite" (literally, "More-than-perfect") liqueur from a back door at Versailles, Roze de Chantoiseau's *Almanach* offered to bring the accoutrements of court life into Parisian daily existence.[52] Roze's *Almanach* would make the material benefits of aristocracy, like royal privileges and venal offices themselves, available for purchase.

Among those privilege-carrying merchants was Mathurin Roze de Chantoiseau himself. In January 1768, a year before the first edition of the *Almanach,* he purchased a privilege as one of the twelve "cook-caterers following the Court."[53] Though he paid 1600 livres for this title, or approximately 1000 livres more than he would have for the various fees attendant on becoming a master in the Paris *traiteurs'* guild, the terms of this patent exempted him from the need to serve an apprenticeship, spared him entanglement in other guild regulations, and placed him under the legal jurisdiction of the Versailles-attached Prévôt de l'Hôtel rather than the Paris-based Châtelet.[54] The purchase of the post gave him immediate access to the marketplace, and attached instant prestige to the restaurateur's bouillons. (His almanac entry advertised that the restaurateur specialized in the production of true bouillons, also known as "princely consommés.") His new title, much like the almanac's subtitle, functioned as an indication of royal endorsement and sanction, and thereby as a powerful enticement to prospective patrons.

The aura of official approval extended to other early restaurateurs as well: Jean François Vacossin, described in Roze's *Almanach* as the "second restaurateur," was such by the king's favor; Nicolas Berger, who organized many restaurateurs in a 1780s legal battle against closing-hour regulations, was another "privileged cook following the Court"; Anne Bellot, who took over Roze's restaurant in the Hôtel d'Aligre, also belonged to that category (though as a single woman, this daughter of a *rôtisseur* would have found the other routes into the retail food businesses barred to her).[55] Quite the opposite of a commercial innovation made impossible by the Old Regime (as the old tale of the cook-caterers' lawsuit against them would have it), these first restaurants were, in fact, all supported by royal privileges. Like the furniture makers studied by Michael Sonenscher, or the patent-medicine vendors analyzed by Colin Jones, the first restaurateurs were venal office holders deeply implicated in the growth of urban commercialism.[56]

These first Paris restaurateurs were, in large part, the beneficiaries—and not the victims—of the Old Regime's system of privilege and status. As successful and comfortable merchants and entrepreneurs, they shared in the intellectual and cultural life of Paris; their customers included dukes and actresses, clergymen and philosophers; they numbered minor office-holders, lawyers, and fellow merchants among their friends.[57] They worked within and between established systems, not hampered by them but manipulating them to their own advantage. This is not to suggest that they were somehow distant from the ordinary run of tradesmen; since the Crown did not grant privileges to upstarts likely to poison the population or besmirch its good name, these early restaurateurs also had close business and family ties to the established Paris food and drink trades. Before Berger became a privileged *traiteur,* he was a master retail wine merchant connected by marriage to one of the most important families in that trade, and of the eight restaurateurs who joined him in his 1784 lawsuit, seven were not privileged merchants but regular guild masters.[58]

In these earliest decades of the restaurant business, corporate or professional background was not the key factor that differentiated restaurateurs from *traiteurs.* Rather, it was by proclaiming their concern for the health and well-being of their customers that the first restaurateurs explicitly distanced themselves from the existing retail food trades. Suggesting that the discoveries of medical science would provide the basis for their new ways of interacting with patrons, early restaurateurs emphasized their bouillons' "restorative" powers. Like Roze de Chantoiseau's almanac, the first restaurateurs made much of their novelty, serving the eighteenth-century's version of "nouvelle cuisine" to an audience easily intrigued by claims of modernity's advances. Like the business directory, they promised a subtle blend of pleasure with profit: profit for the restaurateur, to be sure, but also for the individual customer, and, by extension, for the nation at large. All, in short, could be improved and benefited, restored and delighted, by means of a small cup of bouillon.

"... *et ego vos restaurabo*"

Like many of the other products and services publicized by Roze de Chantoiseau's *Almanach* (and often endorsed by the Academy of Sciences and announced in the daily or twice weekly classified advertisements), restaurants addressed a semi-medicinal need in a busy urban setting. While perhaps more genteel than the purgative and vermicidal spicecakes manufactured by the gingerbreadmaker Boquy, Roze's and Vacossin's restaurants could still be found along with Keyser's anti-venereal pills and Madame Villard's laxative waters under the *Almanach*'s heading "Remedies and Medical Secrets." Like their fellow venal officeholders, the *médecins du Roi,* the first restaurateurs were participants in, and beneficiaries of, the enormous eighteenth-century marketplace of medicalized consumerism.[59] They expanded that market well beyond anti-venereal salves and smallpox inoculations; thanks to their place at the intersection of medicine and diet, they marketed not just health, but taste and sensibility as well.

As much a scientific innovation as a culinary curiosity, the opening of the first restaurant responded to eighteenth-century elite culture's preoccupations with the pursuit of health as well as to its fascination with cuisine. Throughout this period, intellectuals, merchants, and courtiers alike were obsessed with physical well-being and captivated by the possibility of its secular and scientific attainment. A large number of the eighteenth century's most prominent thinkers (including Mandeville, La Mettrie, de Jaucourt, and Bordeu) had received formal medical training, while Voltaire and Rousseau, notorious for their maladies, read widely on the subject. Quesnay, first of the Physiocrats, was also court physician to Louis XV. Diderot planned a work on the elements of physiology and habitually kept his correspondents informed about the state of his digestion.[60] Famous doctors who had never seen a particular patient nonetheless often gave recommendations in epistle form, consultations comparable to the immensely popular genre of published legal briefs.[61] Medical authorities such as Samuel Tissot, Pierre Pomme, and Anne-Charles Lorry were among the most celebrated figures of their day, and medical books, long available only as weighty tomes with expensive bindings and Latin texts, began to be published in a comparatively inexpensive, portable, vernacular format. Reading medical treatises became such a common pastime that physicians and other experts criticized the availability of these texts, much as moralizing social commentators bemoaned the popularity of novel-reading.[62]

According to the era's respected (and often reprinted) expert on happiness, Louis Jean Levesque de Pouilly, physical health was a necessary precondition for any sort of deeper spiritual or emotional happiness.[63] At the same time, its converse, illness, seemed both conquerable and ever-threatening; the plague made its last appearance in France in 1720, but other epidemics (such as influenza) continued to pose regular threats. The subject of the proper treatment of syphilis and gonorrhea sparked endless debates, sending sufferers to experiment with an enormous inventory of purgatives, enemas, and mercury salves.[64] The theories of Mesmer, who promised to re-establish a balance of the body's electrical fluids through his use of tubs and wands, generated far more interest than any of Rousseau's political writings.[65]

Across social divisions and professional allegiances, health was a shared goal of Enlightenment culture: the impetus behind experiments with spiritualism and the proliferation of other pseudo- and semi-sciences, it also shaped thinking about cookery and diet. Already in 1750, the anonymous *Dictionnaire des alimens (Dictionary of Foods)* claimed that the interest in health characteristic of "the newest and most interesting" cookery had created a new public, one free of the old distinctions between rich, bourgeois, and "sensuous"—each of whom already had numerous cookbooks to consult. In 1758, Menon, the most prominent eighteenth-century French cookbook author, broke with his previous pattern of writing books addressed to particular socioeconomic groupings (for example, *Les Soupers de la cour*, "for grand tables," and *La Cuisinière bourgeoise*, "for middling ones") to publish *La Cuisine et l'office de santé*, a work specifically directed to the common urban concern with individual health.[66] The pursuit of health united, rather than distinguished, bourgeois and aristocratic Parisians (though it never encompassed "the people"). While socioeconomic distinctions might still hold sway among those individuals so old-fashioned as to be vigorous, healthy eaters, members of those same classes might also form a new eating (or non-eating) public, thanks to the universal culture of regeneration. According to medical and culinary literature alike, the natural simplicity and harmony of good health found its base not in rigid social divisions or hierarchies but in more mutable and expansive cultural markers.[67]

While the search for a state of health influenced intellectual and literary productions at many levels, it also entered the marketplace and affected commercial developments. Roze de Chantoiseau's *Almanach* was hardly alone in emphasizing salutary innovations: across the tightly printed pages of the twice weekly *petites affiches* (classified advertisements), purveyors of everything from tortoises to chocolate touted the healthful benefits of their products.[68] Maille, mustard manufacturer to the king, marketed his two hundred varieties of mustard and vinegar as health and beauty aids (ideal holiday gifts), while his philanthropic winter distributions of mustard to the poor earned him several congratulatory articles in the *Année littéraire*.[69] The city of Paris even entered the lucrative health business by sponsoring fund-raising *bals de santé* ("health balls"), which began in the late afternoon and closed by midnight, for "the sick, and those who must follow a strict regimen."[70]

Within this context of the elite pursuit of individual health, the first "restaurateurs" hung out their shingles. Throughout the 1770s, restaurants styled themselves as *maisons de santé* (also the name for private infirmaries), and the author Nicolas Restif de la Bretonne asserted that a decade later they were still known as "health suppers" *(soupers de santé)*.[71] Jean François Vacossin, one of the first restaurateurs, stressed the healthful aspects of his fare by telling potential customers that he served "only those dishes that contribute to the conservation or re-establishment of good health"; he also alluded to potential spiritual, as well as physical, benefits to be derived from his carefully chosen menu by decorating the shopfront of his rue-de-Grenelle restaurant with the vaguely blasphemous witticism, *Accurite ad me omnes qui stomacho laboratis et ego vos restaurabo* ("Run to me all you whose stomachs labor, and I shall restore you"). This maxim, widely recognized as a paraphrase of Christ's "Come unto me, all ye that labor and are heavy laden, and I shall give you rest" (Matthew 11:28), made the Gospel into a promise of material nourishment and the words of Christ into a charlatan's slogan (especially in some advertising, where the Latin verb was conjugated incorrectly), but it also, by its similarity to a doctor's Latin sign, gave notice of the restaurateur's medicinal pretensions.[72] Jacques Minet promised the "weak chested" that they would find strength in his restorative consommés, while Duclos, another early restaurateur, apparently certain of his menu's salutary qualities, hastened to announce that the food he served was "as tasty as it is healthful."[73]

In positioning themselves at the semi-learned intersection of medicine and cookery, the first restaurateurs at once drew on longstanding traditions that linked the two fields, and, more immediately, responded to attacks on cookery being made by the professionalizing medical trades of the late Old Regime. For centuries previous, cookery and medicine had worked together, almost like two branches of chemistry; the Middle Ages and the Renaissance barely distinguished between medical and culinary knowledge, and single manuscripts often combined recipes with remedies.[74] During the 1700s, however, doctors (like apothecaries and surgeons) increasingly emphasized their own specialized scientific knowledge and distanced themselves from the arts of the kitchen. Self-styled practitioners of the "liberal arts," physicians more and more firmly rejected comparisons with the manual trade of cookery (even though the mid-century prevalence of materialist science meant that their basic tools actually continued to overlap considerably with those of cooks).[75] A "war" between cooks and doctors, an educated retelling of the traditional folkloric conflict between Fat and Lean, Carnival and Lent, ensued, surfacing in a wide range of literary contexts: for example, in *Le Nouveau Gulliver* (a 1730 French supplement to Swift's work), followers of the god "Gastrimythes" live most of the year on the island of cooks, but they take regularly timed holidays to the island of doctors, where they feast on purgatives, laxatives, and enemas.[76] Painting a less benign picture of the battlefield, the *Encyclopédie* article "Seasonings" bluntly asserted that there were in the world two sorts of men: "cooks who work ceaselessly to kill us . . . and doctors who try desperately to cure us."[77]

While all kitchen employees were, by this reasoning, suspect, it was the "public cooks" of inns and cookshops who received the full weight of enlightened opprobrium (in parallel with wineshop-keepers, who were regularly accused of adulterating their wines). Household servants were part of an extended network of nearly familial relations and hence might conceivably be loyal and trustworthy, but no such ties of obligation and dependence guaranteed the reliability of unknown caterers.[78] Medical dissertations and cookware advertisements therefore agreed wholeheartedly that "public cooks," who cared only for making money, posed a grave threat to the hapless eater's well-being. The jurist Des Essarts, in his 1786 *Universal Police Dictionary*, explained that economic considerations determined a *traiteur's* preferred recipes and cooking methods, and that these cheap and shoddy preparations (chosen by "avarice alone") often gave rise to a panoply of illnesses; an aristocratic family obliged to travel long distances might try to avoid this hazard by sending their kitchen staff ahead in a postchaise loaded with bottled broths and ready-prepared sauces.[79]

Though *traiteurs* who manufactured bouillon cubes had been among the first to promise reliable foods for travelers (claiming in the early 1760s that their easily carried, nonspoiling products guaranteed safe and healthy voyages on land and sea alike), their reputation (however little deserved) for poisoning their customers meant that they were unlikely to find many takers for their "meat-extract bouillon tablets."[80] If public cooks were to become the defenders of public health, far more than a change in recipes was required.

As far as the medical and scientific communities were concerned, the master caterer's attachment to his copper cookware most clearly proved his dedication to poisoning his unwary customers. According to dozens of articles in Vandermonde's monthly *Periodical of Medicine, Surgery, and Pharmacy,* copper residue was an ever-present danger, most to be feared because it was, like so many other dietary impurities, menacingly invisible.[81] While the unlined pot stayed hidden in the kitchen filth, toxic verdigris "combined," in the words of one horrified barrister, "with all the most delightful dishes and all the stews most likely to please our taste and senses."[82] The Paris cook-caterers' guild, beginning in 1779, conducted monthly inspections for dangerous cookware, but this was too little, too late: a self-proclaimed restaurateur had preemptively pounced on the issue more than ten years earlier, assuring his customers that he prepared his bouillons in utensils not of copper, but of "glazed Flemish clay."[83]

From the accounts in the medical and more general press, one might conclude that the cook-caterers of Old-Regime Paris delighted in selling spoiled food and thought nothing of poisoning their customers by cooking in dilapidated copper utensils. Were this true, it would seem not at all extraordinary that early restaurateurs, by emphasizing their concern for health and cleanliness, could successfully challenge the established trade. Indeed, given the number of Parisians who relied on public cooks, one would be left to marvel that the entire city had not long ago succumbed to food-poisoning-induced imbecility. But, of course, these denunciations told only one side of the story: it was far easier for a doctor or legist to condemn public cooks than for a neighborhood *traiteur* to issue a rebuttal. Furthermore, these criticisms were not unique to social reformers or public health advocates. Instead, they were but one version of the complaints common among a wide range of travelers, all of whom griped bitterly about the quality of food made available by the public cook-caterers of Paris.

Since any successful *traiteur's* business depended largely not on occasional foreign travelers, but on regular, local customers, visitors passing through the French capital were perhaps justified in complaining of the city's public cooks. Most *traiteurs'* rhythms and menus were geared to a steady clientele, and their rigidly fixed schedules were as useful for the many diners who reappeared at their tables day after day as they were aggravating for the one-time visitor. Eighteenth-century French-to-English dictionaries translated *traiteur* as "public cook," but they perhaps led their readers astray, for that translation obscured the extent to which the guild's members relied overwhelmingly on their repeat customers, each of whom thought of a particular master as "*my* cook." (Interrogated by the police, a potential witness to a crime contextualized his remarks by saying he had been "dining at my caterer's [*traiteur*].")[84] The daily customers at a table d'hôte knew each other and formed a community based in the repeated patterns of informal, quotidian sociability. When something de-

parted from this routine, they noted it: when silverware was stolen from
the *traiteur* Grapin, suspicion immediately fell on the one non-regular
customer. Similarly, when his colleague Pour de Lamothe realized that a
silver fork had disappeared, he told the police that he had more reason to
suspect his new apprentice than the familiar "people who come to eat in
my house."[85] So central were regular patrons to a *traiteur's* business that
one, at least, noted in his account book whenever a regular customer did
not order a meal, while the sale contract of others' businesses specified
that the "equipment" being sold included "the patronage of regular
customers."[86]

Even aside from the table d'hôte, it was local neighborhood business
that sustained the average *traiteur*. Thus he might sell an unadorned roast
turkey to somebody who then went to eat part of it in the tavern across the
street, or he might direct a customer who wanted a salad to the fruit-and-
vegetable retailer next door.[87] Working with his wife, a single apprentice,
and perhaps a female domestic servant, the typical Paris *traiteur* made
cooked foods available to the vast population of urban workers and artisans who did not have their own kitchens or cooking equipment. Travelers
who remained in Paris for a considerable period of time could establish a
rapport with a local *traiteur* as well, who provided them with silverware
and crockery in addition to food and drink.[88] If a client preferred to dine
in his or her hotel rooms, the caterer's apprentice, who delivered the food
and returned later to pick up the silverware, went into the customers'
rented rooms as if he were a domestic servant bringing food from the
household kitchen. The relationship between the cook-caterer and his
longstanding regular customers was based in trust: trust that the eater
would not pocket the silverware, trust that he or she would eventually pay
the bill.[89] Quite frequently, a regular customer would be allowed to run a
tab for a month or more.[90] When somebody carried this logic to an extreme, a hotel guest could have meals delivered for nine months without
paying, a *traiteur* could be stuck feeding a parrot for sixteen months, or an
imprisoned aristocrat might borrow considerable sums from her well-
established and affluent *traiteur*.[91]

Even in the least routine branch of his work—furnishing wedding dinners and other celebratory banquets—the *traiteur* was well integrated
into his local community and its customs. The banquets he prepared, often occasioned by important moments in the life cycle (marriage, christen-
ing, death), marked the passage of human time as surely as the regular
one-o'clock table d'hôte did. More than an obscure or purely legalistic

definition, the announcement "serves weddings and parties" decorated the front of many *traiteurs'* places of business; for the chronicler and novelist Louis Sébastien Mercier, the link between the specific trade and the family event was sufficiently strong for him to devote much of the chapter entitled "Weddings" in his *Tableau de Paris (Picture of Paris)* to the business difficulties of *traiteurs*.[92] A celebratory meal in a *traiteur's* banquet room marked the creation of a new family and reaffirmed the family's importance as a locus of festivity. The wedding party, the solidarity of the table d'hôte—both suggest that the *traiteur's* shop formed an integral part of the web of family and neighborhood sociability characteristic of popular life in eighteenth-century Paris.[93]

For all of these people, then—for the thousands of Parisians who dined regularly at *traiteurs'* tables d'hôte, and the many others who had celebrated the major events of their lives in a cook-caterer's banquet room—a medical practitioner's repeated warnings about the dangers of copper poisoning probably did not give rise to much alarm. Much as a *traiteur* allowed his regular customers to run a tab and trusted them to pay at the end of their specified terms, so his clientele expected to survive each and every dinner. Since his business depended largely on regular customers, it was hardly in a cook's best interest to poison them—in fact, it was all the more crucial that he did not. So for this large group of eaters, the horror stories about poorly tinned pans, or about glass beads and other potentially fatal ornaments accidentally mixed into stews, would have been just that: horror stories about "somebody else's cook."[94] However, for those who did not have their own cooks (literally or rhetorically) the dangers seemed far greater, and the threat, far more immediate.

The restaurant, which guaranteed beneficial bouillons prepared in scrupulously clean stockpots, did not address the many groups of regular neighborhood eaters who relied on their familiar *traiteurs*. Rather, Roze de Chantoiseau directed the restaurant at the same population of merchants, entrepreneurs, men of letters, and venal officeholders targeted by his other ventures. "Le Restaurateur," like the other hoteliers and innkeepers with whom Chantoiseau initially catalogued him, catered to the needs of those from out of town, those who were "traveling through"—those who were, literally, in circulation. More dour critics of the commercial spirit (for example, the author of the *Encyclopédie's* article "Hospitality") bemoaned the expansion of the market and the increased movement of goods that, by converting the world to a monetary system, had (at some ill-defined moment in history) destroyed the links of simple person-to-person human generosity.[95] Roze de Chantoiseau's restaurants (the one he briefly operated, the several others he endorsed, and the many he inspired), on the other hand, implied that commerce itself could be perfected to offer the comforts of modern hospitality. If the first restaurateurs were not quite "friends of all the world," they did nonetheless open their doors "at all hours" to ladies and gentlemen who required a cup of restorative bouillon or some other "dainty and salutary dish."[96]

Where the *traiteur*'s usual sign ("Fait noces et festins") promised general family- and community-based festivity, the restaurateur addressed a much more specific audience of debilitated, perhaps Latin-reading, individuals. Restaurants grandly announced to passersby: "I shall restore you"—how did that promise come to take precedence over the traiteur's cheery "prepares weddings and parties" or the quotidian patterns of the table d'hôte? For, as we know, restaurateurs did in a sense triumph: today, even the humblest eatery or the smallest takeout stand offers not large festivals and ceremonial banquets but restoration for individual eaters.

2

The Nouvelle Cuisine
of Rousseauian Sensibility

M. DelaMorgue: I imagine that even though you're a restaurateur,
you might still be able to serve me supper?
Arlequin: But why wouldn't I be able to?
M. DelaMorgue: Well, if you followed the customs of your Parisian
colleagues—they overwhelm you with dishes, then starve you to
death! . . . for my part, I eat to live, and I have no intention of saying
I've supped, when my stomach makes a liar of me.

ARLEQUIN, RESTAURATEUR AUX PORCHERONS (1769)

In March 1767, *L'Avantcoureur (The Forerunner),* a journal dedicated
to innovation in the arts, the sciences, and "any other field that makes
life more agreeable," announced that a new type of establishment had
opened in Paris's rue des Poulies. The new business specialized in "excellent consommés or *restaurants* always carefully warmed in a hot water
bath." These *restaurants* were available at all hours, at reasonable prices,
and were served in gold-rimmed, white faience dishes. The restaurateur, a
master *traiteur* named Minet, provided a takeout service, but his announcement particularly stressed the pleasures to be had on the premises:

> Those who suffer from weak and delicate chests, and whose diets
> therefore do not usually include an evening meal, will be delighted to
> find a public place where they can go have a consommé without of-
> fending their sense of delicacy, as one might have a *bavaroise* in a café
> while enjoying the pleasures of society.
>
> In order to leave nothing to be desired, it was also decided to make
> available the many new periodicals that appear every month in the
> capital, such that this new establishment offers both solace for the
> body, and distraction for the soul.[1]

Culinary historians have assumed that the first restaurants offered food
that countered sudden, debilitating pangs of urban hunger.[2] Yet this advertisement for one of the very first restaurants makes clear that the *salle de
restaurateur* appealed instead to the more specific and medicalized sensi-

bility of those Parisians who, on doctors' orders, ate almost nothing. The new business's storefront was decorated with a Latin couplet that emphasized the same point: "Here are tasty sauces to titillate your bland palate; here the effete find healthy chests."[3] The restaurant catered not to the hungry, but to the enervated who had lost their appetites and suffered from jaded palates and weak chests.

Why would anyone care to replace supper (the evening meal; "dinner," in eighteenth-century Paris, was the meal eaten in the early afternoon) with a small cup of potent broth? What, in short, needed to be restored? To answer these questions, we must suspend our twentieth-century understanding of what a restaurant is, for restaurants were neither originally nor necessarily about lavish dining. Rather than originating in Rabelaisian excess, the restaurant's emergence as a cultural institution distinct from the inn, the traiteur's shop, or the café owed much to a particular style of *not* eating. Conspicuous consumption, as Peter Burke has noted, need not always take the form of prodigality: abstemiousness, too, may prove quite remarkable.[4]

Several months after the first "restorer's rooms" opened, another long advertisement for a new restaurant, this one run by Jean François Vacossin, self-styled "truc restaurateur," again appealed to a public afflicted with "delicate chests":

> We shall serve, and at a modest price, only those dishes that contribute to the conservation or re establishment of good health . . . For those who have weak and delicate chests, and who rarely eat two large meals, it will be convenient to find some decent place where they can go both to enjoy the benefits of society and to take their *restaurants*.[5]

What was this weakness of chest that so plagued Enlightenment-era eaters, and sent them to seek restoration in a soup-cup? In this period, pulmonary weakness served both as a synecdoche for general fatigue, and (in some understandings) as a symptom of intellectual sophistication and emotional acuity. In an age of vapors and miasmas, when the "unfathomable mixture" of elements composing the atmosphere posed a constant threat to human well-being, weak-chestedness became a modish complaint and lungs were widely considered the most fragile organs.[6] Respiratory ailments were among the most common and least specific of complaints: anybody—from the asthmatic to the intellectual, from the tubercular to the allergic, from the blasé to the syphilitic—could claim to be "weak of chest." Medical doctors busied themselves regrouping ailments into a variety of technical categories, but Paris restaurateurs of the 1760s remained deliberately vague, content to cast their net wide by advertising bouillons and other dishes that might restore all and sundry.

Physicians gave a wide range of scientific names to the various conditions that manifested themselves in weakness of the chest and published multi-volume works to describe the complicated symptoms and etiologies of these numerous maladies, but all diagnoses depended on widely accepted physiological models that stressed the importance of proper digestion for each of the body's processes. Although there were heated debates in the early eighteenth century over digestion's mechanical or chemical basis, all parties agreed to its significance. Digestion clearly worked the most miraculous transformations: hay was transformed into horses, mice became cats, and bread turned into people. As Diderot promised to demonstrate, digestion could even bring statues to life. If, he wrote, one pulverized a statue, then mixed this dust with dirt and planted seeds in it, a plant would grow from the nutrients of the soil. A person could then eat the plant, digest it, and thrive, thereby completing the conversion of marble bust into sentient human.[7]

The miracles of digestion were not unfailing, however, and so vital a bodily process could easily be deranged by ill-prepared foods, intellectual exertion, or emotional anguish. In the medical imagination of the eighteenth century, *indigestion* therefore posed a constant and serious threat: Samuel Tissot, the Swiss physician, began his very influential *De la santé des gens de lettres (On the Health of Men of Letters)* with the statement that all ills—including consumption, madness, and early death—could be traced to deranged digestion.[8] Non-specialists, too, feared indigestion: years before it heralded the opening of the first restaurants, *L'Avantcoureur* told its readers that a sound stomach was the first prerequisite for "stable good health"; in his diary entry for November 6, 1767, Paris man-about-town Simeon Prosper Hardy remarked worriedly that reports had come from Versailles of the queen suffering "serious indigestion" but, with evident relief, he added that the malady in question had proven to be merely a tubercle on her lung.[9]

While scrupulous attention to diet was always advisable, it was especially significant in the treatment of respiratory and circulatory complaints. According to the dominant physiological models, if one's food did not move freely through the gastrointestinal tract, then one's blood was sure to become sluggish as well, losing its necessary liquid qualities. The stated relation of the three processes (digestion, circulation, and respiration) was both causal and analogical, relying for its explanatory powers on the very graphic image of undigested pieces of food rotting in the stomach. When hastily eaten or poorly chosen foodstuffs sat solidly and stubbornly in the belly, they clogged circulation and hence overcharged the lungs. Over-consumption of food caused over-production of blood and hence necessitated blood-letting. (All these bits of medical wisdom are not, after all, so unlike a twentieth-century physician's warnings that a diet rich in red meats will raise cholesterol levels and lead to a thickening of the arteries.)[10] The physician Rozière de la Chassagne, one of the eighteenth century's greatest experts on lung diseases, repeatedly emphasized the necessity of strict adherence to a prescribed diet and concluded his description of a patient's ideal regimen with the threatening comment that "the most minor mistake or the slightest deviation may have deadly results."[11] In 1767, Coste's *Traité des maladies du poumon (Treatise on Maladies of the Lung)* credited ragouts, sauces, and essences with causing most pulmonary maladies, while another specialist rejected all "succulent" dishes as likely to cause the body to rot and spoil.[12] Though celebrated in the early nineteenth century as the archetypal French meal and the site of delightfully witty conversation, the supper (or evening meal) was denounced by eighteenth-century physicians as a pernicious custom sure to overload the digestive system.[13]

As if the threat of tuberculosis and early death were not sufficient warning, experts insisted that overeating and the careless consumption of stimulants could have almost immediate effects on mental, as well as physical, health. While difficult-to-digest items sat rotting in the stomach, they produced clouds of noxious gas that befuddled thought and eventually triumphed over reason. Foods were said to "cook" in the stomach, and if this process were to go wrong and the pot somehow to "boil over," the heated foods gave off vapors which rose to the head, impairing intellectual and emotional functions.[14] In his *Traité des sensations (Treatise on the Senses)*, the noted Rouennais surgeon Claude Nicolas LeCat recounted the cautionary tale of a delicate young man, seduced by his friends into drinking a cup of coffee and a few sips of liqueur. This rash experiment first resulted in the anticipated gaiety and vigor, but as the liquids began to evaporate they left a residue, a "heaviness in the stomach," which "agitated his nervous organs and crushed his spirit." Nerves confused and soul oppressed, the youth began to suffer from the "phlogiston" fermenting in his stomach. Then, resolving to rid himself of the putrefying mass, he took an emetic, but the rotting of the "phlogiston" had proceeded apace, and the strong emetic failed to induce vomiting. Instead, it only exacerbated the situation, inflaming his stomach yet more, and eventually leaving him the incurably mad victim of hallucinations.[15]

LeCat's ominous little morality tale attributed a central role to the suffering patient's stomach. Though one historian has claimed that the eighteenth century's concept of "nerves" has guided medical theorizing ever since, we should note that, for thinkers of this era, the processes of digestion (or their dread counterpart, indigestion) mediated much of the external world's impact on those nerves. Nerves, then, did not so much replace the stomach as the century's "magical human organ" as they extended its domain.[16] When, in the late 1750s and 1760s, mechanistic physiology intersected with the cult of sensibility, medical categories and dietary proscriptions increasingly converged with aesthetic and ethical judgments (and vice versa).[17] A "nervous sensibility" manifested itself in a visceral response to any and all stimuli: beautiful landscapes and strongly seasoned foods alike. The more delicate one's nerves, the more likely one was to weep at a tale of woe, or fall ill after a poorly prepared meal. By this logic, to be "weak of chest" was also to make a statement about nervous sympathy, and to have good taste in food was to be exquisitely sensitive to the stimuli of nature.

"Weakness of chest" was therefore far more than a simple physical condition. Instead, the eighteenth-century diagnosis of "weak-chestedness," like that of "consumption" in the nineteenth century, condensed a variety of cultural meanings into a set of specifically physiological attributes. (In many respects, the weak-chested bouillon sipper of this period was the immediate precursor of the Romantic *poitrinaire*.) Maladies such as "weak-chestedness" and the even more vague and widespread "vapors" brought together physiology and affect in a spiral of science and sentiment that precluded the designation of either term as solely the cause or uniquely the effect.[18] Moral, artistic, and personal sensitivity were all to be expected from the physically debilitated individual, and nervous or pulmonary maladies were taken to be reliable indicators of emotional responsiveness.

Since weak-chestedness was both a function of nervous acuity and a factor contributing to its development, French men and women were not all equally susceptible to the effects of bad air or suspect diet. All humans were sensate, but some were more sensitive than others. Intimately linked to other predispositions and inclinations, weak-chestedness and its symptoms were among the many signs by which spiritual worthiness could be deduced. To be a sensitive soul was to be awash in empathy, passion, pathos, and pain. Moved to extremes of feeling by beautiful sunsets, resolute orphans, unhappy lovers, or Roman ruins, the man or woman "of feeling" most stereotypically revealed his or her sentiments by copious tears and occasional fainting spells, but the same condition might just as well manifest itself in the "inability to eat an evening meal."[19]

Such assumptions about the transparent correlation of moral and physical states allowed, of course, for the manipulation, whether conscious or otherwise, of symptoms and outward appearances. If spiritual sensitivity and moral awareness betrayed themselves in fits of weeping or by a delicate appetite, then surely alimentary fastidiousness necessarily indicated a caring heart and a tortured soul? In this almost obsessive discussion of vapors, phthisis, and other maladies, health may have been the putative goal, but the search for it made a spectacle of ailments and afflictions. "Weak of chest" or no, as they sipped their consommés, restaurant customers demonstrated (to themselves, and to anybody else who might be watching) the delicacy of appetite that indicated a sensitive soul and a refined spirit. Like the "bals de santé" (health balls) sponsored by the city, restaurants made frailty into a quality to be exhibited and shared with others. Describing the restaurants of the Palais Royal as late as 1788, one observer wrote, "Even if he is not sick, a pretentious little fop [*petit maître*] often orders consommé in the evening, because that gives him the aura of ill-health."[20] To be as healthy as some mythical peasant or remote savage might be the delicate eater's putative aim, but at the same time the fastidious city-dweller carefully asserted that she or he was not a coarse peasant by exhibiting the delicate degeneration caused by urban existence. After all, how could a truly sensitive body and soul be healthy breathing the fetid air of Paris? (In 1755, a dissertation defended at the Paris School of Medicine argued that Parisians—because of the city air—had dietary requirements that differed from those of all other peoples.)[21]

Even as it formed an ideal shared by the bourgeoisie and the nobility alike, the achievement of health through science and through a simple existence still served as a social marker, as a way to differentiate the sophisticated urbanite from the coarse worker capable of digesting whatever was placed before him.[22] To suffer the ill effects of digestion gone wrong was to prove the worth of one's intellectual life: one aspiring author, Mauvelain, regaled his publishers with tales of headaches and stagnating humors, perhaps to impress upon them the seriousness of his commitment to the life of the mind.[23] The eighteenth century's new mechanistic models of physiology taught that perception and intellect were functions of bodily organs that were necessarily constructed from the same nutrients as the rest of the human body; therefore, as diet affected physical health, it also shaped emotional and intellectual life.[24] Since gustatory and aesthetic sensibility were equally grounded in the senses, someone's taste for meat might actually cause, rather than merely parallel, his fondness for bellicose epic or proclivity for murder. The sensitive soul—the philosophical young man or the tender-hearted woman who burst into tears in front of a painting by Greuze, or while reading Rousseau's *La Nouvelle Héloïse*—was inherently delicate of body as well as of mind and heart.

Those who were "delicate," either by nature or from overexertion and the resulting disequilibrium, were therefore advised to pay the closest attention to the condition of their lungs and the suitability of their diets. And the category of "the delicate" accounted for no small percentage of society; according to the *Encyclopédie,* "we should classify as such, women in general, as well as most residents of large cities . . . especially men of letters."[25] Men of letters needed to take particular notice of their diets because their overactive brains easily disturbed the balance of the human machine; as they struggled to digest difficult ideas, no energy remained for digesting their food.[26] For Anne-Charles Lorry, physician author of the influential 1754 *Essai sur les alimens (Essay on Foods),* intellectual and emotional meditation led directly to the failure of the stomach: "the senses are distracted, and so the basic bodily functions are suspended; the body-machine's maintenance is overlooked . . . All the energy is in the soul, little is left for the body." Writing as if he were describing the care and feeding of a rare pet bird or a tropical fish, Lorry termed the "man of letters" both "humanity's most brilliant ornament" and the most difficult decoration to keep alive. Men of letters, he asserted, nearly all suffered from melancholia and constipation—two conditions that could be treated with a gentle and limited diet.[27] With their unctuous bouillons and, just as important, their Latin signs, restaurateurs addressed the many dandified aspiring men of letters and would-be philosophes who flocked to Paris, all armed with little but a smattering of Latin and the manuscripts that would make their fortunes.[28]

According to the literature on ailments, women were nearly as likely as bookish men to suffer from weak chests and fragile tummies. By one physician's account, women's vulnerability stemmed not from their naturally overactive minds, but from their profound mental and physical laziness. With no occupation other than the pursuit of "the silliest amusements," women yielded easily to their passions and fancies, both dietary and sexual. In their search for stimulating pleasures, they often rashly ate strongly flavored items which had particularly deleterious effects on their inactive and easily irritated stomachs. Even though experts traced women's susceptibility not to their fast-paced intellects but to their general physical and mental indolence, the recommendation remained the same: gentle, light foods in small quantities.[29]

Identified as a condition exacerbated by feminine sloth and febrile intelligence, weakness of chest might, in the minds of some, be little more than a euphemism for general decadence or immorality. (Several doctors specifically argued that pulmonary consumption remained incurable until patients admitted that their conditions were the secondary symptoms of syphilis.)[30] The condition could connote licentiousness specifically because it seemed to plague the feminine or effeminate; yet it might mean attentive virtue, precisely because it affected those rare individuals who responded to all impressions. The modishness of cure seeking, the rapidity with which remedies rose and fell in popularity, the emphasis on past "excesses" contributing to present poor health: all gave to the manifestation of illness and to the restoration of health a series of expanding, and increasingly self-contradictory, connotations.

Nouvelle-cuisine Restaurants

To treat these many different sorts of delicate sufferers, the restaurants of the 1760s and 1770s presented dietary innovation in a form that combined forward-looking science with more conservative, pastoral impulses. Restaurateurs advertised that they kept their consommés warm in *bains-marie*, instruments usually considered complicated pieces of scientific equipment, but they also insisted that extreme "simplicity" characterized those same soups.[31] By means of scientific knowledge and technology, restaurateurs claimed to simplify nature itself. "Modern cookery," wrote one of their advocates, "refines away the coarse qualities in foods and rids them of their earthy essences [*sucs terrestres*], thereby perfecting, filtering, and, in a way, spiritualizing them."[32] In this common model, here outlined by the academician Etienne Laureault de Foncemagne, nature needed to be cleansed in order to be fit for human consumption; cookery, by civilizing the raw materials of human diet, could propel humanity further from its brutish origins.

The foods and clothes marked by eighteenth-century literate culture as "simple" were, however, rarely those actually eaten or worn by the more humble segments of the population. In one famous sartorial example, Marie Antoinette's shepherdess costume—though certainly austere in comparison with the robes of court ceremony—was also far finer, and infinitely cleaner, than the wool garments of real sheep farmers. Dressmakers, artists, and authors all created representations that betokened natural simplicity but were composed of more sophisticated materials. Jean-Jacques Rousseau extended his stirring critique of "civilization" to the table, but in *Les Confessions, Emile,* and *Julie, ou la nouvelle Héloïse* he celebrated neither the dark bread of peasant fare, nor the acorns eaten by the "primitive man" of his *Discourse on the Origins of Inequality,* nor even the "pot-au-feu" of the ancient Gauls. Instead, Rousseau's sensitive characters inhabited a milk-and-honey world of (comparatively expensive) fruits and dairy products.[33]

When restaurants served "simple" bouillons, they similarly contributed to the construction of a mythical version of sincere, healthful country life which proved acceptable to an urban, elite population. The *restaurant,* as the emblematic ingredient in the eighteenth-century's fashionably scientific "nouvelle cuisine," was a restorative well suited to the ailments of the sufferingly sensitive. While the bouillon as remedy addressed medicinal needs, the same liquid as delicacy assured that the cure was no worse than the malady.

Though the word *restaurant* had historically been derived from a verb meaning "to repair" or "recuperate," contemporary connotations linked it much more intimately with novelty. *Restaurants* and other condensed broths featured prominently in the mid-century version of nouvelle cuisine: a 1742 manifesto, entitled *La Nouvelle cuisine,* began with two recipes for "*restaurants,* or the reductions used in the new cookery"; a 1757 play, *L'Ancienne et nouvelle cuisine,* personified the modern cookery in a protagonist named "Restaurant," as did the 1779 boulevard success, *Blanquette et Restaurant.*[34] In all of these contexts, the *restaurant,* a tiny amount of bouillon requiring hours to prepare, offered a neat emblem, a convenient way to synopsize the nouvelle cuisine's most salient attribute: its paradoxical promise of "restoration" by means of innovation. Well before historians had traced the restaurant, as an institution, to the Revolution, cooks and eaters had treated the *restaurant,* in its bouillon form, as a symbol of culinary upheaval. Grandiose as it may sound, the restaurant was inscribed—right from its beginnings in a tightly sealed soup kettle—in debates about modernity and historical change.

As a badge of novelty, the *restaurant* played a key role in the debates between "ancient" and "modern" cookery which raged in cookbook prefaces, medical texts, and fashionable conversations for over forty years.[35] The new cookery created a "schism," in the words of one late-eighteenth-century writer, that quickly divided Paris's most influential intellectual circles, but the debate over the nouvelle cuisine was hardly limited to elite culture.[36] Like other Enlightenment-era controversies, this one appeared simultaneously in a variety of contexts: in published writing, in salon conversations, and on stage at the most successful boulevard theater, Nicolet's Grands-Danseurs. Made into a mock family drama by Beaunoir's popular work, *Blanquette et Restaurant,* the struggle between veal in white sauce and stewed beef with onions delighted crowds of master-craftsmen, shopgirls, idle young men, domestic servants, apprentices, and incognito aristocrats.[37] Accompanied sometimes by a pantomime entitled "Pierrot, King of Cocaigne" and on other occasions by "The Fricassee Dance," *Blanquette et Restaurant* loosely borrowed the plot of Voltaire's Babylonian tragedy, *Sémiramis,* to tell the story of Restaurant's conquest of the charming kitchen maid, Blanquette.[38] For the audiences at the Grands-Danseurs, wisecracks about the nouvelle cuisine, the *restaurants* that were among its key ingredients, and the restaurants that were its chief institutional support were as much a part of contemporary Paris life as freemasonic temples, hot-air balloons, and mesmerist mumbo-jumbo (all of which also found their way onto the stage of the boulevard theaters). Like these other great vogues, the nouvelle cuisine promised to extend the scope of science and to bring the marvels of modern knowledge into Paris life on a daily basis.

Though not the first cuisine to be dubbed "nouvelle," the eighteenth-century variant—launched into polemic by the continuing Quarrel of the Ancients and the Moderns and furthered by the spread of materialist science—was the first to be discussed beyond the realm of chefs squabbling for precedence in cookbook prefaces.[39] Proponents of both the old and new cookeries agreed that a culture's gustatory preferences might provide evidence of its moral fiber and physical strength, but they disagreed on the standards by which those preferences were to be evaluated. Partisans of the modern cuisine (such as Foncemagne, cited earlier) argued that cookery, like the other arts and sciences, had progressed and improved with the passing of centuries. Hence, French cookery's positive reputation indicated France's advanced state of civilization and generally high level of culture. On the other side of the Quarrel, the "ancient" cuisine's champions (including most of the Encyclopédistes) asserted that only decadent, feminized cultures considered cookery an art, and that virtuous and virile societies, such as that of classical Greece, were content with the most rudimentary cooking methods.

Like the Ancient and Modern *littérateurs,* who agreed that art should imitate nature but who quibbled over how best it might do so,[40] advocates for the two culinary styles agreed that human diet, ideally, was composed of "pure" and "natural" foods—but split over the definition of these terms. The debate turned on competing definitions of "simplicity": was, for example, a *restaurant* simple because in the cooking of it, all the non-nutritive excess had been boiled away, leaving only purified meat essences, or was it complex because it required such lengthy and intricate preparation?[41] Looking at recipes of the period, one may have little inclination to consider the new cookery particularly simple. For example, the 1742 *Suite des dons de Comus,* a key text of the debate, contrasted a wide range of "modern" preparations with an occasional old-fashioned item included for the obdurate reader/eater. As the base recipe of the "old Gallic cookery" the author suggests a "juice" of beef alone, prepared by the rather straightforward method of pricking a piece of half-cooked meat with a knife, and moistening it with a bit of bouillon. The recipe takes half a page, and the preparation an unspecified, but fairly brief, period of time. In comparison, the recipe for a modern *restaurant* (composed of onions, carrots, parsnips, turnips, celery, chicken, partridge, veal, beef, fatback, ham, cloves, basil, and "excellent, very gentle bouillon") occupies nearly two full pages, and admonishes the preparer to seal the kettle hermetically with thick pastry in order to prevent the nourishment-laden steam from escaping. Then, after four hours of carefully supervised simmering, the *restaurant* was to be passed through a silk strainer, and allowed to cool.[42]

Depending on one's definition of "simple," one might well wonder which of these recipes was the basis of a new and simpler cookery. But that was precisely the point: new food seemed to depend on new ideas. (Whether new ideas grew from new foods would become a point of heated contention.) As liquefied meat, as food in an unexpected format, *restaurants* signified innovative artistry as much as regained vitality. The nouvelle cuisine therefore had ramifications far beyond the kitchen: minor academicians penned learned introductions to cookbooks, many of which were then reviewed, by other scholars, in the leading literary journals. Famous doctors questioned the benefits of the proposed change in diet, while socialites and philologists earned immediate notoriety by hosting ancient or modern dinner parties.[43] The nouvelle cuisine made its way into Diderot and D'Alembert's *Encyclopédie* and, as we have seen, onto the popular stage.

It also confused and annoyed some of the greatest minds of eighteenth-century France. Writing to his friend the Comte d'Autrey, in the autumn of 1765, Voltaire grumbled:

> I swear my stomach can not get used to this nouvelle cuisine. I can not tolerate a veal sweetbread swimming in a salty sauce which rises far above the little piece of meat, and I refuse to eat some hash of turkey, hare, and rabbit which they want me to think is all one meat. I like neither *pigeon à la crapaudine* nor bread that has no crust. I drink moderately, and find people who eat without drinking, or without knowing what they are eating, very strange . . .
>
> As for cooks, I can not stand the ham essences, mushrooms, pepper, and nutmeg with which they disguise dishes that are, left by themselves, perfectly fine and healthful.[44]

Interpretations of this passage have, until this point, fallen into two distinct categories: the culinary and the anti-clerical. Cookery pundits, seeing Voltaire's complaint as an accurate description of the new cookery's distinctive features, have delighted in his commentary's detailed description. For these readers, Voltaire's rejection has suggested just how very innovative and challenging the nouvelle cuisine actually was.[45] In a somewhat more nuanced approach, the sociologist Stephen Mennell found Voltaire's account of nouvelle cuisine at odds with the definitions offered by cookbooks, and concluded that no agreement existed on this new cookery's actual content.[46] Mennell asserted that, rather than describing a specific cooking style, the label "nouvelle" worked as a marker of cultural class, an indicator of the continuing civilizing process.

Intellectual historians who concentrate on the Enlightenment have unearthed yet another set of meanings in Voltaire's letter. Unlike the culinary historians who cast the wise old philosopher of Ferney in the rather unlikely role of curmudgeonly food and wine columnist, the editors of his correspondence unanimously agree that this letter satirizes the Eucharist and other Christian ceremonies.[47] In their readings, the phrase "turkey, hare, and rabbit, which they want me to think is all one meat" veils an ingenious attack on the doctrines of transubstantiation and the Trinity: anybody so naive as to accept the nouvelle cuisine's "turkey rabbit" as a single meat might well believe that the communion wafer was really Christ's body or that God existed equally in Father, Son, and Holy Ghost.

To achieve the fullest understanding of Voltaire's letter we would be best advised to see it negotiating—as all commentary on the nouvelle cuisine did—between the material and the cerebral, the specific and the general, the gustatory and the philosophical. Rather than being either a response to a dinner party or a critique of Christian doctrine, Voltaire's complaint may easily prove to be both. In this letter, Voltaire—a notoriously finicky eater, as well as a famous critic of religious superstition—combined his hypochondriacal obsessions with his intellectual concerns in the traditionally two-edged genre of table talk.[48] In satirizing theology in terms of a dinner party, Voltaire relied on a lineage of impossible banquets and mock symposia rooted in the classical models of Horace's satires and Petronius's account of Trimalchio's feast.[49] Within Catholic custom, the centuries-old Feast of Fools tradition of the wanton Last Supper had presented "King David" and his harp providing after-dinner entertainment. With accompanying tales of the martyrdom of "Saint Ham" and "Saint Sausage," hagiography had taken a decidedly Rabelaisian turn. Later, Protestant critics appropriated these Catholic festival parodies (part of the traditional cycle of Feast and Fast, Carnival and Lent) in order to single out stereotypically jolly monks and stout churchmen for derision.[50]

While drawing on this tradition, Voltaire's condemnation of Catholic ritual took a distinctly eighteenth-century form. Neither wine-guzzling monks nor sausage-draped and pancake-bearing figures of Mardi Gras appeared in his critique. Instead, his satire, if such it was, abandoned the common image of a heavily laden banquet table in order to describe a meal both minimal and mystifying. His portion of veal was minuscule, lost in a sea of sauce. The scandal was no longer gross excess but the opposite extreme: "delicacy" of taste had become the newest gastronomic sin. The nouvelle cuisine subsumed the Carnival/Lent dyad by offering neither vulgar gluttony nor abstemious piety. Rather, preaching a timeless doctrine of good taste and pure art, it promised to cleanse foods of all their material baseness.

When Voltaire wrote of the nouvelle cuisine that it concealed and disguised what would better be left in its natural state, he was commenting on far more than his slice of veal and its strongly flavored sauce. I do not mean to suggest that Voltaire—or any of the nouvelle cuisine's numerous other critics—was "really" writing about the Eucharist, or about any other single identifiable ritual phenomenon. The nouvelle cuisine was neither a mere shorthand for theological debate nor a simple coded message to be deciphered by some set of one-to-one correspondences (a sort of *cuisine à clef*); nor, however, was it a specifically gastro-culinary subject confined to questions of cooking times and sauce preparation. Rather, the perceived conflict between old and new—be it simple meat juices versus *restaurants*, Homer versus Pope, or "primitive" social contract versus the intricacies of absolutist court society—structured discussion of nearly every topic in this period. Given an explicit form by the literary Quarrel of the Ancients and Moderns led (in France) by Boileau and Perrault, the battle between tradition and modernity reappeared everywhere, to the point of being nearly drained of meaning. It became, quite simply, a topos, a commonplace.[51]

As part of an ongoing debate that encompassed topics from architecture to artillery, the nouvelle cuisine was at the heart of attempts to define an enlightened life-style.[52] When the Marquise de Créquy declared the nouvelle cuisine to be "bitterly stupid" and the result of "idiotic refinement," she was commenting both on what she perceived to be the general shape of modern life and on the serving of foods prepared *en macedoine*.[53] Pessimism about the nouvelle cuisine, like other criticisms of modern, seemingly luxurious, or indulgent living, expressed what could best be described as a set of profoundly "historical" questions—questions about the place of traditional models in eighteenth-century life.

The debate over the nouvelle cuisine translated the central question plaguing French thinkers of this era—Was humanity in progress or decay?—into the burlesque, almost billingsgate, idiom of stomachs, stews, and digestion. Lurking in the discussion of poison and appetite, stewed hare and meat essences, was a far broader, perhaps graver, concern: Did the supposed advances of the sciences and the arts (including, perhaps, cookery) actually help humankind? Rousseau's 1750 *First Discourse* had answered famously in the negative, but the inquiry was far from settled and continued in debates about landscape gardening, educational methods, and political change for decades to come. Literary, economic, and artistic debates, each with a potential moral component, all contributed to making the nouvelle cuisine (and hence, implicitly, *restaurants*) a vivid topic. In their verdicts on the nouvelle cuisine, eighteenth-century commentators revealed both their understanding of human biology and their attitude toward the possible perfectibility of man and the meaning of innovation. The mutually defining categories of the good-to-think and the good-to-eat reshaped each other in lighthearted scrutiny of questions that nonetheless bespoke real anxiety over the possible substantive link between a nation's culinary style and its moral fiber. Were the playwright Beaunoir's protagonist, "Restaurant," and his namesakes the latest state of the art, the advance of culinary knowledge to a point where it could appeal to "those too weak to eat an evening meal"? Or were restaurants, be they broths or business ventures, fraudulent and dangerous, made popular only by the whims of fashion and the degeneration of Frenchmen?

Those who supported the nouvelle cuisine described a natural state in which essential nutrients existed in an alloyed state, mixed with coarse and tainting elements. The new cookery would, in condensing foods to their component parts and, hence, purifying them, effect a sort of chemical equation, a scientific advancement.[54] Its partisans contrasted the old-fashioned eater, weighed down with extraneous and heavy, earthy foods, with a modern eater, released from corporeality by his subsistence on "essences." Even a somewhat skeptical reviewer, writing in the Jesuit *Journal de Trévoux,* admitted that "it seems certain that coarse or poorly prepared food slows digestion, and causes heavy, animal spirits to rise to the head, where they communicate their weight to the mind and the imagination."[55] In contrast, the modern cookery would free the eater's mind, soul, and bowels. The nouvelle cuisine could satisfy the eater's physical tastes and needs while it liberated him from his body. Thus eighteenth-century modern cookery would make it possible, Foncemagne and others suggested, for the intellect and the spirit to dominate. Animal coarseness, represented by "laborious digestion," would no longer contaminate human thought.

For the partisans of nouvelle cuisine, the new, more delicate cookery indicated but another of civilization's triumphs. They granted that "Hottentots and Hurons" might reject the new cookery's sensibly subtle mixture of ingredients—but added that the same populations would neither understand nor appreciate the music of a brilliant European composer. Genius in any field, Foncemagne wrote, condemned one to misunderstanding and obscurity. The greatest cooks "are sometimes those least able to satisfy the common palate; they need discriminating eaters, as a musician needs fine and well-schooled listeners."[56] As Mandeville and his followers had argued that delight in luxurious living benefited society because it employed artisans and encouraged industry, so the partisans of the nouvelle cuisine claimed that the pursuit of culinary pleasures could become a generalized social virtue by encouraging the forward march of French culture.[57]

In contrast to this vision of progress and perfection, the criticisms voiced by opponents of the nouvelle cuisine expressed a belief in the ideally simple state of already existing nature. Medical and philosophical critics of the nouvelle cuisine fantasized about the straightforward and honest fare of early civilizations, and bemoaned the time when people first contrived to "make an art out of the simplest and most natural act."[58] Culinary "refinement," they maintained, posed a danger to moral and physical well-being alike: as the body, accustomed to delicate morsels, grew unable to digest plain food, so the mind would avoid weighty intellectual matters and content itself with frivolous witticisms. For these doctors and philosophers, cookery was an artisanal activity that ought, ideally, to be transparently obvious to all. While they occasionally inveighed against specific dishes, sauces, or preparations, they more regularly concentrated their energies on refuting the notion of cookery as an art. Rejecting any possibility of artistic genius in the kitchen, they presented cooks as masters of deception, as jealous keepers of sneaky trade secrets. For its critics, the vaunted variety and subtlety of modern cookery was but another example of "art" gone to unnecessary extremes.

The confluence of aesthetic and physical taste, a parallel transformed from vague metaphor into direct causality by materialist thinking, was central to the logic of the nouvelle cuisine. Brumoy and Bougeant, Jesuit authors of the preface to *Les Dons de Comus* (a 1739 inventory of dishes, favorable to the nouvelle cuisine), claimed that "physical and spiritual taste depend equally on the shape and condition of nerve fibers and their related organs."[59] Such assertions were bitterly challenged by the nouvelle cuisine's detractors, who saw them as indicating a corruption of the senses and a parody of reason. The *Encyclopédie* article "Goût" ("Taste"), for example, carefully separated cookery from the true arts by concentrating on the key question of necessity.[60] The author (the article has alternately been attributed to d'Alembert or Voltaire) began by grounding both gustatory and aesthetic taste in an intimate and discerning relation with nature: as the "man of taste" recognized a mélange of styles, and rejected burlesque in favor of the "naturally beautiful," so the "gourmet" perceived adulterated wine, and preferred simple foods to spicy concoctions. The end results of these two processes were equally quick, certain, and natural, but the means by which one arrived at these conclusions were far from equal. Aesthetic reaction might be as prompt as that of the tongue, but it only became so through training: for the eyes to "see" and the ears to "hear," education was required. In contrast, the physical sense of taste could not and should not be educated. Gustatory sensitivity, the philosophe argued, depended solely on untrainable physical organs. Were the palate to learn to taste, nature's plan would be contradicted: "Nature did not intend for man to have to learn to sense what he needs."[61] Education, as a characteristic of aesthetic taste, and necessity, as an attribute of the palate, separated the terms of the metaphor "goût."[62]

In his article "Cuisine," the physician de Jaucourt (who also, tellingly, wrote the *Encyclopédie*'s articles on "Frugality" and "Gluttony") used similar ideas of need and art to outline more specifically the argument against any but the plainest cookery.[63] According to de Jaucourt, early man, like the eighteenth century's "sober and poor," defined cookery as "the most common means of preparing foods in order to satisfy his needs." As time passed, however, "the habit of always eating the same foods, always cooked in the same way, gave birth to distaste, which led to curiosity, and then experimentation and sensuality; man tasted, tried, varied, chose, and managed to make the simplest and most natural act into an art form."[64] The spirit of experimentation, that characteristic tool of scientific endeavor, contributed to making cookery a ruinous art. For de Jaucourt, like the other *encyclopédistes,* cookery erred when it left the realm of need and entered that of the arts and sciences.

The *encyclopédistes* and sympathetic medical doctors saw the history of diet as a tale, not of art's perfection, but of society's decay. Extreme simplicity, they claimed, had characterized ancient human diet: Homeric heros roasted their own sides of beef and varied their diet with seasonal fruits and vegetables. Contact with luxury-loving Asiatics had, however, corrupted this honorable austerity, contaminating first the Greeks (with the exception of Spartan law-givers) and then the Romans.[65] Spices and other exotic ingredients, while acceptable in their places of origin for which Nature had intended them, became the seeds of decay when transplanted to republican Rome. These "drugs," as one mid-century physician called them, benefited those somnolent beings who inhabited the hot climates of the East Indies, but they incited others to indolent living; their use, menacingly enough, was particularly "dangerous in Europe, for by delighting, seducing, and snaring the sense of taste, they covered Reason with a mist that soon eclipsed it."[66] Degeneration in the dietary sphere quickly contaminated all others, easily spreading from personal vice to political fiasco. As de Jaucourt wrote (in the *Encyclopédie* article "Frugality"), sobriety of diet ought to provide the base and the "most firm support" for moderation in all other expenditures. Once a state's leaders occupied themselves with food, drink, and dinner parties, the state was on a sure road to collapse: "Gourmandise is a merit in countries of luxury and vanity, where all

the vices are held up as virtues: it is the fruit of soft living." Virtuous republican Rome, de Jaucourt implied, had tumbled headlong into sloth,
decay, and tyranny when it adopted the spiced concoctions of the debauched Persians.[67]

According to those who were skeptical about the possibility of culinary
"progress," innovation in cookery did not strain away impurities; instead
it aggravated the appetite, enticing one to eat far more than was necessary.
Rousseau, in his 1762 educational tract, *Emile,* decried the "salt, seasonings, and made dishes" that led children away from their natural and
wholesome tastes and into the contrived and artificial world of debauch.[68]
Culinary embellishment, by tempting the satiated to eat yet more, destroyed the unity of desire and need that once had existed. Once people
craved more than they physically needed, they could no longer trust (as
animals did) that what tasted good was also good for them. The nouvelle
cuisine, like other elements in a too sophisticated, degenerate culture, ca-
joled the senses into responding to false, unnaturally acute stimuli. Doctors and philosophers saw cooks using all their wiles to stimulate "unnecessary" yearnings and "perverse" desires, and viewed the nouvelle cuisine
as a seductive and dangerous tongue-tease. Liquefied meats, according to
a reviewer in the *Journal de Trévoux,* were particularly likely to confuse,
delight, and, eventually, corrupt: "The Author of Nature gave us our
senses to guide us in our choice of necessary foods; how can our senses be
a sure guide when, in order to tease our appetites, meats are mixed,
blended, boiled down and turned into essences?"[69] The Versailles physician Dupré de Lisle similarly worried that socialization and habit had so altered humanity's natural tastes that "wanting to stimulate appetites, foods
have been given an unnatural taste and converted into poisons."[70]

This leading astray of "taste" had dire implications for the organs of
the social body as well. By perverting man's original and natural tastes, *restaurants* and other shows of culinary refinement broke the great chain of
being and destroyed any sense of responsibility between fellow men. While
a few privileged members of society busied themselves condensing ever
more meat into ever smaller bouillon cups, the remaining members of
society faced shortage and dearth. In his 1786 *Traité philosophique et
politique sur le luxe (Philosophical and Political Treatise on Luxury),* the
abbé Pluquet calculated that the foods assembled to serve one lavish table
for ten finical gourmets would, in their unadorned state, provide solid,
hearty, and honest nourishment for three hundred hungry people.[71] From
this vaguely physiocratic perspective (later echoed by the sans-culottes),

the nouvelle cuisine was not a triumph of culinary science, but an affront to the French peasantry and a sad commentary on national morality. As advocates of the nouvelle cuisine had removed discussion of cookery from the kitchen in order to describe the new cookery as evidence of society's delicacy and perfection, so its critics brought it into the salon to hold it up as proof of the same society's decline and corruption.

Were we to map the debate over the nouvelle cuisine onto more canonical moments in eighteenth-century intellectual life, we might say that the advocates of the nouvelle cuisine sketched a basically worldly, Mandevillean position (not unlike Roze de Chantoiseau's belief that increased circulation would benefit the nation at large), while its opponents outlined an austerely neo-Classical critique. Yet both saw dining as a privileged moment in the definition of society and of the individual, as a means to gauge France's general well-being. The fastidiously set table—lavish not in quantity but in hours of preparation—became the predominant site for debates about the social and personal consequences of opulent living. There was solid precedent for this: the serpent in the Garden of Eden, after all, enticed Eve not with silks to wear, but with an apple to bite.

The questions surrounding the nouvelle cuisine were not particularly new—they were, in fact, the familiar chestnuts of the Quarrel of the Ancients and Moderns—but when the focus shifted from problems in the translation of Homer to sauces and seasonings, the issues became accessible to a broader audience. Questions once confined to the scholarly and erudite could be posed at the table on a daily basis; the traditional joviality of table talk made the nouvelle cuisine a learned debate on which any wit could easily take a position. Cookery provided a standard reference point, an easily understood comparison. Pluquet, in the rousing conclusion to his *Treatise on Luxury,* instructed his readers to turn from luxury, as they would from "a delicious dish that has previously provoked pain or illness," and to live simply, as one would "confine oneself to a diet of bland foods" in order to recover one's health.[72] An extravagant diet was both luxury's standard allegorical representation, and among its most common manifestations; thanks to the medicalization of society, it was also one of the most quickly perceived dangers.

Rousseau in the Restaurant

The invention of the restaurant (as a business where *restaurants* were sold) marked far more than the triumph of the culinary Moderns and the nouvelle cuisine. In a sense, the restaurant's appeal reconciled the Ancients and the Moderns; like the former, it agreed that something needed to be "restored," but by the very serving of *restaurants,* it announced itself as a strong partisan of the latter. When Duclos, inheritor of Roze de Chantoiseau's restaurant, advertised the availability of "English-style nouvelle cuisine," he was simply adding modish anglomania to the already long list of attributes linking restaurants to innovation.[73] Indeed, there may never have been a "nouvelle cuisine à la mode anglaise" (Mary and Philip Hyman, specialists in the arcana of French culinary history, have never encountered it), but that is hardly the point. Rather, Duclos was claiming to be fashionably au courant in any number of ways. Like the confiseur whose novelty sugar sculptures for the New Year in 1779 included a large set piece in which the marzipan figure of Immortality led equally saccharine models of Rousseau and Voltaire to join the composer Rameau and "Antiquity's wise men and poets" in a pastillage reconstruction of Apollo's Temple, so the first restaurateurs took the icons of "high" Enlightenment culture and presented them in an accessible, ostensibly edible, fashion.[74]

To soothe the weak-chested, the vaporous, and the generally delicate, the first restaurateurs offered a range of healthful foods in addition to their eponymous bouillons. At a time when the traditional *traiteurs* of Paris were preparing mutton cutlets, spiced sausages, dense pâtés, and stewed spinach, Vacossin promised his patrons "Breton porridge, orange-flower-flavored rice creams, semolina, fresh eggs . . . fruits in season, preserves from the most famous manufacturers, fresh butter, and cream cheeses."[75] The foods he advertised were both common to other restaurant menus (they are very much like the ones listed in Roze de Chantoiseau's almanac), and familiar fare for any reader of medical books or sentimental novels. Among them, rice creams (very soft, sweet rice puddings made from a little rice, a lot of milk or cream, and generally egg yolks, sugar, and orange flower water) were at the same time prescribed by Rozière de la Chassagne as the best foods for pleurisy; mentioned by Vandermonde's *Dictionary of Health* as a regular component in the diet of a healthy man of letters; endorsed by Joseph Raulin, former Royal Inspector of Mineral Waters, as suited to the treatment of phthisis; and recommended by Rousseau as one of the first foods to feed a weaning child.[76] Vacossin's fruit, eggs, and butter, like the barely congealed soft cheeses, were more idyllic than therapeutic: foods of the countryside picnic, they evoked the lush, green plants from which the berries had been plucked; the contented hen from whom the egg had been taken; and Rousseau's beloved heroine, Julie (whose regular diet they were).[77] Milk had its greatest significance in the context of the polemical celebration of breast-feeding championed by Rousseau and Beaumarchais, but milk products—especially ass's milk—were also central to many therapeutic diets for adults.[78]

Rousseauian myth, and the practices it inspired, drew on centuries of tradition to mark sweets and dairy products as the foods of women and children, of beings uncontaminated by the extravagances of overly civilized cookery. As Rousseau explained in *La Nouvelle Héloïse,* "Sweets and dairy foods are the natural favorites of the gentler sex, symbolizing the innocence and sweetness that are her most appealing ornament."[79] Mild, white foods such as these stood in opposition to the regularly brown (or black) bread of the common people, as they did to the sanguine meat and red wine associated with Homeric heroes and the sturdy early Gauls. The colorless foods of women, like the white sauces and meats of the nouvelle cuisine, distinguished restorative cookery from the strong flavors and dark colors of ordinary fare. (In Beaunoir's play about the nouvelle cuisine, Restaurant's beloved is named "Blanquette" and dresses, aptly enough, all in white.) The foods necessary for health and available in a *salle du restaurateur* reinscribed an austere beauty on the bodies of the already delicate. As sugar had done since the early Middle Ages, these other white foods combined medicinal and gustatory functions with those of social differentiation.[80]

Vacossin's menu intimated pastoral delights and colorless purity, but it did so as Roze de Chantoiseau might have planned: by bringing together goods and products from the varied regions of France, and thus contributing to increased economic circulation even as it drew on Rousseau-like dreams of local self-sufficiency for its effectiveness.[81] Combining the promise of purity with the allure of social distinction, Vacossin served no water except that bottled from the king's fountain[82]—water which only a few months earlier had first become available to the Paris public. Though royal and of the court, its promoters described the spring of Villedavray as "water in its original state," recognizable by its "limpidity" as well as by its healthful effects.[83] Only the court, they implied, had had the delicacy of taste necessary to appreciate pure, uncivilized water—water now served by "the true restaurateur." Vacossin's puddings, pastries, and conserves all required sugar: a refined and hardly "simple" product, sugar was a colonial good shipped from France's jealously guarded possessions in the Caribbean. Though in its raw and natural state, sugar was almost unusable (and certainly far from white), that was one of the factual details to which the mythologies of restorative natural simplicity did not pay attention. Similarly, Vacossin advertised "preserves from the best places"—no time spent in transportation was too long, no circuit of exchange too arduous, if it guaranteed high-quality jams, jellies, and pâtés. The "biscuits du Palais Royal" that he sold—fragile, pale cookies similar to present-day ladyfingers—were by their very name more evocative of luxurious high society than of unsophisticated village life.[84]

In its furnishings as well as its menu, Vacossin's restaurant combined references to the joys of archaic nature with celebration of the benefits of modern civilization. Like the poshest cafés and the homes of the most affluent Parisians, restaurants were lined with mirrors.[85] In the 1769 play *Harlequin Restaurateur,* Harlequin has been in the restaurant business for two days, but he is reluctant to spend money on covering his walls with mirrors. To this his sophisticate friend replies:

> Oh you wanted to economize! If that's the case, you shouldn't be in the restaurant business. The ladies, the dandy young men, the handsome lawyers and the prissy abbés, what will they do here if there aren't any mirrors? This little Sunday lawyer who has just bought his mistress a *restaurant,* what will he do? What will she do, in the hour they sit here, if they don't have a mirror in front of them to tell them that at each instant, they have the air, the manners, the appearance, he of a president of Parlement, and she of a marquise?[86]

Real-life restaurateurs wisely followed the advice of Harlequin's knowledgeable friend. In 1779, ten mirrors (each approximately 45 inches high by 28 inches wide) decorated the largest dining room in Vacossin's rue de Grenelle restaurant, while a thermometer and an expensive clock filled the little remaining wall space. Mirrors and landscape paintings also hung in the restaurant's smaller dining rooms, such that every room evoked (and, in the mirrors, reflected) the sentiment of nature, its beauty, and its scientific measurement. (Sensibility predominated over science in the Vacossins' private living quarters, however: in 1779, six framed engravings of paintings by Greuze hung on the walls, as did one of Rousseau's tomb in Ermonenville.)[87]

From its menu and its Latin street-sign to its comfortably furnished salons and the cooking utensils hidden in the kitchen, everything about the restaurant bespoke delicacy, even as it promised to restore its clients to a more robust state of health (Figure 1). In the consommés and other foods

Figure 1. "The beautiful restauratrice," one of Louis Berthet's many vignettes for Nicolas-Edme Restif de la Bretonne's *Les Contemporaines,* a nearly endless series of love stories about eighteenth-century Parisians. Others in the series, such as "the adorable meat-roasting girls" or "the four fetching pork butchers," show the young women in homely kitchen settings surrounded by the totems of their trade. Here the restauratrice is also depicted in an easily recognized context, but her emblems are far less edible. She poses not in a kitchen or a larder, but in a dining room decorated with chandeliers and an ornate wall clock. Note the tempting pyramid of fruit on the central table and the very small consommé bowl and round soup spoon on the table to the far left. Evidently, the male protagonist's appetites have been sufficiently restored and he is now eager to sample the restaurant's fruits.

they offered, as well as in their style of furnishings and method of service, there was little we might call "simple" about the first restaurants. Nobody ever established businesses to sell the "hearty pot-au-feu of our forefathers" so beloved by critics of eighteenth-century luxury; despite their purported frugal simplicity, the restaurants of the 1760s and 1770s were spaces for the display of "delicacy" and the appreciation of "sensibility." The pale foods and limpid liquids sold by the "true restaurateur"; his *restaurants* prepared with scientific exactitude; his fragile, china serving dishes; his elegantly appointed and splendidly lit dining room ("In addition to the room's numerous lamps, each table will be candle-lit")[88]—all combined to make the restaurant a place for the most comfortable sort of rusticity. A restaurateur's rooms appealed to the equation of happiness with health, but required no sacrifice of sentiment. Thanks to the restaurant, sensitivity could be reflected in bodily suffering, without necessitating that delicacies be traded for slabs of beef, hunks of rye bread, or medicinal decoctions of bitter herbs.

Serving dairy products, sweet foods, and fresh fruits, the restaurants of the 1760s and 1770s drew their menus neither from the daily diets of peasants nor from the most dour medical texts, but from the cuisine of Swiss villages as idealized in Rousseau's best-selling epistolary love story, *Julie, ou la nouvelle Héloïse* (1760), and his equally popular, barely novelized educational tract, *Emile* (1762). In both these adored texts, Rousseau argued (as he did in his more forthrightly polemical *Discourses*) that the customs and habits of modern urban civilization had corrupted human nature. The shallow conventions of civility and the fashionable affectations of worldliness—like all other tokens of good behavior—limited the expression (and even the feeling) of honest heartfelt sentiment or simple natural needs. Life in society, as Rousseau saw it, was based in artifice; it required wit, grace, good manners, and style; supremely rational, it left no room for childlike innocence, no space for spontaneous virtue. Social life, which had long ago replaced man's natural solitary state, created distinctions between people, making inequality acceptable, debauchery amusing, and nature repugnant.

Of obvious political import, Rousseau's critique of social convention had a culinary edge as well: no longer a matter of freshly gathered fruits and hand-picked nuts, European diet had become divided between the "overly refined foods of the rich, which nourish them with binding juices and overwhelm them with indigestion" and "the bad food of the poor, which they do not even have most of the time, so that they tend to overburden their stomachs greedily whenever the occasion permits."[89] In contrast, Rousseau described life in a small village, or in the Savoy hills at the foot of the Alps, settings distant enough from urban corruption to allow childlike shows of honest sentiment and the expression of simple, unadulterated taste. Raised far from any major city, Emile (Rousseau's ideal pupil) prefers "good fruits and vegetables, sweet cream and kindly people" to a dinner where "beds of artificial flowers were served on mirrors with dessert."[90]

Rousseau's fictional, political, and autobiographical writings all denounced modern urban society as perfidious and cruel, but they kept their author in its limelight. For decades, Rousseau treated his own life as a perfect exemplar of fashionable people's malevolent attitude toward honest individuals—indeed, as the only exemplar. As he recounted in his autobiographical *Confessions* (written throughout the 1760s and then read aloud to several elite gatherings), he had spent years of his life attempting to gain fame and fortune in the artistic milieus of Paris, only to discover that its tributes were meaningless and the friends he found there, false. He had been secretary and music master to noble families, he had written articles on music for the *Encyclopédie,* but only when he published his *Discourse on the Sciences and the Arts*—in which he rejected said arts and sciences because of their corrupting effects on humanity—did he become the darling of Parisian high society. Yet his social success was brief, and he tired of incessant dinner invitations; vowing to live the rest of his life in honest poverty, he gave up his secretarial position to become a freelance copier of music. This retreat did not bring him inner peace or personal stability, however, and in the following years he quarreled with his friends the philosophes and was threatened with arrest after the publications of *Emile* and *The Social Contract.* Persecuted and misunderstood, hounded and ridiculed, the public figure "Jean-Jacques" wandered across Europe, his suffering thoroughly catalogued by his untiring and far from disinterested (auto)biographer, "Rousseau." Mocked by Voltaire and betrayed by Hume, Jean-Jacques sought anonymity only to find it obstinately denied him. Repeatedly and vociferously resolving to spurn society, he seemed surprised that every such resolution brought him all the more clearly and paradoxically into its view.

In the eyes of modern cynics, Rousseau's public parading of his lonely virtue may make him little more than an incurable hypocrite, but for thousands of eighteenth-century readers he was a limitless source of inspiration. As Robert Darnton has shown, readers in the 1770s were devoted to their "friend, Jean-Jacques," treating *Emile* as a practical volume on baby and child care and understanding their own trials of the heart by reference to those of Julie d'Etange, Saint Preux, and Wolmar.[91] They wept over the end of *La Nouvelle Héloïse,* and shed copious tears at the news of Rousseau's death in 1778. Moved by sentiment and curiosity, they later flocked by the hundreds to the Marquis de Girardin's Ermonenville estate, where Rousseau lived his last days and where he was buried on a poplar-planted island in the middle of a lake.[92]

Years before his death had turned Ermonenville into a site of secular pilgrimage, however, the restaurants of Paris offered the sensitive soul a nearly perfect setting for genteel imitations of Jean-Jacques. They promised the exquisite pleasures of an Alpine repast, without the expense of traveling to Switzerland, and the delights of Julie's simple meals, without the inconvenience of spurning polite society. As the first restaurants reconciled the Ancient and the Modern, so they paradoxically seemed to incorporate Rousseau's isolated martyr into civilization by providing a social space for one of the chief physical manifestations of "sensibility"—the inability or reluctance to eat an evening meal. In the words of Minet's 1767 announcement, the restaurant, "for those who are not in the habit of eating an evening meal," would make it possible for them to heed their physicians' warnings even as they enjoyed "the pleasures of society." For all that the somewhat paranoid Jean-Jacques might have scoffed at the notion, the restaurant offered many Parisians what they believed to be a Rousseauian opportunity for shared, frugal melancholia, for the semi-public display of sensibility.

When Rousseau himself visited Vacossin's restaurant, however, the delightful illusion of plenty was promptly shattered. Rousseau's experience *chez Vacossin* forms the central example of the fourth "promenade" in his *Reveries of a Solitary Walker.*[93] As he tells the story, friends invited him one day (in 1776 or 1777) to dine "Pic-nic" style at the Vacossins' restaurant. Accompanied by Thérèse Levasseur (Rousseau's longtime mistress and then wife), they were joined as well by Madame Vacossin and two of her three daughters. During dinner, the eldest daughter, Henriette Sophie, recently married and several months pregnant, stared boldly at Rousseau and pointedly asked him if he had had any children.[94] Blushing to his hairline, Rousseau sputtered that he had not had that pleasure, but he suspected that his discomfort was clearly obvious and that Henriette was slyly grinning at his expense. For Rousseau's notorious, haunting "secret" was that he had, in fact, fathered five children, all of whom Thérèse's mother had abandoned on the steps of the Paris foundling hospital.

In the tortured world of Rousseau's memoirs and reveries, Henriette Sophie Thevenin (née Vacossin), the mere daughter of a restaurateur and the wife of a very minor legal official, became a traitor as sly as Hume or Diderot, an enemy as conniving as Voltaire. She caught the famous man in a trap, posing her question in such a way that the self-proclaimed disciple of truth had to speak what "everybody" knew to be a falsehood. "They were waiting for my negative response," wrote Rousseau, "they provoked it even, in order to have the pleasure of making me lie. I was not so stupid that I did not know that."[95] In the restaurant, by Rousseau's logic, not his own answer but Madame Thevenin's malicious question, not his blush but her stare, had proved immoral.

Using the remainder of the fourth promenade as a rebuttal, Rousseau left the restaurant table behind in order to explain that his answer to Henriette Sophie had been neither premeditated nor desired, but simply a "mechanical effect of embarrassment."[96] Moved by "mechanical effects," Rousseau discovered in the restaurant that he was like other people; contrary to his self-proclaimed utter singularity, which was meant to reside in his unwavering commitment to truth, he told the table a falsehood. Rousseau in the restaurant did not confess, he did not pay up or own up; instead, he told a convenient lie and kept his secret to himself like any other embarrassed fool. The restaurant, with its emphasis on personal *sensibilité* and its departure from the shared model of the table d'hôte, offered nearly all its customers the illusion of public privacy, of sociable idiosyncrasy, of individual taste. But Rousseau, with his already acute sense of isolation, found himself confronted instead with the far more terrifying truth of his fibbing similarity to all around him.

The meal with the Vacossins is the final scenario in a chain of Rousseauian tales associating the table with childbirth. In his *Confessions*, Rousseau framed the first of these by evoking the months he spent in the summer of 1747 at Chenonceaux with Madame Dupin, wife of a farmer-general, and Monsieur de Francueil, aspiring gentleman scientist. Rousseau, present nominally as their secretary, passed several happy months there and, by his own admission, "became fat as a monk."[97] Upon his return to Paris, he discovered his beloved Thérèse also considerably larger than she once had been, but "for another reason." Alarmed at this potential "complication," Jean-Jacques sought solace in the conversation of his daily dinner table, a pension where the food was "bad" but the company "good."[98] There, he first learned that it was "the custom of the land" to leave unwanted infants at the foundling hospital.

Throughout this account, the stages of Thérèse's pregnancy seem to mimic, or to appear in sympathetic reaction to, the states of Rousseau's digestion. Rousseau, enjoying the pleasures of an aristocratic country estate, gained weight, while his lover, living in a cramped apartment in Paris, became visibly with child. When he took to eating at a table where the food was not particularly good and where he no doubt lost his monastic pudginess, then his new "table friends" told him how to rid himself of the baby. Ranking the tables at Chenonceaux and in Paris on the basis of culinary quality, it is no surprise that Rousseau found the food better in the countryside, or that it was the pastoral table that figured pregnancy, the urban one that flagged abandonment. Into the binary oppositions of Chenonceaux and Paris, pregnancy and babylessness, good food and bad, Vacossin's restaurant introduced a third or hybrid term: the all-satisfying refined simplicity of the nouvelle cuisine.

Of his meal at the Vacossins', Rousseau wrote that it was "contrary to his habit" and "pic-nic style." It was contrary to his habit to eat in a restaurant, for while the restaurant's menu of pastoral-syle delights was Rousseauian, it was too urban to be suited to Rousseau himself. In addition, though "picnic" to Anglophone readers immediately suggests a rustic spread—a style of dining well suited to the happiest meals in Rousseau's oeuvre and to the landscapes that decorated Vacossin's restaurant—it had in eighteenth-century French a different sense, a meaning much closer to what Americans might call a "potluck." At a *pique-nique* each guest brought his own dish, or paid his own share; to dine at a restaurant "en manière de Pic-nic" was to have each guest pay his own check *("chacun son écot")*. While today it is utterly commonplace for each customer in a restaurant, or even at a particular table, to pay his or her own way, to pick up his or her own check, that behavior is nonetheless far distant from the logic of "buying rounds" and sharing hospitality. Even at a table d'hôte, each patron paid a set amount—dining "by head," it mattered not if he had been the first and the hungriest to set upon the roast, or the last arrived at table, obliged to make do with the remaining side dishes. In contrast, the restaurant picnicker in the eighteenth century ate alone, not sharing, not participating in hospitable give and take, but paying his own way. At a *pique-nique* everybody owed something: built into its pastoral promise was the moral and economic imperative of the divided bill.

In the seemingly hospitable and comfortable setting of the restaurant, in the familiar surroundings of a meal with his friends and wife, Rousseau, like anybody else, found himself obliged to pay (or to run out on the check).[99] Like all the other trappings of city life, of social life, the restaurant in the *Rêveries* emerges as a place of lies and deceit: in Rousseau's model, the introduction of payment falsifies festivities and corrupts all pleasure. Even as the restaurant appealed to others by its simplicity and honesty, it repelled Rousseau by its fictions and deceits. The restaurant's mirrored walls allowed the customers to see themselves, so everyone said. And yet, Rousseau most certainly would have responded, mirrors could not force people to see themselves as they "really were," as fawning fops posing in front of mercury- and tin-backed sheets of glass.

The restaurant's hospitality, that illusion predicated on the absence of a host (for the restaurateur, in general, though he might survey the room, did not dine with his "guests"), endured in the period created by the consumer's desires (for the hour spent looking in the mirror). In Rousseau's story, though, the company of Madame Vacossin and her daughters, the unmediated presence of the restauratrice, brought bills due before the meal had ended. Rousseau in the restaurant may or may not have owed the truth about his children to his dinner companions, but he certainly owed for his dinner—and though he, in a way, paid off the former by writing the fourth promenade, it remains unclear whether he ever paid money for his dinner or not.

Perhaps it is not surprising that we do not know if he paid his share, for tales of ordinary restaurant going that include this detail are rare, except when the bringing of the check becomes a moment of surprise or embarrassment. Such moments have a special name in French: they are called "le quart d'heure de Rabelais" ("Rabelais's fifteen minutes"), after a legend concerning the often penniless author of *Gargantua* and a bill-bearing Lyonnais innkeeper. Needing to return to Paris, but unable to pay for transportation, the destitute Rabelais ingeniously set aside little packages labeled "poison for the King" and "poison for the Dauphin," with the result that the innkeeper discovered them and had the apparent conspirator arrested and transported to Paris—where François I welcomed him with open arms and laughed heartily at the story. His unhabitual meal at the Vacossins' was Rousseau's far less happy "quarter hour": a moment of picnic reckoning with no munificent and smiling monarch at the end.

Rather than eliciting royal guffaws, Rousseau's fifteen minutes brought him into contact with the smirking Henriette Sophie. Having paid for his meal (or, at least, having been expected to pay), he owed Henriette Sophie nothing. Thanks to her question, then, he could write the fourth promenade, confessing to not confessing, confessing that he owed her nothing but confessing all the same. As the restaurant promised the natural goodness of the countryside in an urban setting, so it allowed Rousseau the exquisite pleasures of suffering through a confession without enduring the more mundane aggravations of raising five children on a music-copier's salary; in short, it allowed sensibility without sacrifice, picnic without payment.

A restaurant meal also allowed others to be like Rousseau. With its private rooms, intimate tables, and particularized service, the restaurant made isolation available to everybody. The eighteenth-century cult of sensibility did not exist only when sobbing at a family drama, or in confronting a dead canary. As an emotional or intellectual state with physical manifestations, the cult of sensibility also conjured up its own spaces: the farm where Marie Antoinette played milkmaid, Rousseau's grave, and the restaurant. The restaurant introduced Rousseau's desires—not just the paradoxically refined simplicity of his ideal meals, but the equally perplexing publicity of his privacy—into the marketplace.

3

Private Appetites in a Public Space

> On arriving in the dining room, I remarked with astonishment
> numerous tables placed one beside another, which made me think
> that we were waiting for a large group, or were perhaps going to
> dine at a table d'hôte. But my surprise was at its greatest when I saw
> people enter without greeting each other and without seeming to
> know each other, seat themselves without looking at each other, and
> eat separately without speaking to each other, or even offering to
> share their food.
>
> ANTOINE JOSEPH NICOLAS ROSNY, *LE PÉRUVIEN À PARIS* (1801)

How did restaurants, those urban spas for people who "do not usually eat
two full meals or supper," survive as a distinct institution, even when they
had become the place, par excellence, to eat an enormous evening meal?
When restaurateurs expanded their offerings, as many quickly did, from
consommés and other gentle restoratives to salt cod, mutton cutlets, and
cauliflower, why did the word "restaurateur" remain in use? When café-
keepers, recognizing the needs of the non-supping and the weak of chest,
began to serve rice cooked in milk, how did the restaurateurs hold onto a
clientele?[1] Why was their "restorative" function not simply absorbed into
the caterers' or café-keepers' business, a momentary spasm no more enduring than the specialized trade in soup turtles or the later short-lived fad
for "Dutch dairies"?[2] As the foods and beverages available in a number of
venues came increasingly to overlap, what made the restaurant a distinctive and enduring feature of Paris life?

Well into the nineteenth century, at least some restaurateurs remained
faithful to their origins and continued to include restorative bouillons on
their menus. Verjus, a restaurateur and pastrycook with a large establishment on the rue de Madeleine, advertised in 1799 that he served "*restaurants* in all the newest flavors"; many years later, an undated menu from
the Grand Véfour, a famous Palais-Royal establishment (not founded until
1817), specified that "*restaurants* and soups are available at all hours."[3] All
twenty-one restaurants surveyed in 1815 by Honoré Blanc's *Guide des
dîneurs (Diners' Guide)* had "consommé" on their menus, as well as a
wide range of other soups; many also served "potage de santé" (literally, a

"soup of health"); two restaurants made special provisions for those customers ordering "only soup"; and most provided fresh eggs, fruit, and butter (though now these items, along with blood sausage, stuffed pigs' feet, and marinated tuna, were suggested as hors-d'oeuvres).[4] Yet from an early date, many restaurateurs elaborated on their repertories, incorporating a wide range of meat, fish, and vegetable dishes. Even Roze de Chantoiseau's 1773 almanac announced that the "first restaurateur" served, in addition to those preparations related to his restorative function, full meals prepared with the expected attention to delicacy and cleanliness.[5] Wise to the varied preferences found in a population eagerly engaged in medico-culinary polemics, the restaurateur had quickly expanded his business to please not only the "weak of chest," but any and all who delighted in the possibility that careful attention would be paid to their meals.

By the early 1780s (and perhaps far earlier), Jean François Vacossin was serving fish stews, sauced partridges, ray in black butter sauce, artichokes, and spinach, in addition to his still popular *potage au riz.* His account book tells us that for dinner on August 20, 1780, a customer residing at the Hotel Royal ordered a full meal of two soups, two chicken fricassees, six mutton cutlets, a roast chicken, and a side-dish of artichokes, as well as bread and wine, while another takeout customer, either more frugal or more in need of restoration (or simply inclined to purchase his meat elsewhere), ordered only a cucumber salad, a dish of green beans, and bread. The same day, the duc de Chaulnes, a regular customer, dined on some indefinite poultry *(volaille)* and vermicelli (the fowl unspecified by Vacossin's account book, but perhaps not by the duke), and supped on poultry and consommé.[6] While the duke's evening meal would certainly seem to fit within the medical literature's guidelines for dietetic suppers, an unnamed customer's meal, of roast mutton and fried calf's ears, just as clearly does not.[7] Producing a variety of meals and keeping his Latin promise in a number of ways, Vacossin moved easily between restorative and more outright nutritive functions, seeming to erode the very specificity on which his trade had once been based.

The distinction threatened to collapse from the other end of the spectrum as well, for any *traiteur* could easily enough cook up a cauldron of bouillon and style himself a "restaurateur." The restaurateur who served only delicate and healthful foods and the *traiteur* who offered stuffed calf's head quickly came to overlap in the vague category of the "traiteur-restaurateur," who experimented with a variety of forms that combined the cookshop's practices and the restaurant's innovations. For example, David, a *traiteur* at the Hôtel de l'Empereur, located on the same street as Vacossin's restaurant, evidently felt it necessary, or advantageous, to compete with his neighbor. In March 1781, he advertised two tables d'hôte (one at 30 sous per person, and the other for 40 sous) while specifying that he offered "the same advantages in terms of cookery" as any restaurateur. By October, he apparently recognized that serving the same quality food as a restaurateur, but in a traditional table-d'hôte setting, would not suffice to attract a new clientele, so he announced the opening of a new *salle du restaurateur* "at a reasonable price" and "at whatever hour one desires." By April of the following year, he had settled so fully into his new role that he advertised himself no longer as "David, *traiteur*" but as "David, restaurateur" (who continued nonetheless to offer a 30-person table d'hôte for 30 sous); eight months later, however, perhaps fearing he had overstepped the boundaries and alienated his former patrons, he settled for the hybrid "*traiteur* and restaurateur" who offered two afternoon tables d'hôte (at 1:30 and 2:00, both for 26 sous) and continued to provide restaurant service as well.[8]

In fact, throughout the 1780s and 1790s, as merchants widened the range of their offerings, it was increasingly common for a single establishment to provide both "ordinary" and "restaurant" service—and to claim, somewhat confusingly, that the same foods were served, and the same niceties observed, for each. One *traiteur-restaurateur* offered meals either "at 2½ livres, per head, or in restaurant style," while several years later, one of his colleagues served meals either at 2 francs per head or "au restaurant."[9] Given that one individual, at one address, was fulfilling both functions (often by serving the same food), what was the basis of this lasting differentiation? In 1793, a restaurateur named Venua directly contradicted the earlier definition of a restaurant by advertising that he specifically provided "all sorts of large meals and suppers"![10] What, then, made his restaurant, or any other restaurant, "a restaurant"?

It was as much its style of service as its menu of bouillons and rice creams that distinguished the restaurant from other, already existing, public eateries. In the restaurant, the eater enjoyed a new kind of personalized treatment, one that he or she would previously have rarely (if ever) encountered, so that even when restaurants came to serve full meals they were hardly the equivalent of an inn, tavern, or cookshop. Instead, the restaurant gave new significance to the individual's emotions, utterances, and actions, and elaborated a whole new logic of sociability and conviviality.

While the serving of salutary dishes was the restaurant's initial raison d'être, fans of the restaurant spoke with equal enthusiasm about the many other delights available there. Diderot, for example, writing to Sophie Volland only a few months after his first visit to a restaurateur, extolled not the restorative bouillon and limpid ice water, but the comfortably individualized settings and the "beautiful restauratrice."[11]

"Healthful foods" and a new way of serving them proved inseparable, for the "weak-chested" were at least as much a socio-cultural category as they were the victims of an epidemic, and the restaurateur's bouillons derived many of their salutary qualities from the context in which they were served. Not for long did restaurateurs limit themselves to bouillons and rice creams, but they always distinguished themselves from *traiteurs* by the use of a menu, the option of service at any moment, and the presence of female bouillon sippers. The serving of delicate and healthful bouillons actually seemed to demand a new urban forum, a new social venue, a new kind of public space. The restaurant's effete clientele required a host of attentions unheard of at an innkeeper's or cook's table d'hôte, and those new modes of interaction would long outlive the fashionable ill health that originally provoked them.

In 1777, defining the "Founder's intention," Roze de Chantoiseau repeated that the goal of the first restaurateur had been to provide "delicate and healthful foods" and specified that they should be "served not at a table d'hôte, but at any hour of the day, by the dish, and at a fixed price."[12] His description immediately set the restaurateur's establishment apart from the *traiteur*'s or innkeeper's, not only by the menu it provided, but also by its style of service. Even as he tended to the weak-chested and catered to the sensitive, the restaurateur—with his door open at any hour and his printed menu (which "fixed" prices even as it stimulated desires)—promised respite from the hazard and awkwardness of the table d'hôte.

With extraordinary regularity, the descriptions of early restaurants—be they the advertisements of restaurateurs or the chronicles of astonished travelers—all emphasized that restaurants were open "at any hour," as if this convenient departure from the rigid hours of the innkeeper's table were their most salient feature. Why, however, did Roze de Chantoiseau, Vacossin, or some other restaurateur not serve his restoratives at a two-o'clock table d'hôte? What was it about the providing of succulent consommés, stewed capons, and delicious conserves that necessitated a rejection of standard mealtimes?

The restaurant's open-ended business hours, modeled probably on the pattern of service found in a café (where only beverages were served, and hence preparation time was minimal), depended upon assumptions about its therapeutic function and its fragile clientele: the delicate people of Paris, after all, would not necessarily all fall weak at any one particular moment. Unlike mealtimes, which might be set by shared social convention, the need for restoration could never be so routinized. The common *traiteur* might set his ordinary at the same time every day, but the restaurateur's commitment to his customers' well being obliged him to serve his extraordinary bouillons and rice puddings at all hours. At any moment, the feeble Parisian or exhausted foreigner might need to find a genteel atmosphere in which to drink his or her *restaurant*.

Restorative bouillons could in fact be ready at any hour; prepared in advance and kept warm in a hot-water bath, they required no more finishing touches than would a cup of coffee or a carafe of wine. (Thus, when Vacossin's stock was inventoried after his wife's death, the notary noted "soups and bouillons worth sixteen livres" stored on the premises.)[13] The other advertised restoratives were similarly easy to keep always available: *chapons au gros sel* could come from a *marmite perpétuelle* (perpetual kettle), where the analeptic juices of one bird would forever imbue the succulent flesh of the next;[14] soft-boiled eggs would cook in a few minutes; "preserves from the most reputable manufacturers," like fruit and dairy products, required no preparation; only the rice creams might spoil. The foods served by the first restaurateurs made their flexible hours physically possible without requiring a huge expansion of staff or space, while at the same time, the prevailing medical logic necessitated the serving of those very foods and no other. If eighteenth-century models of physiology had singled out the soufflé for its restorative powers, the restaurant could not have taken the form it did; if Roze de Chantoiseau, Vacossin, and their colleagues had not been as innovative in their style of service as they were semi-medicinal in their menus, the restaurant might well have become no more of a cultural institution than the purveyor of soup turtles. Material conditions and scientific developments intersected; one did not produce the other.

The regular quotidian pattern of the table d'hôte had suited the *traiteur's* or innkeeper's local clientele, but precisely by virtue of its regularity, the table d'hôte could also prove inhospitable to newcomers. Suspicion fell easily on the most recent arrival, and even if no silverware were to disappear and no brawl to erupt, the table d'hôte was not necessarily a warm or friendly experience for the person passing through Paris. Louis

Sébastien Mercier, writing with characteristic hyperbole, declared tables d'hôte "insufferable," and described with obvious delight the fate of the timid stranger seated with the regular crowd of "cormorants" and "vultures."[15] Johann Volkmann, a German traveler, appreciated the possibility of meeting local people at a table d'hôte, but he took it as a matter of course that he would be obliged to arrive at a set hour (most usually, 1:00 or 2:00 P.M.) and might well have to try several establishments before he would find an empty seat at a loaded table.[16] The British agronomist Arthur Young, as well, liked the opportunity tables d'hôte afforded to "see something of the manners of the people," but he complained (in typical English fashion) that the French were rude, the food was insufficient, and "the ducks were swept clean so quickly that I moved from table without half a dinner."[17] (In reasoning worthy of the restaurant's inventor himself, Young then went on to attribute the French economy's failure to keep pace with the British to the comparatively poor quality of inns and other travelers' accommodations.)[18]

A meal at a table d'hôte, by all accounts, necessitated interaction with, and awareness of, one's fellow diners. It required a certain willingness to plunge into the fray, if one did not want, like Arthur Young, to see the ducks stripped bare before one's very eyes. Granted, these particularly disgruntled descriptions present the table d'hôte in caricature, as Protestant foreign travelers saw the parsimony they had long learned to associate with Catholic France. But even the most lavishly set table d'hôte required the guest to arrive at a dictated hour and to converse, at least minimally, with fellow diners. (It is no coincidence, then, that the table d'hôte was often endorsed as an excellent means of learning another language, and that foreign-language teachers in Paris offered table-d'hôte-style pensions well into the nineteenth century.)[19]

So if the table d'hôte had its comforts for hearty eaters who kept to a regular schedule, it had considerable inconveniences for those given to more erratic hours and fastidious appetites. Whether one understood a less regular clock to stem from libertine indolence, invalid restlessness, or entrepreneurial commitment depended, of course, on one's outlook on urban French society, but they all could be translated into physical suffering and the very real "inability" to conform to the strictures of the table d'hôte. Lazy, sickly, or simply busy, the restaurant patron needed bouillons available at any minute. (And once restaurants began to offer the requisite flexibility of service, it became possible for more people to behave in a "lazy," "sickly," or "busy" fashion.) While mealtimes had always been something of a marker of place in the social order—to cite one common formulation, "artisans dine at 9:00 in the morning, provincials at noon, Parisians at 2:00 in the afternoon, businessmen at 2:30, and nobles at 3:00"—the restaurant made it possible to differentiate one's mealtime (and oneself) still further, or to do so without regard to the habits of one's family and relations.[20]

But what did it really mean for restaurateurs to offer bouillons "at all hours" in a time when the streets of Paris were poorly lit, and the work day largely determined by the hours of natural light? In the 1770s and 1780s, a series of police ordinances attempted to limit the hours in which restaurateurs did business, and eventually provoked them to appeal their case to the Paris Parlement. As of 1775, Paris police decrees had assimilated restaurateurs to other wine- and food-sellers, all of whom were required to close by 11:00 P.M. in the summer (10:00 in the winter), and who fell under the jurisdiction not of the police commissioner but of the night watch (*la garde*). This, the first attempt to subject restaurants (still known as "houses of health" [*maisons de santé*]) to closing-hour regulations, roused immediate opposition among restaurateurs, who argued that it was an insulting misnomer to class them with cookshops, inns, cabarets, and taverns. To their delight, a ruling of 1777, while reiterating the 1775 closing hours for all other establishments, made no mention of restaurants. Yet the matter was not completely settled, for a police ordinance of spring 1784 once again included them in the purview of this ruling.[21] As their owners quickly realized, it was the continued existence of restaurants as businesses distinct from cabarets or cookshops that was at stake in this dispute. In arguing against the proposed measures, restaurateurs and their lawyers amplified the place of restaurants in Paris life, shading medicinal connotations into theories of political order and social hierarchy.

Shortly after the 1784 decree that reinstated restaurants in the category of nightwatch-regulated spaces, eight restaurateurs organized to appeal this decision (an appeal that eventually cost them over 2000 livres in legal fees).[22] Nicolas Berger, a rue-Saint-Honoré retail wine merchant and restaurateur who complained that the *garde* regularly harassed him and his customers, led his colleagues in a legal battle to establish that restaurants were not the equivalent of other places that served food and drink. The police insisted that Berger and his associates were merely ordinary caterers and common cabaret-keepers, fraudulently operating "under the supposed title of restaurateur."[23] Not so, argued the lawyer hired by the restaurateurs: restaurants uniquely offered "help always ready" for "people who are forced, by their feeble or impaired health, to consume only salutary dishes."[24]

As was the norm in any court case at that time, the trial of the late-night restaurateurs provoked the production of a factum, a published and widely circulated judicial brief or mémoire.[25] Though initially written for the benefit of presiding magistrates alone, legal mémoires had become, in the second half of the eighteenth century, an enormously popular literary genre. They were issued in what were, for the era, extraordinary numbers—as many as 20,000 copies might be printed of a mémoire pertaining to a particularly sordid or notorious case, such as the Diamond Necklace Affair (which involved the Cardinal de Rohan, several sly con artists, and a prostitute disguised as Marie Antoinette).[26] The mémoire on behalf of the restaurateurs was not, in comparison, among the great narrative factums of the Old Regime; it is difficult to imagine how it could have been, when its protagonist was neither a wily libertine nor an innocent victim of religious persecution, but an entire category of business. Still, the anonymous lawyer, well versed in the tricks of the genre, did the best he could to personalize the tale: how could the reader not sympathize with the nameless restaurateur who, having closed early one night because business was slow, then found himself roused from his sleep by the imperious pounding of the *garde* at his door? Abruptly awakened, the restaurateur stumbled into his clothes and hastened to the door—only to be cited and fined for failure to open at the first knock.[27]

In arguing for Berger and his colleagues, the lawyer included a mass of this sort of description: material unrelated to the specific problem of regulating hours of business, but very much germane to the broader agenda of arguing that restaurants were, quite simply, utterly different from any other "maison publique" (public house).[28] Though less than twenty years had passed since Vacossin, Minet, and Roze de Chantoiseau had first advertised their restorative bouillons and other salutary dishes, the lawyer emphasized not the foods prepared, but the style of service. Describing the advantages brought by the restaurant to Paris life, he wrote:

> To order your own meal, or to bargain over it, would be, for many people, an irksome task [lit., *corvée* or "forced labor"]. The restaurant spares you that.
>
> A menu indicates the price and the variety of dishes prepared, so you can limit your expense before spending a penny. Unlike at a table d'hôte, you neither have the disagreement of waiting for a specific

number of fellow eaters; nor of being required to arrive at a certain set time; nor of watching two warring gluttons snatch the morsel that you would, at least, have liked to see them share with you.[29]

The lawyer for Berger and his colleagues admitted that if going to a restaurant constituted a "luxury" indulged in by a few debauched Parisians, then the case for exempting restaurateurs from the regulations governing taverns, open-air dance halls *(guinguettes),* and inns would be weak indeed.[30] Restaurants, however, he claimed, were not frivolous luxuries but obvious necessities, required by the "revolution" of life-styles common to the city's inhabitants.[31] Like mid-century partisans of the nouvelle cuisine arguing that the new cookery was not an extravagant decadence but a healthful purification, the writer described restaurants as useful, as necessary for the well-being of a modern urban population: "Those who merely provide pleasure must submit to the letter of the law, but it would be wrong to place restaurateurs in this class."[32]

In emphasizing that restaurants provided a "meeting-place for the delicate and sickly, whose health could not tolerate the food served by most caterers," the mémoire's author also made claims for the socioeconomic standing of the weak-chested. He argued that in order to guarantee the health-giving properties of the foods prepared, restaurateurs were obliged to use high-quality ingredients and to hire the most talented chefs. These constraints meant that prices were generally higher in a restaurant than in any other drinking place or cookshop, hence "one is morally certain to meet there only guests who abide by the proper and urbane rules that regulate all discussion and action among members of good society."[33] Anybody affluent enough to enter a restaurant, the argument went, was obviously polite and fragile enough to be allowed to stay. Yet the *garde* had had the temerity to refer in its reports to Berger's delicate patrons as "fifteen drinkers" as if they were but another group of "turbulent fellows, abandoning themselves to an excess of wine."[34]

The lawyer for the restaurateurs moved easily from questions of medical or physical need to those of social differentiation. He began in a universalizing register: restaurateurs met a "true need"—they were beneficial friends of all the world, bouillon cup and soothing broth at the ready in times of crisis. But his text slid quickly into a far more particular scenario; the "revolution in our way of life" that made restaurants necessary seems to have touched only a certain portion of the population. Apparently, it had had no effect on the cabaret and tavern patrons, whom the mémoire described as "unwilling to leave the scene of their debauches" until chased away by the night patrol. To have those rowdy locales closed by the *garde* at a reasonable hour was, the factum argued, to do a favor to the workers who would otherwise have drunk away an entire week's wages and been unable to work on the morrow. Truly, as a character in the play *Harlequin Restaurateur* remarked, "drunkards and peasants have no need of restoration."[35]

In the mémoire's terms, however, it was equally clear that other members of society certainly did need restoration, and that there was no reason for the police to challenge them. Immediately following the allusion to some dramatic change in life-style, the mémoire for the restaurateurs explained that "for a long time now, the cabaret has been out of fashion for those we call respectable people [*gens honnêtes*]; and a *traiteur's* house is no better suited to serving them."[36] The "revolution" in habits to which the brief referred may have described a newfound attention to a healthful diet, or a growing pattern of urban socialization, but it even more significantly denoted a process of social stratification whereby "honest people" were no longer willing (nor, it was implied, were they able, as a result of physical, moral, and aesthetic "delicacy") to frequent inns, taverns, or cookshops.

Restaurants, in this argument, may have been a necessary part of contemporary urban life, but they were not for everybody. Instead, the mémoire described the average restaurant patron as perhaps a rich foreigner, bored with eating in his rooms, and "hardly desiring to eat in an inn, where he would feel out of place"; or a financier whose business had kept him from home at mealtime; or, even, somebody who had spent the evening in a "great household," expecting to be invited to sup there, but when the time came he noted more guests than place-settings and slipped quietly away.[37] Where could any of these people go, if not to a restaurant? What difference could it make to the safety of the streets of Paris, if a few rich financiers and guests of prominent households were supping in a restaurant, rather than sleeping snug in bed?[38] By definition, restaurants did not pose a possible threat to public order; instead, they remedied private, physiological disorder.

In addition to appealing to keep their businesses open until midnight, the restaurateurs also requested that they be placed under the jurisdiction not of the *garde,* but of the police commissioners. The police came only if called, while the *garde* made nightly (and, in the eyes of restaurateurs and their patrons, intrusive) rounds. Furthermore, the *garde* was responsible

for the unsavory tasks of emptying taverns and brothels, as well as reporting on inappropriately located rubbish heaps. By what logic, the lawyer
demanded, could a restaurant's peaceful, genteel, and law-abiding customers be compared to the uncouth clientele that frequented taverns? To
give the *garde* jurisdiction over restaurants was to insult "honnêtes gens"
by confusing them with "vagabonds, drunks, and trouble-makers."[39] As a
distinct type of establishment, with its own specific (and important) patrons, the restaurant also merited its own administration, separate from
the nightwatch which supervised possible disturbances of the peace. "Order," explained the restaurateurs' lawyer summarily, "does not truly con-
sist of putting everything in the same place, but of putting each thing in its
rightful place."[40]

This, obviously, was only one side of the picture. The mémoire's author,
after all, had been retained by Berger and the other restaurateurs; he
wanted to win their case; and, quite possibly, he exaggerated the genteel,
inoffensive qualities of the restaurants' customers. In their competing accounts, the officers of the watch certainly noted that they were often the
explicit targets of restaurateurs' far from polite animosity: the restaurateur
Després threatened to lock a reporting officer in his restaurant and then
turn him over to the Commissaire de Police; Berger made a similar threat
and demanded to know "who gave him [the officer of the *garde*] the right
to enter" his restaurant.[41] The reports of the night watch, though rarely
naming the customers present, give some indication that restaurant patrons joined restaurateurs in protesting the intrusion of the *garde* and its
attempt to supervise restaurants—and not always in the delicate language
of "good society." A chevalier de Saint Louis (an honorary knight), found
after 11:00 at Després's rue-de-Grenelle restaurant, told the officer of the
watch that he had no right to enter there and should "go fuck himself and
not come back." The Comte d'Asson, one of five people having supper at
a restaurant on the boulevard des Italiens, also threatened the watch, while
the restaurateur's wife vaguely hinted that she had "friends."[42]

Though they were, in almost every respect, diametrically opposed texts,
both the mémoire for the restaurateurs and the reports of the *garde* emphasized not the food provided in restaurants, but the consumers found
there. The reports of the night watch differentiated the restaurateurs of
Paris from other violators of closing-hour regulations not by the bouillons
they served, but by the late-night customers to whom they served them.
According to the legal brief defending the restaurateurs, the latter followed from the former—only the best sort of people required restoration,

and they should be allowed to have it. Dietary needs and sociocultural identity would prove to be one and the same.

In June 1786, the Paris Parlement accepted this logic and ruled in favor of the restaurateurs and their powerful "friends," allowing them to stay open one hour later than any other purveyors of food or drink.[43] The restaurant might ostensibly cater to all who were delicate or enfeebled, but by common usage, if not technically by definition, many were excluded from those categories. The eighteenth-century restaurateur might be "the friend of all the world," but not everybody belonged in his world.

Public Spaces, Individual Tastes

Some twenty years after they were first established, restaurants no longer specialized in providing delicately healthful soups to a genteelly weak-chested clientele but in catering to individual tastes. While the *traiteur* fed large groups, the restaurateur offered single servings and small, intimate tables. As Diderot noted, writing of Roze's restaurant only a few months after it opened, "everybody eats alone there, each in his own little cabinet. . . . It is truly marvelous, and it seems to me that everybody sings its praises."[44] Service "au restaurant" named not a demitasse of bouillon, but the individualized meal available at any hour to the single eater. While the hybrid or intermediary establishment of a *traiteur*-restaurateur might well have a large banquet room or two in addition to secluded alcoves and cabinets, specifically restaurant service was reserved for, defined by, and perhaps instrumental in creating, individuals.[45] The restaurateur invited his guest to sit at his or her *own* table, to consult his or her *own* needs and desires, to concentrate on that most fleeting and difficult to universalize sense: taste.

With their exquisite furnishings, varied menus, and flexible business hours, restaurateurs offered their customers "distractions for the spirit"[46] and solace for the digestion that only slightly resembled the nourishing camaraderie of the traditional cookshop or inn. While the caterer's business depended largely on a regular clientele and on the established rhythms of neighborhood life, the restaurant emphasized the delicate, the unexpected, and the individual. Advertising in 1797, the *traiteur*-restaurateur Bouvrain declared that his establishment offered both the "useful," in the form of his 40-sous, wineless table d'hôte, and the "agreeable," in the form of private rooms or tables served with the "greatest care and cleanliness."[47] Whereas traditional table-d'hôte service placed all comers at a single large table, restaurants were innovative in the use of small tables and private rooms. While the caricatured table-d'hôte customer needed to seat himself strategically beside the roast and the green peas, the equally stereotypical restaurant patron could leisurely admire his own poise and graciousness without fear that every time he lifted his eyes from the table to a nearby mirror, his neighbor might snatch a choice morsel from the serving dish.

The restaurant, unlike the table d'hôte, presented its patrons with at least the appearance of choice. Even when it served not 88 entrées, but bouillons, vermicelli, capons, wafers, and rice pudding, the restaurant seemed—in comparison with the table d'hôte's dependably "overcooked beef, so-called stew, veal cutlets, and a few vegetables"—to offer an enormous range of options.[48] The restaurant allowed for variety, and insisted on the individual, much as medical science of the period departed from theoretical wisdom by arguing that each patient might well require a slightly different remedy. Like the relativist aesthetics of the abbé DuBos, the restaurant conceded that tastes might be individual and unreconcilable, without thereby condemning society to meaningless fragmentation and cultural anarchy.[49]

Furthermore, the eater could choose exactly what to eat, in keeping with the dictates of his or her delicate constitution (and pocketbook). From the early 1770s, at the latest, the use in restaurants of a printed menu, or *carte,* that allowed each customer to choose his or her own restoratives marked another distinctive innovation in service.[50] Before the emergence of the restaurant, a menu had always been a list of all those foods to be served during a particular meal (as at a banquet today). Cookbooks recommended them and chefs in wealthy households composed them, but all the items on the menu were brought to the table in the course of the meal. A table d'hôte had no menu; the eaters (whoever they might be) and the food (whatever it might be) arrived at the same moment. The restaurant's role as a place for the exhibition and treatment of individual weaknesses, however, necessitated a new sense of the menu: the creation of a list of available items from which each consumer made personal choices at the most convenient moment. In the restaurant, the vagaries of each customer-patient's malady demanded different dietary treatments; no two souls or nervous systems were "sensitive" in the same way. When ordering from a restaurant menu, the patron therefore made a highly individualistic statement, differentiating him- or herself (and his or her bodily complaint) from the other eaters and their conditions. By the mere presence of a menu, the restaurant's style of service demanded a degree of self-definition, an awareness and cultivation of personal tastes, uncalled for by the inn or cookshop.

When a *traiteur* in the 1780s added "restaurateur" to his sign, he probably began to serve some sort of bouillon, but he also, if at all possible, made provisions for more particularized repasts, for service à la carte. The restaurant made it possible, for the first time, to partake of a meal in the company of others without actually sharing their provisions. In 1794, one would-be restaurateur identified serving single portions as a rare new talent, and thus advertised specifically for a cook who knew how to "carve dishes for à-la-carte service" and price single servings.[51] Yet even if restaurateurs and their kitchen staffs knew that restaurant service was intended for individuals, their novice customers might not, and so menus throughout the 1790s carried reminders in large and boldface type informing eaters that prices listed were for *single* servings only.[52] A change of format as well as of cuisine, the restaurant depended on its own mini-technologies, which altered the lives of restaurant workers and customers alike.

Restaurants had printed menus because they offered their customers a choice of unseen dishes. Whereas a table d'hôte offered little individual choice, and a fishmonger's or sausage-maker's wares were all visible (and olfactible) to anyone entering his shop, the restaurant—which separated kitchen from dining room, and left foods hidden in the former until specifically called for in the latter—offered the variety of the invisible and the unknown. Neither obliging the eater to perform the "forced labor" of composing a meal independently, nor surprising him or her with an unanticipated bill, the restaurant's printed menu made standardized transactions possible in a time when printed prices or fixed charges were still far from the norm in most shops or markets. Tradesmen so innovative and so publicity-oriented as to advertise in the citywide classified advertisements often listed prices, but most shops of the 1760s and 1770s did not. Instead, their owners preferred to name prices orally at the moment of sale, often leaving open the possibility of bargaining. This practice among innkeepers struck travelers as especially barbaric; Philip Thicknesse, writing in 1778, noted with alarm that it was as necessary to haggle over the price of a meal in a French inn as it was to "bargain with an itinerant Jew for a gold watch."[53]

While a restaurant's fare might not be uniform (one serving of *pigeon à la crapaudine* might be larger or better cooked than another), its monetary transactions were. As Berger's advocate had noted, the printed menu allowed restaurant patrons to calculate costs "before spending a penny."[54] There in print, set and fixed before his or her very eyes, the restaurant customer saw prices and dish names, concoctions and costs. No longer required to share each of the dishes brought to a table d'hôte, but permitted to concentrate on the ones he or she explicitly requested, the restaurant patron could make preference as much a matter of finance as of taste. As the restaurateur Duclos advertised: "Each dish is reasonably priced, such that everyone can adjust expenses to means."[55] In a restaurant, the ostentatious potlatch of baroque expenditure was replaced by the equally conspicuous and significant economy of rationalized calculation.

After perfecting a bouillon recipe and printing a menu, a *traiteur* who was converting his cookshop or cabaret into a restaurant often undertook extensive architectural renovations as well. For example, in 1775 Jean-Baptiste Henneveu was, like his father before him, a highly successful tavern-keeper *(marchand de vin–traiteur)* at the sign of the Cadran Bleu, on the corner of the boulevard du Temple and rue Charlot. His establishment consisted of one very large room furnished with 27 tables and 78 stools, and two somewhat smaller rooms (each seating nearly 40 people). He also provided two rooms for more intimate drinking parties—a single *chambre* seating maybe 10 people, and one small *cabinet*.[56] By 1792, Henneveu (a distant relation of Roze de Chantoiseau) termed himself a *traiteur-restaurateur;* alterations to the physical layout of his business marked this shift. The largest dining room, containing a single large table for the table d'hôte that was still a central part of a *traiteur's* business, was now more lavishly decorated, hung with two wood-framed, built-in mirrors and an elaborate clock. The major change, though, came in the addition of eighteen "cabinets" or private rooms, each furnished with a small table, a mirror, and two to six chairs. Better suited to confidential tête-à-têtes than expansive sociability, the restaurateur's new spaces emphasized the private, the intimate, and the potentially secret.[57]

The rejection of the table-d'hôte tradition indicated far more than a move toward flexible mealtimes and away from shared provisions; the restaurant also altered the relation between provider and customer, marginalizing the former and cosseting the latter. The table d'hôte had literally been "the host's table"; semantically at least, the *traiteur* hosted his local associates, or the innkeeper welcomed the weary diner. The restaurateur offered a different sort of hospitality: he promised to provide each customer, or group of customers, with his or her or their (even at the level of pronouns, difference proliferated) *own* table. The restaurant, in the words of Berger's lawyer, promised the comforts of home, each restaurant table or private room briefly serving as the eater's "chez soi." As the restaurateur Duclos advertised in 1769, the rooms of his restaurant were "well arranged for those who would scarcely want to eat in public"; his colleague Dujardin, in 1796, also guaranteed "small separate apartments, where one is served just as one is at home [*comme chez soi*]."[58]

The restauratrice of the rue des Poulies, Diderot commented (implicitly comparing her behavior to that of innkeepers or *traiteurs*), did not seek out her customers or try to engage them in conversation. Instead, she left them alone and let their "attentions wander."[59] Nor were all the customers under a restaurant's roof or in its dining room there to interact with each other (though, perhaps, by means of each other). Two people seated at neighboring tables were nonetheless each seated at their "own" tables, left to think their own thoughts and order their own restoratives. In fact, neither common English nor French usage has, or had in the eighteenth century, a word for the relation that obtains among all the people in a restaurant. (To the restaurateur they might be "patrons" or "customers," and to a materialist they might be simply "eaters," but what were/are these people to each other? Sociologists could conceivably call them "consociates," but this term is hardly common usage.) "Personal" needs and "private" desires dominated the mythology and rhetoric of the restaurant; they were what separated the restaurant from other forms of public eating.

By its creation of discrete spaces, the restaurant's model of service and sociability differed as greatly from the café's as it did from the cookshop's. In 1789, in the full flush of shared revolutionary optimism, the proprietors of the new "Cirque de Palais Royal" (a multivenue center of enlightenment and entertainment in the center of Paris) advertised that their ample establishment included both a café and a restaurant.[60] The café, which held up to 500 people at any one time, served light lunches and beverages; like most cafés of the time, it also provided newspapers and other reading materials. In the restaurant, 200 more patrons might find seating. However, unlike the one huge open space of the café, the restaurant consisted of "24 small rooms, set up for parties of 2, 4, 6, or 8 persons, such that there need not be any communication between the groups." "Restaurant" service—as unlike the café as it was distinct from the table d'hôte—characterized not commonwealth but compartmentalization, a world of dividing partitions and individual isolation. Café patrons read newspapers, and thought about the world around them; restaurant customers read the menu, and thought about their own bodies.

The gendered analyses of medical science meant that the bodies found in a restaurant were far more likely to be female than those in a café or at a table d'hôte. Roze de Chantoiseau's almanac announced that women could easily order their meals at a restaurateur's, and his pseudonym, "Everybody's Friend," had none of the gender implications of the notoriously rakish Mirabeau's "Friend of Man." Vacossin explicitly invited ladies into his establishment: "Ladies may, without offending either their sense of decency or the rules of public propriety, go to a well-decorated suite of rooms intended only for them."[61] In one of those rooms that Vacossin reserved for ladies and decorated with two plaster busts of women and two of cupids (and one of Louis XV), a weak-chested victim of "the vapors" could sit in any of six crimson-velvet-upholstered "queenly armchairs" *(fauteuils à la reine)* and sip her *restaurant* from a dainty porcelain cup. In the other room, which looked out on the courtyard, the chairs were blue, and the walls covered with a fashionable new invention—wallpaper. A mirror, of course, hung over the mantelpiece in both rooms, and an extensive set of fireplace tools below helped to ensure that the rooms were "very warm during the winter," to protect delicate constitutions.[62]

The stated goal may have been restoration, but in the fashionably decorated and delicately furnished upstairs rooms of the restaurant, just which appetites were being restored? After the 1760s, restaurateurs no longer advertised special "apartments" for ladies alone, but they were quick to offer private rooms for intimate meals. For all the pastoral joys of these quickly assembled urban picnics, the notion of a restorative diet necessarily implied that something had been lost and therefore needed to be restored. Indeed, the simple diet of dairy foods, eggs, and vegetables made available by the first restaurateurs bears a striking resemblance to the menu recommended in the *Treatise on the Whip and its Effects on Physical Love, or the External Aphrodisiac* (1788) as a remedy for the exhaustion of appetites wrought by debauchery.[63] Connotations of indolence and seduction clung to the idea of relieving personal maladies and stimulating individual appetites.

The restaurant's potential for libertine sensuality was broadly hinted at in a 1782 print based on a watercolor by the Swedish artist Nicolas Lavreince, famed as an author of suggestive artwork and the illustrator of Choderlos de Laclos's *Dangerous Liaisons*.[64] An immediate success (one reviewer gushed, "nothing could be more charmingly spicy than this print"),[65] "The Restaurant" depicts an alcove richly hung with lavish fabrics and furnished with delicate upholstered furniture, a profuse floral arrangement, and a vaguely "antique" urn (Figure 2). A buxom young woman draped in a revealingly negligé costume reclines on a small sofa, while her fawning suitor sits beside her, encircling her waist with his arms, pressing his knee into her skirt, and gazing soulfully into her eyes. A third figure, a lady's maid, stands facing them, holding a small tray—really, not

Figure 2. Nicolas Lavreince's "The Restaurant" (1782) derives its title not from its setting, but from the small bowl of restorative bouillon that the maid is bringing to the lovers.

much more than a saucer—on which sits a small porcelain bowl. The whole thing is standard fare for eighteenth-century semi-licentious or "gallant" art: a scene of seduction decorous enough to be polite, while suggestive enough to be titillating.[66] If the pose of the two central characters did not reveal enough for the viewer's tastes, a more careful perusal exposed the chevalier's virilely upright sword in the lower left corner and his dangling watch chain glinting on his crotch. His beloved holds a dainty demitasse; the spoon with which she stirs its contents calls attention to her cleavage. The light, as well, from a window behind and to the side of the settee, directs our eyes to the young woman's very white décolletage.

The eponymous "restaurant" is not, as one might have initially suspected, the setting or frame for this scene. Rather, it is what that image frames: the *restaurant* presented by the maid and stirred by the young lady is the detail that gives this scene its title, and distinguishes it from countless others in which comparable figures hold a letter, a kitten, or a nosegay. The interweaving and confusion of sexual with gustatory appetites made the *restaurant* an appropriate detail for a gallant image. For a learned culture fascinated with Tissot's work on masturbation, delicacy of diet naturally factored into a generalized economy of appetites. According to Tissot's model of finite and comparable amounts of vital energy, the expenditure of sexual energy was said to leave one debilitated, less able to digest one's own food.[67] The hot-water-bath preparation of a *restaurant* was a means of pre-digesting meat, of cooking it into a more easily assimilated liquid state for those otherwise too dissipated to eat. Without any exertion of digestive energy, the *restaurant* drinker could be reinvigorated, stirred by the strong flavors of condensed meat, once again endowed with a range of appetites and the energy to pursue them.

According to critics, *restaurants* and other similarly potent delicacies actually overstimulated the senses and provoked pernicious eating without appetite, much as pornography and lewd thoughts prompted dangerous masturbation. Relying on a tradition begun with Plato's *Gorgias,* moralizing critics likened culinary artistry not to the perfection of painting or sculpture, but to overblown eloquence and feminine ornamentation.[68] They denounced the pernicious effects of these condensed broths in terms that made clear their inflammatory effects on more than the organs of digestion: one author characterized the products of the nouvelle cuisine in terms ("these fraudulent dishes that under seductive and appealing dress hide a secret poison") that sound like the words of a doctor issuing a warning about well-dressed, fetchingly made-up, and quite possibly syphilitic prostitutes.[69] In the case both of food and women, attractively disguised temptation provoked desires unrelated to needs. Appetites, sexual or alimentary, were too quickly roused and the senses too easily deceived. The consumption of curative bouillon shaded quickly into a scene of seduction.

As a business as well as a bouillon, the restaurant, with its private cabinets and late closing hours, seemed to promise far more than mere gustatory delights and to hint at the arousal, if not necessarily the satisfaction, of multiple appetites. Was a restaurant then somehow "decent" (unlike a tavern or café) because it was an appropriate place for women (Vacossin invited them, and they came), or was the restaurant a dangerous, sexually charged space, comparable to a theater or brothel? By 1788, one description of the restaurants of the Palais Royal commented, "Honest women, and those of good reputation, never go there"—but an 1803 guidebook instructed its readers: "one may not lunch with a lady in a café, but one may have dinner with her in a restaurant."[70] Who was that woman in the restaurant, and how could one know for sure? Whoever the women were, their presence immediately separated a restaurant from a table d'hôte or a café. While political pamphleteers in the 1780s issued tracts that claimed to represent the deliberations of a café's assembled clientele, no one ever authored a similar diatribe in the name of a restaurant.[71] Instead of reform programs and angry polemics, restaurants promised pastoral temptations and illicit innocence.

Spheres and Spaces

The eighteenth-century restaurant has previously been the focus of little, if any, scholarly research, but historians and political theorists have thronged to this era's cafés, seeing in them arenas of debate central to the rise of the "bourgeois public sphere" and the development of modern political culture. Scholars have often compared "café society" to social forms as dissimilar as the art exhibit and the freemasonic assembly, on the basis that all three provided the contexts within which notions such as "the public good" were first formulated. The men of letters who, as the physician Lorry had it, so delicately "ornamented" eighteenth-century French society have of late been more often described meeting in academies and cafés than suffering from constipation and insomnia. (Though we might wonder whether the former activities were not responsible for the latter conditions.)[72]

Much of the recent scholarship on eighteenth-century institutions of sociability has been directly inspired by the work of the German political philosopher Jürgen Habermas. In his 1962 book, *Strukturwandel der Öffentlichkeit* (translated into English in 1989 as *The Structural Transformation of the Public Sphere*), Habermas discussed the changing fortunes of public life in the transition from the Early Modern to the Modern period.[73] For him, the "public" in the absolute monarchies of the Old Regime (such as the France of Louis XIV) had been an arena of spectacle, the space reserved for the monarch's presentation and representation of his power(s) to the people. Habermas then posited that the late-seventeenth-century increase in the size and significance of a literate, urban bourgeoisie sparked the development of a different sort of publicness: the so-called "bourgeois" public sphere, characterized by dialogue and discussion, and putatively open to all "private" (that is, independent), rational individuals. No longer was publicness an attribute of rulers alone; instead, the new kind of public life was constituted by all "autonomous, relatively equal persons who in public discourse might address the general or public interest."[74] Participation in this novel form of publicness depended, according to Habermas, on individual, subjective opinions formed by reading and experiences within the family, and not on social rank or status granted by birth.[75] Thinking about ideas, not orchestrating spectacles, would henceforth be the basis for involvement in public life.

Habermas saw the emergent bourgeois public sphere based physically in provincial academies, urban cafés, freemasonic lodges, and aristocratic salons.[76] These innovative semi-public institutions served as meeting places for individuals from varied socioeconomic backgrounds, all united by their capacity for rational dialogue. The new physical spaces of the cafés, academies, and salons made possible the development of new discursive and linguistic "spheres" as well: in these new contexts of interaction, Habermas argued, people came to think and behave differently than they had formerly done in the market square, the church, or the royal court. As much by its formal emphasis on accessibility and rationality as through the substance of discussion, the exchange of ideas that took place in a café, a lodge, or even in the columns of a newspaper constituted a new "civil public sphere" and provided a framework for political engagement and action.[77] When opinions in the "bourgeois public sphere" clashed, the disagreement was to be settled not by a display of state-based power but through the egalitarian processes of enlightened communication. By the late eighteenth century, the dominant model of publicness had moved, we are told, from theater to courtroom, from presentation to participation.[78]

Within the broadly Habermasian framework, the vaunted cafés of Paris have been more significant for how they functioned as part of a metaphorical public "sphere" than for their role as actual public "spaces." This emphasis on new forms of interaction has had a number of curious effects: it made it possible for Dena Goodman to include the salons hosted by aristocratic women in her definition of the "public sphere"—though Madame Deffand's drawing room was certainly never a "public" space in the sense of being open to all—and for restaurants to be omitted from the general working definition of the public sphere's localization.[79] For while in terms of its admission policy, the restaurant was at least as public as a café (maybe even more so, since the restaurant explicitly invited women), in terms of its presiding ethos the restaurant was a decidedly different sort of place. And so, although the chronology of its development coincides perfectly with the late Old-Regime time period that many historians consider crucial, the restaurant has remained an emblem of the nineteenth century, and a subject studied almost exclusively by culinary connoisseurs, zealous tourists, and guidebook writers. Too "private" for an eighteenth century studied as the era in which a public sphere and public opinion coalesced, yet too "public" for a nineteenth century troped as "the golden age of private life, a time when the vocabulary and reality of private life took shape," the restaurant seems, for most historians' purposes, to have been neither public nor private but instead nearly invisible.[80]

When the restaurant is reintroduced into discussions of eighteenth-century France, however, a far more complex and nuanced picture of the "public" aspects of modern life emerges. For in the restaurant, new forms of publicness could be as much about consumption, display, and spectacle as they were about dialogue or discussion. Modern innovations in public *space* did not necessarily coincide with the expansion of a public "sphere": urban topography and political engagement never matched up so neatly. Disputes in a café might well be just as physical and unreasoned as conflict in any other forum: in January 1767, the owner of the Café de la Paix summoned the police after a brawl erupted between one of his apprentices and a customer who said that the coffee he served "was not worth a thing."[81] The idealized meeting place known as the coffeehouse certainly thrived in the writings of Addison, Steele, and their epigones, but in the rue du faubourg Montmartre, individual preferences and disagreement over the definition of "good coffee" made café society in the not-so-aptly named Café de la Paix (Peace Café) far less philosophical or contemplative.

According to Habermas and many of the historians who have taken up his model, the bourgeoisie's "audience-oriented privateness" led to the discovery of common, shared interests: the emergence, that is, of "public opinion" as a weapon for political debate. Learned societies, café coteries, widely circulated legal briefs: all at least claimed to speak for a broad-based "common good." While historians recognize that access to freemasonic lodges and provincial academies was, in fact, sharply limited by gender and social class, nonetheless they emphasize the significance of the formal equality governing members, and the supposed universality characterizing their utterances. But interaction in new common spaces would not necessarily have to lead to the discovery of shared opinions or enlightened universals (as the eruption of violence over the definition of "good coffee" makes clear). This is where the restaurant provides an important counterexample: restaurants, after all, only addressed the common good by means of the individual and the particular. Insofar as they were ostensibly open to all, restaurants were among the eighteenth-century's new institutions of public life. But as a public roof over a series of private tables (or even rooms), the restaurant would seem to confuse the now standard picture of the "public sphere." For if the restaurateur's door was open to all (with the caveat that they appeared sensitive), the doors of a private cabinet and the seats at specific tables just as definitely were not. One could gain access to a restaurant by shared social codes, a part of public knowledge; but once seated at the table, one was left to confront one's own sensibility.

To the degree that they promised individual attention to personal preferences, restaurants differed strikingly from many of the other new institutions of the eighteenth-century public sphere. In the freemasonic lodges and academies, we are told, members who spoke as private individuals (with no *acknowledged* regard for rank or status) might eventually discover a shared common interest. In a restaurant, however, the customer supping on bouillon at one table did not enter into rational debate with the stranger at the next table who had just ordered chicken and vermicelli. Nobody has ever expected restaurant customers to reach a consensus, or even to strive for one; nobody has ever imagined that beef-eater and chicken-eater could agree for the common good to compromise on veal. Instead, restaurant patrons are assumed to make their *own* choices regardless of the orders placed by those around them.

Like a conceptual lens, the restaurant here focuses issues and problems of where and how the "public" in the sense of the visible, the "public" in the sense of the accessible, and the "public" in the sense of the common, do and do not coincide. The restaurant was a publicly private place: Minet promised the weak-chested "a public place where they can go to take their consommé," but (and in no less certain terms) another restaurateur advertised his establishment as perfectly suited to "those who would hardly want to eat in public."[82] Neither expansively "public" nor narrowly "private," the restaurant offered the possibility for a public display of private self-absorption. Public life as it developed in the late eighteenth century was—and is—as much about the ability to ignore other people (even while being aware of their presence) as it was about the common good.

4

Morality, Equality, Hospitality!

The need to eat unites all men, and creates a sort of bond; as one of the Ancients tells us, it seems that at a meal, all the guests form a single body, and have but a single life.

ABBÉ PLUQUET, *DE LA SOCIABILITÉ* (1770)

In February 1783, Alexandre Balthazar Laurent Grimod de la Reynière, son of a wealthy tax-farmer, nephew of Louis XVI's minister Malesherbes, sometime lawyer, and future author of the *Almanach des gourmands (The Gourmands' Almanac),* hosted a dinner party that instantly made him the talk of Paris and established his reputation for years to come.[1] Invitations to the meal took the form of ornate burial announcements, and "tout Paris" gossiped that a black-draped coffin had served as the table's macabre centerpiece. After one course composed solely of pork dishes, Grimod announced that the food had come from the shop of his father's cousin, a talented pig butcher. After the next course, in which all the dishes were prepared with olive oil, he again announced that the oil had been furnished by one of his father's relatives, this one an affluent grocer. Surrounding his guests with reminders of their inevitable demise, and literally stuffing them with evidence of his noble family's shopkeeper origins, Grimod staged a message of "vanitas" and "memento mori" that kept Paris talking for many months.[2]

Like a banquet of freemasons, to which contemporaries compared it, Grimod's supper made heavy use of arcane ritual and semi-democratic pretensions.[3] Just as freemasons in their mysterious temples separated themselves physically from the "profane," so Grimod's guests had to pass through an entrance hall and a series of chambers before reaching a darkened waiting room, and, finally, the inner sanctum of the dining room. In one room, heralds dressed in Roman robes examined the guests' invitations; in the next, an armed and helmeted "strange, terrifying monk" subjected them to further scrutiny; beyond, a note-taking fellow in lawyer's garb greeted and interrogated the twenty-two guests, each of whom answered that he (or she: the guests included two women in men's clothing) sought "Monsieur Grimod de la Reynière, defender of the people"; in the final stage of initiation, two hired hands dressed as choir boys perfumed the guests with incense. Unlike the secretive freemasons, however, Grimod teasingly flaunted his supper party's idiosyncrasies and exposed the mysteries of his dinner to noneating observers. Turning his cryptic supper into a highly visible spectacle, Grimod allowed hundreds of spectators to observe the proceedings briefly from a gallery ringing the room, only to find themselves ushered away in order to make space for other eager audience members.

Grimod de la Reynière's supper is often cited as proof of its host's eccentric tastes and obsession with the table.[4] While neither could be disputed, the focus here is on the audience, on that public of three hundred who dawdled in the gallery and spread tales of Grimod's supper across Paris.[5] What might it have meant in 1783 to invite noneating observers to a dinner party, to convert hospitality into spectacle? What comparisons did his contemporaries make, and how would they have evaluated this rather extraordinary gesture? One guest had no doubt what it meant: the young lawyer de Bonnières claimed to have told Grimod that the audience was the perfect final touch for getting the host and all his guests declared utterly and stark-ravingly mad.[6]

To an Old-Regime mind, the presence of spectators at a meal would more generally have suggested monarchial or civic ceremonial. In his diary, Simeon Prosper Hardy, an eighteenth-century Parisian, mentioned observing the future Louis XVI and his young bride, Marie Antoinette, dining in state at the Tuileries Palace.[7] Such events were quite common: on the annual feast of Saint Roch, audiences at the Hôtel de Ville watched the dinner of Paris's newly chosen municipal magistrates; at Versailles, hundreds were routinely admitted to the *grand couvert,* the centuries-old custom of the royal family's public meal.[8] On these latter occasions, the monarch and his family dined in regal, public splendor, to the delight of the ticket-holding public. Admission was open to any properly dressed individual, but, in the 1780s, those too threadbare or too busy might enjoy the same pleasure in central Paris, where Curtius's Palais-Royal wax museum offered a very popular, lifelike reproduction.[9] By admitting observers to his supper, Grimod (the "defender of the people") mocked court spectacle, audaciously intimating that any Parisian meal could just as easily merit an audience's observation and a host's theatrical treatment. The audience members at Grimod's supper, and the published attention the meal received, implied that everybody had the right to eat in *grand couvert,* that anybody's dinner was worth observing, that all could be king.

All could be king—except, of course, for those in the audience, whose presence as spectators, rather than as performers (as subjects, rather than as monarchs) was as necessary to the dinner's significance as was the course composed solely of pork or the esoterically calculated number of table candles. Without those three hundred or so people in the balcony, Grimod's meal would have been just another carnival farce, just another scene of gothic aristocratic debauch no more interesting or memorable than the duc de Chartres's "widow's supper" in honor of the comte de Fitzjames's impending wedding, or the Marquis de Brunoy's exaggerated show of filial piety at his parents' funerals.[10] With an audience, however, Grimod's meal invited a new sort of publicity, a new power of social and political commentary. The model set by Grimod de la Reynière's supper— and it was a model of sorts, for though nobody dared repeat it, everybody discussed it, and from the early 1780s through the First Empire (1804– 1815) Grimod struck as notorious a figure as Talma, Beaumarchais, or Sade—celebrated the spectacular and the idiosyncratic, while at the same time pronouncing, in an engaged and critical fashion, on the corruption of the wealthy tax-farming elite.

Grimod inflected his hardly original critique of aristocratic debauchery (which many saw as evidence of that very decadence) with a new and powerfully pessimistic message. In staging his dinner as he did, Grimod created a moment that indicted both the *grand couvert* and the exclusionary logic inherent even in the Enlightenment's more universalist aspirations. Freemasonry's mysteries and the academies' libraries were no more open to all comers than was Grimod's funereal supper table. Grimod's meal—a series of obscure and pseudo-democratic rituals performed in front of an audience—commented simultaneously on the ceremonies of the absolutist court and on the new institutions that claimed to abolish ceremony and establish brotherhood. Both were subject to scrutiny; nobody escaped the bite of Grimod's satire.

By passing out tickets to spectators, Grimod highlighted the tensions between conceiving the realm of "public life" as that which is widely visible and as that which is easily accessible. Audience members could see the meal, but, forced to leave after a brief visit and prohibited from the evening's central mystery (eating), they were excluded from understanding it. Grimod de la Reynière's supper ritual, despite its notoriously open admissions policy (Friedrich Grimm referred to the guests as "a happy motley"),[11] drew clear distinctions between the nescient, who watched, and the cognoscenti, who ate. Allowed to see, but not guaranteed to understand, audience members by their very presence (and ignorance) lent credence to the notion that Grimod's funeral supper required interpretation. While the events of the evening did not offer any single clear moral, the easy availability of first-, second-, and third-hand accounts gave all Parisians the idea that something of great importance had occurred in the mansion on the Champs Elysées.

Grimod de la Reynière's macabre supper was hardly the last meal to attract attention or notoriety in the final decades of the eighteenth century. Throughout the period, a nearly endless variety of state-sponsored meals, extravagant dinners, and touchingly frugal suppers occupied the popular press and the Paris police, as well as the kitchens of prominent restaurants. Governments and individuals, whether revolutionary or otherwise, proposed myriad versions: from the fraternal festivals of 1790 to the ritualized pleasure of dining in a famous restaurant; from the republican repasts of 1794 to Bonaparte's triumphant victory banquets; from the little old lady who earned her place in the police archives by her obsessive insistence on inviting Napoleon to dinner, to Grimod's rejection (in the *Almanach des gourmands*) of ceremony as the death knoll of fine cooking.[12] Truly, Paris in the years between the calling of the Estates-General and the battle of Waterloo seemed gripped by a "manie des dîners."

In the decade of the Revolution, all these tables had specifically political import. The sorts of questions that preoccupied revolutionaries—debates about fairness and equity, questions about finance and food, problems of fraternity and Frenchness—could be (and were) easily mapped onto the dinner table. The development and circulation of new models of table-based sociability, new arguments about the association of taste with virtue, new notions of the relation of individual appetite to social cohesion: all marked a profound interrogation of the meaning, function, and status of the shared meal. Site of frugal repast or decadent feast, the table became a material and symbolic battleground, as important as street names, festivals, and the tricolor patriotic cockade.

Little wonder, then, that when historians have looked beyond the gastronomic and the culinary for broader social and cultural factors explaining the restaurant's emergence, they have insisted on the noteworthy role played by the French Revolution of 1789. For nearly two hundred years, historical commonplace has cited the development of the restaurant as an incidental and unexpected result of that revolution. From the guidebook writers of 1800 to an American journalist covering the Revolution's bicentennial, from the French aesthete brothers Jules and Edmond Goncourt to the British Marxist Eric Hobsbawm, rumor and received wisdom have inextricably linked the origin of restaurants to the political, economic, and cultural upheavals of 1789.[13]

In the highly charged political climate of early nineteenth-century France, as well, observers from across the ideological spectrum invoked the Revolution's aftermath in order to account for the proliferation of restaurants. Restaurants featured in the analyses of counter-revolutionaries and radicals alike: the aristocratic Madame de Genlis (former governess of Louis XVI's young cousin, the future King Louis Philippe) saw the spread of restaurants and the development of gastronomic literature as further signs of revolutionary barbarism; the writer Louis Sébastien Mercier, whose republican fervor only cooled with his imprisonment under the police-state of the Terror, denounced restaurants for breaking up the family meals (real and imagined) that had characterized the Revolution's great fraternal moments.[14] It remained for Pierre Jouhard, a successful lawyer during the First Empire, to outline a more optimistic perspective, concluding that the restaurants of Napoleonic Paris promoted republican ideals in the form of democratized cuisine.[15] Though each was affected differently by the Revolution, all these commentators concurred in seeing restaurants as somehow among its by-products. Convinced that the Revolution had actually managed to begin time and space anew, royalists and republicans alike saw the restaurant as certain evidence of the Revolution's rupture of daily rhythms.[16] All, we might say, accepted the Jacobin notion that true revolution necessitated a complete upheaval in every aspect of existence—eating habits and mealtimes included.

What all these writers somehow managed to overlook (or perhaps rejected as irrelevant) is, of course, that restaurants had actually first appeared in the 1760s. Invented by the inexhaustible entrepreneur Mathurin Roze de Chantoiseau and hailed by the polymath philosopher Denis Diderot, parodied by dramatists writing for the popular boulevard theaters and sanctioned by the Paris Parlement (the highest court in the land), the restaurant did not require the Revolution to make it a fixture in Paris life. If we are to understand how the restaurant came to *look like* a creation of the tumultuous revolutionary era rather than a product of Old-Regime commercial medicalized sensibility, then we must examine it in conjunction with the numerous *other* possibilities for "eating out" that were invented in that decade. To understand what was unique (revolutionary, even) about the patterns of conduct and consumption associated with the restaurant, we must also consider political banquets and fraternal suppers, for it was these other forms that in the 1790s did the most to call attention to acts of public eating.

In general, these revolutionary tables offered a stark contrast to the individualized service and attention to style that already characterized the earliest restaurants. Whether proposed by a philosophically-minded nobleman (the Marquis de Villette), a group of angry sans-culottes, or a lawyer member of the Terror's Committee of Public Safety (Bertrand Barère), the Revolution's ideal tables functioned as spaces of solidarity and uniformity, not of idiosyncrasy and preference. They promised equality and sustenance, not distinction and restoration. Directly challenging the modes of social and cultural differentiation to which Old-Regime restaurants had catered, the Revolution's communitarian meals necessarily focused attention on all forms of table-based sociability.

If the proliferation of public tables placed restaurants within a set of newly expanded and overtly political contexts, their function was also highlighted by revolutionary uses of medical rhetoric—uses that often deployed that language of distinction and individuality in novel and confrontational ways. Responding to Louis XVI's August 1788 request for advice on the assembling of the Estates General (the French parliamentary body, not convened since 1614), pamphleteers deluged readers with evaluations of France's enfeebled state of health; diagnoses of the kingdom's condition were as common as bulletins on Voltaire's or Rousseau's health had once been.[17] In dozens of polemical tracts on the condition of the body politic, the discourse of health and well-being acquired a pointed national significance. For as authors diverted medical language from human beings to all of society, it became a tool for denouncing social injustice rather than a means for defining physical ailments. What had formerly been a matter of personal restoration became a topic of political disputes and the focus of angry calls for reform: an anonymous pamphlet, *Letter from a Little Old Lady, Margot, Aged 102, to the Estates-General,* condemned French nobles as just so many "stomachs that take in everything, but can digest nothing."[18] As more and more writers treated the state's fiscal difficulties as physical maladies, and the regime's swollen budget as an ill to be cured by a more balanced distribution of resources, the proclamation of "delicacy" that once had helped restaurants to prosper threatened to consign them to the class of the ideologically suspect and politically dubious. For whereas restaurant patrons had sought solace in savory broths and creamy puddings, these authors proposed far more drastic cures: the "little old lady's" pamphlet recommended that "such bellies, which with their cookies, their consommés, and their sugars, are only good for fancy cooking" should be surgically excised from the state.

The Nation's *Grand Couvert*

The "fraternal" banquet remains one of the French Revolution's most enduring images.[19] Whether gathered by the thousands on the Champs de Mars for the July 1790 Festival of Federation, or seated at long tables in the streets for the frugal shared meals of Messidor Year II (as "late June 1794" was labeled in the new republican calendar implemented in September 1793), the emblematic Parisians of the Revolution affirmed their solidarity with a loaf of bread and a bottle of wine. In the heady excitement of August 1789, Louis XVI took the epithet "Restorer of French liberty," and the sobriquet *Restaurateur de la liberté française* appeared on medallions and popular prints diffused across the land.[20] Louis truly was the friend of all the world, and all of France could be restored. Later, when the monarchy's reputation had plummeted, and even well-known restaurateurs like the Véry brothers described themselves as simple *traiteurs,* municipal authorities maintained that it was still the Spartan fraternal supper that "most truly characterized" the sincerity, devotion, and dogged elation of the Festival of the Supreme Being.[21]

If, as many historians have argued in the past twenty years, the French Revolution was, in large part, a struggle over the definition of meaning, an effort to create a new symbolic order (and hence a new political order), then there is no reason to expect the shared meal to have escaped this debate.[22] Yet the table was not only a symbol; or rather, as a symbol it could stand effectively neither for an abstract good such as Liberty, nor for a political right such as freedom of the press. Instead, it insistently pointed to a real and pressing material need. For as other historians have argued, the French Revolution was also driven by a series of actual material crises: bankruptcy, food shortages, bad harvests, threats of invasion.[23] Though the effort to define political life played no small part in that period we call "the French Revolution," and though that struggle did necessitate the reassigning of meanings, the table, precisely because of the indisputable materiality of subsistence, resisted being fully or satisfyingly symbolized. As a category of universal consumption, food was not a symbol that could be claimed or monopolized by any one faction or group. Food, which was ingested as well as depicted, which was good to eat as well as good to think, could not be purely metaphorical. Metonymical as well as metaphorical, a physical part of the symbol-maker as well as a symbol to be made, food united quotidian preoccupations with more grandiose aspirations.

I am not arguing that material conditions somehow took a sort of "vulgar" precedence over equally necessary social logics; rather, people needed both food, clothes, shelter, *and* some sort of coherent belief system.[24] But when belief system and material conditions were sharply at odds with each other (say, when one argued that a shared meal created equality and then stumbled upon the servants who were responsible for preparing that meal), then conflict, confrontation, and unstable meanings resulted. The table refused to be simply theorized—whenever an attempt was made, there was always a critic to the Left or Right (usually Left) to ask who was providing the food and who was washing the dishes. And yet, concurrently, the shared meal proved too powerful an icon and too important a dream for the French to reject it as merely one of despotism's hollow superstitions.

In order to understand what happened when people partook of a meal together, philosophes and journalists often proposed analogies with antiquity.[25] Interest in, and knowledge of, the "daily life" of ancient Greece and Rome had grown throughout the eighteenth century, stimulated by numerous archaeological discoveries and popularized in a wide range of contexts. Central to this project was a fascination with ancient cookery and a celebration of classical symposiac civility: the mid-century archaeological digs at Herculaneum and Pompeii unearthed pie crusts that predated Christianity; LeGrand d'Aussy's 1782 three-volume *Histoire de la vie privée des françois (History of French Private Life)* traced his countrymen's diet to its Gaulic origins; in 1788, Jean Jacques Barthélemy's lengthy, fictional travelogue, *Voyage du jeune Anarcharsis en Grèce (Voyage of Young Anacharsis in Greece)*, presented the findings of classical history and archaeology in a page-turning format that went through numerous editions and included several chapters on diet; later that year, the court portrait painter Elisabeth Vigée Lebrun, inspired by her reading of Barthélemy's novel, hosted a famous meal in which she offered guests her version of Spartan fare; and, in one of the lesser-noted events of 1789, LeFebvre de Villebrune began publishing, in gorgeous gilt-edged folios, the first full French translation of the *Deipnosophists,* Athenaeus' extraordinary compilation of ancient table lore.[26] But as so often happened when the men and women of the 1780s and 1790s turned to the Classical period for inspiration, a superfluity of models awaited them (as this only partial listing suggests), each ready to undermine the next. Some said that the shared meals of the Revolution indicated "a return to Spartan simplicity and hospitality"—but critics of the same meals saw them as imitations of the "feasts where Caesar fed the Roman people" in order to make his dictatorship more palatable.[27] The table's connotations in this period twinned round each other; decades of the history of "private life" and of the culinary playing out of the Quarrel of the Ancients and the Moderns had left a double legacy. The quasi-classical "fraternal" model of the bare minimum divided into equal parts inevitably collided with a countermodel of the table as the initial, and not so innocent, sign of luxury, debauch, and moral corruption.

In one version, the honestly divided frugal repast would cement society, creating new bonds and forging a deeper sense of shared commitment. This, according to the philologist Anne Dacier and many other panegyrists of the Ancients, had been the habit in ancient Greece.[28] Unsurprisingly then, of the three cardinal Republican virtues, the one most often invoked at the banquet table was neither "Equality" nor "Liberty" but the ever-amorphous, and difficult to legislate, "Fraternity." In the excitement of July 1789 (only a few days after the storming of the Bastille), the Marquis Charles de Villette proposed that fraternity could be achieved simply if the people of Paris all dined together in the streets. Saying nothing about groups having their *own* tables, or about service being available "at any hour," the reform-minded marquis painted a utopian picture, describing a moment in which "the rich and the poor would be united, and all ranks would mix . . . The capital, from one end to the other, would be one immense family, and you would see a million people all seated at the same table; toasts would be drunk to the ringing of church bells and to the sound of a hundred cannon blasts. On that day, the nation will hold its *grand couvert.*"[29] As the historian Mona Ozouf has commented, Villette saw this idealized meal not as the celebration or commemoration of an event, but as a revolutionary action in and of itself, a dramatic enactment of unity with commensality at center stage.[30] Like the monarch's ceremonial meal, this patriotic banquet would have symbolic effects far exceeding any incidental nutritional benefits.

For centuries, the *grand couvert,* the protocol-wrapped meal open to an audience, had impressed the observer with the distance separating him from the monarch. The king ate from gold and silver dishes; three men, each with a slightly different task, were required to fill his regal glass. Like other ceremonies of the absolutist court, the *grand couvert* turned the king's most plebeian physical actions into an ornate, and closely observed, ritual.[31] By the late eighteenth century, however, the *grand couvert,* along with other court ceremonies, had become to many an empty formality; no longer inspiring awe, it instead provoked slight embarrassment. Arthur Young termed it "more odd than splendid," while one French author commented that only in France did the ancient custom of the king's public meal continue, and nobody understood why: "There are some who are pleased by it," wrote the anonymous observer, "but they don't know why; others are indifferent to it, but they go automatically; . . . and how many of them, in leaving the sight of these sumptuous tables, have nothing on which to dine or sup?"[32]

What form could the *grand couvert* take if it were not to have those hungry spectators, not to depend on the distinction of king from subjects, of participant from observer? How could all of France dine *en grand couvert!* These questions had perturbed critics of the absolutist state for decades, prompting at least one well-known work of "philosophical" (that is, illicit or underground) literature to propose an ingenious answer. In his utopian fiction, the 1770 best-seller *The Year 2440, a Dream if Ever There Were One,* Louis Sébastien Mercier described a future fantasy Paris that his eighteenth-century narrator only barely recognized as his own home city.[33] In the world "dreamed" (in considerable detail) by Mercier's narrator, credit has been abolished, churches stripped of ornament, and the works of Anacreon, Horace, and Bossuet burned. The luxury of the few no longer contrasts with the misery of many, and laws reign, rather than men. In the future, hunger and gluttony have both been abolished—for when the rich are not greedy, the poor are not starving. Travelers, like elderly people, pregnant women, and orphaned children, all know that they can find nourishment at open tables joyously laid by the princes of the land. Invited to partake of a tasty soup, vegetables, fruits, and a little meat, the time-traveler enjoys the fairly distributed wealth of what Mercier titled *le prince aubergiste* ("the innkeeper prince"), and participates in a "decent and animated conversation."[34]

During his "simply prepared" meal, the narrator appalls the people of the future by describing living conditions and cuisine in eighteenth-century France. Back then, he tells them, three hundred cooks might have worked to feed a dozen people, and hunting was an expensive pastime of the idle rich. He regales his guide with tales of adulterated wine, spoiled grain, and mismanaged harvests—crimes he attributes to the parasitism of the indolent rich, and the greed of *traiteurs* and wine merchants. In identifying these as the major difficulties in eighteenth-century provisioning, and in imagining governmental intervention as the basis of improvement, Mercier shared the assumptions of many of his contemporaries. Like numerous others, Mercier blamed profit-hungry merchants and shopkeepers, and appealed to a munificent monarch to set things aright. His twenty-fifth-century innkeeper-prince was but the old myth of "the King, father and feeder of his people," actualized into a local and easily visible street-corner phenomenon.[35]

By 1789, tens of thousands of readers were familiar with Mercier's "innkeeper-prince." In fantasizing about the nation's *grand couvert*, Villette worked with a similarly dichotomized vision of private greed and public generosity, but he went one step beyond Mercier's still rather myopic picture. For whereas Mercier's Paris of the future still needed princes with emblazoned entranceways and magnificent reception rooms to provide ample and nourishing repasts, Villette's city seemed able to generate its feasts almost spontaneously. Nowhere in his musings on the nation's *grand couvert* did the nobleman mention what was to be set on those tables in the streets, nowhere did he suggest from where the food might come—and yet it would be there, providing the pretense for sociable interaction. Appealing primarily to the table's power to forge social bonds, Villette was moved to imagine a ceremonial meal in which there was no audience, no representation, and, often enough, no food: the prandial equivalent of Rousseau's idealized, spectatorless festival.[36] As Villette described it, his version of the *couvert* would feature neither spectators nor etiquette; his was a meal of and for the public, not staged in front of a public. At the Nation's table, all would eat, and eat as they pleased, free of odious protocol. The sharing of such a meal would do more than demonstrate or indicate; unlike the king's meal, which with every detail emphasized social difference, the patriotic banquet would create solidarity, melding rich and poor together into one gigantic family.[37]

Villette used the model of the biological family to construct a metaphorical one; later he declared winter the appropriate season for fraternal meals because it was "the season of marriages." He offered a comforting picture of nuptial revelry: his *grand couvert* respected the traditional calendar and preserved the familiar patterns of daily life, even as it profoundly restructured the social and political order. Just as the *traiteur*'s daily table d'hôte and wedding festivities had done, Villette's banquet reaffirmed basic, routine patterns of sociability: "At these civic banquets, we shall see the reunion of families, the forgetting of hatred . . . these periodic feasts will remind us of the course of human life."[38] In his picture, the Revolution would not overturn the social order; it would simply return it to its lost state of familial innocence.

The meals associated with the celebration of the national Festival of Federation (July 14, 1790) perhaps most closely approximated Villette's scheme.[39] Much has been written about the Fête de la Fédération: at the time and in the years to follow, as well as in the present historiographical tradition, republicans and historians have evoked the Federation as the high moment of revolutionary optimism, the pinnacle of honest communal labor. At a single joyous moment of unison on the first anniversary of the fall of the Bastille, voices from all across France took the same oath of national loyalty, thousands of mouths miraculously speaking the same words.[40] As related by a flood of popular prints, stirring descriptions, and commemorative plays, the now constitutional monarch Louis XVI participated in the scramble to convert the parade ground of the Champs de Mars into an amphitheater and then swore his devotion to the Nation; tens of thousands of provincial and military participants traversed France in order to take part in the spectacle; women and children, aristocrats and artisans, all happily and patriotically volunteered to drive wheelbarrows through the mud of the fatherland.[41]

For over two weeks, it would seem, Paris was awash in patriotic songs, joyous dances, and fraternal banquets. Throughout the second fortnight of July, the National Guard promised "a meal in every district."[42] On July 13, the day before the Federation itself, over 2000 spectators "attracted by the novelty of the scene" watched as the members of the National Assembly shared a "patriotic meal" in the Palais Royal's "circus" (or amphitheater)—thus was the *grand couvert* expanded if not to all the people, then at least to their representatives.[43] On another happy occasion, General Lafayette invited the provincial participants to feast at "endless tables" set under the trees of the parc de la Muette; after the official meal, the poor of Paris (by one count, as many as 5000) were admitted and allowed to partake of the leftovers.[44] At a slightly earlier patriotic meal (this one to mark the anniversary of the Tennis Court Oath), the citizens of Versailles invited several deputies to a joyous repast that ended with "a young and beautiful child, dressed as the spirit of Liberty" emerging from the ruins of a cardboard Bastille.[45]

Scenes of spontaneous mealtime unity filled the theaters at this time as well. For ten days in mid-July, the Théâtre du Palais Royal performed Ronsin's *The Patriots' Dinner,* while the Théâtre français et lyrique offered *The Supper on the Champs de Mars* during this same period.[46] The playwright Jean-Marie Collot d'Herbois (later famous as a member of the Terror's ruthless Committee of Public Safety), in his tribute to the Federation, relied, as Villette had done, on the civil family in order to make sense of the political one: in his play, *The Patriotic Family, or the Federation* (1790), the main female character weds her honest, hard-working fiancé early on the morning of July fourteenth, thus saving herself from the arranged aristocratic marriage planned by her evil uncle. When her father returns from the solemn ceremonies on the Champs de Mars, he brings with him four *fédérés* (three provincial representatives and one veteran) whom he invites to share in his daughter's wedding banquet—in this depiction, the *traiteur's* wedding feast literally confirms the solidarity of France asserted by the Federation.[47] Unable to bring the Federation itself to the stage, Collot d'Herbois chose the less spectacular, but more familiar, image of the wedding banquet with which to end his play.

Yet if the moment of Federation was one of incomparable "exultation,"[48] and the shared meal a particularly convenient shorthand for that lofty sentiment, the entire event was also any party planner's nightmare. Fifty thousand participants, assembled from all across France and beyond, descended on the capital with little idea of where they were to go or what they were to do.[49] We are accustomed now to the images of the Festival itself: General Lafayette and Bishop Talleyrand (both utterly drenched, for it had rained all day) standing at the Altar of the Fatherland; the participants swearing to "remain united, by the indissoluble bonds of fraternity, to all the French"; Louis XVI's oath to uphold the Constitution and enforce the laws.[50] Yet this moment of mystical unity came only after weeks of hard work, for the once flat Champs de Mars had to be graded, the imposing (if slapdash) triple arch had to be built from scratch, and all those associated had to be housed and fed.

While the laborious toil of thousands to prepare the terrain offered the painter Hubert Robert and the engravers Duplessis-Bertaux and Swebach-Desfontaines ideal subjects for commemoration, other logistic headaches proved harder to resolve than the moving of all that rock, and less easy to recuperate symbolically.[51] For example, the Constituent Assembly debated for hours on how representative members of the armed forces were to be chosen—by election, lots, or seniority? They eventually decided on the last, since it was, in the words of the deputy d'Aubergeon de Murinais, Nature's own lottery.[52] On another thorny issue, it was noted that provincial representatives to the Federation, since they were required to pay their own travel expenses, were likely to be among the wealthier citizens of their communities—should they also be expected to pay for food and lodging in Paris?[53] Certainly, many merchants thought they would do so, and allowed the euphoric spirit of the Federation to set the tone for money-making ventures as well. While a member of the Butte-des-Moulins section decried the hotel-keepers and restaurateurs who hoped to profit from the influx of provincials, Gaëtan Velloni, café-keeper/restaurateur and festival impresario, enticed customers by offering free military music to any party of fifty or more dining in his establishment.[54] Landowners tried to rent their Champs-de-Mars-front property to restaurateurs or café-keepers, and the pastrycook LeSage advertised that his varied pâtés and almond cakes were perfect picnic foods for "the Champs de Mars, and other festivities."[55]

Still, for all this flourish of commercial activity, the proposals made in municipal "section" meetings implied that the regenerated Nation would soon need neither innkeepers nor restaurateurs. "Since hospitality is one of the Revolution's first blessings," one patriot claimed, "all good citizens have rushed to offer their homes to the deputies arriving for the Festival of Federation."[56] Another advertised that he would happily lodge and feed ten delegates (though his sense of "fraternity" seems, by his expressed preference for visitors from his home town of Rocroy, to have been rather literal).[57] The Englishwoman Helen Maria Williams, who described the Federation to her British correspondents as "indescribable," nonetheless found the words to salute the "most cordial hospitality" that all provincial participants found waiting for them in Paris.[58] The radical journalist Louis Prudhomme, slightly less giddy than Williams, had harsh words for the local and national authorities who planned the Festival, but he too showered praise on the simple Parisians whose "private civility and most gentle hospitality" intervened in the face of what he considered a rude and disorganized public welcome.[59]

Despite all the talk of France's great dinner party, some, like Prudhomme and his fellow radical journalist Camille Desmoulins, saw the celebratory meals of July 1790 in a not quite so favorable light. Writing of the Parisians who were allowed to take the leftovers from the dinner Lafayette hosted in the park of La Muette, Desmoulins said they had had "no party dresses" (that is, no National-Guard uniforms) to wear to the official Federation banquet. The nation's *grand couvert,* like the monarch's, had a dress code. Desmoulins categorized the banquets as self-congratulation on the part of Lafayette, and pointed out an obvious difficulty: "when you want to invite a great many people to dinner, your first concern must be to find somebody who will cook and serve."[60] It was, Desmoulins wrote, all well and fine to talk of the French people gathered together in a joyous feast, but if all were sitting down to eat, who would serve? Who would provide the food for these hundreds of thousands? Most important, who would foot the bill? Who was the host at this dinner party and who the guests? The fraternal meal, he implied, could easily turn into a variation on the bread and circuses with which "the aristocrats of Rome corrupted the people."[61]

Desmoulins's abiding distrust of Lafayette, his suspicion that the general was perhaps too closely tied to the court to have the nation's interests at heart, no doubt initially stimulated his skeptical account of the fraternal banquet's pleasures. Yet he easily gave this prejudice critical weight simply by looking beyond the table, beyond the moment of fraternal communion, to ask how the food and wine had arrived on the table in the first place. Desmoulins's critique, in effect, invoked the specter of Rabelais's fifteen minutes. When the bill came due—which, he implied, it inevitably would—to whom should the waiter give it? In Villette's or Lafayette's ideal of the nation's patriotic banquet, food needed to be neither harvested, nor prepared, nor served, nor paid for; it simply appeared in all its honest, decent bounty, and offered the occasion to convoke people to a single spot. Their models of the Nation may have had a *grand couvert,* but they had no accompanying "Service de Bouche"—no kitchens full of talented chefs, no pantries and hallways crowded with ceremonially significant platter-bearing noblemen.

In fact, most accounts of the Federation avoided any discussion of the practical conditions of fraternal hospitality whatsoever: a pamphlet promising *Detailed descriptions of the patriotic festivals, illuminations, banquets, etcetera, that have occurred since July 18, 1790* in truth mentioned not a single banquet; Prudhomme's *Revolutions of Paris* celebrated the Federation at length as the first festival in which the people had been its own host, while alluding but briefly to "some tables set up by tavern-keepers and caterers."[62] All of these texts so idealized shared national conviviality as to leave it almost no material form. Even in Collot d'Herbois's *The Patriotic Family,* the wedding banquet was, according to the script, "in the next room" (that is, offstage and invisible, hence non-existent). For with a feast on stage, *The Federation* would have concluded with a tableau that, in some sense, would have reinscribed the logic of absolutist ritual: an audience watching as others ate. The exemplary lesson of the play (revolutionary theater tending as it did to heavy-handed morals) was meant to prompt audience members to offer their hospitality to all the Nation's supporters (servants, veterans, and *fédérés* alike), but to stage this didactic point would, paradoxically enough, have also invoked the "cold and empty etiquette"[63] of the absolutist court. The wedding banquet, here serving as a more immediate, intimate, and personal version of the Federation, nonetheless had to be banished from the stage. Collot d'Herbois solved the problem of depicting an appropriately revolutionary repast by alluding to it, without showing it, shunting aside the actual logistics of feeding provincials and Parisians. With no thought for *traiteurs* to be paid or waiters to be tipped, the hack playwright and future terrorist provided a bountiful feast just beyond the stage's frame.

By the terms of the Federation's ideals, hospitality was a basic virtue to be respected, not a service to be sold for five or fifteen livres per head. As theorized, the Festival of Federation, like Villette's *grand couvert,* created a bond and forged a nation. Its organizers attempted to institutionalize fraternity on a national level in a fixed moment of union, rather than leaving that important work to the thriving and piecemeal market in military music, restaurateurs' tables, and patriotic fireworks. In the new Nation, there was to be no market in hospitality. The idealizing moments of the Revolution—recalling, perhaps, Montesquieu's and Rousseau's lessons about the exemplary hospitality common to earlier peoples—attempted to distance the providing of food, drink, and shelter from the corrupt realm of commerce.[64] Since indissoluble ties of brotherhood and friendship linked all Frenchmen to each other, and since every dinner table was a fraternal banquet in miniature, what need had the Nation of a restaurant's private rooms?

Hospitality, if practiced properly, with everybody's home open and hearth ready, would render the division of domesticity from publicity nearly obsolete. France's new criminal code, passed into law a year after the Federation, came very close to doing just that, by indiscriminately stressing the sanctity of all apparently hospitable interactions no matter where they occurred. The Penal Code of 1791, debated throughout the summer and passed in September as one of the last acts of the Constituent Assembly, broke with the past in a number of remarkable ways, some better known to us than others: it established a uniform sentencing code, one that took no account of the perpetrator's rank or status; it abolished the "imaginary" crimes of heresy, blasphemy, and witchcraft; it made taking up arms against France a crime to be punished by death. The code also established, without any debate or discussion in the Assembly, two distinct categories of theft, articulated in terms of hospitality. In most cases, conviction for theft would result in a standard four years of forced labor, but the penalty was to be doubled to eight years in the cases of servants convicted of stealing from their masters (or masters from their servants), guests who stole from their hosts, and hosts who robbed their guests. The latter category, protecting the domestic sanctuary of the home, built on well-established tradition, since Old-Regime legal precedent had allowed the death penalty for cases in which servants stole from their masters (though it was, by the late eighteenth century, rarely actually levied).[65] The 1791 Code expanded that category in a striking fashion, however: it extended the protectively harsher penalty to include "thefts committed in hotels, inns, cabarets, cookshops [*maisons de traiteurs*], furnished rooms [*logeurs*], cafés, and public baths" while expressly excluding "theaters, shops, and other public buildings" from this category.[66]

The revolutionary penal code did not divide the world into anything we would recognize today as public and private spheres. It separated "public" buildings from "public" baths, and while it assimilated shops to "public buildings," it left the more jealously guarded cabarets and cookshops or restaurants in another domain. Some practical considerations almost certainly featured in this division: it was, after all, far easier for a criminal to pocket a fork from an innkeeper's table than to take a bolt of fabric from a dry goods shop surreptitiously, and a restaurant (where each table usually had its own salt cellar, flatware, and napkins) probably presented far more temptations to the nimble-fingered than did a theater. But simple material concerns such as these cannot fully account for the Penal Code's logic, for the value of the object stolen clearly did not determine the severity of the sentence: the theft of three napkins from Girardin, caterer-restaurateur on the rue Honoré, resulted in a former monk being sentenced to eight years of hard labor, while the theft of a far more valuable watch from a jeweler's shop got a used-goods dealer, Berteau, sentenced to four.[67] Nor did the legislation particularly protect "public morality," for if theorists of eighteenth-century public life (past and present) have considered the café far more public than the boutique—public in the sense of shared, common, and accessible without reference to wealth or rank—they have also tended to treat the theater, here grouped with the shop in opposition to the café, as among the revolutionary decade's other archetypally "public" spaces.

In short, the Penal Code's division had as much to do with ethical considerations as it did with physical spaces or idealized "spheres": its opera-tive concept was neither "publicity" nor "privacy" but the more amorphous and classical virtue of "hospitality." Hospitality was what Parisians showed to their provincial brethren, what Philemon and Baucis offered to Jupiter and Mercury, what Nestor showed to Telemachus. Once upon a time, friends, relatives, and even entire towns had simply broken a coin in two, so that the halves, when matched again, would remind them and their posterity of the hospitable commitment that linked them together.[68] When young Anacharsis, the abbé Barthélemy's hero, made those fictional travels through ancient Greece that so impressed the reading public of 1788, did he stay in inns, eat in restaurants, or sit in cafés? Of course not, for as Barthélemy "knew" from all his reading in ancient history and archaeology, "hospitality" was the "ordinary usage" throughout the Classical world. The early Germans, too, had often been hailed for their society based on rigorous equality, courage, frugality, and hospitality. These, according to the journalist Prudhomme, should provide the inspiration for the newly reborn France.[69]

By including inns, taverns, cookshops, and restaurants in the category of protected, hospitable spaces, the Assembly redefined their place in the economy, privileging form over finance. According to Montesquieu in the *Esprit des lois* and to de Jaucourt in the *Encyclopédie*'s article "Hospitality," such a transition was unimaginable, for the institutions of the market, the products of trade and commerce, had in fact been responsible for abolishing hospitality: in modern society, the faceless coin of the realm and streams of filthy lucre had replaced the simple talisman broken in two.[70] But in writing the laws that were to govern the regenerated and virtuous France, the authors of the Penal Code simply decided that such institutions would, henceforth, be hospitable. Like Villette describing the nation's *grand couvert* without once suggesting how the food was to get to the table, so the laws of 1791 simply made stealing from a restaurant equivalent to theft from a house "where one was received as a guest," without noting that the restaurant customer rarely saw his "host." The legislation blithely overlooked the fact that while a café-keeper's or restaurateur's door may be open to all, and therefore he does, in a sense, demonstrate exemplary hospitality, the conditions for getting back out of the restaurant or the café involve payment. In its Penal Code of 1791, the Constituent Assembly attempted to legislate the restaurant and the table, unlike the shop or the theater, out of the marketplace and into the realm of civic virtue.

Of Fraternity and Frugality

In his 1780s display of carefully sculpted wax figures representing Louis
XVI and Marie-Antoinette at table with the Queen's visiting brother, the
Hapsburg Emperor Joseph II, the Paris showman Curtius had offered
the *grand couvert* to an audience far greater than the one that actually
witnessed the ritual meal at Versailles. Several years later, in the spirit of
revolution, he broadened the dinner's guest list a bit, adding mannequins
of General Lafayette, commander of the Paris National Guard, and of
Jean-Sylvain Bailly, first revolutionary mayor of Paris. Paralleling real life,
Curtius had expanded the scene of politically significant eating to include
the Revolution's notables, as well as the monarch's relatives.[71] After another few years, however, the wax museum's exhibit presented a scene of
individual sacrifice rather than of happy commensality: Curtius now featured a dummy of the martyred Jacobin deputy Le Peletier, murdered in a
restaurant for having voted "Yes" on the question of the former king's ex-
ecution. In the pages of his *Révolutions de Paris*, the radical journalist
Prudhomme applauded the waxworks' new tableau, but suggested that
the same venue be used to present an even more uplifting scene: that of
Louis XVI's beheading by guillotine in January 1793.[72] The National
Convention, brought to power by a moment of rupture rather than a continuation of etiquette, would have no *grand couvert*.

The years between the Festival of Federation and Curtius's exhibition of
revolutionary martyrdom witnessed the fall of the monarchy, the outbreak of war, the declaration of a republic, the rise to power of the Jacobin
Clubs, and the eventual radicalization of the national government. For a
time, food prices rose dramatically; crops planted by farmers, who were
then drafted into the Republic's armies, went unharvested; the assignat,
the Revolution's paper currency, was issued in such quantities that
inflation inevitably resulted. Attempting to impose fraternal solidarity by
means of food distribution programs, more than one revolutionary demanded that bakers stop preparing their typical range of breadstuffs and
combine brown, white, and rye flours together to make one single "Bread
of Equality."[73] In the capital, in February of 1792, shortages led to the
outbreak of popular street protests, but, as William Sewell has noted, the
men and women of Paris were rioting not for bread, the totemic staff of
life, but for sugar, soap, and candles.[74]

Sewell's point is particularly well taken, for the radical revolutionary
rhetoric of "subsistence" has long led historians to believe that the danger

of famine was the driving force behind many of the National Convention's economic policies. True, the Convention passed "the Maximum" in September 1793, putting into effect a broad series of wage- and price-fixing regulations in a wartime effort to control the cost of "articles of prime necessity." Yet these "necessities" included not only bread and wine, but cheeses, butter, honey, and sausages as well.[75] In the district of Paris, governmental decrees set fourteen sous as the maximum price for a pound of butter from nearby Chartres, but allowed Longjumeau butter to rise to twenty-two sous per pound, and permitted the same quantity from Isigny (one of the most renowned butter-making villages in the prime dairying region of Normandy) to sell for twenty-eight sous, eight deniers. Nor did the authors of the Maximum display a gourmet's sense of fine differentials only in their treatment of butter: a pound of honey might vary from twelve sous five deniers for "ordinary honey" to two livres, eighteen sous, and one denier for the prized product of Narbonne.[76] "Subsistence" was certainly at the heart of much revolutionary rhetoric; but revolutions do not subsist on bread alone.[77]

In the months following the passage of the Maximum, "Terror" was institutionalized in the form of a radical police state, and a republican calendar (in which days were assigned not to saints, but to fruits, vegetables, and other products of nature) was implemented. Newspapers solemnly reported that flower gardens were being uprooted to make space for legumes, and one militant argued that the central marketplace, les Halles, should be renamed "Republican Frugality Square."[78] Leading members of the National Convention replaced the utopian vision of tables stretching into infinity with the brutal boredom of quiet and frugal home life, and even theatrical meals declined: in the original 1790 version of Ronsin's *The Patriots' Dinner* (an uplifting play about an émigré aristocrat's return to France), the duke had asked his steward whether he could have spent less on the celebratory feast and the steward had replied that only a truly lavish meal could convince the suspicious people of the nobleman's good intentions. In late 1792, when the play was modified for performance in a somewhat less giddy and more austere political climate, this interchange was cut completely.[79] The title meal, now firmly confined to the symbolic, no longer needed any material basis whatsoever.

Though meals were more frugal, hospitality—of a sort—remained a virtue. Dedicated to fighting the Republic's enemies (both inside France and out), revolutionaries just as adamantly welcomed its supporters. Jacques Louis David, the artist and Jacobin ("Pageant-Master to the Revolution," as he has been called), suggested erecting a colossal statue of "The People, Eater of Kings" somewhere along France's border with the German states; Prudhomme's *Révolutions de Paris* supported this idea and proposed that the giant's base be inscribed: "Hospitality to free men, death to tyrants and their slaves."[80] During that same winter (Year II, 1793–1794), citizens of the revolutionary section of the Mountain (named after the most radical faction in the National Convention, though the district had been known, less than five years earlier, as that of the Palais-Royal) agitated for legislation that would require the restaurateurs of the Maison Egalité ("Equality House," as the republicanized Palais Royal was known) to be more welcoming and to keep their prices within the range set by the Maximum. Though the Maximum did not technically cover prepared foods other than bread, it fixed prices and enumerated goods, giving administrative, judicial, and marketplace muscle to the metaphors of paying and reckoning that pervaded so much of revolutionary discourse. Supported, so they thought, by the provisions of the Maximum, the section militants saw prosperous restaurants as an insult to the Republic and a clear affront to properly egalitarian hospitality.[81] Denouncing, on an almost daily basis, the restaurants' ostentatious plenty, the sans-culottes demanded police action that would force restaurateurs to serve not their usual variety of high-priced dishes, but a more standardized fare: "dinners for two livres per head," for example. It was, they grumbled, an impermissible scandal that a restaurateur should purchase half a cow, a calf, and a side of mutton, when "an honest sans-culotte with a sick wife" could not afford enough meat for the simple pot-au-feu of his ancestors. "If they want to provide food, let them serve potatoes and beans, which are what most decent people are now forced to eat," one man told a police informer. The moral economy had come banging at the restaurateur's door, demanding that he either leave the market and show true patriotic hospitality or pay the price for his counter-revolutionary insolence.[82]

Even when restaurateurs were charged with the treasonous crime of hoarding (defined as treason because it might "starve the Nation"), symbolic, as well as economic, motives were at work: the restaurant's cachet of individual service, private rooms, weak chests, and delicate stomachs could not easily endure the re-evaluation of symbols central to the Revolution. Throughout the Terror, the restaurants of the once "royal garden" preoccupied Parisian revolutionaries. In early summer 1794, the members of the radical and powerful Jacobin Club listened in alarm as one of their fellows briefly denounced the restaurateurs of the Maison Egalité. Their rev-

olutionary indignation mounted as the ever-alert member told of shop
signs he had recently noticed: the Véry brothers' restaurant advertised, in
Spanish, that "we welcome *people of the best sort.*"[83] A few doorways down,
Postal's restaurant bore a Latin slogan that was familiar to many eighteenth-century restaurant patrons, but regarded suspiciously by the reporting commissioner who paraphrased it: "Come to me all you with tired
stomachs, and I shall restore you."[84]

The Jacobins, and the Revolutionary Committee of the Section of
the Montagne, into whose local jurisdiction the restaurants fell, voted to
send commissioners to investigate these evidently counter-revolutionary
inscriptions. Later that week, the commissioners Freté and Boubon reported to their section that the restaurant run by the Vérys offered insults
to liberty and equality in several foreign languages. Along with the Spanish
slogan and the standard Latin greeting, their sign also featured disturbing
proclamations in German and Italian, all audaciously announcing that the
restaurant catered to "people of distinction" and offered "the most delicate dishes." One of the Véry brothers had even admitted to having had
the signs painted, seven or eight years ago, when the restaurant had gone
by the cosmopolitan name of "The Four Nations." But, he insisted, he
had long ago regretted that folly, and hired a sign painter to efface the incendiary advertisements directed at foreign aristocrats (many of whom
had been at war with the Republic for the past year). He was, he protested,
merely a humble *traiteur* committed to the task of feeding his fellow patriots, a bachelor who had adopted his orphaned niece and nephew.[85] Nonetheless, and despite Jean François Véry's commendable record of service—in addition to taking up arms in both July 1789, when the Bastille
was stormed, and August 1792, when the monarchy was abolished, he had
outfitted two of his waiters for the Republic's armies—he spent time in the
Terror's jails for his once-clever multilingual advertising.

While Véry fretted in jail and militants ferreted out other purveyors of
distinction, the streets of Paris filled with tables, and all honest sans-
culottes rejoiced in the simple pleasures of a "family meal." Or so, at
least, songs, engravings, memoirs, and nineteenth-century historiography
would have us believe. Throughout the spring and summer of 1794, many
of the forty-eight sections across Paris decreed their own civic meals, impromptu street festivals to which every household contributed what it
could.[86] According to one newspaper account, these feasts had just the effect the Marquis de Villette would have expected: "There, all distinctions
disappear entirely; there, the rich mix with the poor and, as they eat a sim-

ple meal, they learn the lessons of equality."[87] In the depictions that survive of these meals, people unanimously lift wine glasses, dance joyously around liberty trees, and wave flags exuberantly. Garlands of flowers decorate the houses, and dogs share the contents of a single dish without a snarl. Decreed by neighborhood committees, these localized civic meals actually forced conviviality, demanding that people eat in the street or risk being denounced for unfraternal selfishness and nefarious isolation. All residents of a neighborhood were invited to bring a table and whatever food or drink they could supply into the street, for the stated purpose of behaving in a fraternal fashion. So explicit was this motive that an elderly *rentier,* Célestin Guittard de Floriban, describing the meals in his diary, repeatedly used the verb "to fraternize [*fraterniser*]," as if he could find no other word to describe what he and his neighbors were doing.[88]

As an exercise in mandatory fraternity and unity, these patriotic banquets required that the most basic modes of differentiation, of self, should disappear. All food was to be shared, all good will to be allotted equally: François Hanriot, commander of the Paris National Guard, reminded his fellow "brothers in arms" that in a Republic toasts should be drunk not to the health of individuals, but "to all virtuous men."[89] Very little flatware was available, since silverware, like church decoration and the ostentatious ornament of despots, had long ago been melted down or hidden, so Parisians were encouraged to eat, like "children of Nature," with their hands.[90] In one contemporary image (Figure 3), a child seated on the ground drinks directly from a wine bottle; to the left of him, two more children are tethered together by the piece of food they both hold. At the table, a man suggestively holds an entire sausage over a woman's wide-open mouth. Beside her, a hale and hearty sans-culotte gnaws on an enormous hunk of meat. A man fiddles, a boy plays a tin whistle.

The suppers appeared and appealed as hostless functions, very much like a potluck or *pic-nic*. Everybody was to bring whatever proved available; one person's meat ration would supplement another's vegetables. By an Englishman's account (he was twelve at the time), one needed to choose one's offering carefully: "If you presented a luxurious article, you were called an aristocrat, who fed upon dainties, while the people were starving; and if, on the contrary, your contribution was humble, you were accused of being a monopolist, insulting the indigence of your neighbours."[91] Historians actually know these civic meals, which apparently filled the streets in July 1794, best through Bertrand Barère's denunciation of them; since the Committee of Public Safety's spokesman attacked them, nineteenth-

Figure 3. One of the French Revolution's idealized fraternal meals, in which even dogs peaceably share from a single dish and nature's bounty is available to all good citizens.

century republican writers treated these meals as evidence of the people's genuine, as opposed to the Convention's police-state, sense of fraternity.[92] As mandatory meals in the street, accessible to all, visible to all, held for the purpose of cementing bonds between neighbors (and guaranteeing that if one's neighbor had a roasting chicken one would get a bit of it), the banquets of July 1794 would seem the most public meals imaginable. Yet Barère denounced them as too particular, too private, because they were mandated by the sections, and Robespierre rejected them because they reduced the people to specifics and sat them at separate tables, where dissension too could find a place.[93]

In a report to the National Convention, Barère explicitly outlined the many dangers posed by what he termed an "epidemic" of fraternal banquets.[94] Instead of rejoicing at the sight of all those shared meals, he adopted the longstanding critique of cookery as fraudulent dissimulation and introduced it squarely into politics.[95] At the heart of his report lay the idea that the amicability found at the table was passing, ephemeral, superficial; a mere bite or drink would not forge true fraternity. The reactionary could always assume a revolutionary facade; this was particularly true at the table, Barère implied, for poisons had often appeared there in attractive guises. He commented that it cost the aristocrat nothing to sit in the street, drinking his heady, expensive wine, and occasionally mouthing the words "Vive la République," for these were only the external signs of revolutionary zeal, easily donned by the protean counter-revolutionary.[96]

For the Convention's benefit, Barère began by comparing the past weeks' "contagious" meals with scenes of true republican hospitality. In the latter, two or three families, no more, calmly enjoyed their frugal meal; or perhaps a mother and several aged citizens, gathered around a table, patiently taught the woman's five-year-old son the words of a patriotic song and saw in him "the hope of their household and of their fatherland."[97] Yet even if no such child was conveniently available, other features distinctly separated the real patriotic meal from the mass event that passed for one. Until the revolution was "completely finished," Barère insisted, the republican meal would have to take place within the natural family, and not in a dangerous street "saturnalia" where the sexes mingled wantonly. Republican morals could not be regenerated "with this strange confusion of citizens, this unplanned mixing of the sexes . . . after a meal where wine and the most immoderate joy have presided."[98] If women were to be present, Barère implied, then the celebration belonged within the safe confines of the actual family; otherwise, indulgence in the pleasures of the table could too easily lead to the provocation of other desires. As the *restaurant* had restored amorous as well as digestive capabilities, so too, according to Barère, might the aristocrat's well-set table turn the patriot away from his love of country, and send him in search of a more palpable love object.[99] (One song written for the occasion of a fraternal supper elaborated just this theme and turned a traditionally raunchy drinking song to patriotic ends by bidding "young husbands": "Let each man here besiege his love / And with her sweetly altercate / That each might make this very night / Another citizen for the State.")[100]

By Barère's definition, "frugality" characterized any true fraternal meal.[101] His emphasis on frugality was in part practical; in February, he appealed to citizens to give up eating meat for a time, lest breeding stocks be depleted.[102] But it was also highly moralistic—aimed at creating an egalitarian distribution of austerity—and symbolic, meant to recall the classical culinary virtues of Sparta and the ancient Gauls.[103] The emblematic foods of the Revolution were Lacedaemonian, Rousseauian, or American foods—bread, cheese, fruits, and vegetables—items untainted by the flattery of cooks.[104] Describing their own patriotic meals, provincial revolutionaries often emphasized this feature by using the words "*sans apprêts* [without preparation]," intimating that citizens of the French Republic celebrated with raw vegetables and just scavenged nuts.[105] Denouncing the phantasmatic dainties served at the so-called fraternal meals as opportunities for "the chefs of aristocrats" to cook up a counter-revolution, Barère saluted temperance and "economy" as "the sources of all virtue."[106]

Narrow definitions of "fraternity" and "hospitality" underlay this emphasis on frugality and family. In the Terror's world-view, fraternity was neither innate nor universal; gone were the days when all were brothers. Instead, Frenchmen had to learn fraternity through a specific set of procedures in which patriots mingled with patriots—and only with patriots.[107] Only those who had already proven their revolutionary commitment should have access to the frugal republican table. Unlike Villette, Barère did not see the shared meal as an experience with the potential to unite and purify its participants. Instead, the Spartan repast could only confirm already established revolutionary worthiness; and it might fail to do even that, were counter-revolutionaries to insinuate themselves into the party. For while Barère doubted the table's ability to convert aristocrats into sans-culottes, he saw all too clearly the ease with which it could, by appealing to individual, physical wants, corrupt patriots.[108] Though the table in ancient times had been a "temple of Friendship," it could not serve the same purpose now, for the Republic's enemies, armed with delicate morsels and strong wines, had converted it into a "temple of Discord." Because of the differentiation of foodstuffs, no modern hospitality could compare to that found among the virtuous ancients; what had once been a generous gift had degenerated into a dangerous exchange, and the supposedly fraternal banquets were but poisoned presents.[109]

Barère concluded from this that the Convention alone should host public meals, for only the Convention represented the general will of the nation rather than the particular desire of a faction. When a section or committee ordered a feast, it sacrificed the overall well-being of the Republic to the selfish interests of a few. While the real fêtes in honor of the Republic's victories had featured poetry and the "sublime art" of music, the fraudulent repasts, according to Barère, substituted intemperance and prodigality of food. The latter appealed not to the General Will, but to hungry and thirsty individuals—how could that be an appropriate celebration for a besieged people? The local civic meals, in the eyes of the official Terror, were too much about really eating, too little concerned with the expression of a single shared belief. The disembodied Will should subside on neither ambrosia nor *restaurants,* but on stirring speeches and food for thought, and it had no use for the individual tables set close together in the once-busy streets.[110] The Nation could not really dine at its *grand couvert;* for if the Terror discovered that speaking for the General Will required constant expulsions of the specific, eating for the General Will proved clearly impossible. The same words could, in the singing of patriotic hymns and the swearing of national oaths, all issue in unison from many mouths, but the food that went in one mouth could not go in another. (Rousseau, in a story from the *Confessions,* offered a rule-proving exception: as his beloved "Mamma," Madame de Warens, put a bit of food in her mouth, he claimed to see a hair on it. She spit it out and he, madly enamored of all she had touched, pounced on it, devouring it in a gulp.[111] But what was possible, even called for or desirable, in the world of hypertrophied Jean-Jacquean sympathy was impossible in the still-unfinished Revolution.) Representative eating proved at best insufficient, at worst, counter-revolutionary. The Nation spoke with one mouth, but that orifice could not eat.

The Marquis de Villette had called all people to join in the street—but because he did not specify whence the food on the tables was to come, he had avoided the questions of who was to preside at the table, who was to host the party, and how everybody was to eat at once. His utopian vision abolished not only the roles of king and subject, but those of host and guest as well, thereby interrupting any circuit of exchange or reciprocity. Nobody needed to offer hospitality in return. Instead, the Nation's *grand couvert* occurred in a perpetual, time-stopping moment, at which individuals' positions in real networks of exchange no longer obtained; in this lovely image, Nature played host to all the children of Liberty, and the bill never came.[112]

Camille Desmoulins's vision, in contrast, had been firmly anchored in the historical, the sequential; he contemplated not just the single minute, but the before and the after as well. His description of Lafayette's banquet evoked not only the thousands of *fédérés* under endless trees, but also their march through the rain, and the disposal of festival leftovers. In doing so, he necessarily raised the question of who was hosting the party, and why. Barère saw this broader picture, and saw it with the Terror's careful eye for plots and conspiracies; with characteristic attention to detail, he clearly outlined the problem:

> Without doubt, fraternity, that sparkling sign of the union of hearts and spirits, is a republic's most precious coin; but it loses its value and is debased, when it is suddenly converted into a negotiable currency [*effet de commerce*]. Fraternity suffers a great loss in being traded too frequently, for this sign of our moral wealth acquires its value only by its imperceptible circulation among citizens.[113]

Fraternity for Barère was a coin, "la monnaie la plus précieuse des républiques." Like any money, fraternity was a convenience, a shorthand; it pointed to other, substantive, sorts of wealth (be they stockpiles of gold or caches of moral conviction). But fraternity was not to circulate freely, not to be frequently exchanged, for—like a sad comment on Roze de Chantoiseau's wonderful banknotes that, by losing one percent of their value each time they were handed along, would eventually disappear completely—fraternity decreased in value as it was exchanged. The public street banquet therefore was unsuitable and dangerous because it involved the indiscriminate spending of fraternity's small change; when the true patriot gave his brotherly welcome to a disguised aristocrat, he got nothing in return (and in this economy, far from any Judeo-Christian notion of alms, gratuitous giving served no purpose). Barère's model of fraternity depended on reciprocal uniformity, on the possibility of a perfectly equitable exchange. Until the Revolution was complete, fraternity was to be hoarded at home like a mercantilist's gold.

Barère made each honest participant in a civic meal into a host whose hospitality might be violated by a deceitful counter-revolutionary. The latter had no sense of the obligations of hospitality and could not learn from sans-culotte generosity, for he was a creature of selfishness and of the unscrupulous market. Yet even as Barère flagged commerce and trade as contrary to the workings of Nature, he had recourse to just those metaphors in order to explain his understanding of fraternity. Barère was working with a "famine model" of fraternity; in the summer of 1794, he asserted, fraternal sentiment, like meat and vegetables, was in short supply:

> The sentiment of humanity evaporates and weakens as it spreads across the Earth: a friend to the Universe has never known the delicious pleasures of loving his country [*amour de la patrie*]. The same is true of fraternity; for it to have a useful function [*activité utile*] it must be limited and restrained [*comprimer,* also meaning "to squeeze in at the waist"] . . . During the Revolution, Fraternity must be concentrated among patriots united by a common interest . . . our enemies cannot be our brothers.[114]

In decrying what he and the Committee of Public Safety saw as the commerce in fraternity, Barère obliquely criticized the logic of the restaurant, which promised the pleasures of being "chez soi" (that is, at home, within the family) for a price. He claimed that no true hospitality was possible within the structures of the market; the optimistic Penal Code of 1791 had actually made almost the opposite argument, suggesting that market conditions of "publicness" were irrelevant when hospitality was for sale. In condemning the fraternal meals, Barère rejected the liberal notion that modern society might rely upon the market to supply hospitable bouillons or any other comforts of home.

Barère argued that the patriot needed to conserve his tender feelings of brotherhood with humanity; distributed too liberally, fraternity was like too little butter spread across too much bread. The Friend of the Universe, said Barère (but he might as well have said, "the Friend of all the world"), "has never known the delicious pleasures of loving his country"—small wonder that when Mathurin Roze de Chantoiseau wrote to suggest his banking scheme to the Committee of Public Safety he signed himself no longer "Roze de Chantoiseau, Friend of all the world," but "Roze Chantoiseau, Friend of those who are good and true."[115]

The Revolution's fraternal suppers, as public meals intended to efface differences of opinion and sentiment, would seem to offer few points of contact with the restaurant's world of personal tastes and private preferences. Neither Barère's paranoid nor Villette's idyllic description of the fraternal meal mentioned a single restaurant. Neither the family of all humanity, nor even the core group of the Republic's true brothers, would have fit into the largest banquet room of any Paris restaurant (much less into the *cabinet particulier* that was among the restaurant's most distinctive features). Nonetheless, the revolutionary festival, in its elaboration of the table as a space of unity, a space open either to all or to the restricted worthy, did give new significance to the public meal of whatever variety, and exemplified the strong communitarian impulse in French culture with which the restaurant continued to compete.

It is almost certainly because of the decade's pervasive interest in the table as a place of possible solidarity, corruption, or final reckoning that the restaurant looks like a product of the Revolution. If that is the case, then the restaurant is not a peripheral, chance, or even purely utilitarian offshoot of that turbulent period; rather, in the era's re-evaluation of symbols and cultural forms, it was not only political culture but restaurant culture as well that would eventually take on its distinctive modern shape. Reading every aspect of daily life as a political statement, revolutionaries, famous for their attempt to delineate an austere republican wardrobe, regarded the pantry with a wary eye as well.[116] In the early 1790s, as Jacobinism confronted the gentle, proto-Romantic Rousseau of *La Nouvelle Héloïse* with the more politically didactic analysis of *The Social Contract,* the urban sophisticate's pleasure in "delicacy" was sent into an irretrievable decline. Rousseau had once been the touchstone of all who were fashionable and literate, but their claim on him was increasingly rejected by those who were explicitly revolutionary and dourly anti-chic. During the Terror, mere outward manifestations of sensitivity were exactly the sort of duplicitous performance that Barère and others expected from hidden counter-revolutionaries.

If we examine again Villette and Barère's opposing positions, we discover that each of their arguments resonates with claims that would later be made about the restaurant, and about the place of the table in modern life. Villette argued, as Brillat-Savarin would do in his 1826 *Physiology of*

Taste, that the table was a means of effacing difference and creating unity. His table open to all, the nation's *grand couvert,* made court ceremonial public, shared, and accessible; in the nineteenth century, widespread agreement that former chefs of émigré aristocrats had been among the first restaurateurs would literalize this image, substituting the restaurant for the patriotic repast in the tale of cookery's democratization. Barère's table, on the other hand, did not create solidarity or popularize once-exclusive privileges. Instead, it tested for worthiness in a manner reminiscent of an Old-Regime restaurant, but with one significant difference: the revolutionary showed true sensibility not by being too weak to eat an evening meal, but by being too strong to do so. As we can read Villette's national feast as a precursor to Brillat-Savarin's gastro-liberalism, so we might see Barère's parsimonious paranoia as an avatar, however unlikely, of Grimod de la Reynière's exaggerated strategies of distinction. (Like the ideal eater of Grimod's *Almanach des gourmands,* Barère demanded that all his guests be true believers, and that women be banned from the table.)

Barère's July 1794 speech to the Convention did not dwell on the wonderful moment of sitting down at the table, nor on the pleasures of dining on food prepared by others. Instead, in his economic account of fraternity squandered, he emphasized the other key moment of any restaurant meal—the *quart d'heure de Rabelais,* the point at which one must pay the bill. In this preoccupation he was hardly alone, for much revolutionary symbolism might well be read as an extended meditation on the question: "Who gets the check?"

5

Fixed Prices: Gluttony and the French Revolution

A peasant from Montrouge, full of common sense, called the French Revolution the battle of the eater and the eaten.

LOUIS SÉBASTIEN MERCIER, *NÉOLOGIE* (1801)

In the spring and summer of 1789, as the Estates-General prepared to meet for the first time in 175 years—and then, as its members did meet, and as the deputies of the Third, most populous, and unprivileged Estate insisted on voting by individual deputies rather than by order—the image of paying the check in a café or restaurant gained new importance. A popular print of the time showed three men, one from each estate, sitting at a small table in an elegant café (Figure 4). The caption, presumably the words addressed by one of them to the mistress of the café, reads: "A la bonne heure . . . Chacun son écot" ("That's right . . . separate checks").[1]

The political significance of this seemingly innocuous request for the bill is not difficult to fathom. The clergy and the aristocracy, the privileged First and Second Estates, had long counted exemption from most taxation among the benefits of their exalted status. In consequence, the far more numerous members of the Third Estate (which included everybody else, from the poorest peasant to the wealthiest merchant) felt unfairly taxed, forced to shoulder the burdensome load of paying the *taille,* the *gabelle,* and a host of other taxes. For the three delegates in the café to request separate checks, then, was for the nobility and the clergy to agree, finally, to pay their share. Life in France was no longer to be the Third Estate's "treat."

Scenes of paying the bill occurred as well at the theater, that other great forum of public instruction and communication. In DeVérité's *The Deputies' Dinner* (1789), representatives of the three orders meet in a roadside inn on their way to the assembly in Versailles.[2] The jolly innkeeper welcomes them all—in fact, he suggests in tones reminiscent of the Marquis de Villette that a meal together might be the best way to end their disagreements—and promises to serve them whatever they desire. For

119

Figure 4. "That's right . . . separate checks," says one representative of the Three Estates.

most of the play, the characters discuss the *cahiers de doléances* (the grievance lists drawn up in each of the local electoral assemblies and by representatives of the first two orders) and other major issues of the day in a fairly caricatured and didactic fashion. At the conclusion, as they prepare to continue their voyage, the innkeeper presents them with the check: his friendly hospitality is revealed as a commodity selling for "six livres per head." "Per head!" exclaims one of the aristocrats, "but it is by Order that we intend to proceed; we shall do nothing by head!"[3] (Paying by order or estate would actually not in this case benefit the privileged groups economically. If each estate were to pay a certain flat sum for the meal, then the individual members of the numerically smaller First and Second would each pay a proportionally higher amount.) After some further discussion and allusion to the difficulty of eating by orders, the delegates resolve to pay their own shares. The play ends, however, not on this happy scene of conciliation, but on a somewhat harsher note: "Never mind," says a lawyer, "the Third has paid for all."[4]

Given that the 1788 calling of the Estates-General had, in fact, been provoked by de facto state bankruptcy, it is hardly surprising that moments of requesting (and receiving) a bill were common currency in the political imagery of 1789–1790. It is, however, rather curious that such scenes were so frequently set in a café, tavern, inn, or restaurant, for those were hardly the only eighteenth-century contexts in which one might owe money for goods or services rendered. Tailors, carpenters, and bootmakers certainly all had to be paid as well, and it was common enough for furniture makers or carpet merchants to furnish their wares on credit and present bills for the amount due months later.[5] In an era when France had no state-backed banks and no public credit system, private credit (often mediated and arranged by notaries) permeated relations between individuals.[6] Considering just how important credit was in so many branches of the economy, then, it seems particularly strange that these scenes of reckoning came so often to be staged in restaurants, inns, cafés, or taverns. With so many other tradespeople extending credit, what made restaurateurs and café-keepers such common personifications of monetary obligation? Images of calculation might well have been set in warehouses or gaming rooms, at markets or merchants' counters, but such scenes were set just as often in public eatinghouses, as if getting a bill were a more distinctive feature of those places than having a meal.

Many of the decade's forays into the symbolism of the table invoked the family of man gathered together for a simple, joyous meal, but many others, perhaps a majority, depicted the moment of paying the check. Sums and quantities, this latter imagery tells us, must be closely watched and accurately calculated. The "sans-culotte rhetoric of subsistence" (to borrow William Sewell's phrase) treated all merchants and middlemen as potential scoundrels or hoarders, but none was more hated or suspect than the one who sold food and drink. "We have no greater enemies," snapped a pamphlet of 1791, "than these voracious creatures who daily gulp down our money . . . so that we may obtain the necessities of life."[7] Operating within a model of finite resources (as most revolutionaries after 1790, facing uncertain harvests and foreign wars, wisely did), one man's overeating, one woman's demand for sugar, one farmer's fattening of geese on nuts, would inevitably result in somebody else's hunger and possible starvation.

Revolution-era imagery assigned multiple functions to the table: it might be a space of utopian fraternity and equality or of dystopic greed and selfishness. What it could not legitimately be, however, was a site for the expression of socially neutral personal preference. Either as the effete aristocratic obsession with delicacy, or as the uncivilized slaughter of "blood drinking" anarchy, dietary habits insistently marked membership in a social group. As Barère argued in condemning sneaky royalists who toasted the Republic with the vestiges of some aristocrat's wine cellar, enemies revealed themselves not by the public, avowedly political positions they took, but by their private behavior (be it communicating with émigrés, inciting riots, eating babies, drinking blood, or roasting partridges). Thus the robust Republic called on its citizens to reject the "delicacy of appetite" dear to Old-Regime sensitive souls as a mark of foppish degeneracy and unpatriotic selfishness. The *Père Duchesne* (a radical journal that was the mouthpiece of the populist Jacques-René Hébert) launched its customary colorful and vituperative epithets at "selfish aristocrats [who] curse and swear because they can no longer restore themselves [*se restaurent*] with succulent consommés" after their sordid nights and wasted days of debauchery.[8] The decreeing of civic commendations for soldiers who "generously sacrificed" their meat rations for the sake of children or the infirm recurred throughout the meetings of the National Convention and across the pages of the daily press.[9] Claiming to subsist on bread, French wine, and revolutionary fervor alone, the frugal sansculotte scrupulously concealed any evidence to the contrary: one revolutionary section, faced with an itemized bill from the cook-restaurateur who catered its daily meetings, asked the Committee of General Security to order payment of 2539 livres from the national treasury for "secret expenses," rather than admit the nature of the bill.[10]

And while the revolutionaries of the Year II were condemning aristocrats and clergymen for worshipping their stomachs, counter-revolutionary rhetoric reversed the direction of satire's arrow to decry the "blood-drinking cannibalism" of the animalistic sans-culottes.[11] In the anti-republican version, the fall of the Bastille had been but an excuse for bacchanalia, and the most important action of August 1789 had been not the declaration of the Rights of Man, but the repeal of hunting laws. As one aristocratic parody had it, the true words of the *Marseillaise* called the French people not to a defense of *la patrie,* but to a feeding frenzy: "Allons, enfans de la courtille, / Le jour du boirc cst arrivé . . ."[12]

By the prevailing logic, you inevitably were what you ate and, more important, you were interchangeable with all who ate their meat in the same way (whether it was condensed into bouillon or spit-roasted).[13] The Revolution's rhetoric of eater and eaten, of fat and lean, based as it was in loose socioeconomic groupings deployed to sharply pointed political ends, left no room for the individual's personal likes or dislikes, no opportunities to exercise a talented palate. Rejecting notions of individual or relative taste, revolutionary definitions of the gastro-culinary instead tied each individual to the community by notions of debt, obligation, and payment.

Running Out and Paying Up

When, less than a year after the joyous Festival of Federation, the royal family famously attempted to flee France, many of the King's critics argued that he had attempted to run out on a check. Anti-monarchial pamphlets and caricatures asserted that Louis XVI had treated the entire affair as a *repas champêtre:* pausing for a snack of pigs' feet and relishing his arrest in Varennes because it gave him the chance to eat once again, the King in those satires suffered from a moronic and short-sighted bulimia that made him no match for the honest, abstemious, and responsible Constituent Assembly. In this moment, the King's gourmandism, like Marie-Antoinette's fabled licentiousness, marked him as an unfit ruler.[14] Perhaps in previous centuries, when divine-right kingship had rested firmly on what the medievalist Ernst Kantorowicz has called "the mystic fiction of 'the king's two bodies'" joined as one (the ordinary, physical body of whoever happened to be monarch, and his official and theological body "that never dies"), then the fatter the king's visible body, the wealthier was the state and the better fed the body politic.[15] By the spring of 1791, however, Louis XVI had been desacralized and secularized, reduced like all the French to only a single body, forbidden to eat more than his fair share.

Late in the evening of June 21, 1791, as the shadows filled the court-yard of the Tuileries Palace, Louis XVI, Marie-Antoinette, their two children, the King's sister, and the children's governess sneaked out of Paris disguised as a German baroness and her retinue. In a four-wheeled covered carriage of the type known as a berline, they attempted to flee France and escape to the monarchist comfort of lands held by the Queen's brother, Emperor Leopold II of Austria. Historians agree in seeing the Flight to Varennes, as this ill-fated dash to the border is called (after the name of the town in which the royal family was eventually arrested), as an important turning point for popular sentiment during the French Revolution. By attempting to escape France, Louis and his family seemed to demonstrate that their true sympathies lay not with the France of the Federation and the Rights of Man, but with the forces of aristocratic counter-revolution and foreign repression massing on France's borders. On the day after the royal family left Paris, even the royalist brothers Royou changed the title of their newspaper from *l'Ami du roi (The Friend of the King)* to *l'Ami des français (The Friend of the French)*.[16]

The intricacies of the carefully arranged plan to meet troops at a frontier garrison—details of which were revealed in the weeks following the scheme's failure and which implicated a number of once highly placed officials—have been minutely studied by antiquarian, military, and royalist historians. In brief, the royal family, partly angered by the civil constitution of the clergy, partly enticed away by the promise of foreign support, and partly scared of what the Parisians might do next, made a run for the border, assisted by the Swedish nobleman Axel Fersen. As one would expect, historians, depending on their methodological and political allegiances, have described the attempt in a number of ways. (Or, rather, in their varied tellings, they have staked out a range of ideological positions.) The particularly pathos-laden accounts of royalists and their sympathizers stress Louis's dignity and determination, Marie-Antoinette's calm regal composure, and the sleepy looks of confused horror on the faces of the royal offspring.[17] Jules Michelet, the great Romantic republican historian of the mid-nineteenth century, reproached the Queen's foolish girlish amusement at the disguises of her children, and Louis's treachery in abandoning his supporters (Lafayette, Bailly, Montmorin) to the anger of the Paris crowd. The Marxist Albert Soboul included virtually no colorful narrative detail in his version, for he emphasized the struggle between bourgeois revolution and aristocratic reaction, and had little energy for character development or plot-level flourishes.[18]

Yet there remain a few details on which nearly all accounts agree. Narrators concur on the major role played by Marie-Antoinette's dashing Swedish "friend," the Count Axel Fersen (though whether they depict him as a Nordic bastion of chivalry or as her partner in debauch is, of course, another question), and often linger over the details of their getaway carriage's secretive construction.[19] In addition, many of the contemporary accounts, seconded by nineteenth- and twentieth-century histories, mention that the royal family, after being stopped at Varennes, took a little light refreshment (or, maybe, were offered some vile swill, or, perhaps, demanded an extravagant supper). In fact, this particular network of details, this specific semiotic constellation, appears with curious regularity, striking an oddly prosaic note among the many tales of foreign conspirators and betrayed confidences.[20]

As a plethora of quickly printed pamphlets and abbreviated newspaper accounts told their readers, the carriage carrying the royal family had first caught the eye of Jean-Baptiste Drouet, the postmaster of Sainte Ménéhould, a small town in Champagne through which the royal family passed. Suspicious, but uncertain, Drouet had let the heavily loaded berline continue on its route, but quickly persuading himself of the correctness of his intuitions and of his patriotic duty to his nation, he had roused a friend and made all haste to arrive at Varennes, the carriage's next scheduled stop, before the King. Once there, Drouet instructed the community's *procureur* (elected public prosecutor), a grocer-candlemaker named Sauce, to refuse the carriage passage. When the berline arrived, its accompanying paperwork was examined and judged to be in order, but Drouet insisted that it be detained. Given the late hour (nearly midnight) and the unrest in the streets, Sauce decided it would be best to hold the travelers until the morrow. Then—and this is the setting for the relevant detail—he invited "the Baroness Korff" and her associates into an upstairs room of his house-cum-shop. With an angry pitchfork-bearing crowd below, Sauce, according here to Prudhomme's *Revolutions of Paris,* "offered his hospitality to the travelers who asked to refresh themselves."[21]

Across the pamphlet literature, and throughout the nineteenth-century retellings of the King's arrest, accounts varied as to the King's motive and to how the plan went wrong, but they all picked up on the detail of Sauce's hospitality. One pamphlet, claiming to be an eyewitness account by a local resident, described Louis eating the candlemaker's cheese and toasting him with his Burgundy; the official version produced by the Imprimerie Nationale mentioned the King eating several meals before his captive return to Paris; Pierre François Palloy, famous as the entrepreneur who masterminded the distribution of the disassembled Bastille across France, claimed to have traveled to Varennes at his own expense, and reported that he too had seen the King pacing around a table cluttered with the leftovers of a meal.[22] The duc de Choiseul, who was to have provided the escaping family with a military escort for the trip's final leg (but who got lost in the woods instead), finally arrived in Varennes to find the royal family held in a bare little room, where he saw a table holding bread and a few glasses; later royalists relied on the duke's memoirs, published in 1822, for a description of the "very meager meal" Sauce provided to his king.[23] Even Larousse's comparatively brief entry "Varennes," in his *Great Dictionary of the Nineteenth Century,* noted the King sharing a meal and clinking a glass with Sauce.[24]

How can we account for the insistent reiteration of this hardly plot-turning detail? What was it about the King's late-night supper in Varennes that made it a significant point, even a seemingly necessary one, for those describing one of the Revolution's most famous incidents? Depending on the narrator, the detail's meaning might well shift considerably, highlighting either greed or simplicity, gluttony or parsimony. So, for example, royalist memoirs stressed Sauce's "meager" hospitality of bread and local wine in order to flag the town's lack of respect for its king, while republican accounts touched on the same detail as evidence of the public prosecutor's simple, yet decent, frugality. Still, the table of leftovers remained, as if the story could not be told without a break for refreshment. Not until Ary Scheffer, drawing master to the royal family in the 1830s, painted the scene do we get a version of the arrest in which a writing stand with inkpots replaces the table covered with crumbs.[25]

Since the shortest and safest route to a garrison town required that the royal family traverse the province of Champagne, perhaps it was inevitable that their itinerary reads like a gastronomic guide: first to Meaux, famous for its Brie; through Sainte Ménéhould where, by one apocryphal account, Louis insisted that they halt for a sample of the prepared pigs' feet that had made that town's name famous; arrest in the home of the aptly named Monsieur Sauce; passing through bubbly-bottling Epernay on their return trip to Paris—all seems set up as a progression of pilgrims through the Land of Cockaigne. In several accounts, it was actually the surgeon in the town of Varennes, a man with the allegorically appropriate name of Mangin (sharing a syllable as it does with *mangeant,* "eating"), who finally recognized the King. One image of the time even depicted Louis fleeing

Paris in a cook's costume, with knives projecting from the white apron around his midriff and a small pig tucked under one arm, while another version of the story claimed that Marie-Antoinette had been the one to leave the Tuileries so disguised.[26] In fact, nobody in the famous berline wore chef's whites, but so pervasive were the gastro-culinary thematics of this moment that it is hardly surprising that they erupted in the form of misperceptions and mirages: an insistence on seeing cooks where none existed.

While cooks proliferated, so too did eaters, with Louis first among them. Scenes of the King peacefully stopping to eat a few pigs' feet in Sainte Ménéhould before continuing his mad dash to the border made much of royal gluttony, transforming the "Restaurateur of Liberty" into a restaurant patron of libertine propensities.[27] Louis, in short, was a pig: in the Tuileries garden, some wag posted a "lost pig" notice, and in the printshops of Paris over a dozen caricatures depicted the royal family with markedly porcine features.[28] Hence, in eating pigs' feet, the King was a cannibal. Nothing could interfere with his appetite; nothing edible repulsed him. But there was more at work in these satires than the cardinal vice of gluttony: these texts reproached Louis not only for crapulence, but also for failing to pay his bill. The King's crime was both moral and, in a sense, economic.

This theme, explicit in some texts, more gently suggested or hinted at in others, was most fully developed in radical language, where metaphors of engorging, swallowing, and digesting intertwined with discussion of payment and reckoning. The very widely circulated *Revolutions of Paris,* in discussing Louis's absence from the capital, commented: "The regal man-eater has devoured all our wealth; and after having converted the people's bread into his gold, he leaves us starving for money . . . far from being *starved for the sight of the King* [original emphasis], the reaction of the people to the news of Louis XVI's flight shows that they are *fed up* [emphasis added; the French here is *saoul*, which most often translates as either "stuffed" or "falling-down drunk"] with the throne and disgusted by paying its bills."[29] Appetites in this account were disordered and deranged, with need and consumption in inverse proportions to each other. Eating men, eating money, eating bread, the King nevertheless continued to gobble; yet it was the devoured people, who had been deprived of gold and sustenance, and not the monarch, who were said to be "stuffed." In his next issue, Prudhomme continued his account by describing Parisians lining the King's route and holding upright pikes onto which they had all thrust loaves of bread, thereby demonstrating that Louis's brief absence had caused them not hardship, but plenty.[30]

Parisians may or may not have massed in the streets with their bread standards; what really matters is how very omnipresent such imagery became. According to the *Courrier français,* the carriage was actually halted in Varennes not by Drouet's alertness or Sauce's insistence, but by the King's gluttony (because "he wanted some refreshment").[31] Images of the precise moment at which Sauce or some other official positively recognized Louis argued sharply for the conjunction of intemperance and final payment, with artists frequently placing the soon-to-be captive King at table, or at least in the vicinity of some bread and a bottle or two. In one of the most frequently reproduced engravings of his arrest (from Desmoulins's *Révolutions de France et de Brabant*), Louis's apprehension actually takes place at Sainte Ménéhould, where he sits at a restaurant or inn ("At the Sign of the Runaway"), peacefully munching pigs' feet (Figure 5).[32] He looks blissfully into the distance, seeing neither the Queen who gestures to him to hurry, nor the clean-cut, polite fellow who has come to arrest him, nor even the strangely spectral pig inked in at his side. With a penile pig's foot in one hand, such that royal gourmandism shades into equally self-indulgent masturbation or similarly degenerate fellatio, and a glass of wine in the other, Louis is oblivious to the moment of reckoning and inclined, like many a restaurant customer, to prolong his pleasures and postpone his departure by ordering more food. The caricature depicts the officer's moment of epiphany when he compares the King's image on an assignat (the Revolution's paper money) to the pudgy man sitting opposite him. To make this point all the more clear, the officer holds out the note and gestures at Louis: he appears to be giving the King the bill for his pigs' feet, rather than matching likenesses. The scene of recognition becomes also a scene of reckoning; the assignat the officer holds slides from mode of payment to bill to be paid. His bill enumerates no sum, it only depicts the eater: for his pig's feet, the King must pay with himself.

Other versions of the arrest sat Louis at the table and put the rest of the royal family there as well, omitting any sign of the berline or any other reference to flight (Figure 6). Prieur and Berthault presented a bare, dark room, where upright pikes and smoke billowing from torches suggested a stark, pseudo-Davidian stage scene, but they kept the table and set it with meats and patés. In another version, Louis sits at table with his hand on a wine bottle and a white napkin highlighting his belly, as a dozen or so officials rush into the room (Figure 7). At the front, a solemn fellow with a sword at his side points to Louis's portrait on an assignat, but the most visible figure on the left is the one whose white Phrygian bonnet and apron may mark him as an honest artisan, but also make him look very much like a chef. The arresting officials look for all the world like the entire staff of a

Figure 5. One of many popular images that showed Louis XVI being arrested at table. Here, he is absorbed in eating his pigs' feet *à la Sainte Ménéhould* and seems oblivious to everything else.

Figure 6. "The Glutton, or Big Birds Fly Slowly," an especially nasty version of the arrest at Varennes. Seated beneath a painting of the storming of the Bastille, Louis, busy with dinner, appears unaware of the situation's gravity and responds to the arresting official's warrant by saying: "I don't give a fuck about all that. Leave me in peace." The heir to the throne has finished his dinner, and grimaces as he sits on his chamberpot.

Figure 7. Another scene of gluttony and reckoning at Varennes: note the man in white who looks much like a chef.

restaurant come to prevent a notoriously deceitful customer from running out on his bill.

During the final week of June 1791, as the royal family made its captive return to Paris, the Constituent Assembly debated the monarch's fate and eventually recuperated the incident by issuing a proclamation announcing "great joy" at the return of Louis who had been malevolently "king-napped" by France's enemies. Having preserved Louis, however awk-wardly, from the accusation of abandoning the nation, there was nonetheless little anyone could do to absolve him of the charges of gluttony. As if all the scenes of arrest were not sufficient, several reports of the Capets' return trip to Paris also commented on the family's pauses for refreshment. (To such an extent, in fact, that André Castelot, writing in the twentieth century from a monarchist perspective, saw fit to furnish a copy of the menu in order to argue that the return to the capital had been conducted with utter frugality.) Prudhomme and Desmoulins both noted that his arrest had not agitated Louis, for he ate heartily at Claire, and had another snack at Pantin.[33] The latter journalist, continuing to trail the King's digestion, further claimed that the sealed trunk in the regal carriage, imagined by some to be crown jewels or state secrets, had actually proven to be a porta-toilet.[34] Returned to the Tuileries Palace in central Paris, Louis was said to have eaten his roast chicken for supper, no more bothered than if he had returned from a tiring day of hunting.[35]

The conjunction of payment with gluttony in these anecdotes and images repeatedly transformed the site of Louis's arrest into a restaurant—where else but in a restaurant would the financial consequences of overeating be so very clear? While simple gluttony alone might have been just one more instance of aristocratic debauch, and while a scene of reckoning could easily enough have taken place in any shop, market, or counting-house, the two together required a restaurant, such that Varennes emerged as the monarchy's *quart d'heure de Rabelais*. The Bourbons' fifteen minutes was a striking inversion of their former *grand couvert*. Where once the king at table had radiated regal, godlike dignity, he now projected nothing but vulgar gluttony. The *couvert* was now only a place setting; the scene, one of expenditure.

Louis, of course, was not actually stopped in an inn or restaurant, but that did not matter; putting him at table made his offense immediate and tangible in a way that more historically accurate scenes of stopped carriages and unfolded paperwork did not. By moving Louis from the berline to the table, these images made the greed often predicated of the monarchy into a corporeal attribute, much as basing the recognition on an assignat made it possible to treat the confrontation between revolutionary publicness and monarchial duplicity as a problem of fiscality. In all these accounts, Louis gets the check but neither understands the lengths to which his tally has grown, nor realizes that, for the monarchy, the days of free lunch have come to an end. Instead, in all these phantasmatic restaurant scenes, the King appears utterly surprised to receive a bill, baffled by the implicit narrative sequence of cause and effect. Proponents of the new model of service had noted in the 1780s that the menu permitted customers to adjust their meals to their purses, but Louis, rather touchingly like Rousseau, proves an inept customer, one conversant with neither menu nor bill. The King, it would seem, still inhabits a world where prices cannot be fixed, where a meal may cost more, less, or nothing depending on the identity and the "quality" of the person who eats it—a world, in short, where some people's *couverts* are, by definition, far grander and more appropriately public than others.

While Louis at his arrest in Varennes offered an example of how not to behave in a restaurant, the Revolution's first martyr, Michel Le Peletier de Saint-Fargeau, who was killed in a restaurant, demonstrated the contrary. One of the wealthiest men in France and a magistrate of the Paris Parlement, Le Peletier had been elected to the Estates-General in 1789 as the representative of the nobles of the Yonne. He quickly turned "patriot," then Jacobin; he authored the report on the 1791 Penal Code; he served a stint as Secretary of the Assembly; and he voted, as did all the members of the Jacobin Club, for the former king's death sentence. Shortly after that fatal vote on January 20, 1793, and less than twenty-four hours before Louis was guillotined, Le Peletier was stabbed in a restaurant by an angry royalist named Pâris, a former member of the royal guard.

Le Peletier's death has interested historians primarily for the elaborate funeral ceremony orchestrated by Jacques-Louis David, and for the deathbed portrait painted by the same Jacobin artist.[36] Representations of Le Peletier's stabbing may, however, be as revelatory as those of his apotheosis since, as a scene placed in a restaurant, his murder begs to be read as a pendant, or counterexample, to the scenes of the king's arrest at Varennes. In place of the king's gluttony, we find Le Peletier's abstemiousness; as we have seen, details of Louis XVI's meals play an unexpectedly prominent part in pamphlet and journal accounts of late June 1791, but menus, bread crusts, and pickled pigs' feet featured not at all in the later tales of murder in the restaurant. Linked by tableside settings, depictions of the two moments shared a pervasive economic resonance as well. While caricatures of Louis XVI's arrest in Varennes commented both on his eating and on his inability to pay for what he had eaten, many of the images of Le Peletier stressed his willingness to pay—balancing the former's spendthrift ways, the latter hastens to settle all accounts before he dies.

Dominique Février, owner of the Palais-Royal restaurant where Le Peletier was killed, told the Committee of General Security that the deputy had been seated in a room separate from the one where he (Février) generally presided, standing behind his counter. Because of the long hours of debate over Louis's fate, Le Peletier had arrived later than usual for his dinner, and Février, rather than going to greet him, had stayed at the counter taking payment from other customers who had already finished their meals. Suddenly, though, a shout had rung out, and with what he modestly described as an "extraordinary movement" Février had dashed to the second room, arriving just in time to see a stranger plunge a saber into "Monsieur Saint Fargeau's chest." By his own account, the gallant restaurateur had struggled with the attacker, but in vain: Pâris escaped and Février turned his attentions to the suffering deputy, sending his *garçons* to fetch doctors and police commissioners.[37]

Interviewed by officials, the restaurant's two waiters told very similar stories: Lepine, the waiter in the second room, said he was well acquainted with Le Peletier, who regularly ate his evening meal at the restaurant. The deputy, according to Lepine, had been seated across the table from another man and had just finished his first dish, such that Lepine had gone to the kitchen to get the next course. Absent for barely a minute or two, Lepine nonetheless had returned to the back room only in time to see Février struggling with Pâris. Durand, *garçon* in the front room, said that although he had seen nothing of the murderous attack, he had heard sharp words and had run to Février's assistance when summoned.[38] According to all these eyewitness accounts, Le Peletier definitely still sat at his table while the attacker first interrupted his dinner and then quickly silenced the deputy and made a fiendish escape.

Later images and pamphlets, like the speeches made at his funeral, offered a different version of Le Peletier's last minutes, embellishing and refining the assassination for full patriotic effect. Most famously, David's portrait of the dead man (which, though now destroyed, hung throughout the Terror at the front of the Convention's meeting hall alongside his equally famous portrait of another martyr, the populist journalist Marat, murdered in his bathtub in the summer of 1793) replaced Le Peletier's far from attractive head with that of a young Greek god.[39] In a comparable fashion, Le Peletier's final words were considerably transformed as well, changing from a plaintive "I'm cold," in the deputy Maure's first report to the Convention, to the heroic and more expansive "I am content to spill my blood for my country; I hope it will serve to consolidate liberty and equality, and to reveal their enemies" on the banner carried as part of his funeral procession.[40] So too, Le Peletier after his death continued to move around Février's restaurant—and as journalists, memoir-writers, and artists shifted the hero from his small table to Février's counter, so the meanings of the scene changed as well.

The very first official reports of Le Peletier's murder largely reiterated the accounts of the restaurateur and his staff, but within twenty-four hours the demands of revolutionary martyrology had begun to revise the details. In the tribute authored by Félix Le Peletier (brother to the slain deputy), Le Peletier had gone to Février's restaurant for his customary "frugal meal." Seated there, alone (that is, not across the table from someone else as he had been in the waiter's story), in a dank "sunken basement," he was attacked by Pâris, who had first harangued Madame Février.[41] The deputy from Auxerre, Nicolas-Sylvestre Maure, first to describe the murder to the Convention, also spoke of Le Peletier sitting alone: "he had barely begun his dinner, when six individuals, leaving a neighboring *cabinet*, presented themselves to him."[42]

This, then, was the scene that illustrated Prudhomme's *Revolutions of Paris* for January 19–26: Le Peletier, recognizable by his dignified serenity and patriotic cockade, is seated alone at a table in an alcove where Pâris, supported by a group of hired killers, has just accosted him. The thugs block the doorway and effectively separate Le Peletier from the other diners in the room, so that even before death he is already isolated and strikingly alone. In Brion's considerably more detailed engraving, a far better dressed Le Peletier—his napkin spread from buttonhole to pocket, providing a convenient target—sits completely alone, in a room decorated with pastoral, restorative murals (Figure 8). Through the archway we see not Février but his wife, standing at the counter, peacefully reckoning with other customers. Here, even though Le Peletier's surroundings and dress are not particularly modest, the swarthy attacker's grimace and dark clothes still suggest a battle between good and evil staged over a bare table.

In his formal account to the Convention, Minister of Justice Dominique-Joseph Garat reported still another version: "Le Peletier had dined in the Palais Royal [*sic*], at Février's restaurant. He was at the counter, paying for the dinner he had eaten, when Pâris entered."[43] It may seem a minor matter, but this alteration in detail was at least as significant as the funeral banner's transformation of the martyr's final words. For it moved Le Peletier from the table, site of Louis's crime and his conviction, to the moment of payment.[44] Though it would seem possible that, as a regular and reliable customer (according to the waiter, Le Peletier had only "missed four meals"), the deputy might have paid at the end of a week's or month's term rather than after every meal, in the official account of his murder he hurries to settle accounts. Several artists' renderings, as well, presumably based on Garat's version of events, show Le Peletier and

Figure 8. Brion's "Assassination of Le Peletier" put the deputy at a table in a comparatively opulent alcove. Through the doorway, other guests are seen settling with Madame Février, but Le Peletier will not have the chance.

Février together at the counter, where the former settles with the latter, even as Pâris finishes with him (Figure 9). Even in death, the true patriot could not leave the nation a tab to pick up.

Stories about the runaway monarch and the murdered Jacobin thus presented a series of didactic tableaux on the workings of hospitality and social change, dwelling obsessively on the fundamental economic logic of restaurant going: the customer consumes a product and then pays for it. These varied accounts mocked the King and honored the martyr, but they also turned the restaurant into a veritable icon of standardized payment

Figure 9. The assassination of Le Peletier reworked so as to show the murdered deputy being stabbed at the counter as he pays his bill. The much more spartan setting, with shared tables and bare walls, brought the scene into harmony with Jacobin rhetoric.

and obligatorily visible exchange. Like Barère's warnings about the dangers of indiscriminate fraternizing, revolutionary images of tableside reckoning served as a reminder that the generosity implicit in a restaurateur's willingness to provide what an eater desired was based in relationships of the marketplace, that—1791's definition of hospitality aside—"chacun son goût" depended on "chacun son écot."[45]

"Fussier Eaters than Formerly"

With the coup against Robespierre on the ninth of Thermidor (July 27, 1794, less than two weeks after Barère denounced the fraternal suppers), the most radical phase of the Revolution came to a close; on the tenth of Thermidor, it is often suggested, all of Paris breathed a collective sigh of relief. One sign of this relief is widely taken to be the great surge toward entertainment, and the great importance attached to fashion and other physical delights. A. V. Arnault, the one-time royalist and playwright, wrote of this period in his 1833 memoirs: "Pleasure was a universal need, and an insatiable one . . . we borrowed on the future and made up for the past . . . so far as pleasure was concerned, we were greatly in arrears"; and he was hardly alone in his assessment. Other authors, including men as ideologically different as the émigré comte d'Allonville, the republican writer Louis Sébastien Mercier, and the Englishman John Millengen, highlighted this phenomenon in their memoirs as well, further contributing to a sense of Paris in the second half of the 1790s as a whirl of diaphanous dresses, tiny toy dogs, and pineapple ices.[46]

In keeping with this image of an inexhaustible appetite for delights, the regimes of the Thermidorean Convention (August 1794–October 1795) and the Directory (November 1795–November 1799) have been identified as the restaurant's first period of full-blown extravagant splendor, and histories of this time have marked Paris as the premier city, not for politics, but for fun.[47] Personified in the figures of the *incroyable,* with his high starched collar and lorgnette, and his scantily-clad female equivalent, the *merveilleuse,* the period has come to stand for idle frivolity and wanton pleasure seeking, as if an entire nation suddenly awakened in autumn 1794 and could think of nothing but drinking champagne, swallowing oysters, and changing its clothes. While historiography was perhaps its most eloquent on this point in the nineteenth century—when Thomas Carlyle's chapter on the Thermidorean Reaction instructed his readers: "Do but look at the cut of clothes," and when the Goncourt brothers gasped, in their typically breathless prose, "And the restaurants, how many new marvels!"—the basic story has remained the same.[48] Jean Robiquet, contributing to the politically conservative *History of Everyday Life* series, attempted to salvage the Directory's reputation by assuring his readers that aside from a few thousand libertines, people had all been happy to lead a "completely bourgeois existence,"[49] but he was fighting a losing battle: even the author of a risqué work of popular history, *Love during the Revolution*, conceded that the sensuously self-indulgent ethos of the period after Thermidor was so well known that there was no reason to belabor the point.[50]

These seemingly giddy years have often fared poorly with historians, at least in comparison with the Revolution's trademark zeal and fervor, or in contrast with the masculine military splendor of Napoleon's Empire. Seen widely as the Revolution's end, rather than its continuation, the years from summer 1794 through 1799 have provoked generations of historians to summary judgments and barely disguised expressions of disgust.[51] The early twentieth-century Robespierrist Albert Mathiez, not surprisingly, declared the after-Thermidor period "an open sewer into which the Convention now plunged"; and even the more sanguine American historian R. R. Palmer, attempting to defend it several decades later, ended up writing: "The Directory looked like a government, and indeed was one . . . but from the beginning there was a certain lack of substance."[52] Though historians have lately made concerted efforts at re-evaluation, they still have not grappled in any serious way with the predominant image of the Thermidorean Convention and the Directory as eras of high frivolity.[53] How did "pleasure" become the emblem of a period just as truly characterized by inflation, war, and continued ideological conflict? And how did the restaurant become one of the primary icons of the many pleasures Paris had to offer?

At the time and ever since, anecdotal history has chosen to attribute the proliferation of restaurants in this period to the entry of former private chefs into the public market. According to this claim, the aristocrats who fled France left their household staffs behind; chefs who suddenly found themselves unemployed put their experience to profitable use and opened restaurants, often in buildings that once served as aristocratic private residences.[54] The Goncourt brothers, who advanced this explanation at mid-century, explained that the advent of the Revolution had produced a situation in which "the cooks of great noble and clerical households found themselves on the street, and decided to treat the public, rather than cooking only for their masters."[55] Another mid-nineteenth-century observer optimistically hailed these early restaurateurs as "the first step in a new aristo-democratic social order," while Jean-Paul Aron, writing in the twentieth century, termed the move of chefs from private homes into restaurant kitchens "the kick-off of a new gastronomic regime."[56]

Antoine Beauvilliers, by far one of the most famous early nineteenth-century Paris restaurateurs, did, in fact, come from a nobleman's private kitchen, leaving his position as pastry chef to the household of the King's brother (the future Louis XVIII) in order to establish a restaurant in the busy arcades of the Palais Royal. Depicted in Brillat-Savarin's *Physiology of Taste* as acting the part of affluent host to his numerous customers, and cited by the Marxist Hobsbawm as evidence of the triumph of the bourgeoisie in the early 1800s, Beauvilliers stands as the first and most easily recognized example of the restaurateur as a democratization of what had once been an aristocratic privilege.[57] Yet Beauvilliers did not move into the public realm because his former royal employers emigrated across the Alps and left him stranded on the street. Instead, he set up business in the mid-1780s, well before the eruption of the Revolution. Beginning with a furnished lodging house on the posh rue Sainte Anne, he moved his business to the Palais Royal in 1787, when that royal residence was divided into rental shopfront parcels by the financially strapped Orléans family, cousins of his ex-employer.[58] He may, perhaps, have left the service of the Bourbons because he was seized by an entrepreneurial urge, or because that branch of the family (like all others) was already cutting back the size of its staff. In either case, however, Beauvilliers did not wait for the Revolution before moving into the restaurant business.

Other, less famous, former employees of private households also opened restaurants; many, however, had gone into business for themselves well before the outbreak of the Revolution.[59] So, for example, Jean-Baptiste LaBarrière left private service in 1779, to establish himself as a *traiteur* on the rue St. Honoré.[60] In 1782 he rented space in the nearby Palais-Royal arcades, which he quickly turned into the most widely acclaimed restaurant of the period.[61] Five years after that, he acquired the ornate Café Militaire, moved into the café business (note how easily he moved among the retail food trades), and sold the Palais-Royal restaurant to his former employees, two recent arrivals from the Meuze, the brothers Jean François and Jean Baptiste Véry.[62] Under the Directory and the Empire, the Véry brothers' two restaurants certainly were among the most famous of the capital's gustatory attractions, but only by their locations—one in the

Palais Royal and the other in the Tuileries gardens—could they be called the descendants of aristocratic privilege.

At any number of moments after 1789, being the former chef of an Old-Regime aristocrat would hardly have been the sort of rousing recommendation sure to make one's restaurant a smashing success. With the fall of the monarchy, such a history could offer testimony neither to the republican nature of one's associations, nor to the necessarily desirable quality of one's cookery. Consider the case of Versailles native Gabriel Charles Doyen, who had worked for ten years in the kitchens of the Queen's household. After the royal family moved from Versailles to the Tuileries in October 1789, Doyen also relocated to Paris, where he worked for a year in Robert's famous Palais-Royal restaurant. But this perfect example of the democratization of privilege and the migration of private servants into public kitchens collapses on a minor detail: in May 1794, Doyen was arrested, hastily tried, and sent to the guillotine, having been convicted of "longing for the Old Regime and missing his former employers."[63] In the eyes of those who denounced him, and of Fouquier-Tinville, who chaired the tribunal that convicted him, Doyen—who stated his occupation as "scullery boy"—was Marie Antoinette's "chef de cuisine," her personal servant, a powerful and dangerous lackey. Nor was he the only former kitchen employee to suffer at the hands of a regime that saw servants as counter-revolutionary sympathizers and as the soft and easily manipulated "creatures" of their employers.[64] Aristocrats knew that their domestic staffs were suspect: when the ultra-royalist Auguste François Frénilly fled Paris after the attack on the Tuileries Palace in August 1792, he made sure that his family's servants, including the chef and maître d'hôtel, also had the necessary passports.[65]

To say that restaurants were opened by the former chefs of aristocrats has become a convenient shorthand for the idea that the restaurant both was the product of, and resulted in, a sort of cultural democratization. As Brillat-Savarin's *Physiology of Taste* put it, "Any man who can spend fifteen or twenty francs, and who sits down in a first-class restaurant, is sure to be treated at least as well as if he sat at a prince's table."[66] But when the writer Louis Sébastien Mercier (cited by the Goncourts, Aron, Héron de Villefosse, and probably many others) first asserted that "the cooks of princes, of *parlementaires,* of cardinals and canons" all became restaurateurs, it was not as a tribute to the Revolution's leveling of culinary hierarchies. Rather, in his chapter "The People, Fussier Eaters than Formerly," he argued that the common people of Paris, once so fine and honest (in the glorious moment, predictably enough, of the Festival of Federation), had been corrupted by aristocratic indolence and patrician vice. "Fine food," Mercier's article begins, "made him [the worker] insolent, lazy, libertine, greedy, and gluttonous."[67] For Mercier—who had supported the Revolution enthusiastically until he was denounced and jailed during the Terror—the notion of former chefs of aristocratic households turning their hands to feeding all of Paris was a way of condemning the Revolution's shortcomings. In short, Mercier argued Barère's point: aristocratic delicacies corrupted republican decency and contaminated honest citizens. When Mercier dwelt on the great advances of culinary science since the Revolution, it was not as praise, nor even as social commentary divorced from politics. Rather, it was an acutely political form of criticism, one that employed the Revolution's rhetoric of fat and lean in an era that was fast becoming, at least insofar as the table was concerned, postrevolutionary. When he singled out the separate tables and dreamy selfabsorption characteristic of restaurant service, Mercier was not singing the virtues of proto-Romantic introspection, but condemning the vice of selfishness; when, in an often quoted and overblown bit of description, he alluded to the goddesses who descended from chariots in the Roman dining rooms of Méot's rue-des-Bons-Enfans restaurant, he was arguing not that the Parisians of 1798 dined on Mount Olympus, but that even the prostitutes of the Palais Royal had taken "antique" nicknames and adopted neoclassical dress.[68]

In the utopian fiction of his youth, *The Year 2440,* Mercier had thought that France's future princes might someday host perpetual tables d'hôte, free and open to all.[69] When, nearly thirty years later, he wrote his *Le Nouveau Paris (The New Paris),* Mercier painted a very different picture of the changes in French table manners wrought by the Revolution. Whereas in the early 1770s, two possibilities had occurred to him—what he saw as the then-current system of private exploitation for personal gain, or the idealized picture of public state intervention and innkeeper-princes—in 1797 he found that a third and unanticipated state of affairs, the reign of the restaurateurs, had actually come to pass. In the palaces where he had hoped to find innkeeper-princes, he instead saw restaurateurs, the one-time intimates of nobles and bishops. In the salons of Méot's restaurant, "the dish appears on the table as soon as it is ordered, and since all who eat there are stuffed with gold, they are treated and fed as kings, princes, and ambassadors."[70] Instead of ushering in the reign of the innkeeper-prince, the Revolution had brought the restaurateur-kings to power.

Restaurants, then, interested Mercier neither as idealized meeting places of the post-Terror public sphere nor as proof of the democratization of privilege. They were not primarily enticing because they served oysters, truffles, turbot, and a host of other exotic delicacies; nor even because, in the notoriously licentious Directory, the restaurant's private little room was a perfect place to entertain one's mistress. Rather, restaurants fascinated Mercier and other journalists because they were, to put it quite simply, extraordinarily expensive.[71] Mercier was hardly alone in privileging the restaurant as a site of greedy expenditure: Jean-Baptiste Pujoulx guaranteed his readers that only "our modern Croesuses" were to be found eating fashionable "fork breakfasts" at the Café Hardy, and *The Foreigners' Guide to Paris* suggested that the post-revolutionary perfection of the culinary arts was one point on which the newly rich should be congratulated.[72] Newspapers and police spies did not regale the varied readers to whom they reported with descriptions of roast turkey or recipes for stuffed sole, but with bills, accounts, and reckonings. One anonymous description of the capital's restaurateurs began: "Some make fortunes, and others lose them. In general, their establishments are very expensive . . . They would do more business if they lowered the prices on their menus, but they prefer to keep most dishes at a price one cannot approach."[73] The grand Paris restaurant may have become, in the early years of the nineteenth century, an emblem of splendor and bounty, but in the late 1790s it was a symbol of greed.

According to the standard tale, the apparently wanton cultural life and unrestrained gluttony of Parisians during the Directory should be understood as a predictable period of hedonism after the anxieties of 1793–1794, as a sort of political Carnival that, in the new inverted calendar of the Republic, followed the civic Lent of Terror. But long before restaurant reviews and tourists' memoirs had spread the rumor of Méot's posh dining rooms or Corcellet's lavish display windows to the far corners of France and beyond, the whisper of starvation had been heard in all the streets. Police spies in the Year III reported not great outbursts of joy at the end of the Terror, but hunger, want, and near-famine conditions: "Everybody complains that they are not able to buy food"; "we lack everything, only the rich have anything." People grumbled that restaurateurs and *traiteurs* bought fifteen loaves of bread, when a mother could afford not one; police agents reported their own disgust at the opulence of restaurant dinners.[74] The restaurant patrons of that horrible year of inflation, shortages, and revenge (1794–1795, Year III)—for restaurant patrons there certainly were, filling the salons of Beauvilliers, Naudet, Robert, Méot, and the Véry brothers as surely as the era's famous *dansomanes* thronged to the ball-rooms of Peroni, Buté, and Mauduit (all of them also restaurateurs)—did not whisper in polite and genteel tones, or hint quietly at their sensitive di-gestions.[75] Rather, they seemed to flaunt their appetites and glory in their hungers, only too happy to eat large evening meals and pass into the notes of police spies for their suspicious extravagance.[76] In periods of shortage and severe inflation, "necessities" rather than luxuries were the first to dis-appear from the market. Bread may, in the Year III, have been very hard to find, but the shop windows seemed to be full of cheese and pastries.[77]

"Pleasure seeking," in the years immediately following the ninth of Thermidor, was not an innocent release of tension but a politically en-gaged and critically attuned activity. The so-called Gilded Youth, a group of sleekly garbed young dandies who smashed busts of Jean-Paul Marat (the revolutionary journalist and martyr) and of Michel Le Peletier, earned their notoriety specifically as a political strike force, a sort of private well-dressed army enlisted by the editor and politico Louis-Stanislaus Fréron to repress those Parisians who had been most militantly and radically active in local politics.[78] In this period, being well dressed, wearing a green or black collar, or frequenting the restaurants of the "Palais Egalité" were not signs of frivolity but of earnestness, matters as serious as the wearing of a liberty cap and a tricolor cockade had been in 1792 or 1793.[79]

In anecdotal history, life in Paris during the Directory appears to have been one big party, but many of the sources for that picture come from the writings of those who could not attend. Gourmands and poor devils alike passed hours every day talking about what they had (or had not) eaten.[80] The glories of the restaurant particularly merited noting in the diaries of those who did not themselves go to the party, those who presented them-selves as suffering and cold, appalled by the spendthrift ways and expand-ing girths of the Directory's nouveaux riches. In 1796, it was both former nobles, stripped of their possessions, and sans-culottes, who never had many, who loathed the restaurants of the Palais Royal and the wealthy who ate in them. As one police report put it, conflating Jacobins and royalists in a single clause: "Some want Robespierre and some want a king, but all want a regime in which they can eat."[81]

Restaurant reviewing in 1795–1799 was table talk in its still politi-cal mode, bitter and caustic, celebratory only long enough to torment, cornucopic only to tantalize. It was politically engaged and harshly satiric; whether eater or eaten, one could not help noticing, when pineapples appeared in the market and sold for 36 francs apiece—and when stories about those who could afford them littered the popular press—that the Revolution's promise of equitably divided bounty had fallen far short of the mark, that "égalité" was now but a palace's fashionable surname.[82] Gastronomic rumor, the suspicion that somebody else is eating better and the desire to do so oneself, was born in this period, as an acutely political form of criticism, a reinscription of the revolutionary conflict of the eater and the eaten. For a brief time in the early and mid-1790s, discussions of the restaurant's place in Paris life had come to be as much about justice and human equality as they were about sensibility and medical conditions. But the language of the fat and the lean was rendered ineffective when stripped of any legal, judicial means of enforcement: no Maximum but a return to the free world of the market; no revolutionary sections but singing societies that banned explicitly political topics from their monthly competitions, and whose members diverted their ode-writing talents from Robespierre and the Montagne to midnight, garters, and champagne.[83] In May 1795, Gilbert Romme spoke passionately to his colleagues in the Convention about the need to reinstate the "Bread of Equality" policy and to prohibit the making of brioches, but he persuaded no one and was arrested shortly thereafter as a dangerous and unrepentant terrorist. On his way to being guillotined, he committed suicide.[84] The communitarian critique of selfishness had been divested of its power; the "hungry and suffering," in the words of the Ministry of the Interior's Houdeyer, "do not even get the cooking steam" from the Palais Egalité's restaurants, and were left with little recourse but envy.[85] A light radiated from the restaurants of the late 1790s, but it was the harsh glitter of ill-gotten gold, not the rosy glow of democratized haute cuisine.

6

From Gastromania
to Gastronomy

O strangers to the laws I lay,
Put your errant tastes away,
Let Appetites by Habit ruled,
In my learnèd Art be schooled.
Choice and Method, diners dear:
Of these, my pupils, come and hear.

JOSEPH BERCHOUX, *LA GASTRONOMIE* (1801)

Few pronouncements could have been further in tone from Bertrand Barère's denunciation of the wasteful frivolity of supposedly "fraternal" suppers than the following excerpt from a satisfied police report, written a mere seven years later: "Paris is perfectly peaceful; people now are only concerned with having a good time."[1] The law of the fifth of September 1793 had famously pronounced terror "the order of the day"; less blunt, perhaps, but equally significant was the bulletin circulated in March 1800 by Dubois and Piis, recently appointed heads of the Paris police: "Liberty of religion, of dress, of pleasure: all must convince you that the government has no other intention than to treat you as the free men that you are."[2] Moral hospitality, mandatory cockades, and the Cult of the Supreme Being—the new political regime of the Consulate dealt them all a final blow, as it officially "freed all loyal citizens of the formal regulations with which they have been burdened during the transition from monarchy to republic."[3]

Paris as the capital of pleasures, as the City of Light—the home of champagne parties and showgirls, dressmakers and cafés—is among the commonplaces of modern life. Yet the very differentiation of "pleasures" from policing emphasized by Dubois and Piis's declaration was a strategic political move on the part of the Consulate, the new order brought to power by Napoleon Bonaparte's military coup of Brumaire 18, Year VIII (November 1799). If suspected royalists, foreign sympathizers, and former Jacobins all needed to be closely watched and supervised, official policy had it that the state would henceforth leave honest citizens to do as they pleased. You can have your private and spiritual pleasures, the police in effect said; we are interested only in maintaining public order, in "apprehending plotters, and foiling conspirators."[4] As First Consul Bonaparte himself reportedly muttered about the gossips, journalists, and scandal-mongerers of the capital: "Let them amuse themselves, and let them dance! But don't let them stick their noses into the counsels of government!"[5] Hence the regime separated pleasure from policing, fashion from ideology, and individual taste from communitarian truth. It also thereby distinguished itself from previous revolutionary governments, for under the numerous governments of the 1790s, such divisions had been largely unthinkable.[6] But in 1800, now that the Republic had achieved what the Consuls intended to be its "final" and permanent form (that is, the Consulate itself, headed by Bonaparte and his fellow Consuls, Cambacérès and Lebrun), further regulation of daily life would prove unnecessary, and the drastic, quotidian revolutions wrought since 1789 (new calendar, new church, new toponyms) could be brought to an end.

One of the two signatories of the police decree promising "liberty of pleasure" was Antoine Auguste Piis, previously best known as a remarkably prolific songwriter.[7] While his fame at the time rested on his inexhaustible musical talents, any notoriety Piis may today enjoy derives from his equally extraordinary ability to survive and prosper under all the regimes that governed France from 1780 to 1815. Though he had begun his professional life as secretary to Louis XVI's brother (the future Bourbon king, Charles X), by the spring of the Year II revolutionary sections were singing Piis's vaudevilles about the benefits of printing and properly didactic theater troupes were staging his earnest plays about adoption, frugal living, and the pleasures of hospitality.[8] Once a court retainer, then the manager of a popular theater and the writer of revolutionary hymns, this most changeable of *girouettes* (or "pinwheels," as social satirists termed men who moved with the prevailing political winds) ended his career in public office as secretary general of the Paris police throughout the Consulate and the First Empire.[9]

During this entire four-decade period, Piis continued to toss off bits of doggerel, and his name was often linked with those of prominent musicians, noted actors, and minor academicians. In the late 1790s, he was a central figure in the "Dîners du Vaudeville," the singing society that met monthly in Juliet's rue-Vivienne restaurant to eat, drink, and compose avowedly unpolitical ditties; newspapers commended him for his witty improvisations (his song on the disappointments of an oyster's life was particularly noted) and his heartfelt toasts.[10] When, in 1807, the Académie Française voted to make his singing buddy, Pierre Laujon, one of their members, Piis's verses of tribute claimed that "since the police know all" this honor came as no surprise to him.[11] Yet in 1813, when the *Gazette de France* mentioned a song of Piis's published in the most recent volume of the *Caveau moderne* (the monthly journal of the then-preeminent "epicurean" singing society), he quickly dashed off a letter of denial which he sent to the *Gazette* and other Paris papers. "Sirs," he remonstrated, "just because the editors please to include a song I composed several years ago, you would be wrong to conclude that my current duties [at the head of the Paris police] leave me any leisure for sacrifices to the Muses."[12]

The change in Piis's public persona—from Republican bard to solemn police functionary—exemplifies the shifting relations between pleasure and politics, consumption and community, in the first decades of the nineteenth century. Reasons of state may not actually have required Antoine A. Piis, the person, to put aside the amusements of his youth or to shun his more literary and polyhymniac friends, but they did demand that the putative second-in-command of the Paris secret police *appear* divorced from the world of song, champagne, and shellfish and make public notice to that effect. Officially and deliberately, across the fifteen years of the Consulate and the First Empire, amusement and administration were increasingly to be distinguished from each other. While the creation of a zone of pleasurable freedoms was, in truth, as calculated a regulatory move as spying on freemasons or interrogating foreigners, the world of pleasure became, by official definition, that which was not policed, that which spontaneously occurred among loyal, civilian citizens. Yet in order to ensure that the differentiation of pleasure from politics took the sanctioned form, the state had to survey the former almost as carefully as the latter. And so the secret police's daily reports to the Minister of the Interior and to the Emperor Napoleon tracked the progression of comfort almost as closely as they followed the pattern of bread prices. "Several branches of the luxury trades, especially the fake pearl manufacturers, are in a slight decline," noted Police Chief Dubois in his daily report for April 14, 1805, before commenting on the rumor that the Army's 17th Division was to be sent to the Italian border.[13] Though in the hierarchy of police concerns, seditious speech in cafés and attempts to assassinate the Emperor certainly took priority over slumping lace sales, the memoranda of police spies in this era nonetheless bear a striking resemblance to guidebook prose ("foreigners are attracted to Paris by the amusements it offers"), or to the writings of fashion columnists ("an ornament of feathers and diamonds to decorate a dress").[14]

As public life came increasingly to be demarcated from private affairs, the meanings and values associated with the restaurant followed a trajectory that was the reverse of Piis's. At the Revolution's radical peak, in 1793–1794, both musicians and restaurateurs expressed explicit political positions (whether they cared to or not): Piis's songs demonstrated support for the Revolution as surely as the latter's pantries or street signs suggested the contrary. Twenty years later, though, Piis had been identified as a "serious" administrator (too preoccupied by his duties to frolic in restaurants), while restaurant going was consigned to the class of "frivolities" (too enjoyable to have any social or political import). Instead of being seen to occupy competing positions within the framework of politics, police and restaurants were now opposed as the two terms of a work/play, governmental/civilian, or public/private dichotomy. Dominique Février, who owned the restaurant where Le Peletier was killed, certainly benefited when his own career followed a comparable pattern: a year after the assassination, Février was arrested, charged with counter-revolutionary sympathies, and jailed for months.[15] By late 1797, however, the liberal Republic no longer imagined it could hold him responsible for the crimes committed in his restaurant or for the political attitudes of those who dined there and, instead, granted him a concession to run the snack bar within the confines of the Council of Five Hundred's recently refurbished assembly hall.[16] Once a valiant hero who had rushed to assist the Republic's first martyr, and then a suspected dangerous counter-revolutionary, by 1797 Février was again but a restaurateur, his activities constrained only by his menu.

An upper-level conspiracy was not required to make the restaurant a common feature of French life, nor was the early nineteenth-century celebration of the Paris restaurant a Napoleonic version of bread and circuses—after all, the First Empire did not usually give away restaurant dinners. But governmental attitudes toward the uses of the table did shift dramatically in the period from 1789 to 1815: from Villette's optimistic vision of the people's banquet as a spontaneous state of natural, calm effusion or Barère's paranoid suspicion that the enemies of the Revolution were skimming the fraternity from the small remaining stock of sociability to the decision, less than ten years later, to control public life by leaving certain delimited arenas, such as the festive table, officially untouched. In the early nineteenth century, gastronomic literature, working within the strictures of police-state "pleasures," helped to reconfigure further the previous decade's discussion of the restaurant, bringing oysters, pheasants, champagne, and turbots center stage. No longer would it matter if a restaurateur treated his clientele fairly, or if his guests comported themselves in a fashion consonant with displays of republican virtue.

By describing a world in which eating was not a biological imperative but an artistic passion, and in which food came not from farm or field but from ornately decorated boutiques, gastronomy exempted itself from incendiary questions of subsistence, and placed the table squarely in the realm of literary or artistic debate. From 1801, the Ministry of Police instructed censors to strike all references to the grain trade from the press, while avidly endorsing articles that might celebrate the regime's freedom of "pleasure" and religion.[17] Rather than strictly limiting journalism on the arts and sciences, the censors' office encouraged (we might even say, fomented) heated argument about theater or music in order to create a sort of diversion, to fill the press with "debate" rather than with monotonous repetitions of the *Moniteur's* official announcements. To this end, one censor alerted his superiors to the impending danger of a new subsistence crisis: a "shortage" (literally, *disette*) of "literary and theatrical gossip," which he termed the "best diet" *(le meilleur aliment)* for idle Parisians. Censor Lemontey warned the administration that if angry crowds and dissatisfied citizens ever ceased to be preoccupied with comparing the talents of rival actresses, or with rehashing the debated merits of Italian versus French music, they were sure to assemble in the streets. Without cultural squabbles, he predicted in a memorandum to his bureau chief, Parisians would turn their attention to politics and to military campaigns, such that "Spain will replace the Théâtre Français, Russia will take over from music, and the government will become the focal point of all conversations."[18]

Gastronomy—defined by the dictionary of the Académie Française as "the art of good eating"—emerged, in that first decade of the nineteenth century, as one means of satisfying the incessant hunger for aesthetic debates. Gastronomic literature, led by Grimod de la Reynière's *Almanach des gourmands,* evoked a world where restaurateurs and pastry-chefs were the equivalent of theater entrepreneurs and playwrights, and where one candymaker charged admission simply to look at his new bonbons.[19] For eight years in the early nineteenth century, Grimod annually sketched an oneiric, Bosch-like tableau of heroic partridges and pyrotechnic pastries, describing a realm of fantasy where sardines rose like Venus from the sea, and fresh green peas offered "the most unspeakable delights."[20] Repeatedly pushing food and cookery from the realm of quotidian necessity into that of delirious fantasy, the *Almanach des gourmands* pronounced dinner a magical activity unlike anything else in daily life.

Denying the relevance of pre-existing categories and genres, First-Empire gastronomic literature set the model for future writing about food and established a *code gourmand* as enduring as any of the legal codes over which Napoleon so famously slaved. Interspersing anecdotes about meals eaten (or missed) with helpful hints, hyperbolic descriptions, restaurant reviews, and occasional elaborate recipes, the *Almanach des gourmands* combined the Classical and Renaissance traditions of the symposium with the increasingly popular forms of the guidebook and the almanac. Within these texts, and by the increasing codification of everyday practices they both accompanied and stimulated, the restaurant became a real cultural and social institution, an easily identified landmark. For by concentrating exclusively on food and dining, gastronomic literature gave the restaurant new prominence, and transformed it from a space of scandal into one of celebration. Delimited within two important new discursive institutions—the specifically "gastronomic" literature inaugurated by Grimod and the "epicurean" singing societies with which his name was also linked—early nineteenth-century discussions of restaurant going came to focus neither on the extravagance of expenditure nor on the inequitable distribution of resources, but on the grand restaurant's ability to stimulate and satisfy any desire, on its exemplary place in the spectacle that was Napoleon's Paris. Taking their cues from the commercial success of these gastro-epicurean publishing ventures, travelers, guidebook authors, and even the weariest observers of Paris life all included restaurants in their accounts of the capital's marvels. But unlike commentary about the restaurant in the immediate post-Revolution years, the new gastronomies and guides of the Empire and the Restoration demarcated the table as an autonomous realm, one structured by rules distinct from those that governed other aspects of social life. Within this newly circumscribed context, authors might interpret meals without reference to overtly political concerns, either aristocratic or republican. With the development of gastronomy, the restaurant table would become significant in its own right, independent of both the court society's *grand couvert* and the Revolution's fraternal repast.

The New Gastronomic World of Grimod de la Reynière

Alexandre Balthasar Laurent Grimod de la Reynière is widely credited with having invented the restaurant review and being one of the founding fathers of modern gastronomic discourse.[21] Neither a restaurateur nor even a regular restaurant patron, Grimod de la Reynière nonetheless must be central to any history of the restaurant, for he was, unquestionably, the single most famous eater in First-Empire France. Foreign visitors to the capital and local chroniclers of city life routinely wrote of Grimod and of restaurants in a single paragraph (and probably spoke of them in a single breath)—as if reviewer and restaurants could not be known one without the other. With the *Almanach des gourmands,* Grimod (who had briefly edited a theater weekly, the *Censeur dramatique*) expanded the established form of the drama review to make it a genre applicable to another ephemeral, but decidedly more edible, art. "The table," he wrote smugly, "is a stage on which there has never been a flop."[22]

One of the great literary and publishing successes of its day (the first volume alone sold out four editions), Grimod's *Almanach des gourmands* confirmed its eccentric author's position as among the most familiar of Paris celebrities. By the sixth year, he grinningly styled himself France's "Ministre de la Gueule" ("Minister of the Maw"), a title few would have disputed, though some might have suggested that the honor involved was small indeed.[23] Popular vaudeville plays featured characters based on Grimod: "Monsieur Gourmandin" named Strasbourg (home of the finest pâté de foie gras), Mayence (famous for its hams), and Pithiviers (specialist in lark-filled pastries) as the three principal cities of France.[24] The *Journal des dames et des modes* claimed that theater audiences could be relied upon to applaud wildly at any scene mentioning "capons, partridges, or gluttony in general."[25] Chocolate manufacturers advertised Grimod's endorsement, while the German dramatist August von Kotzebue incorporated pages of the *Almanach* (unattributed) into his account of a visit to Paris. The Scots antiquarian Pinkerton, as well, copied long sections from Grimod's oeuvre, asserting in passing that its author's pre-eminence in all manners gustatory made any other research or references unnecessary.[26]

It was not simply that Grimod described restaurants or fanciful meals, for that had of course been done before. But whereas earlier authors had generally treated these topics as symptomatic of economic conditions and social relations within the capital, Grimod made restaurant going into an affair of "taste" alone. Combining the gastro-criticism of the past decade with parodies of aesthetic discourse and flights of gothic fancy, the *Almanach* sketched a complex and often self-contradictory form of government—part constitutional monarchy, part theocracy, part idiosyncrasy—for the land of gourmandism alone. In his wryly self-censoring, self-parodying *Almanach,* Grimod described exquisite meals, praised new inventions, and offered stray bits of medical and household advice. One item guided the reader in removing stains from table linens, another congratulated the chemist Appert on his successful canning of vegetables, and still another advised the serious eater on the purchasing of clocks for his dining room.[27] A manufacturer of nets merited the gratitude of all gastronomers for the fish and fowl caught in his creations, while a purveyor of fast-drying paint was congratulated for making it possible to redecorate in the morning, and eat dinner in the same room that evening.[28] Throughout the *Almanach,* the table provided an interpretive "table," a chart that enabled the reader to make sense of the entire world.

Indeed, Grimod seemingly mapped a whole new world: a region with its own saints, calendar, and geography, separated from Napoleonic France by its own hierarchies of conduct, gender, and taste. The *Almanach des gourmands* established its own Academy (the "Tasters' Jury") and distributed its own laurel wreaths and martyr's palms. Gastronomy offered a new calendar of saints—neither Catholic nor revolutionary—led by François Vatel, the mid-seventeenth-century maître d'hôtel who served first the financier Nicolas Fouquet (for whom Vaux-le-Vicomte was built) and then the Bourbon prince Condé, and who became famous for committing suicide when the delayed arrival of a delivery of seafood ruined Condé's planned dinner for Louis XIV.[29] For Grimod, Vatel's story proved that the search for emblems, icons, and heroes never needed to extend beyond the kitchen. Owing beatification to his courage alone, Vatel was the gastronomer's Joan of Arc and his Le Peletier de Saint Fargeau.

As Grimod wrote, he created not only his own pantheon but his own Paris as well, a city strikingly different from the one with which others were acquainted. Travelers had long had recourse to guidebooks, but the First-Empire proliferation of restaurants and food sellers produced (and, in a sense, was produced by) a sort of guidebook for residents. In his famous "nutritive strolls," Grimod, described by one writer as "a sovereign in his Louvre," invented the restaurant review as he exercised his rule over candy-makers, butchers, and restaurateurs, making and breaking reputations (or so he claimed) with a single sentence.[30] In the first nourishing promenades, the "editor" of the *Almanach des gourmands* claimed to be

guided by a "gourmand." Together they wandered the streets and neigh-
borhoods of Paris, infallibly led by the gourmand's "subtle sense of smell."
As they walked, they commented on the storefronts they passed, and
paused to examine particularly delightful specimens. If the "gourmand,"
beagle-like, followed his nose, the reassuringly human and literate figure
of the "editor" ensured that the less olfactorily gifted could still find their
way in Paris, as well as in the Land of Gourmands. In this early version, the
gastronomer's map followed the visible contours of Paris cartography. The
novice (unacquainted with both Parisian topography and the delights of
Rouget's pastries), instructed to follow the rue Traversière to the rue de
Richelieu (via the Cour de Saint Guillaume) and turn right, could easily
follow these directions.[31] The walking tour seemed to make the capital's
culinary delights available to all—even the poorest reader could repeat the
narrator's progression, smelling the roasting meats and ogling the sugared
pastries along the way.[32]

In the fourth year of the almanac, however, Grimod dropped the image
of walking along a city street and integrated the characters of the guide-
gourmand and the editor-translator into one omniscient narrator. The
new organizational strategy, "less amusing than it is useful," depended on
a categorical, rather than a geographical, schema that listed all pastry-
shops together followed by all wine merchants and then all roast-meat sellers.[33] The *flâneur*'s meandering path no longer governed the steps of the
Almanach's readers; instead, the new itinerary rejected the logic of Paris
streets to follow one based on the diner's most pressing concerns. Grimod
made excuses, insisting that the *Almanach*'s readership had imposed the
new guidebook arrangement that scrambled Paris geography, further distinguishing the gastronomer's city from the cartographer's. For example,
Grimod listed a cook-caterer on the Boulevard du Temple, and immediately thereafter mentioned one on the rue du Vieux-Colombier, jumping
from the city's northeastern limits to a street on the other side of the river,
near the Luxembourg Palace, in no more than an instant. As he often did,
Grimod here claimed neither to invent nor to create, but to transcribe and
to report. If there was no distance to be covered between the Boulevard
du Temple and the Left Bank, that was only because his city was no longer
the "Paris" that appeared on everybody else's maps. Instead, Grimod's
was a new city: the gastronomic capital of the nineteenth century.

Grimod's newly specific criteria and altered urban topographies produced a picture of Paris purged of the momentous events of the 1790s,
and of the Revolution's political understanding of the table. The careful

diner shared Paris not with urban crowds, plotting conspirators, or the specter of beheaded aristocrats, but with succulent piglets, gargantuan oysters, and appealingly trussed rabbits. Wherever the gourmand traveled, he would of course sample the native specialties, but only in cornucopic Paris could he find macaroni and "pouding," sauerkraut and bouilla-baisse—in short, all of the planet's bounty, assembled in one place.[34] Paris, according to the *Almanach,* owed its reputation as the capital of Europe as much to "the high quality of its food" as to the "splendor of its monu-ments" or the sophistication of its inhabitants. So central was the myth of an ever-ample Paris that Grimod exempted the Parisian alone from the in-junction to voyage to the Mediterranean coast in order to eat fresh sar-dines.[35] In a similar vein, he informed his readers that the best beef in France originated in Poitou and the Auvergne, but only reached its point of perfection upon arrival in Paris. The meat improved immeasurably in its travels: "like those young idiots whose minds only grow in traveling, these succulent beasts must voyage to Paris before developing their full merit."[36] The beef cattle of France ran to the Paris slaughterhouses and to Grimod's table, happily throwing themselves into his waiting, cavernous mouth. The gastronomer never claimed to be friend of all the world, but all the world's products were his.

In this new world, the most scrumptious morsels appeared, semi-miraculously and fully formed, in the Bohemian-glass display cases of Grimod's favorite pastry chef. Paris, the unquestioned capital of gastron-omy, nonetheless "produced" not a bit of food: "not a stalk of wheat grows there, no lambs are born and not a single cauliflower is har-vested."[37] As in the Land of Cockaigne, cooking was no more required than harvesting, and sheeps' feet (in sauce) ran eagerly across Paris, for a price.[38] Gastronomic literature—which told the would-be gourmand to buy his butter "at Theurlot's" and his macaroni "either at Corazza's or at the Magasin d'Italie," but which did not hint at the quantities of these goods to use in concocting "soup à la Camerani"—offered instruction in purchasing, not in preparing.[39]

Indeed, whenever the cook's art seemed so clean, so proper, and so sim-ple that it might be allowed to leave the kitchen and enter the dining room (to leave the cookbook and enter the *Almanach*), Grimod turned his ver-sion of the recipe into a Gothic horror tale, swathed in macabre overtones. He introduced one simple dish, a salmi of pheasant or woodcock, with the claim that it was the perfect thing for the host himself to prepare in the dining-room chafing dish, but ended the recipe with an ominous warning:

"It is absolutely necessary to use a fork on this occasion, for fear that one would eat one's own fingers if they were to be coated with this fabulous sauce."[40] The collapse of the division between cook and diner, the crossing of the threshold between kitchen and dining room, when it occurred, could easily precipitate the abolition of the line between the eater and the eaten. Despite its many advances and improvements, the art of cookery needed to remain in the realm of private, semi-alchemical, arcanum. As Grimod wrote about one restaurant's ability to make oysters available in the summer: "To attempt to penetrate this extraordinary mystery, to unveil the secret, would be perhaps to destroy it."[41]

For the greater glory and decency of the dish prepared, the preparer needed to remain hidden from view. Concealment and secrecy enticed the diner, as they did the lover.[42] In the twenty years since the Revolution, according to Grimod, Paris pastry shops had, by banishing a blackened oven and "several cook's boys" to the back rooms, demonstrated progress surpassing that of all the other arts and sciences. Though disdainful of camouflaged or masked dishes, he nevertheless applauded the marble counters and elegant light fixtures that ornamented the renovated pastry-shops and hid the odious work-spaces.[43] The "arts of the oven," by this argument, demonstrably advanced when they hid the oven and brought "art" center stage. According to the *Almanach des gourmands,* actresses, rather than technological developments or the availability of colonial ingredients, motivated the First Empire's greatest pastry innovations, so that the pastry chef Rouget appears as an inspired portrait painter, one moved by the delicate, sugared charms of vaudeville actresses to invent tiny cakes bearing the names, not of the women themselves, but of the roles they had created on stage.[44] The *Almanach*'s oft-repeated parallel between theater and cookery, between feminine attractions and edible enticements, worked to establish the table as a space not of dire nutritional necessity, but of light-hearted urban frivolity and the fusion of multiple appetites.

When Grimod permitted a few creative artists to emerge from back rooms and offstage areas, they were neither the hundreds of ordinary caterers and restaurateurs whose listings filled the pages of the commercial almanacs, nor even the score of names he mentioned annually. The *Almanach*'s real dramatis personae consisted of a few exemplary figures such as Rouget, that veritable Watteau of pastry cooks, or Balaine, the seafood magician whose necromancy produced oysters in July. Almost as if he were eulogizing the dead, Grimod lavished praise on a small handful of idealized culinary artists. He celebrated their genius in lengthy encomia, calling Balaine the true "Apollo" of the gourmet's Parnassus, and comparing Rouget to a playwright of the French "Golden Age" in a verse that concluded: "Two Names canst thou e'er but in Rapture say: / Racine for his Verse; and for Pastries, Rouget!"[45] These leading characters, the *Almanach* made clear, were stars in their own right, gifted with the calm, reasoned genius required of a military commander or a head of state.[46] Like Grimod de la Reynière himself, these few individuals became iconographic reference points in the urban gastronomic imagination. Gastronomic literature formed a mythology which posed (like all myths) as real explanation, and which became, by its repetition and codification, a set of meaningful examples: an epicurean singing society in Lyons celebrated its host restaurateur by comparing him not to a Greek god, but to the already apotheosized Balaine, and during the peak seafood season of Lent in 1813, the *Gazette de France* made a point of reporting that elegant carriages crowded the streets leading to his rue-Montorgeuil fish restaurant, "Le Rocher de Cancale."[47] For another thirty years, the Rocher remained a landmark restaurant: in the 1830s, a Russian nobleman sent members of his household there to serve apprenticeships, and its eventual passing provoked tear-stained editorials from several newspapers.[48] And even when the chefs and menus that Grimod praised had long since died or disappeared, the institutions by means of which he evaluated them—the nutritive strolls, the taste-testing panels, the published commentary—lived on.[49]

But perhaps the *Almanach*'s most famous character and most enduring creation was "the gourmand" himself. Grimod's protagonist (uniformly read as a simple account of Grimod himself) was as infamous as he was famous, as notorious as he was noted. To the gourmand, nothing was sacred—except dinner. Grimod's *Almanach* compared women to food and found the former sadly lacking; he wrote of the innocent charms of little robins, only to encourage eating them; he commented not at all on Napoleon's many conquests, but marveled at the wonderful new sugar "artillery" invented by the Fidèle Berger ("The Faithful Shepherd," a well-known candy shop).[50] In his obsessiveness and his discrimination, Grimod's gourmand or "gastronomer" was a truly new configuration of attributes, a character impossible to classify by the typologies of Old-Regime medicine or 1790s politics. For in defining the nineteenth-century eater, Grimod both rejected "hunger" as a vulgar and common sensation, and scorned "delicacy" of appetite as a "feminine" attribute.[51] Thereby distancing himself from two standard Old-Regime images (the vaporous, aristocratic, delicate weakling and the animalistic, vulgar, rustic glutton), he characterized the gourmand as "someone endowed with great delicacy, only his health must be vigorous."[52] Concerned not with the satiation of mere hunger, but with the provocation of educated appetite, Grimod's gastronomer was a new character—the virile, healthy, tasteful eater—in a new world.

Impossible to categorize by Old-Regime medical terms, the gourmand stood resolutely outside social characterizations as well, endowed in his own world with a status that corresponded only poorly to any more mundane system of estates or classes. Defining the gastronomer as someone who appreciated any well-prepared dish, no matter how humble its origins, Grimod de la Reynière pointedly distinguished the subtleties of "savoir-manger" from the easily calculated vulgarities of wherewithal.[53] Gastronomic sensitivity, he asserted, did not depend on social position and was not guaranteed to the materially solvent; money alone would never assure the newly enriched arms dealer of a fine dinner. Even in the best restaurants, where true connoisseurs enjoyed "many excellent dinners," the merely wealthy would find only indigestion.[54] In the meritocratic land of gourmands, there were to be no venal office holders and no inherited titles.

Grimod often emphasized the table's theatrical qualities, but perhaps his most significant contribution to modern gastronomy was to define this spectacle as explicitly apolitical (or, often enough, impolitic). Dinner was a spectacle solely for the satisfaction of the individual, with no ceremonial function, no thought for serving nation or monarch. Since the gourmand lived in his own world, the titles he bestowed might have little relation to those earned in other realms, and honors granted in one world might be balanced by their loss in another: the *Almanach* singled out the Emperor's new roast-meat man, a longtime favorite of Grimod's, not to congratulate him but to comment on the domineering haughtiness he had acquired along with his title.[55]

Insisting on the space separating private good taste from "public affairs," Grimod resolutely banned politicians and political discussions from the serious dinner table. When confronted with an elaborate pheasant pâté or a truffled roast turkey, the true connoisseur often could not control his own eating—how could he attempt, Grimod asked, to govern others?[56] Even selfishness (of which gourmands were very often accused) the *Almanach* treated not as a sin or crime, but as evidence of how little time the dedicated eater had for anyone else's activities; busy researching the etymology of the word "mayonnaise," purging his cook of palate-altering impurities, or evaluating the samples sent by fame-seeking restaurateurs, the gastronomer had no interest in spying and snooping, or meddling in politics.

In his use of a funeral announcement for his famous 1783 supper, and in a notorious subsequent adventure—a parodic legal text for which he was exiled from Paris and banned from practicing law—Grimod de la Reynière had exploited two of the Old Regime's few uncensored forms.[57] In his most famous accomplishment, the *Almanach des gourmands,* he carved a new niche in the thick wall of Napoleonic censorship, explicitly marking dinner and its accompanying conversation as an area exempt from Fouché's prying police spies. This may seem paradoxical, for outlining the government of an imaginary land is one of the most common forms of political satire (think of *Gulliver's Travels* or *Utopia*), and one might well wonder whether Grimod's gastronomic rewriting of France was not an extended piece of political commentary, an elaboration of the critique begun with the famous 1783 funereal supper. Indeed, Grimod's *Almanach* offered copious social criticism for those who knew how to read it, but his references to "most Parisians, whose hearts have been transformed into guts" could almost pass for praise in a text that trumpeted sirloins as preferable to women.[58] In exalting Balaine, he noted that the restaurateur "could have ruled the realm as well as he does his restaurant"—were these simple words a tribute to the chef who coordinated the service in a very busy establishment, or a mocking gibe at the Corsican nobody who now was Emperor of the French?[59] Thus the polymorphously perverse *Almanach des gourmands* certainly could have been read as a work of social or political commentary, but reviewers did not often evaluate it in such terms. Rather, instead of seeing Grimod's new world as a clever satire of the equally new Empire—in the era of the Napoleonic wars, after all, restaurateurs and gastronomers were not the only ones to be regularly drawing up new *cartes* ("maps," as well as "menus"), and Grimod not the only author of law-giving codes—his critics saw it as the product of a deranged mind and an unrestrained appetite.[60]

Rarely has such a polyvalent text been read in such a single-minded fashion; rarely has satire been so blindly ignored. Journalist critics of Grimod (and he had many) attacked the individual whom they saw as the single arch-glutton, rather than reproving the society in which he lived and flourished. They emphasized his "vulgarity" over that of the butchers who supplied him, or even of the foreigners who regurgitated his every utterance. Gourmandism, which during the Year II had been proof of the existence of foreign and aristocratic plots against the Republic, once again became an individual's sin (or perhaps merely a bachelor's peculiarity).

In order for gastronomic literature as we now know it—distinct, that is, from the Rabelaisian confusions and excesses of earlier table talk—to become the restaurant's dominant mode of explanation, Grimod's idiosyncratic text had to be read, critiqued, and sanitized. The demarcation of gastronomy as an autonomous realm, an arena (not unlike Habermas's "bourgeois public sphere") in which wealth and social standing purportedly have no effect on an eater's fineness of palate, required both the extravagant gestures of Grimod's text, and the reading of those gestures propounded by the *Almanach*'s critics and endorsed by Napoleon's censors. The *Almanach* alone, unread, unremarked, and uncommented upon, would have been a far less effective (con)textualization of restaurants and cuisine. Fascinating a text though it may be, it was largely thanks to the ways in which it was cited and circulated in early nineteenth-century Paris that Grimod's *Almanach* became especially notorious. When Napoleon's strictly controlled press lavished attention on the new volume of the *Almanach des gourmands*—rather, say, than on the handful of soup kitchens established along Count Rumford's model, or on the truly bitter responses to the *Almanach* penned by wisely anonymous "poor devils"—it gave any reader the impression that the capital's greatest alimentary danger stemmed not from a potential shortage of staples but from the impending explosion of goodies.[61]

Joseph François Nicholas Dusaulchoy (1760–1835), one of the editors of the *Journal des arts, des sciences, et de la littérature (Journal of the Arts, Sciences, and Literature)*, penned some of the harshest criticisms, calling for an "open war" against Grimod and all his kind. In monthly columns, Dusaulchoy cautioned his readers to stay clear of such dangerous "votaries of intemperance"; to what sin would they next turn their attentions, he asked, once they had accomplished the deification of gluttony? Gambling, theft, and other unspeakable vices surely followed the glorification of "the grossest appetite and the most abject of passions."[62] Launching his crusade in the name of "taste and public morality," Dusaulchoy denounced the gourmands who "build the weaknesses of their private lives into doctrine and propound them in a public forum."[63] His running commentary expressed an abiding fear of contagion, a horror at the spreading perversion of orderly appetite. The weaknesses of the gastronomer's "private life," once made public by the print media, constituted, he implied, a growing problem for the entire nation. Dusaulchoy, in short, denied gastronomy's right to exist as a separate set of guiding principles.

For all his self-righteous indignation and warnings of incipient decadence, Dusaulchoy was hardly a career enemy of spectacle, a model of frugality, or a partisan of Spartan virtue. For the author of this puritanical-sounding criticism had also written a glowing account of Napoleon's coronation, one which lavished praise on the extravagant gifts offered to the new imperial household (especially the gold and vermeil dinnerware) and lovingly described the varied public festivities.[64] Perhaps more tellingly, he was an intimate friend and acquaintance of First-Empire bureaucrats and officials, including those charged with press censorship (in whose offices he worked for a time).[65] Had he wished to shut down the *Almanach des gourmands,* had he desired to silence Grimod de la Reynière permanently, private letters to Fouché or Dubois rather than regular diatribes in the *Journal des arts* would have served Dusaulchoy's purpose far more effectively. Yet he chose instead—perhaps encouraged by his well-placed friends—to rail regularly against the *Almanach* and the monthly *Journal des gourmands et des belles,* sounding his alarm in the most hyperbolic and strident of tones. Reviewing Grimod's 1808 *Manuel des amphitryons (The Hosts' Manual),* Dusaulchoy scoffed at the idea that its author could still have anything left to say after having taught Parisians "how to set the table and how to sit there," but he nonetheless managed to write two long columns commenting on "the gastronomic lucubrations of this bizarre character."[66]

Reviewers like Dusaulchoy, who by according several pages to each volume of the *Almanach* contributed considerably to its fame, focused public attention on it and made a star of its author. The cult of the individual – most often identified in this era with the figure of Napoleon Bonaparte— was not a self-made phenomenon. Rather, it depended on the readers and writers, the observers and polemicists, who willingly credited some individual genius with winning the battle of Marengo, or turning the French into a nation of gluttons. If the gastronomer's way of interpreting the city around him was compulsively focused on the table, so were his critics just as obsessively committed to reading the *Almanach* as autobiography. In the patchwork of aphorisms, advice columns, and curious anecdotes, reviewers identified what they took to be the single authorial voice of a "bizarre character." But it would be a mistake to read the *Almanach* solely as the product of a lone warped psyche. For Grimod's continued fascination with death—he lovingly described one pastry as a partridge sarcophagus where the birds' tufted heads "like so many pinwheels [*girouettes*] . . . served both as ornament and label for this nourishing mausoleum"[67]—spoke to the audience for Gothic literature, and his meditations on taste addressed those readers conversant with the most recent writings of Kant and Cabanis. His narrative persona—as the sole man of taste and the one discerning palate, who gave all for his art and willingly sacrificed family, country, and even midday meal for the sake of dinner—was indeed a bit of a madman; but whether Grimod de la Reynière himself was one, or not, remains another question. That he delighted in the unusual and the maca bre; that he shocked the "bourgeoisie," even as he helped to define its pleasures; that he merits commemoration by satirists, as well as by food writers—all this is clear. Less apparent, however, is the relationship between Grimod, who lived in print-media silence for twenty-three years after the last issue of the *Almanach* appeared, and "the gourmand."

While Grimod's polyphonic, ludic, and often downright disturbing text was forever playing with the heteroglossia and hyperbole characteristic of Renaissance and Classical table talk, reviewers overlooked these generic conventions to concentrate on Grimod himself. They, as much as Grimod de la Reynière, can be said to have invented the ideal nineteenth-century eater.[68] In the many readings of the *Almanach* that treated it as a transcription of Grimod's every desire, perversion, and whim, any distinction between author and text, between what the *Almanach* predicated of "the gourmand" and what Grimod de la Reynière actually did in daily life, disappeared. By reading the *Almanach* as a work of Rousseauian confession, rather than as a work of Menippean (that is, multi-genred) satire, even Grimod's harshest critics actually furthered the triumph of gastronomy.[69] For by insisting that a single authorial presence had to be, in some sense, responsible for the *Almanach,* they contributed to the cult of individual choice and personal taste that the notion of "gastronomy" exemplified. Grimod and his critics shared a language of post-revolutionary individualism, a tendency to emphasize the personal over the political or the social. While eighteenth-century writing about food and eating had pleaded its relevance by demonstrating its civic usefulness, nineteenth-century gastronomy argued for its own autonomy and told tales from Classical sources for reasons more antiquarian than didactic. Making no claims for the morality of the ancients, it recycled the hardly exemplary anecdotes of Domitian asking the Roman Senate how to cook his turbot and of Cleopatra drinking a pearl—much to Dusaulchoy's disgust.[70]

On any number of crucial points, the *Almanach* and its critics took posi-

tions that had curiously similar effects, if not avowedly identical motiva-
tions. From the perspectives of Grimod and his self-identified "sober" antagonists alike, the gastronomer's table needed, for good or evil, to be
distinct and separate. What the *Almanach* described as the creation of a
learned Academy, was, for its opponents, a kind of necessary incarceration.
Where the former wished to bypass women, and demanded that the
gastronomer forsake all joys other than those of the table (better to concentrate his energies on "the stupidest goose, than the sweetest woman"),
the latter insisted that women avoid gourmands' tables lest they be of-
fended, or worse yet, corrupted (or even eaten!).[71] In the debate between their positions, gastronomy emerged as its own possible topic of
discussion, a seemingly autonomous field of inquiry. Shielded from official
intervention by this shared definition of gastronomy as a perhaps peculiar
but nonetheless determinedly apolitical passion, future generations of Parisians would paradoxically find the dining rooms of great restaurants
among the most fruitful and accessible settings for their interventions into
public and political life.

The Laws of Taste

Taking shape across the decade of Grimod de la Reynière's dictates and
pronouncements, gastronomic discourse regularly reiterated the necessary chasm separating preparation from consumption, kitchen from dining
room. "With food, as with the law," Grimod quoted, "to find it good, you
must not see it being made."[72] On this premise, it was not only the
sausageman's stuffing of brains, blood, and ground meat into emptied
intestines, but the gastronomer's savoring of that surprisingly delectable
concoction as well, that needed to be concealed from view. Surrounding his decision-making processes with opaque layers of secrecy,
Grimod separated the gastronomer's table from the potentially contaminating influences of the outside world. He honored the seventeen-
member "Wednesday Society," whose midweek meals had shaped "gastronomic jurisprudence" for the past twenty-four years, by dedicating the
Almanach's fourth volume to them, but he also noted that naming the
members would violate the anonymity central to the Society's continued
happiness. Since "obscurity" and taste formed the heart of their credo,
who was he to compliment them for one while sacrificing the other? Instead of threatening the members' privacy, he abstained from naming
them, and saluted the Society as a whole.[73]

In a modern regime of set prices and abolished privileges, where any-one's money was supposedly as good as everybody else's, the food critic was (and is) a famous figure who nonetheless must ensure that he is treated like an ordinary customer. Dressed sometimes as a modest man of letters, sometimes as an affluent lawyer, and sometimes as a crotchety throwback to the Old Regime, Grimod for all his notoriety claimed to walk the streets of Paris shrouded by a cloak of anonymity.[74] Once he be-came known as the author of the *Almanach des gourmands,* however, Grimod de la Reynière ate his meals in striking privacy, never again expos-ing himself to view as he had in the 1783 funereal supper. While he proved as astute a publicist as ever, he sought public attention by slightly different means, striving to deflect attention from his own role in order to refocus it on the expertise he represented.

Grimod might claim that "our itineraries have become for the food trades, what the exhibition on the Champs de Mars is for businessmen and manufacturers," but the latter was a show in which a year's worth of French products and inventions were publicly displayed for several weeks.[75] These annual industrial fairs (nation-sized precursors of the later universal exhibitions) partook of an Enlightenment logic of publicness and visibility that Grimod's meandering promenades utterly lacked. For whereas the exhibitions brought goods together in a central location where all might come to see them, the edibles Grimod described were spread across Paris, involving the would-be connoisseur not in a parade-ground review, but in a scavenger hunt. Both were public, but in very dif-ferent ways: the expositions, where the Ministries of Industry and Agricul-ture awarded cash prizes and furthered "advances" in all arenas, belonged to Roze de Chantoiseau's world of improved circulation, but Grimod's itineraries were part of a different, darker, tradition, bridging the interval between Réstif de la Bretonne's nocturnal observations of scandal and Baudelaire's mid-century *flâneur.*

From the second year of the *Almanach* (1804), Grimod decreed that he would henceforth pass judgment only on the work of culinary artists who sent samples to be tasted by a panel of experts (as "a sort of letter of intro-duction, like those by which ambassadors recognize and legitimate each other").[76] In the years that followed, the grand ceremonial procession in which these "legitimations" (as he termed them) made their way to the weekly "Jury dégustateur" (tasting jury) supplemented and, increasingly, supplanted the gastronomer's trek across Paris. At the Jury's meetings—meal-length exhibitions staged for a select audience—the fortunate few presided over and "legitimated" a gastro-microcosm of Paris. In the city that was already itself a miniature version of the entire alimentary planet, the honored Jury member had still fewer reasons to venture outside his own world.

Combining diplomatic, legislative, and judiciary functions, the Jury became by far the most important institution within the government of gourmandise. References to its functioning were strewn across the volumes of the *Almanach:* meeting every Tuesday in secretive objectivity, the Jury's members conducted the vital business of receiving gifts, recognizing dignitaries, and, of course, sampling the week's "legitimations."[77] Most important, they prepared their findings for annual publication, and thus while the Jury had other, ceremonially significant, officers (such as a servant-summoning vice-president), Grimod reserved for himself the key position of secretary-for-life. In this capacity, he dictated the Jury's findings and gave them their final form: the *Almanach* frontispiece illustrating the Jury's meetings depicts the key moment at which Grimod turns in his chair to convey a verdict to the scribe-cum-court-reporter seated at a separate desk behind him.

Grimod's role in the Jury paralleled the part he played in gastronomy more generally: not necessarily the most voracious eater, he was certainly the most zealous writer. Combining the key attributes of the two characters, or two parts of Grimod's character, who had gone for the first nutritive strolls (the olfactorily and gustatorily gifted gourmand, and the literate, narrative-building narrator), the gastronomer had necessarily to be as much a writer as an eater. Five of the *Almanach*'s eight yearly illustrations therefore presented the central figure wielding neither fork nor turkey drumstick, but his other key weapons: pen and menu. The Jury's weekly meals (important though they clearly were) could not be separated, Grimod maintained, from the yearly *Almanach* that presented the permanent printed record of gustatory activities and thoughtful decisions.[78] The proof of the tasting, we might say, was in the writing.

Yet, by Grimod's own admission, the *Almanach* could offer only a highly condensed précis, the very briefest abstract, of the Jury's many findings. The perpetual secretary's complete records, those "truly fascinating texts, in which the gourmand displays his eloquence in all its profundity," were circulated only to members of the Jury and remained, by all the rules of the game, top secret, as obscured as any restaurant's kitchen.[79] Early exemplars of the laboratory-based knowledge of modern science,[80] Grimod and his fellow gourmands conducted their experiments in semi-privacy, making only their final conclusions known.

One way to understand the Jury would be to see in the printed form of the *Almanach,* and in the (selectively) open forum of the Jury's séance, an effort to prevent the sense of taste from becoming a matter of erratic individual opinion alone. Henceforth, gustatory sensation, like aesthetics, could be discussed by a public of rational equals. (As Grimod himself wrote, all gastronomers shared a common "tongue.") Grimod's Jury, from this perspective, would have been a quasi-freemasonic attempt to re-introduce men of taste to the table, and to keep the ideals of "bourgeois," potentially republican, debate alive throughout the First Empire. As some described the restaurant as a force democratizing the haute cuisine once reserved for private aristocratic gatherings, so the decisions of a representative table of taste-testers might function as the expression of a general, public culinary will.[81] The Tasting Jury, whose membership, like that of the Wednesday Society, remained largely a matter of speculation, reached its decisions in secret, such that verdicts emanated not from any one individual, who might err or stumble, but from the disembodied workings of "gastronomy" and good taste.[82]

But even as the Jury solemnly went about its own work, its very form satirized other decision-making bodies, offering Grimod the opportunity for further gibes at the Old-Regime lawyers who had stripped him of his legal title in 1786.[83] An alternative reading would reveal the Jury to be an elaborate, tongue-in-cheek charade, and Grimod, its only member. Gastronomy's foes loved to insinuate that the ever-gluttonous and fraudulent Grimod had tricked the merchants of Paris into feeding him for free.[84] Like other criticisms of the *Almanach,* the implied revelation of Grimod as "the man behind the curtain" emphasized the central role of a self-serving individual, and suggested that anonymity shrouded not justice but deceit.

Grimod often emphasized the need for gastronomic "legislation," but he also proposed and passed (with no opposition) extraordinary laws that few others would follow. As the one and only dedicated individual who would willingly determine the freshness of a turkey by sucking a finger he had just inserted deep into the bird's anus, Grimod maintained his position as the true connoisseur, as well as his reputation as a perverse eccentric.[85] Like his cautionary message about the need to use a utensil in finishing the delectable sauce prepared by following the chafing-dish recipe, Grimod's method for testing poultry freshness focused on the gastronomer's proper use of his fingers. A minor biographical detail, never mentioned in the *Almanach* but appearing in Bachaumont's account of the famous funereal supper, casts a particularly poignant light on this apparently incidental issue: Alexandre Balthasar Laurent Grimod de la

Reynière, by all accounts, had no fingers. In all these stories about fingers, about their uses, and about the troubles they might cause, Grimod—who either was born with webbed extremities, or who, as a small child, had his hands gobbled off by a ravenous pig—would prove exempt.[86] Not even fully part of the world of gourmandise, Grimod would here become its licensed fool, its jester, and its gadfly. Gourmandise, in short, gave back the sanction that the lawyers of the Old Regime had stripped from him, allowing him to practice satire with impunity. Perhaps the entire *Almanach* was but an extended practical joke, the most successful of the many mystifications for which Grimod and his circle of friends had once been well known?

Whatever the competing impulses were that motivated Grimod, reviewers and readers proved increasingly oblivious to them all. Throughout the nineteenth century, as the expanding genre of gastronomic literature disseminated the *Almanach*'s model of connoisseurship, new generations of gourmands silenced Grimod's potentially disruptive and bitter wit, even as they preserved his text's outward form and apparent ambitions. Honoré Blanc, for example, in his 1815 *Le Guide des dîneurs de Paris (The Paris Diners' Guide)*, began by discussing Balaine's Rocher de Cancale and promised that his next, larger, edition would "legitimate" more restaurants. In the 1820s, Honoré de Balzac and Horace Raisson combined under the truffled pen name "de Perigord" to write four volumes of a *Nouvelle almanach des gourmands*; Charles Monselet authored several more in the 1850s. Yet even though they depended on the original *Almanach* for much of their structure, these later works relied more on Jean Anthelme Brillat-Savarin's amiable 1826 *Physiologie du goût (Physiology of Taste)* for their tone. Whereas Grimod's text had devoured all of Paris, making the talents of clock manufacturers and tailors little more than subcategories of gastronomy, Brillat-Savarin repositioned the joys of dinner within a continuum of pleasures and pastimes, describing a sense of taste that proved eminently compatible with other social virtues. The pursuit of "fine food" stopped being a life-structuring, world-shaping obsession, and became the amusing hobby of an avuncular magistrate.

In the preface to the *Almanach*'s first volume, Grimod de la Reynière introduced the subdiscipline of "alimentary topography" as a necessary component of any gourmand's education; in 1808, the first "gastronomic map of France" appeared in print. Serving as frontispiece to Charles Louis Cadet de Gassicourt's *Cours gastronomique (A Course in Gastronomy)*, the first "carte gastronomique" redrew the map of France without regard for

Figure 10. "The Gastronomic Map of France" (detail), frontispiece of Charles Louis Cadet de Gassicourt, *A Course in Gastronomy* (1809).

contemporary military or diplomatic events.[87] While the 1807 Treaty of Tilsit and the 1808 invasion of Spain might have occasioned a scramble among other cartographers, it was thanks solely to the innovations of gourmandise that the author of this new map represented Versailles not by a palace, but by a rabbit and a partridge. On the "carte gastronomique," culinary divisions replaced political or national boundaries: gastronomy discovered the inhabitants of the Vendée to be not counter-revolutionaries, but cattle; it replaced Chartres's landmark cathedral with a pâté and substituted a nonsectarian bottle of champagne for the coronation ampoule of Reims. This vision of the map of France—like descriptions of Paris as a city of restaurants, not revolutions—stripped the table of the numerous political meanings under which it had groaned during the Revolution. The gastronomic map, that evocation of what today's Ministry of Culture calls France's "culinary patrimony," drew France as a literal Land of Cockaigne.[88] The ducks of Alençon, the pullets of Le Mans, the wines of Bordeaux—all appeared on the map like rivers or mountains, just so many "natural" features of the landscape, there for ready exploitation.

Perhaps the most telling details of the gastronomic map, though, were not the icons on the map per se, but the "Grotto of Epicure" where the map's authors and muses were honored (Figure 10). Around the entrance, inscriptions commemorated the great epicureans of past and present generations: Favart, who wrote bawdy comedies in fishwives' jargon; Saint-Evremond, soldier and critic, who contributed much to the seventeenth-century revival of Epicurean philosophy; and Henri IV, who brought France peace after the Wars of Religion, and promised a chicken in every pot. A laurel-wreath decorated harp bore witness to the most noted musical members, and a comedian's mask testified to the contributions of the playwright Armand Gouffé. Beside the mask, two more emblems completed the already crowded picture. One, a large military drum with sticks attached for marking time and keeping order, carried the name "Piis"; the other, a jester's scepter with bells and fool's motley, was inscribed "Grimod." Grimod and Piis: the gastronomic map of France was made possible by an uneasy interaction of satyr and drum major, mockery and order—the tense companionship of an unpredictable, autonomous gourmand and a malleable, sycophantish *girouette*.

7

Putting Paris on the Menu

Paris, of all places, for cheap living and for sights; for a constant round of amusement both frivolous and solid. A man may live here for almost nothing . . . But Paris for a steady English family, unless they have already formed an acquaintance in it, must be a wretched hole to live in.

JOHN M. COBBETT, *LETTERS FROM FRANCE* (1825)

Throughout the first half of the nineteenth century, the restaurant's trope was "copia"—cornucopia, to be precise. The restaurant, everyone said, was full to overflowing: full of people, full of stories, full of food. Bedazzled tourists and calm gourmets, philandering husbands and proud wedding parties, Mardi Gras revelers and reform-minded banqueters, silverware thieves and stock-exchange gamblers—all filled restaurateurs' opulent rooms. There were well-mannered old gentlemen, dandies with long black curls and champagne, parents with their children, and "deputies, and proprietors, and gentlemen of fashion, and ladies and young people, and Germans and Italians; throngs promiscuous, differing in ten thousand points, and resembling in two;—they are all hungry and they are all conversational."[1]

To satisfy that hunger, painted horns of plenty spilled their contents past the gilt frames of ornate mirrors and along the margins of four-column menus; truffled turkeys, capered turbots, roast partridges, stewed carp, and stuffed pigs' feet all hurried from seemingly inexhaustible pantries, bringing in their wake sugared peas, smothered artichokes, layered pastries, and brandied apricots; festive parties began their dinners with four dozen raw oysters, *per person,* and ended with innumerable bottles of champagne. As the English traveler and letter writer Francis Blagdon gasped in 1803, "Good heaven! . . . —Beef, dressed in eleven different ways.—Pastry, containing fish, flesh and fowl, in eleven shapes. Poultry and game, under thirty-two various forms.—Veal, amplified into twenty-two distinct articles. Mutton, confined to seventeen only. Fish, twenty-three varieties."[2] Recognizable substances such as veal, mutton, and fish proliferated in unfamiliar but enticing forms: à l'espagnol, à la poulette, à la maître-d'hôtel. To the Philadelphian John Sanderson, who traveled to the Continent because of his ill health, it was clear that in the restaurants of Paris, "Ceres has unlocked her richest treasures . . . and has poured them out with a prodigality that is unknown elsewhere. Fish of fresh, and of salt water; rare wines of home and foreign production; and as for the confectioneries, sucreries, fruiteries and charcuteries, the senses are bewildered by the infinite variety."[3] The restaurant was a space of permanent carnival, an island possession of the Land of Cockaigne, the "gourmet's Garden of Eden."[4]

Such, at least, have been the commonplace impressions shared by generations of Anglo-American tourists and legions of foreign Francophiles, as well as the great majority of culinary historians.[5] Throughout the nineteenth century, plenitude governed the Paris restaurant, defining what real restaurants offered and shaping what accounts of them could describe. For all the efforts to number that variety, the restaurant's fullness consistently surpassed enumeration, such that John Sanderson was hardly the only author to suggest that restaurants approached infinity; others wrote of "infinite choices" and "infinite nuances," or noted that "the superior Restaurateurs specify nothing."[6] Already in February 1792, Jacques Venua, restaurateur at the Grand Hôtel des Etats Généraux, had made so bold as to promise "an *infinite number* of choice entrées, side-dishes, and all that should follow."[7] Decades later, the *Physiologie du goût* asserted that restaurants made it possible for anyone and everyone "to procure, infallibly and immediately, without any more bother than that of desiring, all the delights to which taste is susceptible," and the pleasures of paraphrasing Brillat-Savarin spread that claim across volumes throughout the century.[8]

Historians have generally accepted this picture, waxing eloquent over the pleasures of nineteenth-century restaurant going. Basing their accounts on guidebooks, travelers' descriptions, and the *Almanach des gourmands,* writers as ideologically dissimilar as René Héron de Villefosse, Jean-Paul Aron, and the brothers Goncourt have compiled addresses and referrals as if they were all planning holiday excursions to the gastronomic capital of the past. While the recommendations from which they pieced together their histories had never exactly been secret—recall that the first volume of the *Almanach* sold at least twelve thousand copies, and note that these authors have nothing to say about eating in Lyons, Reims, or Dijon—their chatty collages nonetheless read as inside scoops and gossipy tabloids. Composing a phantasmatic meal from earlier authors' leftovers, gleefully recommending restaurants and pastry-shops that have long since disappeared, these walking-tour histories pick their way along a trail of textual crumbs left in the musings of spectral gourmets.[9]

All such accounts might easily lead us to the conclusion that Paris truly was the culinary capital of the nineteenth century, that restaurants like those of Balaine, Beauvilliers, and the three *frères provençaux* occupied every street corner and satisfied the cravings of every idle gourmet. Commercial statistics, too, marked Paris as the preeminent city for restaurants: in 1815, a nationwide business register noted only a handful outside Paris (four in Bordeaux, to be exact), even though nearly every city had a listing for "principal hotels and cafés."[10] Thirty-five years later, when the Minister of the Interior called for a census of food and drink sellers, he found similar results. Prefects throughout the country counted hundreds of café-keepers and thousands of bar-men: the Dordogne, east of Bordeaux, was home to 828 inns, 2661 taverns, and 404 cafés, while in the north of France, the prefect of the Somme reported 411 inns, 7089 cabarets, and 188 cafés. Their colleague in the Hérault (the region around Montpellier) counted 580 inns, 1289 taverns, and 881 cafés. Thus these departments were well provided with spaces for consumption, popular sociability, and weekend rowdiness, but, like fifty other departments across France, they had *no restaurants*.[11] Certain respondents to the Ministry's survey even made a point of crossing out the category "restaurateurs"—the local official in the Charente Inférieure, for example, who slashed through that heading in broad ink strokes, clearly had no doubt that this classification did not apply to his region (now the Charente Maritime, on the Atlantic coast near La Rochelle). For even by the middle of the nineteenth century, restaurants were still an overwhelmingly urban phenomenon, inventions of the capital and icons of its pleasures. To be conversant with the protocols, rituals, and vocabulary of restaurant going was to be quintessentially Parisian and supremely sophisticated. As late as 1875, an encyclopedic dictionary could confidently assert that "restaurants" were "for many years specific to Paris alone," and append that "even today one finds them only in large cities."[12] Clearly distinct from the many eateries and taverns that dotted the provincial landscape, restaurants became—for memoirists, travel writers, novelists, and playwrights—veritable emblems of modern Paris life.

As the restaurants of the capital became famous for their "infinite" bounty, so did the same rhetoric identify the city as home to "a thousand" restaurants. What the Rocher de Cancale was to oysters, Paris was to restaurants. When Louis Prudhomme wrote a guidebook in 1804, the former editor of the radical *Révolutions de Paris* (now turned author of less overtly polemical texts) boldly stated that Paris was home to over two thousand restaurants—an indication, no matter how wildly wrong or surprisingly accurate his arithmetic, that restaurants had already by this time become a fixture of life in the capital.[13] Yet for all that many authors readily concurred with Prudhomme's claim, the most significant change of the revolutionary decade had not really been the much-touted "birth of the restaurant," nor even its exponential growth.[14] For restaurants had, of course, first appeared in the 1760s, and the *Tableau du nouveau Palais Royal* told its readers in 1788 that "people attach singular importance to the word 'restaurateur.'"[15] Rather than witnessing the invention of the restaurant, the late 1790s saw the *death* of the term's earlier, more particular, definition: set loose from its moorings in the culture of medicalized sensibility, "restaurant" became the fashionable word used for *any* Paris eatery. Already in the 1780s, enterprising cook caterers and anxious innkeepers had begun to add the word "restaurateur" to their street signs and hence to confuse nomenclature, but most nonetheless persisted in claiming that they thereby offered two discrete services: a table d'hôte *and* individual table settings. In the years that followed, however, as political and social turmoil made shuffling names and altering titles all the more easy and advisable, eatinghouse-keepers blurred distinctions that had once seemed crucial. Some added billiard tables and dance halls to their establishments; others promised Lyonnais sausages or moved to premises with private dining rooms.[16] As the attributes separating a restaurant from an inn or a cookshop became harder and harder to identify, categorization became fluid and uncertain. Honoré Boué, though classed in the records of the Committee of General Security as a *"traiteur,"* presented himself to that committee as "Boué, *gargotier* [keeper of a cheap eating-house]" and was described by the investigating administrators as "Boué, innkeeper" (tellingly, however, no one in the period of Jacobin rigor used the word "restaurateur").[17] The Hamille family in the Palais Royal obviously hesitated over the name of their trade as well, for they eventually called their business, with both vivid physicality and some professional uncertainty, a "maison de commerce de bouche" (literally, "a house of mouth business").[18] Members of the retail food trades had a wide variety of possible titles available to them, and often combined several; La Tynna's commercial directory for 1799 reflected this trend by listing them all under the none-too-specific hyphenated category, "traiteurs-restaurateurs." (A decade later the editors relabeled the grouping as "restaurateurs-traiteurs.")[19]

Neighborhood cook-caterers in this period would have had any number of reasons to settle on the appellation "restaurateur." Some, certainly, made drastic changes to their style of service, introducing the private rooms, separate tables, and printed menus that had once so clearly distinguished restaurants from other eatinghouses: in March 1796, Jean-Baptiste Haudebourt, formerly a *traiteur* near the Tuileries, announced the opening of his new Champs-Elysées "maison de restaurateur" and advertised the advantages offered by its intimate individual dining rooms.[20] Haudebourt's strategy was hardly unique: in the late 1790s and early 1800s, the restaurant took over from the table d'hôte as the standard point of reference, as the term in comparison to which other eateries had to be categorized. One self-proclaimed "restaurateur" advertised green gardens, silver tableware, and a choice of three dishes from the menu, even as he announced that customers desiring more regular meals could simply pay forty francs each month; another promised that "notwithstanding his à-la-carte restaurant" he still offered six-course dinners for two francs twenty centimes per person in the large salon or for three francs a head in a private dining room.[21] Still providing a variety of services at many different prices—much as they had in the final years of the Old Regime—the eatinghouse-keepers of Paris all assumed the title that had once referred to purveyors of restorative bouillons alone. As surely as Jean François Véry had told the revolutionary police that he was a simple artisan *traiteur,* now his rivals told Paris that they were newfangled restaurateurs.[22] In 1804, the *Gazette de France* seconded Prudhomme's claim that Paris was currently home to 2000 restaurants—a marvelous figure indeed, until one notes that the newspaper also reported that there had been 1500 "restaurants" in the city in 1789.[23]

Though the men (and, to a much less obvious extent, the women) of the retail food trades certainly played a part in transforming Paris into a city of restaurants, their patrons performed an equally important function. From a foreign traveler's perspective in particular, it was the table d'hôte that proved increasingly rare, the restaurant that seemed strangely ubiquitous. Already in 1792, an English voyager asserted that the French capital's tables d'hôte had all but disappeared, and that the genre was only to be found in roadside inns; a decade later, the author of *A Practical Guide During a Journey from London to Paris* was only one of several Britons to append a footnote saying that the "modern appellation" *restaurateur* had completely replaced the now obsolete *traiteur.*[24] While such travelers' impressions and guidebook accounts may or may not transcribe reality accurately, they speak volumes about changing perceptions and expectations.

Even if Paris at the turn of the nineteenth century still was home to dozens of midday tables d'hôte and hundreds of nuptial-hosting caterers, visitors evidently *thought* they were seeing "restaurants," and by that meant that they were seeing something new, strange, and distinctive.

Though they said that the tables d'hôte had vanished and the innkeepers had gone bankrupt, travelogue and guidebook authors did not therefore treat restaurants as familiar or unremarkable institutions. Rather, they described them as strange by-products of political upheaval, as further evidence of the irreversible changes wrought by an epoch-making Revolution. For decades into the nineteenth century, Anglophone authors and publishers continued to italicize the words *restaurant* and *restaurateur,* marking them and their referents not only as foreign, but as untranslatably so, evidence that something had happened in France that had occurred nowhere else on the planet.[25] Francis Blagdon, who enthusiastically counted the items on Beauvilliers's menu ("Poultry and game, under thirty-two various forms.—Veal, amplified into twenty-two distinct articles," etc.), did so in order to demonstrate the recent growth of public luxuriousness, and included his description of restaurant menus in a book tellingly entitled *Paris as it Was and as it Is, Illustrative of the Effects of the Revolution.* Like many of his compatriots, Blagdon went to Paris during the brief peace of 1802–1803 to see the results of ten years of war and revolution ("traces of havock" was his phrase)—and what did he see?[26] "Restaurants."

In the first decades of the nineteenth century, American and especially British visitors identified restaurants as particularly "French" (even if there were none to be found in most of France, and many more in the rich and heavily-touristed center of Paris than in the city's outlying districts). If these observers were to penetrate the mysteries of "Frenchness"—a task made much more imperative by the apparently never-ending and largely unfathomable changes of the Revolutionary and Napoleonic eras—restaurants offered as good a starting point as anywhere else. Both a strange and confusing world, wrapped opaquely in gastronomy's rules and vocabulary, and a publicly open and available space, a bit of "daily" French life to which travelers had easy access, restaurants were the perfect mixture of the familiar and the exotic, the intimate and the extraneous. In 1814, the Englishman Stephen Weston advised his compatriots that even if they were not very interested in the French capital's artistic, scientific, or industrial accomplishments, they might still derive pleasure and benefit from a visit to its restaurants; some decades later, an American woman counseled that the restaurants of Paris "deserve[d] to be seen as a matter of curiosity, [even] by those who would not otherwise frequent them."[27] Guidebook writers, well aware that a grand restaurant's appeal was not limited to its cuisine, emphasized the uniquely national character traits to be observed there: Edward Planta's *A New Picture of Paris* (the twenty-odd editions of which guided an entire generation of Britons through the capital) urged all travelers to eat at least one meal chez Véry, not because the sole was particularly well cooked or the lobster soup exquisite, but because it afforded the opportunity to "witness and experience the very acme of French epicurism."[28] For the inquiring tourist, "epicurism" was as much something to be espied as to be enjoyed, as much a part of peculiarly French culture as well-dressed women or sober working men, Monday holidays or the Hôtel des Invalides.[29] Tourists also flocked to the Jardin des Plantes and Père Lachaise cemetery, but the pleasures of watching the elephants eat or seeing the tomb where Heloise lay, though great, did not seem to be so very revealing of French "manners and customs."

Though several guidebooks noted that it was considerably more practical for long-term visitors to contract with local cook-caterers, the capital's restaurateurs were an attraction not to be missed.[30] Filling the rooms of the city's restaurants (or, at the very least, filling the pages of their memoirs with cribbed descriptions of those restaurants), these visitors spread the rumor of gastronomic marvels to many who would never taste them. In faraway London, where no one could even smell the delicious aromas billowing from Paris's basement kitchen grates, readers inundated with what the *London Magazine* termed "these innumerable volumes of travel writing" still had time to devour four editions of Lady Morgan's hastily assembled *France* and five editions of Thomas Raffles's *Letters During a Tour of Some Parts of France . . . in the Summer of 1817,* learning from the latter of the French "fondness for publicity" and the "immensity" of Véry's menu in a single chapter.[31] From the United States there came far fewer visitors (on average, one thousand to Paris each year between 1815 and 1848, as opposed to the twelve thousand Britons who passed through the port of Calais in 1820 alone), but they too reacted to the French capital with stunned amazement and volumes of meandering, copious prose.[32]

Known beyond France via travelers' accounts, and portrayed locally by the popular theater and the newspaper press, the restaurants of Paris moved to the center of nineteenth-century descriptions of that city, assuming mythic proportions in the process. The Englishman John Barnes, who traveled throughout France in 1815, brashly claimed that in the Palais Royal alone there were "an innumerable number of restaurateurs"—but how could that well-delimited city-center park really have been home to "innumerable" restaurants?[33] Yet no matter how many (or how few) restaurants catered to Paris diners, their domain in novels, plays, press accounts, and travelers' descriptions expanded to become nearly infinite.[34] The capital's most famous restaurants were within the financial reach of only a tiny fraction of the population, but they were in the view and imagination of all.

The creation of the restaurant as an urban point of reference owed as much to this abundant literature as it did to the somewhat more limited bounty promised by larder and pantry. So frequently were restaurants portrayed and analyzed that one intrepid observer of Paris life was left to comment: "I shall have little to say about restaurants; the minor ones because they have so often been described by the adventurers of realist fiction; the great ones because everybody pretends to know more about them than anyone else."[35] Restaurants figured prominently in novels; they often provided the setting for popular plays; they were the premise for guidebooks and gastronomic manuals that instructed the unwary and the fearful on proper restaurant conduct. From the posters advertising cheap prix-fixe meals to the various instances of the more or less specialized gastronomic press; from offhand references in realist novels to the newspaper editorials that compared the July Monarchy (1830–1848) to a restaurateur's kitchen; from the volumes published by so-called epicurean singing societies to menus themselves—writing about restaurants, in all its forms, was at least as visible as restaurants themselves.

Perhaps it would be just as accurate to call the restaurant's trope simply "copia," rather than "cornucopia," after all. For while there was in the Paris menu-monde no dearth of profusion and plenty, it was not necessarily comestibles that predominated. What spilled from the French capital was not food (Paris, so said Grimod, "produces nothing"), but stories: stories about what had happened in restaurants, what could happen in restaurants, what might happen in restaurants.[36] Novelists and playwrights often set scenes in restaurants, but they just as often neglected to mention any food whatsoever, as if a restaurant's nutritive, restorative, and caloric functions were among its least significant attributes. When Balzac, in *Une fille d'Eve,* has three characters sup at Véry's, they apparently consume nothing but champagne; when Stendhal's Lucien Leuwen obeys his father's order to strike a more dashing figure around Paris, all we know is that he spends "at least two hundred francs" nightly at the Rocher de Cancale.[37]

The importance of restaurants for descriptions of Paris life preceded their integration into that life's more mundane reality. If, in the words of the *Gazette des tribunaux* (the widely read daily that from 1825 reported sensational crimes, court scenes, and legal decisions to an eager public), "everyone knows about Véry's," far fewer individuals were personally acquainted with that restaurant's interiors or had sampled the contents of its wine cellar.[38] The Restaurant Véry of the 1820s no more fed thousands of Parisians than the Bastille of the 1780s had held hundreds imprisoned (on July 14, 1789, the crowd had found seven prisoners to free), but their statistical insignificance did not prevent either from becoming a potent symbol. Even for the novelists, journalists, and playwrights who actually lived in the capital rather than merely visiting it, restaurants were not banal but exceptional. Balzac set so many scenes in the Rocher de Cancale not because dinners there were an ordinary and everyday experience for the average man about Paris, but because they were extraordinary events, the very location of which conveyed much more information than lengthy paragraphs of elaborate description.[39] For all his fabled long-windedness, Balzac never described an opulent restaurant in much detail. Instead, a nonchalant throwaway reference to chez Véry or the Rocher was enough to set the scene; if the reader did not know to what these words referred, then he or she had no illusions about Paris for Balzac to dispel. Only the Left Bank student restaurant Flicoteau's, a less familiar Paris monument, warranted pages of description.[40]

But if the novelist knew that the words "chez Véry" and "Rocher de Cancale" were talismans whose magic he could trust to work without embellishment, less skilled writers often missed that point. To the pens of traveling letter-writers eager to display trophies from their voyages, restaurants offered an especially tempting target. Véry's and the Trois Frères Provençaux were acknowledged Paris landmarks that happily did not require the classical erudition or technical learning demanded by other, more specialized, objects of curiosity. Ladies might demur when it came to recounting military parades or scientific experiments, and medical men might find their expertise of little help in analyzing medieval ruins, but both were comfortable describing restaurants. Surely no extended or specialized education could be needed to count mirrors or gape and gawk at wine lists!

In the decades following the Revolution of 1789, word of Paris's restaurants and of its newfound fascination with all things culinary spread rapidly. War and blockade made Continental tourism all but impossible between 1805 and 1815, but with Napoleon's defeat at Waterloo and the restoration of a Bourbon monarch to the French throne (in the form of Louis XVI's stunningly corpulent younger brother, Louis XVIII), foreign visitors rushed to Paris.[41] Members of the four victorious armies may have paraded through the streets and loaded art treasures onto carts, but their colleagues and commanding officers paid more memorable tribute to the one art that was inoffensive and indigenous enough to leave behind for the Parisians: gastronomy. Fattening themselves on the spoils of French defeat, the Allied armies took pâtés and truffles, as well as territories and antiquities, and while they simply reclaimed the horses of Saint Mark's, they gave hard currency for dinners and banquets.[42] As Charles Rousset's *Code parisien* told its readers, "the menus of the Vérys, the Grignons, the Beauvilliers attracted the gold that these warriors would otherwise have carried away with them."[43]

An often reprinted pair of cartoons (Figures 11 and 12) shows one of the foreign invaders before and after: in the first, a gawky Briton steps ashore under the auspices of his ship's dove of peace. Escorted by an obliging chef, he strides on spindly legs toward a nearby eatinghouse. In the next image, however, he is almost completely spherical as he leaves, pushing his stomach before him on a wheelbarrow.[44] Even the most famous military commanders found their victories intertwined with that of French cuisine: Lady Morgan's quickly published *France* included the Grimod-de-la-Reynière mansion in its inventory of Paris sights both because it was the home of a celebrated author and because it was the temporary Paris residence of the triumphant Duke of Wellington.[45]

Wheeling away gastronomy's apolitical Paris along with their protruding bellies and thinner wallets, these overwhelmingly affluent, generally politically conservative visitors happily reported that decades of social unrest had come to an end. "The French" were just as frivolous as before, but now they changed bonnet styles and fish sauces rather than forms of government. Restaurateurs, often described (not always kindly) as the aristocrats of the new France (obsequious cooks rather than upstart Corsicans), were central to these descriptions, for in their dining rooms travelers observed what they took to be the daily goings-on of French life. Taken as indicative of the capital because they were more common there than anywhere else, restaurants would soon become—like so many other characteristics that made Paris dramatically unlike the provinces (such as political radicalism or, later, the Eiffel Tower)—among the stock features in any representation of nineteenth-century France.

Menu Literacy

Early nineteenth-century travelers to Paris depicted themselves trooping to the dining rooms of Beauvilliers and the Véry brothers as dutifully as they did through the exhibits at the Jardin des Plantes or the Louvre, marveling at the mirrors in one as they wondered at the creatures and creations in the other. Not content merely to taste and observe, foreign visitors regularly felt compelled to try their hand at their own restaurant reviews—even if the ostensible subject was one that had often been de-

Figure 11. "Arrival" ("An Englishman suffering from spleen comes to be treated in France") of an English visitor to post-Napoleonic France. Note that as the skinny Briton arrives, the cook in the background is grabbing cats for the stewpan.

scribed before (perhaps because it had been), and even if they had precious little idea of what to say about it. Edward Fitzsimons, an Anglo-Irish barrister who wrote a volume of letters from the French capital in the summer of 1820, clearly felt the expectation weighing heavily upon him, for at least four of his letters promised to describe Véry's, only to apologize at their end that neither time nor space remained for such an account.[46] Postponed until one of his last missives, Fitzsimons's long-awaited description of the restaurant is in fact only a single paragraph, in which he refers hastily to its mirrors, menus, and "pyramids of peaches grouped with such taste that it is a pity to disturb them" but mentions only one article of food (the predictable turbot) and that to say that "this, too, is cheap."

Figure 12. "Departure" ("Cured by French cooking, the Englishman returns fattened to London"). Well fed on feline delicacies, the foreigner departs, but though he is plump he is hardly healthy—his once-smiling servant gags at his bad breath. At first glance, these two drawings may seem a simple tribute to French culinary supremacy, but they also offer a satirical commentary on vulgar British gluttony.

Edward Fitzsimons obviously knew that Véry's was one of the city's land-marks (described at length in innumerable travelogues, chez Véry was also immortalized by John Nixon's caricature of Madame Véry and in other cartoons, Figure 13), and though he reserved *his* breathless prose for the battlefields of Waterloo and the collections of the Jardin des Plantes, he also knew that he had to include the Palais-Royal dining room eventually.[47] The barrister gasped more convincingly at the natural-history collections: "—and then hundreds and hundreds of Fishes, Serpents, and Shells!—Never!—And yet these are not all—for next come Shells, Pet-rifactions, Butterflies,—Oh such colours!—with Birds and Quadrupeds of every kind!" but the Liverpool clergyman Thomas Raffles said almost the same about chez Véry: "Fish, flesh, and fowl—*rôti*—*bouilli*—*fricasée*—*fri-candeau*—soups—sauces—inconceivable combinations—indescribable compositions—unutterable names—'earth, air and ocean plundered of their sweets' . . ."[48]

The brevity of Edward Fitzsimons's long-deferred account of Véry's suggests the difficulties visitors encountered when they tried to treat something so easily devoured as the arts of the table as one of the fixtures of Paris life. Stymied, they often turned from modernity's quickly chang-ing kaleidoscopes in order to focus on something reassuringly fixed, tangi-ble, and old: the Pont Neuf (the "New" Bridge, built in the late sixteenth century), the Catacombs, the Rubens Marie-de-Medici cycle hanging in the Palais de Luxembourg.[49] The often reiterated, almost formulaic de-scriptions of Véry's (or, later, the Véfour) helped to set the idea of "restau-rants" in the minds of future visitors, but tourists attempting to penetrate the mysteries of restaurant life could also rely on the self-description of-fered by any restaurant itself. Of all the restaurant's distinctive features and traits, perhaps none occasioned more surprise and garnered more com-mentary—French and foreign alike—than the menu. From 1769, when the play *Arlequin restaurateur* featured a lengthy scene centered on the then-novel activity of reading a menu, until well after 1835, when the Académie Française's dictionary definition of "a restaurateur" highlighted his menu, "la carte de restaurateur" remained a source of fascination and wonder.[50]

While the restaurateur's bill emblematized past pleasures for which a price had finally to be paid, the menu—so-called because it offered a small *(menu)*, summary account of the restaurant's offerings—provided a con-venient metonym of the restaurant's delights and anxieties. Heavy with the nonreferential vocabulary of gastronomy ("potage à la Reine," after

Figure 13. It is not always remembered that Paris post-Napoleon was occupied by victorious Prussian, Russian, Austrian, and British troops. Here, two military men are escorted from that emblem of Paris's pleasures, the Restaurant Véry.

all, neither conferred a consort's crown nor produced an heir to the throne), the menu presented myriad conundrums and marked the restaurant as a space distinguished by its own language and script. One Thomas Jessop, a traveling Briton, was only expressing a commonplace when he wrote that "Epicurus himself would stand bewildered at the sight of Véry's bill of fare"; another author chose a more ominous classical comparison, terming the variety "Heliogabalan" (in reference to the notoriously debauched Roman emperor of the early third century, who championed sun worship and promoted his barber to high office). James Simpson, better known as the author of the best-selling *A Visit to Flanders and the Field of Waterloo*, perhaps put it most simply when he said that the menu of a Palais-Royal restaurant was "a curiosity for variety, and, to us, unintelligibility."[51]

Though it perplexed them and often escaped their comprehension, many travelogue writers also had reason to be glad of this new genre, for it offered the most enduring evidence of any restaurant's bounty. Sharing the name "menu" were two linked, but rarely identical, entities: the food a restaurant served and its bill of fare. The first resisted duplication and could be described only imprecisely, but the physical object called the *carte*—product not of the variable kitchen but of the reliable printing press—was infinitely reproducible and easily evoked. In order to convince readers who might otherwise scoff at the notion of any eatery so extravagant as to serve seventeen preparations of mutton or twenty-two of veal, early nineteenth-century visitors recounting their Paris adventures often simply copied a restaurant's menu, reproducing it *in full* in the text of their memoirs.[52] Unable to offer his reader fricandeau à la ravigotte, epigrammes d'agneau, or any other delicacy, Francis Blagdon instead reprinted the entire menu of chez Beauvilliers, spreading it across nine pages of his *Paris As it Was and As it Is* (1803) as the most enduring proof of that restaurant's bountiful existence.

Fixed and susceptible to mechanical reproduction, the menu also had the advantage of being more amazing than any single restaurant meal, or even a series of them, could ever be. A single patron usually ordered four or five dishes, but no one ever sampled everything listed on the menu. Its variety was far greater than the kitchen's; what may have been, in the dining room, "veal, amplified into twenty-two distinct articles," was, in the kitchen, a few cutlets, a steak, two kidneys, and three ears. From a finite number of ingredients, a chef could concoct dozens of dishes, each of which had its own name and occupied its own line on the menu. In merely quantitative terms, it was cooking methods and the names of ingredients that dominated the vocabulary of early nineteenth-century menus; dishes "in broth," "baked," or "sautéed" occupied much more space than those few that were served "à la Soubise" or "à la flamande." Yet the former could be just as difficult for a customer to understand as the latter, because these restaurant patrons were not people who often cooked or read cookbooks. If they had been, they would probably not have been half so impressed, for nearly any cookbook of the previous two centuries included many more dishes than even the longest menu. (Menon's *Science de maître d'hôtel cuisinier,* for instance, presented over seven hundred recipes, including ninety fish dishes.) The restaurant's innovation was to set this list not before a cook, but in front of a diner.[53]

First catching the eater's attention by its format alone, the restaurant menu was an impressive affair, a printed folio text often set in a leather border or affixed to a wooden frame. Little resembling the ornately calligraphed Art Nouveau menus of the Belle Epoque (which to this day provide restaurateurs with one popular model), these early menus were covered with tightly packed columns of tiny print.[54] In the first decades of the nineteenth century, the restaurant menu—by its size, typeface, and layout—resembled nothing so much as a newspaper. As one English traveler commented, "Good Heavens! the bill of fare is a printed sheet of double folio, of the size of an English newspaper. It will require at least half an hour to con over this important catalog."[55] Yet unlike the newspaper which it superficially resembled ("Someone brought me a folio sheet, printed in four columns. At first, I mistook it for the *Moniteur,* but it was, in fact, the menu"),[56] the restaurant's menu referred only to that one restaurant itself. The many different newspapers in a café (in September 1789, the owners of the Cirque du Palais Royal could have subscribed to any of more than a hundred Paris newspapers) visibly offered a variety of perspectives, while the restaurant's text was just as obviously singular and uniform. Even under regimes whose tight censorship restricted the number of periodicals available (1789 admittedly being an exceptional year in the annals of French press freedom), cafés routinely subscribed to a variety of literary publications and classified advertisements.[57] While the reader of a café newspaper learned of faraway events and fascinating new people in at least one, censored version, the uncensored menu, though of similar format and equally informative, told him only about the restaurant.

The menu ostensibly listed a restaurant's offerings, but it did so in a language that few found especially informative. The affluent, educated, and

Francophile travelers of the early nineteenth century did not often fret about their linguistic abilities, but even native speakers of French were not guaranteed to understand a menu (Figure 14). A restaurant customer could be literate and know what the words on a menu "meant" (in some senses), without knowing what they meant on the table. Literal-mindedness and an extensive vocabulary were of little help, for "menu French" was well on its way to becoming a distinct dialect. A "crapaud" was a toad and "crapaudine" was a disease of sheep, so what did that make "pigeon à la crapaudine"? An "epigramme" was a witticism, but what,

Figure 14. "Varieties of the Human Spirit": the patron, faced with the perplexing and specialized vocabulary of restaurant life, is either struggling vainly to make a good impression or is strangely sure of his desires. He orders "India rubber" and *racahout* (a sludgy, chocolate-flavored beverage made from acorn, rice, and potato flours). Note the booklet-style menu face down on the table in front of him.

asked Kotzebue, was an "epigramme d'agneau"? "Financier" had the same meaning in English and French, but in the latter language it was also the name of one of the most common sauces on an early nineteenth-century menu. The American John Sanderson may perhaps be forgiven the hyperbole of asserting that he had "perished several times of hunger" while trying to work out what "this crabbed vocabulary of French dishes" might mean.[58]

When a menu conferred titles and honors, it did so by reference to garnishes and ingredients, not to political events. Like a street map, a menu could be heavy with proper nouns ("à la Béchamel," "à la Barigoule," "sauce Robert," "à la Soubise," "à la Conty") that no longer referred to specific people; though a menu might be thick with exotic place names, they alluded to cooking methods, not military campaigns. Named after one of Napoleon's great victories, *poulet à la Marengo* did not vanish from menus after his defeat, nor did it cast a suspicion of Bonapartism over the many restaurateurs who continued serving it after the Bourbons returned to power. (Napoleon met his Waterloo in late June of 1815, but menus from Billiote, Champeaux, Chion, Ledoyen, Legacque, Hardivilliers, and the Trois Frères Provençaux all listed *à la Marengo* as one of several dozen ways that poultry could be served in the autumn of that year; the last named also mentioned *poulet à l'Austerlitz.*)[59] The Restaurant Véfour did not even open its doors until after Napoleon's exile to Saint Helena, but its menu, too, offered chicken Marengo (listed between the tarragon chicken and the chicken fricassee with truffles).[60] The titles of dishes had no immediately tangible relation with the historical moments toward which they apparently gestured: even the most skilled artillery officer could not count on his tactical knowledge to tell him whether he would prefer his poultry *à l'Austerlitz* or *à la Marengo*. Was it the crayfish garnish, the sauce of tomatoes and truffles, or the name that made chicken Marengo such a popular dish with a Russian major-general stationed in Paris during the 1815 occupation?[61] To call one's dinner after a Napoleonic victory might be to honor the Emperor, as long as he remained in charge; after his defeat, to devour one of his triumphs could be to laugh in his face.

The complicated, increasingly standardized vocabulary of gastronomy may have been largely specific to restaurants, but it was not peculiar to any one restaurant. Rather, a restaurant was a place where this language was spoken (or, at least, read). The logic of the "specialty" had begun to develop—the three Provençal "brothers" had apocryphally brought tomato sauce and *brandade* to Paris (the latter being a preparation of stewed salt cod, puréed with milk, garlic, and olive oil, traditionally eaten on Good Friday)—but aside from a few, oft-noted examples (the other, probably best-known one being the association of the Rocher de Cancale with oysters), an extraordinary uniformity characterized the menus (if not the kitchens) of Paris's restaurants.[62] In 1815, when Napoleon's final defeat meant that Paris was full of occupying armies and curious tourists, Honoré Blanc, a little-known journalist, tried to make his name and fortune by collecting menus from twenty-one major restaurants and publishing them in a little booklet, *Le Guide des dîneurs (The Diners' Guide)*. Blanc explained that "foreigners" and "people without households" could consult his guide every evening before leaving their residences, and hence would be able to plan their meals at leisure.[63] Though it may seem to have been a good idea, Blanc's plans for further editions came to nought, perhaps because foreigners and those without households could not actually learn very much from reading this group of menus. Blanc merely compiled them; he neither annotated them nor attached a glossary. Louis Tronchet recommended Blanc's book in his *Picture of Paris* (1817), but he went a step further—translating all the dish titles *he* mentioned and including only "such of the dishes as can be best understood."[64] Tronchet's strategy was a wise one, for the menus did not, on a cursory reading, provide much information that might distinguish one restaurant from another. In format and in content, they were remarkably similar. All began with "Soups" *(Potages)*, and if Véry's distinguished itself by its four-franc lobster soup, the hungry would-be diner had to page through nineteen other menus (each spread over many small pages) before finding it. (The only soup that approached it for extravagance was Beauvilliers's crayfish bisque for one and a half francs; consommé, more typically, appeared on twenty of the menus, selling in most restaurants for eight or ten sous, though at Véry's it was fifteen sous.)

With many free hours, a clever translator, and perhaps a primitive database, a reader might learn a lot from Blanc; without these, there was not much guidance to be found in *The Diners' Guide*. If an Anglophone tourist in 1815, ignorant of menu vocabulary, had wanted to know what *food* a restaurant actually served, Blanc would have been of little help. But if the reader were someone utterly ignorant of the existence of restaurants, then *The Diners' Guide* conveyed vital information. Each restaurant's menu pronounced the parameters of that restaurant, but its more important task was to mark the establishment as a "restaurant à la carte." Before restaurants could be distinguished from one another, they first had to be separated from all other eateries, and the highly standardized menu structure did just that, making a number of businesses into a specific sort of cultural institution. The shape and appearance of restaurant menus changed considerably during the nineteenth century, but each new format was shared by every place that was "a restaurant." The menu's layout consistently mimicked the century's typographic innovations: first a single large folio, packed with columns of closely printed type; then a small booklet, leather-covered and bound with silken cord; then again a single sheet, hand decorated with languid goddesses and stylized flowers. Thus, while the early menus looked like the newspapers of the Consulate and the First Empire, mid-century menus resembled fat realist novels, and those of the Belle Epoque, poster art.[65] The menu kept pace with the era's literary productions because it was itself a sort of literary product, the restaurant's most marked—and marking generic innovation. When municipal officials categorized eatinghouses for licensing purposes, they separated the à-la-carte restaurants from all the rest.[66]

The closely printed, obviously mass-produced menus of the first half of the nineteenth century made no pretense of individuality. All listed wines in a separate section at the bottom (where a newspaper would put its serialized novel); all had narrow, repeating borders of leaves, grapes, or classical emblems; many bore the words "printed by Gillé" (or whomever) in slightly larger type. Before the print-technology revolutions of the 1830s and the 1880s (not to mention the laser printers of the 1980s), menus were neither cheap to produce nor easy to alter.[67] Instead, they were printed in enormous quantities and listed everything that a restaurant might ever possibly serve, as if there were no calendar to be considered and no market to impose constraints. The restaurant menu effaced time, hinting at a seasonless world in which green peas and venison, truffles, cherries, and oysters would all be ready and ripe at once. Grimod de la Reynière's gourmand, in contrast, relied on his own calendar: one that marked January as good for game and March best for fish, but treated April as the cruelest month (only made bearable by the "distractions" of ham and the "hope" of green peas).[68] Until the growth of canning, rise of refrigeration, and development of railway networks, the marketplace had its own calendar as well, as did even the most opulent and extravagant of gourmet shops *(marchands de comestibles)*. But the restaurant *menu*—if not necessarily the restaurant itself—was resolutely anti-calendrical, seemingly marking the End of History, or at least allowing time to be set aside for the sake of dinner.

If seasons did not feature in a menu's grammar, places were very well represented. A restaurant's dependence on geography may have been most obvious in its wine list, where nearly every line (except the "vin ordinaire") named a different, distinct place, but other categories also emphasized place—oysters from Cancale, or Etretat, or Ostende; veal from Pontoise; ducks from Rouen; cheese from Chester, Holland, Glocester [*sic*], Brie; the many dishes served "Spanish style," "German style," "Provençal style." The menu collapsed time and space into the restaurant's own never-never land, in a manner that abolished the first and reified the latter. All time was present at once, and so was all space—but these comparable gestures produced very different effects. While the logic of "circulation" (vital to the restaurant in so many ways) made it possible for goods to come together from many different places, only a far eerier metaphorics of ghosts and haunting could have allowed both for the passing of time and for the simultaneous presence of things (venison, raspberries, asparagus) from different eras.[69]

Stripped of the signs of passing time, the places the menu named were, for all but the most knowledgeable of code-breakers, "out of time," eternal, without history—like the calves, ducks, and oysters they described, presumed to be naturally existing rather than socially constructed. "A la Marengo" is almost certainly not the way the Piedmontese eat their pullets, but for the non-gastronomically literate, for the many diners who had never heard the fable of the dish's origin, chicken Marengo put that village firmly "on the map." (It did not necessarily specify the village's whereabouts, but it identified it as a place—a place of tomatoes, truffles, mushrooms, and crayfish.) The words "sauce à l'italienne" on Beauvilliers's menu may not have told anyone very much about food as it was eaten in Italy, but they certainly seemed to assert—and the diner can be forgiven for having inferred—that *some* sort of sauce was common to all Italians (in this case, one of ham, herbs, and mushrooms). The cosmopolitan menu made it possible to visualize the world beyond the restaurant, to accept fondue, cod provençal, and "plumpuding" as parts of the world one properly inhabited, even as it consigned everything it did not mention to the unthinkable, inedible void.

On a regular basis, restaurateurs marked the price columns of their menus to indicate what was actually available, but this discreet, almost indiscernible notation did not distract from the menu's initial impact. Travelers looked first at the many columns of confusing words, only later noting the limitations outlined in the facing column. Nor were daily variations uniformly indicated: some guidebooks assured their readers that the handwritten codes on a menu signaled the available dishes, while others just as confidently asserted that the telltale "a" marked the nonexistent dishes.[70] By presenting the patron with a list of dishes that the restaurant did *not* serve, the menu reinforced its pretense to being a complete inventory of all possible preparations. No foods could escape the categories of "available" and "not available"; no mere plate of vegetables could resist such inexorable binary logic. The early nineteenth-century menu presented the entire world on a single sheet, beyond which dwelt nothing but the monstrous unknown. It separated that which could be wished for (even if temporarily unavailable) from the desire that had no name. Simply reading the word "bear" on one menu of the 1840s was enough to prompt a journalist to write that he felt he had already eaten it; merely putting the word on the menu brought bear into the category "food" and hence into the class of "things eaten."[71] On any given day, the menu's handwritten emendations might diminish the sense of cornucopia, but the overall effect—the fantasy of meals that might have been—was only strengthened. Tellingly, in 1843, when Jean-Antoine Arnaud patented a device that would allow restaurateurs to change their menus daily (a wooden panel with a cover hinged along one side), he found few takers.[72]

Many different factors affected the printed text's relation to what was actually served: the availability of ingredients, the popularity of certain dishes, even the provenance of the menu. In 1830, a Monsieur Pique, whose lease only allowed him to run a café, was taken to court because his menu (which listed over one hundred items) was not that of a café, but of a restaurant. In his defense, Pique protested that he had inherited the *cartes* from the previous tenant, a restaurateur, and though he circulated them to his customers, he only actually served what his lease permitted. The judge found this a persuasive argument, and Pique was allowed to continue his business.[73]

As restaurateurs (and café-keepers) copied and reused menus, they disseminated a specialized terminology to a wider and wider audience. Insofar as very similar texts, if not exactly the same dishes, were available in a wide variety of eateries, names could spread semi-independently of that to which they had once referred. With the standardization of gastronomic language, an obvious framework for comparison emerged: the guidebook writer could compare the "blanquette de veau" served by Beauvilliers to the dish of the same name prepared by the widow Edon. In the seventeenth century, no one would have thought to compare a courtier's *paupetons de pigeon* with a silk-weaver's boiled turnips, for those were obviously different foods, eaten by members of different estates. But the spread of the menu's format and language altered this perception of discrete gastronomic classes, since comparable printed texts asserted that "the same thing" was available in many different restaurants. The words "blanquette de veau" might refer to a number of varied recipes, but each of those was then susceptible to evaluation against some platonic ideal. The menu, by fixing names and titles, both addressed the fantasy and further created the expectation of identity and uniformity. Eaters were not meant to be uniform, but the eaten was, and if it was not, then differences ought to be understood and apparent, capable of being erected into a taxonomy.

Before restaurant-going became a common practice, standardization of dishes and their names had not been necessary. There was, of course, a certain degree of regularity (*boeuf à la mode* nowhere meant "hamburger served with ice cream"), and cookbooks gave titles to recipes, but medieval and early modern cookbooks were—at least in comparison to those of the late nineteenth and twentieth centuries—notoriously vague about quantities, cooking temperatures, and seasonings. Until people began eating in a number of different restaurants on a regular basis, they by and large dealt with the same cook from day to day—whether he or she was a domestic servant, a neighborhood cook-caterer, or a family member. In such conditions, the language of food could be a highly specific, unstandardized, local dialect. The restaurant, which for all its insularity was not local but cosmopolitan, put an end to those varied private languages. The first restaurants, where the weak-chested were guaranteed Breton porridge and genuine Burgundies in the heart of the Ile de France, may have saved the traveler from the unpredictably horrid fare of inns, but they also required him to know that the porridge he liked came from Brittany, and the wine his doctor recommended from Burgundy.

National Characters and National Cuisine

La carte, in French, means not only the restaurant's menu but also the city's or nation's map. If the nineteenth-century manufacture of easily reproduced and quickly recognized maps made it easier to visualize territorial nation-states (and hence facilitated accepting them as actually existing phenomena, making a hexagon into "France" and a boot into "Italy"), menus, in a strikingly similar fashion, made it possible to imagine a restaurant's limits, extent, and confines.[74] A restaurant's menu—by its layout, language, and listings—gave the restaurant an identifiable and reproducible icon. It promised the universe on a platter, but it rendered "infinity" in a comfortingly limited, easily consumed, and almost predictable format.

Pierre Jouhard, an early nineteenth-century lawyer and social commentator, delighted in restaurant menus because they rejected no desire as perverse; a menu, Jouhard exclaimed, promised satisfaction of every whim, from the Englishman's blood lust for roast beef to the Frenchman's more refined craving for a salmon fillet. In Jouhard's vision, the restaurateur's *carte* transported every customer until he was "on the land that saw his birth, seated at the table of his forefathers."[75] As surely as the restaurant offered to meet all the customer's desires, it "civilized" them by codifying them. In Jouhard's cosmopolitan restaurant (a composite description of the most famous First-Empire establishments), he imagined all the eaters craving the dishes of their own particular homelands: "Were you born in those burning lands watered by the Indus?" he asked. "Then you are offered a *carrick à l'indienne* [Indian curry]. Dwellers on the banks of the Tagus, if you care to recall the modest repasts that once sufficed to your frugal appetites, then order some *pommes à la portugaise* [Portuguese apples]."[76] For Jouhard, a restaurant's widely varied menu items corresponded on a perfect one-to-one basis with its equally disparate eaters, in a neatly atomized model where the sense of taste neither effaced boundaries nor was amenable to universalization. Rather, diet enforced national differences and made them more tangible, inscribing them in unchanging alimentary structures. Jouhard, in his comments on restaurant culture, thus intimately linked the retention (or perhaps the creation) of a nation's geopolitical boundaries with the stabilization and demarcation of gustatory desire. The Englishman had his roast, the Frenchman had his salmon: both were satisfied and—equally important—identified.

Jouhard was unquestionably working in the realm of caricature and well-established iconography when he assumed that "un énorme rostbeef" was the chosen food of any Englishman. Throughout much of the eighteenth century, British song and stereotype had marked France as a despotic land populated by skinny, effete aristocrats and haggard, starving peasants, while Great Britain was portrayed as the home of free-born liberties and beef-fed prosperity.[77] The mythologizing was hardly one-sided: French medical writers of the period often cited British militarism and proclivity to suicide as evidence for arguments about the dangers of a diet too dependent on red meat.[78] Early nineteenth-century British travelers to Paris may have yearned for a simple cut of meat and indulged in predict-

able complaints about white sauces, but even as they remained faithful to
the roast beef of Olde England they significantly altered the terms of comparison. Substituting the France of gourmets for that of rural penury, Britons emphasized French fickleness and English stability, Gallic ostentation
and English reserve. The editors of *A Collection of Modern and Contemporary Voyages* (1805) blamed "the French Revolution" for all the "absurd
alterations" apparent in French mealtimes and food habits, and though
that explanation conceals much, it still offers an important insight.[79] Fascinated, confused, and awestruck as visiting restaurant patrons routinely
were, their discovery of French cuisine was not tangential to their often
stated project of observing the effects of the Revolution on French daily
life. Expanding on those characteristics that had once been said to describe
the Court—frivolity, obsession with display, a taste for luxury and indolence—visitors concocted a new picture of "France" that was no less caricatured than the old.

John Pinkerton, a noted Scottish antiquary and historian, began his
Recollections of Paris, 1802–1805 by asserting that in that city "the events
of ages crowded into the space of a few years"; unsurprisingly, he went on
to find the local cuisine propelled by a comparable "violent propensity for
innovation."[80] His attribution of causality—not unlike Edmund Burke's
better-known conclusion that the men of 1789 had been driven solely by
the misguided rejection of tradition—made the Revolution into a particularly damning, but by no means exceptional, instance of French fickleness.
To sustain that argument, Pinkerton only needed further evidence of the
inherent French taste for meaningless change—a tendency he quickly located by drawing on fashion, urban design, and semi-erudite hearsay.
Turning to cookery and restaurants, his prose became especially weird and
patchwork-like, combining "the Wednesday club's" meetings at Le-
Gacque's restaurant, the "perpetual pot of Grands-Augustins Street," the
preserving of peas in salt, and the cooking of spinach with sugar all into a
single jumbled paragraph, as if such stylistic haste were the only way to
keep pace with the speed of change and the degree of diversity surrounding him.[81] "They are," Pinkerton concluded of the natives, "impatient of
any little inconvenience, and extremely addicted to change."[82]

Pinkerton's paragraph on peas and spinach, LeGacque and capons is be-
wilderingly varied, and one initially supposes that the national "violent
propensity for innovation" must be the glue holding these disparate elements together—until one realizes that all these topics had been addressed
in the easily-thumbed pages of the *Almanach des gourmands*. Pinkerton's

evidence for French changeability—at least in the chapters he devoted to "French Dinners," "French Taverns," and "The Luxury of Paris"—came in fact almost exclusively from Grimod's annual volumes. Reading that often mocking, sometimes morbid, always fanciful work of satire even more earnestly than its French critics had done, the Scottish antiquary treated Grimod's extraordinary commandments as if they were accounts of average French behavior.[83] The German playwright Augustus von Kotzebue—at the time a darling of literary gossip and reportage—followed a common enough practice when he too took his description of Paris dinner parties and afternoon teas directly from Grimod, but he went even a step further by assuring his reader that "he ought by no means to imagine that he would fare any worse at the houses of the better class of restaurateurs." Having first accepted Grimod's hyperbole as evidence of general French practice, Kotzebue merged this fantasy private life into the world of the Paris restaurant without a word of hesitation. British editors anthologizing Kotzebue's *Recollections* in the first volume of *A Collection of Modern and Contemporary Voyages* (1805) telescoped the perspective still further when they retained the passages lifted from Grimod but attributed them to the German author's own in-depth familiarity with Gallic behavior.[84]

Editors, journalists, and visitors were all eager to document the effects of political change on French daily life (which they expected to be considerable), but their tales of travel almost inevitably depended as much on textual citation and literary collage as on unmediated experience or firsthand observation. Travelers' descriptions, often translated from French texts rather than transcribed from Parisian "reality," produced an overall picture almost postcard-like in its uniformity. One of the few to acknowledge this, the South Carolina rice planter Francis Kinloch, wrote quite frankly to his daughter that since Paris had so often been described, "a good description of the city and its curiosities might be written by one who had never been there," and showed his familiarity with that extensive literature by referring her to several sections of John Carr's *The Stranger in France* (1803) rather than offering his own accounts of the Temple Prison or other thrilling sights.[85] Much as restaurateurs copied one another's menus, their confused and fascinated patrons depended heavily on one another's insights. Visitors writing personal correspondence or travelers keeping diaries saw nothing wrong with pinching references from other authors, and guidebook writers were even more prone to doing so. In typical fashion, the 1802 *Practical Guide During a Journey from London to Paris* combined the author's personal observations of the route

taken with material lifted from—though not attributed to—guides published in France: Villiers' year-old *Manuel du voyageur (Traveler's Hand-
book)*, for instance, provided the *Practical Guide* with its list of recommended restaurants.[86] An especially enthusiastic author, keen to pad the
pages of his guidebook, might well borrow material from several earlier
texts; the author of 1814's *Englishman's Vade Mecum at Paris* actually
stole paragraphs from *A Few Days in Paris* (1802) and the *Practical Guide*
that contradicted each other.[87]

The readily available and annually renewed *Almanach des gourmands*
was the most popular source for visitors to paraphrase, but other texts, as
long as they purported to be simple description, were mined almost as
fruitfully. Henry Redhead Yorke, who traveled to Paris in 1802, wrote in
scandalized tones about the restaurants of the Palais Royal where, he
claimed, banquets were laid like Trimalchio's feast, set in private rooms
the ceilings of which opened to reveal women "clothed like goddesses."[88]
Appalled by the "disgusting" behavior encouraged by such places, Yorke
sagely toured "this Temple of Sin" accompanied by another, married,
Englishman—but he relied on Mercier's *Le Nouveau Paris* for his description of the restaurant where scantily-clad Venuses descended from
above.[89] Though Yorke expressed understandable concern that unscrupulous authors had filled "the English public" with falsehoods about the
Palais Royal's splendor, it apparently bothered him far less to provide
those readers with a perspective skewed in the opposite direction. Like
Pinkerton reading Grimod de la Reynière as if he were an especially well-
informed but still basically representative Frenchman, Yorke found in
Mercier the "inside source" he would otherwise have sorely lacked. His
reference to Petronius's satire implicitly acknowledged the scope of literary invention, but Yorke did not question Mercier's own intentions or
agenda; instead, he contentedly concluded that if a Frenchman could be
scandalized by the Palais Royal, then outrageous it had to be. (Méot's, the
restaurant that Mercier described, was adjacent to, but not in, the Palais
Royal, and it closed in the year of Yorke's visit.)

As they attempted to explain "French" history and behavior, Yorke,
Pinkerton, and Kotzebue (along with their editors and other visitors)
tended to treat all French-language sources as equally valid and impartial.
Struggling—for reasons political, rhetorical, or personal—to identify the
key features of national difference, these authors routinely accepted the
extreme as the norm. To Napoleon's censors, the *Almanach des gourmands* revealed a single warped mind; for foreign visitors, its publication
told of the entire French psyche. Restaurants, like writing about them,

were read as vital indicators of national culture. After dining in the salon of a "superior Restaurateur," James Scott felt justified in concluding that "nothing can be more unfounded than the common idea in England, that they ['the French'] are comparatively temperate" at table; Thomas Raffles decried the Palais Royal as the home of "impurity," but he still dined at Véry's, since a meal there would add so much to his picture of "the national character"; Isaac Appleton Jewett inserted five pages on French, British, and American character traits into his travel memoirs between the paragraph in which he ordered his fish course at the Grand Vatel and its arrival, *au gratin* and "twenty-five minutes" later.[90] The examples could easily be multiplied, but the point remains the same: French "national character" revealed itself to foreign tourists in the dining rooms of Paris restaurants. "Tell me what you eat, and I will tell you who you are," wrote Brillat-Savarin in 1826 (adapting the old German adage, "Man ist, was er isst"). Visitors to France did not ask Parisians what they ate, but that did not prevent them from drawing conclusions about who they were.

Regardless of the fact that Anglo-American tourists—who often commented on how cheaply one could live in France—were among the few who could afford to frequent them regularly, the capital's most sumptuous restaurants became classic sites for meditations on national difference.[91] Restaurants provided visitors with the sustenance they physically needed, but they also offered the vague air of foreign mystery that travelers emotionally craved. Reading the menu, customers immediately realized they had traveled to a strange new world, and yet no special visa was needed. Unlike museums and libraries, which opened their doors only if tourists had letters of introduction from their government's consuls, restaurants were easy to enter—even dinner at the Rocher de Cancale hinged on no bureaucratic formality and demanded no organizational delay. Grimod de la Reynière noted that foreigners visiting Paris for Napoleon's coronation had filled the Palais Royal's restaurants to capacity, and the occupying armies of 1815 had a comparable effect, but aside from those two periods of intense activity nothing indicates that reservations were generally necessary or even that people ever had to wait for a table.[92] People went to famous restaurants as soon as they arrived in Paris, often frequenting them in the early weeks before they had been invited to dinner parties or had moved from a hotel into an apartment: a Philadelphia librarian, desirous of postponing his sightseeing until he had studied his street map and worked out "a proper grouping of objects of interest," did not hesitate to dine at the Trois Frères Provençaux on his first evening in Paris.[93]

The practices and setting of a restaurant meal—the confusion occasioned by the menu, the delay before the food arrived, the mirrors hung on two, or even three or four, walls—invited speculation. Though eager to see and dine in famous restaurants, travelers had very little to say about any meals they actually ate. Since nineteenth-century restaurant culture, like Grimod's gastronomy, endeavored to banish cookery to some faraway netherworld, an evening at Véry's (or wherever) was most often narrated as observations made while waiting for the food to arrive. ("As I had now delivered my judgment [i.e., ordered dinner], and had nothing to do . . . I enjoyed the luxury of quietly looking about me," was how Sir Francis Head introduced his tale of black-bearded Frenchmen in the Café de Paris.)[94] With their menu-waving descriptions and prose of open-mouthed astonishment, visitors to Paris helped to confirm the picture of restaurants as sites of institutionalized cornucopia, but they often refused to accept gastronomy's genre conventions: reserving their critical acumen for their fellow diners, they allowed their actual dinners to go uncommented upon. The Bostonian Samuel Topliff, typically enough, focused on the furnishings and ignored the cuisine; he began his commentary on Paris restaurants by defining them as "apartments on a large scale, lined from the ceiling nearly to the floor with looking glass plates of very large dimensions," and though he continued to comment on the tables (marble-topped, and of various sizes) and the customers (not so numerous as the mirrors made them seem), he said not a single word about the food.[95]

Unlike many of the other places that tourists visited and described, a restaurant dining room had the advantage of being an enclosed space full of people. "French" manners might also be observed at the zoo or in the cemetery, but people in the Jardin des Plantes or Père Lachaise—however interesting they might potentially be—were far too likely to simply wander away. (The deceased and the caged, far less mobile, proved generally better subjects.) Museums, churches, and theaters were more helpfully confined, but there was always something besides the local population— statues, altars, opera—to which the traveler was meant to give his or her attention. In a restaurant, by contrast, there were no antique inscriptions to decipher, no signs of Popish superstition to deplore (nor any traces of medieval devotion at which to marvel), no plot twists to follow. Until dinner arrived, a restaurant patron had "nothing to do," and to show too much attention to dinner even after its arrival was to risk being tarred with the brush of gluttony.

As Raffles, Sanderson, Jewett, Kotzebue, Pinkerton, Scott, and dozens of others tore their attention from counting entrées and puzzling over nomenclature to look at the room around them, one feature immediately struck them: they were stunned to discover that the room they were in was full of women. A lavishly dressed "belle dame au comptoir" combined the functions of household deity and human cash register to preside over the entire scene, but this later-day, commercial *salonnière* was not the only representative of her sex. Central as they were to the definitions of both eighteenth-century sensibility and nineteenth-century opulence, women had never been absent from restaurant dining rooms in Paris. Charlotte Bronson of Boston, on her Paris honeymoon, wrote copious letters to her parents and siblings in which she noted the site of every evening's meal and repeatedly assured her correspondents that eating in restaurants was "quite the common thing for ladies" and "very fashionable" among them. When she dined at the Café de Paris, there were "many ladies"; when she and her husband's niece went to Véry's, there "were numbers of ladies", at Hardy's as well, "there were many ladies besides ourselves"; indeed, as Mrs. Bronson wrote, it would seem that "we always meet numbers [of ladies] wherever we go."[96] Whether those women were as numerous or as ladylike as Mrs. Bronson was eager to persuade her family remains unknown; Emma Willard, who also visited Paris in the 1830s, was not allowed by her male traveling companions to enter a single restaurant, even though she had been told that "respectable ladies" routinely did so and she personally thought that "as I have come to see Paris, I may go to one once."[97]

Gentlemen travelers were equally struck by the women they saw in restaurants. The Briton Barnes was certain that it was because French women had none of British womanhood's "delicacy, decency, and modesty," that they so brazenly dined in public; for others, it was just as evident that well-dressed women added to a restaurant's many civilized delights.[98] Alarmed or charmed, these visitors agreed on one thing: the French, they loved to say, have restaurants because they have no homes.[99] After all, if the French had felicitous domestic arrangements waiting for them by the hearth, there would not be women (and sometimes even children) in restaurants. It was, according to an American chemistry professor, "no unusual thing" for the entire family of a "respectable tradesman or other decent citizen" to eat its meals in a restaurant; another visitor from the New World included the restaurant meals of "father, mother, and children seated together at one table" as one of the noteworthy sights of his eleven weeks in Europe.[100]

By the many women who were to be found dining in them, the restaurants of Paris "proved" what had long been suspected: domesticity was unknown in France. J. W. Cunningham, domestic chaplain to Lord Northwick, strongly cautioned Britons against making any visit to France whatsoever, and though many readers might not have agreed with the intensity of his condemnation, still they would have endorsed his assertion that "a [third] blot in the minds and manners of our continental neighbours, is the almost total disregard and disrelish for domestic pleasures and virtues . . . the word *home* is scarcely known among them."[101] Comfort was something rarely encountered in a land of public grandeur and private squalor (a point Cunningham also made with reference to heat, hot water, and mattresses—all of which necessities were far inferior in France). "If the English have no restaurants," mused the American Isaac Appleton Jewett as he waited for his turbot at the Grand Vatel, "neither have they the anti-domestic state of feelings and habits, which the existence of such establishments implies."[102]

That there should be women in restaurants was strange enough, but that they should eat, drink, laugh, and smile there was really almost unimaginable. "An American lady, when she first commences life in Paris, can scarcely reconcile herself to the idea" (wrote one of them), and yet there the women were, drinking champagne, eating their vegetables in white sauce, and even glancing in mirrors.[103] Women in restaurants who studied their reflections "with as much nonchalance as if they were in their own dressing rooms" struck James Grant (author of 1844's *Paris and its People*) as singular, but his comment—like so many others—highlights how readily visitors assumed that restaurant life was, in truth, a terrarium constructed in order to facilitate their own study of French character. For how could Grant be so certain what French ladies did "in their own dressing rooms"?

In struggling to negotiate an appropriate balance between the pleasures of people watching and the possible consequences of being observed, visitors came to the conclusion that the French behaved in restaurants as they did in their own boudoirs. Martha Amory (another newlywed American) enjoyed looking at the people reflected in the many splendid mirrors of Véry's, but she hastened to assure her mother that "at the same time you are almost as secluded from the rest as in your own home."[104] To enjoy the scene around her, Martha Amory had to insist—to her mother and quite probably to herself—that she was not actually part of it, that her privacy was preserved even as she stripped her neighbors of theirs. Safe and secure at her "own" table (as no doubt James Grant was at his), it seemed that she could see into other people's lives without their ever so much as notic-ing hers.

Thomas Raffles, pillar of Liverpool Non-conformism for over fifty years, was rendered giddily apoplectic by the whole experience. Having already commented upon the French lack of home life (he expected little better in an essentially heathen land), at Véry's he concentrated his energies on the mirrors. He noted with alarm that their "artful distribution" made it pos-sible for "the French" to "gratify their fondness for display and publicity" while avoiding "the vulgar gaze of any individual to whom they might di-rectly turn." Neither directly confrontational nor truly nonexistent, the veiled interactions of people at different tables was almost more than Raffles could stand. He decried this phenomenon, and saw all the custom-ers "engulphed in the dread abyss." Yet he too was almost seduced by its charms: his description of Véry's menu is as studded with exclamation points as anyone's, and his observation of restaurant behavior depended, of course, on those numerous, well-positioned mirrors. Faced with a situa-tion in which he was neither safely alone, nor surrounded by people he identified as like-mindedly righteous, Raffles did just what one might ex-pect from the author-editor of *The Sunday School Teachers' Monitor*: he preached. Taking his meal as the text for a sermon, Raffles ended his de-scription of Véry's with a rousing quotation from Saint Paul: "'Whose end is destruction—whose God is their belly—whose glory is their shame—who mind earthly things'" (Phil. 3:19).[105]

Thundering against the diners in Véry's salon, Raffles indicted not only the hundred-or-so patrons who happened to be there on that summer eve-ning in 1817 (many of them his fellow tourists) but, predictably, the "na-tional character" of the French. The layout and decoration of a famous restaurant's main salon made observation easy, but it was up to the authors of travelogues to conclude that what they had seen was Frenchness. Res-taurant meals excited particularly elaborate fantasies of national identity because during them it seemed that one watched the locals going about their ordinary lives. The complexities of the menu made it obvious that this was a strange institution (one that was, simply by dint of its language, *not* American or British), and yet what people—male and female—did in that place was something as very ordinary and daily as eating. Like Pinkerton assuming that Grimod de la Reynière faithfully represented "the French," other travelers concluded that the gastronomic ethos insti-tutionalized in the restaurant simply had to hold true for French society at large. That which was public—insofar as it was visible and accessible, but which was far less public in terms of its intelligibility—became, for many visitors at least, the national.

How Paris Eats

Much like the Paris Police's decree promising "freedom of pleasure," common nineteenth-century images of restaurants seemed to open festivity to all loyal citizens, and to mark the true beginnings of a national *grand couvert.* As the French ideal of nationhood inherited from the Revolution had neither ethnic nor geographical boundaries—such that anybody who adopted French principles could be part of the nation, and any "Frenchman" who rejected them was no longer French—so did this new *grand couvert* expand to accommodate all who chose to acknowledge the superiority of French cuisine. Instead of feeding the nation, it exported the idea of cookery and nationality to others.

Pleasure as well as privilege—indeed, more so than privilege—had been democratized, and gastronomy, in the words of Brillat-Savarin's *The Physiology of Taste* (1826), presided over both the banquets of kings and the soft-boiling of a single egg.[106] Taste, like sight or hearing, was henceforth an innate faculty that was only minimally linked to social rank or status. Constructing a series of "gastronomic challenges," Brillat-Savarin admitted that a rich man accustomed to truffled quails and Rhine carp would barely acknowledge the chestnut-stuffed domestic turkey so thrilling to a poor gourmet, but he also insisted that the latter's pleasures were no lesser than the former's. Although there could be no single absolute measure of good taste, it was nonetheless not limited to a specific class, profession, or income level.[107]

In a significant reworking of First-Empire gastronomy, Brillat-Savarin integrated the joys of dinner with other pleasures: conjugal love, sprightly conversation, undisturbed sleep. Grimod had banned women from the table as fickle diversions, but Brillat-Savarin welcomed them and painted a charming portrait of the fetching female gourmand with her tastefully draped napkin and eager, shining lips. Rather than sexualizing the table, Brillat named a sixth sense, "*génésique,* or physical desire" that, by perpetrating the species, served humanity as taste did the individual.[108] Alphonse Karr, writing the preface to the 1852 edition of *The Physiology of Taste,* claimed that reading Brillat-Savarin had made him realize that everybody was a gourmand about something.[109]

Making the delights of the table a part of—rather than a replacement for—the other benefits of comfortable Paris life, the *Physiology* derived material prosperity from gustatory satisfaction (rather than arguing that the former should be sacrificed to the latter). As did the utopian socialist Charles Fourier, Brillat-Savarin treated gourmandise as "the most pure of human weaknesses," since it encouraged trade, augmented tariff revenues, created jobs, and "gradually spread that spirit of fellowship which daily brings all sorts together and molds them into a single whole."[110] Wrenching Grimod's gourmand from his self-imposed isolation of notoriety, Brillat-Savarin made the well-ordered table accessible (at least as an ideal) to a far greater number of Parisians. Where Grimod had erected gastronomy as an obstacle course to deny the undeserving access to the table, Brillat-Savarin struck a somewhat more inclusive note, proudly observing that gourmandise, like coquetry, was French in origin.[111] Grimod had established gastronomy as an autonomous, mildly peculiar, realm, one undisturbed by the petty political concerns of states or individuals, but Brillat made it into a recognized, far less alarming cultural institution in which all French people were invited to participate. Restaurants were central to this expanded sense of gastronomy as part of a national inheritance, for it was—according to Brillat-Savarin—thanks to them that eating well had ceased to be the exclusive privilege of the rich and the powerful. Restaurants were nothing less than a "great boon to all citizens [*citoyens*]."[112]

Like the oft-repeated assertion that restaurants were run by the former chefs of aristocratic households, the gastronomic writing of Brillat-Savarin and his imitators contributed to a perception that restaurants were the most modern and democratic form of the *grand couvert*.[113] *L'Officier de bouche,* one of the short-lived gastronomic magazines of the 1830s, enthusiastically hailed restaurants and specialty food stores as products of the Enlightenment, and asserted that cookery, no longer an art but a science, was now actually egalitarian ["régime d'égalité"].[114] By the 1830s, it was a commonplace to say that the restaurants of Paris were "fit for kings" (though it was rarely kings who made such claims).[115] Louis Philippe, the "bourgeois monarch" brought to power by the revolution of July 1830, never did dine *en grand couvert* (instead preferring to show himself to his countrymen on umbrella-toting walks through Paris) or even at Véry's, but the splendor of the capital's restaurants was agreed upon by all.

In the words of one July-Monarchy author, simply entering a grand restaurant, finding himself surrounded by Japanese porcelains, enormous mirrors, and silk wall coverings, was enough to transform him from the "poor wretch" *(pauvre hère)* he had been on the sidewalk into "a prince, a king (king when the king is eating, you understand)."[116] Upon taking a place in a lavish and expansive dining room, any restaurant patron could fancy himself or herself royal, a resuscitated Bourbon dining at a perpetual *grand couvert*. English and American tourists delighted in calling cooks and restaurateurs the true aristocrats of a France that changed political regimes too frequently for any other titles of nobility to have lasting meaning. In such accounts, revered old restaurateurs such as Véry and Beauvilliers were hailed as commanding officers of genius, while the "beautiful lady of the countertop" who, perched on her *"throne,"* first welcomed guests and then took their money, was said to be a monarch "with more than ceremonial duties."[117] As several authors noted, the hostess in one Palais-Royal establishment was widely believed to sit upon "the veritable throne of the Viceroy of Italy"; Caroline Kirkland, an American writer who published two volumes about her European travels, did not hesitate to claim that the damask spread on her table at Trois Frères Provençaux was fine enough for royalty.[118] Vatel, that ill-fated maître d'hôtel, gave his name to a plethora of restaurants and specialty shops as if to suggest that his descendants would commit suicide not only for Louis XIV, but for a whole city of customers; a familiar figure, he was portrayed on the popular stage as well as on shop signs.[119]

Gastronomic sensibility was generalized into a national character trait, and eatinghouses (of a dozen different varieties) were suddenly noticed throughout the capital. Throughout the Restoration (1815–1830) and especially the July Monarchy (1830–1848), authors repeatedly endeavored to outline the complete gamut of Paris eateries. Small books devoted to Paris eateries, such as Honoré Blanc's *Guide des dîneurs de Paris* (1815) or the anonymous *Promenade gastronomique dans Paris par un amateur* (1833) adopted some of the features of Grimod de la Reynière's gourmet strolls, but they never bestowed comparable notoriety on their authors.[120] Instead, these obscure or even nameless authors conferred fame and archetypal status not on themselves, but on the objects of their study. Gastronomy, now the product not of a single, consuming celebrity, but of a faceless Everyman, was no longer marginalized as a perverse aberration or a complicated practical joke.

Slowly constructing a "physiology" of Paris restaurants, urban taxonomists offered descriptions, hints, and anecdotes—all for the benefit of the newly arrived, the easily confused, and the generally ignorant.[121] No single volume entitled *The Physiology of the Restaurant* appeared; instead, countless works broached the topic. Multi-volume compendia of Paris life, from the realist fiction of Balzac's *Comédie humaine* to the fictionalized reality of *Paris, ou le Livre de Cent-et-un,* contributed their part to the description, creation, and classification of restaurant culture, while the illustrated press regularly ran series of images showing "how people in Paris dine" and other dailies were littered with references to the same subject.[122] In 1842, the playwright, adventurer, and artist Jacques Arago published his study entitled *How Paris Dines;* the following year, it was the ultra-royalist daily, *La France,* which promised to "examine the alimentary system of each class."[123] Yet the topic was far from exhausted, and the following years saw the publication of Victor Bouton's *Eating in Paris* (1845) and then of Eugène Briffault's *Paris Eats* (1846). A play such as 1843's popular vaudeville, *Les Cuisines parisiennes,* even presented the whole spectrum on stage. In a series of tableaux ("trois services et six plats"), *Les Cuisines parisiennes* moved from a seamstress's garret and a porter's lodge to the kitchens at the Invalides, a market crossroads, the kitchen of a cheap *gargote,* and the elegantly decorated salon of a proper restaurant.[124]

Grimod's "nourishing strolls" had taken his readers to only the best addresses, and Brillat-Savarin had reminisced about turkey hunting in New England, but the typologies of the 1830s and 1840s introduced their readers to the full range of Paris's public eatinghouses, from the King of Beefsteak to the Queen of the Fork. As one inventory put it, "Today there are restaurateurs for all classes of society: princes, dukes, marquises, barons, generals, deputies, men of letters, judges, lawyers, bankers, stock-jobbers, gamblers, employees, merchants, students, and even for poor retirees; from the dinner for a 40-franc gold piece to the one for the modest sum of 1 franc 50 centimes."[125] Attempting to limit the term "restaurant" exclusively to those businesses with menus, mirrors, and waiter service, chroniclers of Paris's eating habits were careful to distinguish between the "dîner à la pêche" (literally, fishing for one's dinner, in which patrons attempted to catch choice morsels submerged in a soup cauldron) and the "dîner à la seringue" (in which a syringe was used to siphon contents from the cooking pot into the diner's bowl—and back again, if the patron did not pay immediately).[126] There were, by all accounts, dinners to be had for four sous and eight sous, two francs and forty francs. Cheap establishments frequented by workers were not called "restaurants" but *gargotes;* if music and dancing were added to the menu, the *gargote* became, strictly speaking, a *guinguette.*[127]

Members of the legal professions were quick to join this classificatory frenzy, with the result that the hierarchies elucidated in guidebooks were simultaneously being codified by the law courts. As tourists' manuals and scribblers' descriptions tried to make sense of the hybrid "café-restaurant," so too did a jury, deliberating in November 1830 on the pressing question, "If a café-keeper serves hot lunches, is he actually a restaurateur?"[128] When the author of *The Physiology of Paris Cafés* confined his discussion of *estaminets* or so-called "Dutch" cafés where smoking was allowed to a separate chapter, thus carefully marking the distance between the *estaminet*'s "savage, rakish air" and the more refined pleasures of the true café, he paralleled a Paris court's decision that if a lease permitted a tenant to operate a café-restaurant, that did not mean he could allow smoking on those premises, for smoking would transform his business into an *estaminet*.[129] The typologies constructed by the physiology-minded (who eagerly pursued whatever new subspecies they could find, or imagine, for the sake of filling pages and bemusing readers) and those confirmed by the courts overlapped with and reinforced each other.

With their façades visible on some of Paris's most traveled boulevards, their names appearing regularly in the press, and their dining rooms nominally open to all, a handful of famous restaurants monopolized most discussions and established a model that was eagerly mimicked (or parodied, some said) by dozens of lesser businesses. There was only one Restaurant Véry (at least after 1817, when the brothers' second restaurant was demolished in order to build part of the rue de Rivoli) and only a single Rocher de Cancale, but other establishments imitated their names, proclaiming themselves the *Petit* Véry or the Rocher de *Cantale*. Journalists, meanwhile, quickly got in the habit of referring to a nameless or generic eatery as "some Véfour at the city gates" or "some Véry of the suburbs."[130]

The physiologies and guidebooks, the plays about cooks and kitchens, the networks of rumor, lore, and myth in which these were all embedded: all of this apparently bears witness to an intense, generalized obsession with food and cuisine. Urban renewal, it was joked, proceeded on an à-la-carte basis ("a medium rare sidewalk and a neighborhood *aux fines herbes*"), and a circus impresario was almost certainly serious when he advertised the performances of his "Gastronomer Horse."[131] These themes so thoroughly pervade French print culture of the 1820s through the 1840s that one can be forgiven for taking them for granted, or accepting them as indicators of French culinary exceptionalism. For all that they were repeatedly elaborated upon, these themes also seem to "go without saying," to be what one would expect of "the French." Working within this set of assumptions, the noted French historian Pascal Ory has been content to write, "This nation does not have a normal relation to food."[132] But was it really the food that attracted people to restaurants?

8

Hiding in Restaurants

As soon as you enter a restaurant, if your face inspires even the slightest confidence, there is the restaurateur ready to offer you his menu's limitless pleasures. For you, his fires light, his turnspit turns, his wine cellar opens, and you—you sit calmly by, enjoying the products of so much bother, all of which are trustingly brought to you on silver plates. And then what happens? Just as you are beginning to digest your dinner, you suddenly notice (in truth or fiction) that you have forgotten your wallet! What recourse does the poor restaurateur have? Will he drag you through the courts, exercise the full range of his legal rights? Will he have you hauled off to jail—you! a man who has dined as the best of men dine?!

GAZETTE DES TRIBUNAUX, FEBRUARY 3, 1839

During the late fall and early winter of 1832–33, audiences at Paris's Théâtre du Vaudeville roared with laughter at the antics of Xavier and Duvert's new comedy, *Les Cabinets particuliers*. Though the play was dismissed by the stuffy *Journal des débats* as a performance only suitable for the festive, world-turned-upside-down celebrations of Carnival, it was performed daily from late October through January, delighting audiences with its depiction of the confusion and deception found in a Paris restaurant.[1] The play opens with a stage-setting scene in which a restaurateur (Morin) and his staff put the final touches to their menu and dining-room decorations. Then a young couple enter the restaurant, slipping quickly into the private room they have requested. They are closely followed by two men, one of whom (Gavet) insists that he is pursuing the couple because the woman is his wife. He demands that the restaurateur tell him which *cabinet* she has entered, but Morin refuses, pleading that his restaurant is so large that he cannot know all his customers and explaining that "a restaurateur must be discreet." The woman in the *cabinet* then reveals herself to be Madame Gavet; scolding her husband for his groundless jealousy, she proposes that they enter another room for a private discussion. Just as they open the next door, a man cries from the first balcony that he, "Jacquard, manufacturer of phosphorous matches," is the real-life husband of the actress playing Madame Gavet, and that he refuses to let

207

her enter the "cabinet" with the handsome young actor playing the part of "Gavet." Throughout a series of complicated plot twists, "Jacquard" sometimes demands to play the part of "Gavet" and, at other moments, happily relinquishes the part to the other actor. Confusions of identity abound: the "man" originally accompanying Madame Gavet is revealed to be a cross-dressed woman; the actor playing Gavet's uncle leaves the stage to return in his "real-life" role as the theater manager; Gavet demands to see Madame Gavet and instead receives a menu. So numerous and convoluted are the plot permutations that it is hardly surprising that one reviewer simply abandoned his effort at synopsis.[2]

This marital farce of disguise and concealment unmistakably takes place in a restaurant—in the opening scene, several waiters dance with menus as they sing about "fresh fish and vegetables." Yet no food ever appears, or is even ordered. Twice, in fact, his customers bluntly tell the perplexed restaurateur that they do not want anything to eat. In the eyes of the restaurateur (and in the words of almost any dictionary definition), a restaurant exists to provide meals, but for the authors of the play and the audience at the Vaudeville, a restaurant could also serve other functions, as a space for illicit rendezvous of all descriptions (Figure 15).

If foreign writers saw restaurants as proof that Parisians lived in public, many Parisians simply saw restaurants providing the privacy they could not get "at home." Private rooms for small groups had characterized restaurants since before the Revolution. Some larger inns and taverns were also known to have private rooms, but cafés, those other new eighteenth-century urban spaces, most definitely did not. When Mercier, writing in 1798, bemoaned the spread of restaurants, he identified the trend by saying that everywhere he looked, sign painters were drawing hams and writing those fateful words: "private rooms."[3] Well into the nineteenth century, *cabinets particuliers* remained one of the most distinctive features of any place that contemporaries would have termed "a restaurant" (as opposed to an inn, cabaret, café, dive [*gargote*], or dance hall). Legal decisions, popular theater, and fictional accounts all contributed to making private rooms as central as the menu to an eatery's definition as a restaurant.[4] It was no coincidence that à-la-carte restaurants were the ones to have cabinets: like a menu, private rooms lured and enticed patrons with the promise of unknown worlds of delight, hinting at communication between two realms while at the same time separating and defining them. Much as a menu purported to be a window into the kitchen, even as it obscured the reality of that other world, so the cabinet's door marked a threshold across which only few would pass.

Foreign visitors, who insisted that "the French" were so lacking in decency as to take most of their meals in public, rarely had much to say about a restaurant's cabinets. After all, having their meals in private rooms deprived tourists of the opportunity to observe anyone but their all-too-familiar traveling companions. Martha Amory, a honeymooning American of the 1820s, dined with her new spouse in one of the intimate private rooms of the Trois Frères Provençaux, but she did not find it a very "novel" experience and wrote to her mother that she far preferred the main salon at Véry's "as the number of people was greater and of course more amusing."[5] Guidebook writers, too, tended to downplay the attrac-

Figure 15. "A private room, please. Dinner in one hour." This couple are in a restaurant, but they are in no hurry to eat. Can there be any doubt how they will spend the intervening time?

tions of dining in a private room: the author of an English-language guidebook published in Paris in 1842 may have directed his readers to a variety of different-sized cabinets in the Maison d'Or—where he said any number of people, be they two or twenty, could "always imagine themselves at home"—but he knew that Anglophones did not go to Paris to be "at home" and so also recommended the main dining room, which was made interesting by "the variety of visitors by whom it is frequented."[6]

A cabinet, then, was a very different sort of space from the main dining room of a nineteenth- (or twentieth-) century restaurant. Whereas the grand salon was ornately decorated, a typical restaurant cabinet was adequately, but simply, furnished: a mirror, a table, and several chairs were the usual complement, along with curtains for the windows and door and perhaps some fireplace tools.[7] The size and number of an establishment's cabinets varied from restaurant to restaurant, and often contributed little to its reputation with gastronomers or tourists. A comparison of notaries' inventories of two restaurants in 1810–1811 shows that in the more rustic setting of the riverbank Gros-Caillou district, where Parisians might go for a day's pleasure outing, Antoine Jary's "Ecu de France" had ten quite sizable rooms, each furnished with two to six small, nondescript tables and four to fifteen inexpensive chairs (cherrywood, with woven-straw seats), while Jacques Christophe Naudet's much more famous Palais-Royal restaurant (known for its two grand salons lavishly decorated with mirrors and gilding) had only four third-floor cabinets, each of those as modestly furnished as the ones chez Jary.[8] Situated along hallways or stairwells, cabinets abutted other cabinets or perhaps a billiard room, but they were generally far removed from the main dining room. A number of restaurants even had two separate entrances, such that patrons on their way to the cabinets could avoid the salon completely.[9]

A restaurant's *cabinets particuliers* notoriously concealed as much as its main dining room made visible. The perfect place for any sort of vaguely sneaky endeavor—whether a thieves' colloquy, a secret society's conspiracy, or a desperate student's suicide—restaurant private rooms were most intimately associated with tales of seductive food and seducible women.[10] A dense web of nineteenth-century lore, legend, and popular imagery identified restaurant cabinets with honor led astray or laid aside. Even a virtuous woman ("if there is such a thing") was said to be sure to lower her resistance once lured into one of these "public boudoirs."[11] The simian caricature of bourgeois greed, Monsieur Mayeux, was depicted by artists in a variety of settings, but he was perhaps at his most repulsive when Traviès showed him ushering a round-cheeked innocent into a restaurant's clearly labeled *cabinet particulier* (Figure 16).[12] Calling for truffles—notorious for both their cost and their aphrodisiac powers—Monsieur Mayeux comes lurching into the room while the young woman he escorts looks about expectantly, her curiosity piqued by the fine establishment to which she has been led. Traviès's satire may be especially barbed (note the sign),

Figure 16. "Waiter, in God's name bring some truffles . . . like it was raining truffles." The tidy furnishings of this restaurant's private room, the large mirror on the back wall, the anticipated "rain of truffles"—these may all suggest the finest that Paris has to offer, but the sign beside the door asks patrons not to wipe their boots on the curtains or tablecloths.

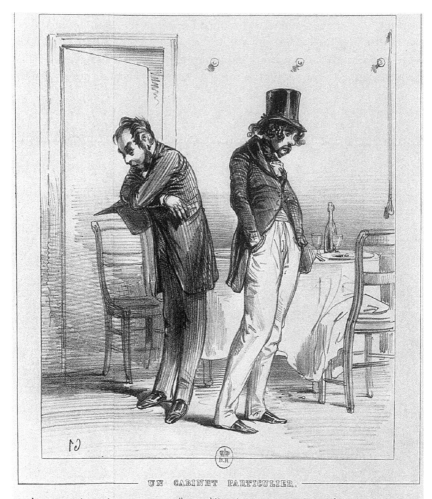

UN CABINET PARTICULIER.

Le garçon a dit un chapeau rose, un voile, un châle noir....... c'était ma Femme, il n'y a pas de doute.....
mais avec qui ?... voilà !... le billet n'a pas de signature... nous sommes arrivés trop tard !....
Anatole! vous qui êtes notre ami depuis si longtemps vous seriez-vous douté de cela ?..... une femme qui a l'air
d'une sainte !..... soyez jaloux, on vous honnit; soyez confiant on ..... ah ! nous sommes toujours dupés !
(Anatole !_oui, nous sommes dupés !

Figure 17. One of Gavarni's many scenes of a restaurant cabinet's interior, this one from the series "A Woman's Ruses." The caption intimates that the husband may be doubly duped—Anatole, to whom he bemoans his cuckoldry, is almost certainly his wife's lover (or one of them)—but he is not so stupid as to ignore the significance of his spouse having been seen in a *cabinet particulier.* There is no woman in the room, but merely her having been there is grounds enough for a conviction.

but his depiction was hardly unusual. Gavarni, in particular, returned to the scene of restaurant private rooms again and again (Figure 17), as he hinted at the parameters of sexual license during the July Monarchy.[13] Nor was Xavier and Duvert's farce the only one to put the private spaces of restaurants on stage; numerous vaudeville productions made use of the convenient device afforded by a restaurant's providing multiple "private" rooms under one widely accessible roof. Transposing comedies that Beaumarchais might have set in an aristocratic household into the anonymous comfort of some Paris establishment, nineteenth-century playwrights from Scribe to Labiche contributed to making privacy a central feature of the restaurant world's public image.[14]

The debauchery often associated with restaurant cabinets may have led some moralists to denounce them as threats to familial decency and hence, by analogy, to French morals more generally, but they were most often understood—like prostitution—to provide polite male society with one of its necessary safety valves.[15] Home to drunken debauches, demimonde scandals, and dastardly schemes, restaurants were also the site of innumerable ordinary dinners. Yet, in many ways, the privacy provided by a restaurant cabinet was less like that of a family dining room (a reception space meant to impress) than that of a bedroom. Since a married woman could charge her husband with adultery only if he actually housed his mistress in their home, restaurant cabinets legally provided philandering (male) spouses with homes away from home.[16] An ambiguous but widely acknowledged loophole within nineteenth-century moralizing paternalism, the privacy that restaurants permitted was one of their most distinctive features.

The dinner table's drunken and ephemeral camaraderie seemed to grant a certain license, and people were imagined to say and do things in a restaurant that they would not (and could not) do elsewhere. It was, of course, precisely this possibility that had worried Barère and other Revolutionary antagonists of table-based sociability, but for later "post-gastronomic" regimes, this same quality made restaurants reassuringly unthreatening. Marked as part of the after-work world of pleasure and festivity, restaurant meals played a central role in rumors of modern prosperity and pleasure. Everything—from the voluminous wine lists and invisible pantries to the smells emanating from a restaurant kitchen's street-level grates—alluded to the copious successes and inevitable progress of modern urban life.

The affluent and amorous were hardly the only people to frequent Paris restaurants, but they lent an air of mildly risqué respectability to all others who did so. In the post-Revolutionary period, the Paris police, though obsessed with plots, conspiracies, and assassination attempts, rarely looked for them through a *cabinet particulier*'s curtained window. Unlike cafés, which were haunted by police informants, restaurants went largely unsupervised. It was, after all, far less expensive to send a spy into a café, where he could sit over a single demitasse for several hours, than to buy him dinner in Beauvilliers's restaurant.[17] (Ne'er-do-wells, agitators, and vagrants were no doubt equally aware of the comparative cheapness of cafés.) Police spies and curious tourists could assimilate easily into the crowds of a carnival ball or a theater, but they had a far more difficult time insinuating themselves unnoticed into a restaurant's private dining room. As early as 1795–1796, two police spies who eavesdropped in a café did not see fit to follow their suspects into a restaurant; during the same period, two supposed accomplices to one of the Revolution's most horrible mass murders, the Nantes drownings, were hounded and heckled from a Palais Royal café, but they were allowed to dine in a nearby restaurant quite calmly.[18]

Restaurant cabinets may have been targeted as potential sites of conspiracy during much of the early 1790s,[19] but by the end of that decade they had come to be much more closely associated with ludic and lyrical outpourings of inoffensive, tipsy wit. Singing societies with names such as the "Vaudeville Dinners" or "Momus's Suppers" (the latter a reference to the Greek god of ridicule) guaranteed that the stereotypical restaurant banqueters of the nineteenth century would all be minor *bons vivants* and generally jolly good fellows.[20] Orchestrated by a few dozen men—most of whom were much like police commissioner A. A. Piis in combining the habit of spontaneous and prolific songwriting with careers in drama, journalism, and administration—these groups met monthly in restaurant private rooms to improvise songs and drink to excess. After the meal, competitive ditty composing continued late into the night, with members drawing topics at random. (Though many titles, such as "Triangles" and "Squares," invited treatments that were patently absurd, songs concerning the table were also common.) Mildly agonistic and overwhelmingly male (serving a vaguely military function in one of the First Empire's few civilian settings), these singing societies were vehemently nonpolitical in their content and roughly egalitarian in their form. They prohibited religion and politics from their songs and conversations; their rhyming statutes specified that each member should pay his own way. Their dinners supposedly drew large crowds of eavesdroppers into a restaurant's other rooms and under its open windows, but singing-society conviviality was as much aggressively promoted as it was serendipitously overheard: the societies published monthly songbooks and quickly made their private and ephemeral improvisations about "Cousins," "Mussels," and "Wells" (to take just three topics from one month's dozen) into a polished and public product.[21] Since many of the men involved were also journalists and/or press censors, each volume was then widely reviewed in the nearly eventless dailies of the Consulate and First Empire—further spreading the idea that restaurant cabinets were primarily frequented by clever men who drank champagne and sang witty songs.[22]

By the first decade of the nineteenth century, merriment had been fully established as a by-product of restaurant life. Along with the "girls" and gambling halls of the Palais Royal, restaurant *cabinets particuliers* appeared as typical features in any inventory of the French capital's slightly lurid, but otherwise basically lawful, attractions. As a space of permanent Carnival, restaurants were part of the status quo. They were the "refuge of erotic gastronomy," sanctuaries into which people entered two by two "like the animals on Noah's ark."[23] A government official in 1824 noted "the well-known fact" that restaurant cabinets were "at the very least, theaters of 'gallantry,'" and no one ever disputed this point or really did anything about it.[24] Theaters were closely policed, brothels were often reorganized, and public balls were made to contribute a percentage of their profits to relief for the poor, but restaurant cabinets, though presenting at least as great a threat to public morality, were protected by law.[25]

Though winking accounts of private-room shenanigans were far more licentious than guidebook descriptions of dining-room splendor, they still supported the notion that restaurants were among the least of the capital's dangers. A grand restaurant presented a series of hurdles, but those were for the individual to negotiate—how a young woman was to maintain her virtue, or the gastronomically ignorant to order a tasteful dinner. Restaurants may have been potentially threatening to personal solvency or eternal salvation, but they posed no overt danger to the municipality or the state. The Paris Prefect of Police wrote in his daily report for February 13, 1839, "we believe the old adage, 'when the people are having fun, they are not plotting' [quand le peuple s'amuse, il ne conspire pas]," and it was this attitude that underlay most official utterances and assumptions about restaurant life.[26] Restaurant conviviality was that of lawful bacchanalia, not illicit conspiracy; the *liberté* found at a restaurant table came from drunkenness, gourmandizing, and bawdy revelry, not from political freedoms and republican brotherhood. Unlike the wedding parties with which the eighteenth-century *traiteur* had been so closely identified, the unions associated with restaurants could easily be treated as illegitimate and fleeting, tainted by the aura of theatricality that surrounded so much of what was said about restaurants. It is not surprising, then, that the repressive regimes of the Restoration and the July Monarchy, which outlawed nearly every other form of meeting or association, did not touch the table, the private meeting-place of happy individuals.

The Many Uses of Public Privacy

On New Year's day, 1833, as audiences at the Vaudeville attempted to follow the twists and turns of *Les Cabinets particuliers,* Charles Philipon's new satirical daily, *Le Charivari* (soon to be the model for the English *Punch*), presented its readers with two pictures. The first was Grandville and Forest's "La Bascule" ("The Seesaw"): a child's toy remade as a political teeter-totter with a pear—the already standard caricatural representation of King Louis Philippe—at the fulcrum.[27] As monarchy rose high into the air, liberty fell to the ground. The implications were clear: Louis Philippe, the putatively constitutional ruler of France since the July Revolution of 1830, was actually augmenting his own monarchial privileges at the cost of his people's liberties. As a counterweight to this harsh criticism of the King, the journal offered "by contrast . . . a simple and true picture": the much more anodyne "Manière dont les jeunes gens font leur droit à Paris" ("How Young People in Paris Study Law," Figure 18). Despite its title, the second scene features neither solemn magistrates nor dusty tomes. Instead, it shows a restaurant scene of chaotic merriment and tipsy debauch: six young people seated at a table in a private room, the floor around them littered with broken bottles, empty dishes, and crumpled napkins. Two share a fond embrace, three others hold their glasses high in a sloppily happy toast, and the last is about to tumble drunkenly from his chair (as he reaches for his napkin). To the rear, a waiter enters the room, bearing aloft a large bowl of steaming punch. It is a perfectly ordinary scene of restaurant life, incorporating many of the menu-monde's icons: the waiter, the broken glasses and empty plates, the sudden outpourings of affection.

"How Young People in Paris Study Law" may have shown a private party, but it still depicted the public face of the restaurant world. Though the image was a "backstage" view of the world of law and learning, and an ironic glance at a supposedly meritocratic educational system, it offered no such critique of the restaurant. As such, it was one among hundreds of instances of what we might call the restaurant's "alibi," its public, widely accepted purpose: to provide, in addition to food and wine, a private place for drunken merriment and irresponsible youthful frivolity. Creating, in effect, its own seesaw of images, *Le Charivari* offset Grandville and Forest's political rendering of a child's diversion with a second illustration of adults at play.

Figure 18. "How Young People in Paris Study Law." This lithograph from the pages of *Le Charivari* (January 1, 1833) was one of many to identify restaurant frivolity as a key component of carefree student life. Note the kissing couple on the right: whether the embracing figures are two men, or whether one of them is a cross-dressed woman, something illicit is almost certainly happening here.

Merrymaking and satire were juxtaposed, but to what end? On the one hand, *Le Charivari's* text clearly stated that the two pictures were unrelated, implying that inebriated revelry in a restaurant—though perhaps not the most conscientious method of studying for a future career—was nevertheless hardly a form of political activity. Restaurant life, in other words, was an autonomous sphere, a realm of holiday unaffected by the political and social restrictions imposed by the increasingly repressive July Monarchy. Yet in publishing the two images together, *Le Charivari* also implied a definite relationship between them, inextricably linking the monarchy's renewed rise with punch-drinking revelers—even if they were tied together "only" as antonyms.

By the time that Philipon published "La Bascule" and "How Young People in Paris Study Law," restaurants certainly had something like their own culture; they clearly had their own setpieces, scripts, and props. Every Parisian needed to know how to eat in a restaurant, but the requisite knowledge was neither innate nor spontaneous nor universally available. Dozens of accounts identified restaurants as a dangerous and baffling institution, demanding their own encyclopedias and special varieties of *savoir-vivre.*[28] "In Paris, nothing is so easy as eating dinner," wrote the novelist Paul de Kock as he briefly described the city's taverns, cabarets, and caterers. But when he turned his attention to restaurants per se, then suddenly de Kock was far less sanguine and dinner much more complicated. "You must know how to order your dinner," he instructed his readers. "It is not enough to have something [in this case, money], you must know how to use it."[29] Specific to restaurants was the gastronomic knowledge that would enable eaters to enjoy as well as to purchase. According to the self-perpetuating claims of gastronomic literature, the acquisition of this wisdom would require patient study. In the words of the *Nouvel almanach des gourmands,* "there can be no question, it is a difficult business, a science of whose principles most people are utterly ignorant . . . to eat dinner in a restaurant is a real battle."[30]

The relation of this specialized restaurant culture—the world of culinary expertise, fruit pyramids, and tantalized appetites—to the other networks of political, social, and cultural activity within the city was far from fixed. For several decades, "No politics spoken here!" had been—at least officially—the motto of all well-appointed dining rooms.[31] Grimod de la Reynière had explicitly banned political conversation from the gastronomer's table and even enjoined against the singing of patriotic songs (which he termed "chants de cannibales"—music for an undiscrimi-

nating group of eaters indeed).[32] His successors had been equally ada-
mant: the authors of the *Nouvel almanach des gourmands* (1827) noted
that "gourmandizing, like gold, has no political opinions" and praised
the Revolution's fraternal meals for having provided respite from tribu-
nals, pamphlets, and bitter debate.[33] The descriptions of restaurant life
so popular throughout the Restoration and July Monarchy were, to all
appearances, equally devoid of political import. Presenting the city as
a space of dietary idiosyncrasies, the many texts and images describing
"how Paris eats" portrayed difference in terms that were predominantly
ethnographic. They promised to take readers on voyages to "another
world," to places where people ate cats or worshipped the great god
Rosbif.[34] Balzac's sometime collaborator, Horace Raisson, maintained
that "however many discoveries one makes, there will always be unknown lands [*des terres inconnues*] in the world of restaurants";[35] Arago's
How Paris Dines was the sister volume to his *Comme on dîne partout*,
which told tales of Chinese banquets, scrawny Hottentots, and obese
"Sandwichians."[36] Treating culinary differences as local, isolated phenomena rather than as social patterns or trends, the ethnologies so characteristic of these tableaux rendered the once powerful rhetoric of fat and lean
obsolete. Like a grand restaurant's menu, Paris seemingly catered to all
tastes.

The great variety characteristic of Paris eateries exerted a powerful fascination over novelists and journalists, who returned repeatedly to the question of "how Paris eats." The habits and preferences they described could
not, however, be those of actual individuals, for the city was made up of far
too many people. Between 1800 and 1850, the population of Paris quin-
tupled (growing from 500,000 to two and a half million), and yet the clientele of any given eatery was, in all this literature, implicitly a constant.
Individual restaurants were presented not as "friends of all the world," but
as socially embedded and fixed locales. Students frequented restaurants
in the Latin Quarter where they were served tough steaks and sour wine;
dandies and rakes were to be found quaffing champagne at the Café
de Paris; the Maison Dorée was full of snuggling couples: in all instances,
it was the patrons as much as the food that made a restaurant into a landmark.[37]

Mapping Paris's restaurants, the authors of the 1830s and 1840s were
also mapping the capital's population. In every case, restaurant patrons
were significant not as individuals but as social types (Figures 19 and 20).
The main dining room of any restaurant was nominally open to all, but

nineteenth-century typologies overlooked this formal accessibility in order to operate with assumptions that resembled the arguments laid forth by Nicolas Berger's lawyer back in 1786. They argued that the food a restaurant served would reliably indicate the social status of its patrons, that a perceptible and substantial chasm separated the clientele of the Grand Véfour from that of a 40-sous prix fixe, the Vendanges de Bourgogne, or Flicoteau's. In a period of rapid social change and dislocation, accounts of the restaurant world's intricacies seemed to offer a stable picture of social

Figure 19. This drawing and Figure 20 depict two cases of "le quart d'heure de Rabelais." For this diner, forty francs is not too much.

hierarchy. Yet the very structure of their descriptions made it obvious that restaurants were public spaces open to all and sundry—if each was really specific to one class of people alone, then how did a single author-observer gain entrance to so many of them?

The generalization of restaurant-style service that had made restaurants into one of the institutions of Paris life and into a popular topos for novelists, playwrights, and "physiologists" had also marked the demise of restaurant culture as a viable marker of specific sensibilities. As the word "restaurateur" expanded to cover an entire spectrum of eatinghouse-keepers,

Figure 20. For this diner, fifteen francs is more than he can afford.

and "restaurants" of all sorts became notable, it was increasingly difficult to link restaurant-going, as a general set of practices, to any particular social position. Numerous writers may have insisted that "Paris has restaurants for everybody, from the cabinet minister to the nameless sans-culottes," but no statute prohibited the former from entering the restaurant that catered to the latter (or, more threateningly, vice versa).[38]

Restaurants certainly differed, but within a restaurant, experience indicated that it was not always easy to tell the peer from the pauper. Again and again, newspapers' tales of unpaid restaurant bills and stolen tableware opened with a description of the well-dressed and impeccably groomed culprit. "A man of elegant and military bearing"; "a very well-dressed gentlemen"; "two fashionable youths"; "a handsome gentleman with his pince-nez around his neck and his riding crop in hand, accompanied by a young and lovely lady"; "a young lady with the most modest air and wearing the most elegant hat": throughout the 1830s, an uninterrupted flood of news stories revealed every one of these (and many more) to be the most common sorts of criminals, intent on dining for free and pocketing the spoons to boot.[39] The stealing of silverware had hardly been unknown earlier—indeed, it accounts for most of what police reports have to tell us about eighteenth-century eateries—but the social significance of these crimes had changed considerably. The Old Regime *traiteur*, accustomed to feeding a fairly stable clientele, had been primarily inclined to see newcomers as the most likely guilty parties. Nineteenth-century restaurateurs, in contrast, had far fewer regular patrons. Because of the city's unprecedented population boom and the association of restaurant meals with occasional, sporadic festivity, any restaurateur who looked warily at all his unknown customers would have to be on the verge of succumbing to paranoia. Faced with a world full of strangers, restaurateurs and social commentators alike were forced to rely on outward appearances as they endeavored to separate confidence men from connoisseurs.

The court-reporting and crime-obsessed press ensured that accounts of fraudulent gourmets circulated to a wide audience. If, as these shocked tales implied, the customers in a restaurant might cunningly present only the appearance of gentility, how was society to know the truly well bred from the cleverly disguised scoundrel? For it was all of French society (some implied) who suffered, brought under suspicion by such violations of hospitality. As one irate restaurateur emphatically told the court: "After all that . . . To run out without paying the check! It's a scandal! It's immoral! In the name of society—which has been injured in my person—I demand justice!"[40]

Lurking within the tidy stratigraphy of restaurants lay the uneasy suspicion that they might actually blur, rather than reinforce, social distinctions. Gastronomy's suitability as a tool for social mapping was subverted by its own claims to autonomy: insofar as the discourse of taste insisted on its own legitimacy, it argued against the viability of using diet as a marker of social class.[41] The sense of taste, after all, was meant to know neither social rank nor economic limits; within a restaurant, where every customer was presented with the same menu, social distinction threatened to collapse into gastronomic equality.

Only to a most uncertain degree did gastro-culinary structures mimic social ones; that mimicry was itself neither perfect nor without dangers. Waiters, the restaurant's omniscient servants, spoke in an abbreviated jargon that made the identity of eater with eaten into a threat rather than a reassurance. "Your chest is being grilled," the garçon might tell one customer, before turning to another to say: "your ear is in the saucepan, your brains are being fried; I'll bring you your tongue, the chef is going to cut off your head."[42] As the guides and manuals warned, a meal in a restaurant was, indeed, a constant combat—a suitable terrain for the male customer to display the military prowess of Napoleon and the gastronomic savvy of Talleyrand. By this trick of language, every successful diner, even the many who did not indulge in the famous "eating duels," became an equally great conqueror. In a restaurant, the locus of violence shifted from the eater's treatment of the eaten (where Grimod de la Reynière's gastronomy had located it) to the restaurant's treatment of the customer. With the kitchen, pantry, and slaughterhouse obscured, the dining room became the real battlefield; rank and status were to be established there in their own right. Serving individual portions, restaurants even banished carving (once an aristocratic art, a sort of swordplay less life-threatening but just as significant as dueling) to the other side of the swinging door.[43]

Certain that one's accomplishments at table had their parallel elsewhere, dozens of authors chorused: "dis-moi ce que tu manges, et je te dirai qui tu es."[44] But the truth of Brillat-Savarin's maxim—already cast into doubt when swindlers supped on pheasant—was further challenged when people did not know what they were actually eating. The aestheticization effected by a restaurant dining room could create a fairyland atmosphere—the author of *The Art of Never Eating at Home* described a restaurant dining room as a bewitched space of enchantment[45]—but it might also raise unpleasant questions about what was going on behind the scenes. In a system of commodities and fast bargains, a restaurant's fare could easily prove as duplicitous as its clientele. (When, in the opening scene of *Les Cabinets particuliers,* the waiters sing about "fresh fish" on the menu, the youngest protests that there is no such thing in the kitchen. The others immediately silence him.)[46]

As early as the 1780s, it had been suggested that restaurant menus were as likely to provoke disappointment as to arouse excitement, since "though you see the price of each dish, you see not the dish itself."[47] Critics of the time may have been commenting on the small portions and delicate flavors popular with non-supping, weak-chested patrons (or perhaps simply expressing their astonishment at individual portions of any sort), but, a decade later, acerbic commentaries on the widespread chicanery of restaurant service remained common. (Mercier made much of this in his post-Thermidor critique of "the new Paris," in which he compared à-la-carte restaurants unfavorably to the *guinguettes* where, he claimed, the food was always visible.)[48] As long as restaurants were comparatively rare, and thus experience with menus was uncommon, it made some sense to accuse all restaurants of deception. But as they became standard elements of the Paris landscape, and were hailed as sites of the nation's *grand couvert,* reputable restaurants had somehow to be distinguished from dishonest ones (lest all marks of culinary and social distinction be lost). When a journalist called modern life deceptive, specious, and (for good measure) "as illusory as a restaurant's beefsteak," he was not, after all, talking about the Véfour or the Trois Frères Provençaux.[49]

If the patrons visible in a dining room might not be who or what they appeared, it was even more difficult to evaluate the contents of the invisible kitchen. Accounts of Paris restaurants from the first half of the nineteenth century—whether novelistic, touristic, or journalistic—nearly always remained firmly in the dining room, venturing only very rarely into the netherworlds of preparation. On occasion, though, an ominous rumor or potential scandal would erupt through the smooth surface of restaurant life. Newspaper editors, who apparently delighted in tales of well-dressed silverware thieves, might then briefly whisper dark hints of what went on behind the swinging doors. In 1838, for example, the Paris press briefly focused on the case of Brutus Bezoni and his two accomplices, all charged with slaughtering stray cats and selling their carcasses to unscrupulous restaurateurs. As with spoon stealing, there was nothing especially novel about substituting cats for rabbits in a variety of recipes, but the story received remarkable and sustained attention. The "Vatels of the rue de l'Hôtel de Ville" (as the perpetrators were repeatedly called, though they seemed unlikely to commit suicide simply because rabbits were unavailable) were paraded through the streets, and their crimes were dragged across the pages of the Paris dailies.[50]

During their trial, Bezoni and his accomplices maintained that their motives had been good, even humanitarian: having sometimes been reduced to eating cat stew, and having saved several poor families from starvation by this means, they were simply making an economical meat available to a broader audience. If fraud was committed, Bezoni suggested, it was by those who put "rabbit" on the menu and not by those who put cat in the skillet. After all, how could he have fooled experienced cooks into thinking he was selling them rabbits? "Rabbits, do they have claws?" he asked the court. "No," responded the prosecuting attorney—before he read aloud the police commissioner's detailed description of the feline limbs he had found, neatly skinned and with the paws carefully removed.[51] (After a trial full of such gruesome details, the cat butchers of Paris were sentenced to six months in prison and a hundred-franc fine.)

To suspicious minds, Bezoni's trial may have intimated that all restaurant cookery was fraudulent, but the commentary surrounding it had a different, more diffuse and ambiguous, effect. Repeatedly referring to Bezoni's customers as "some *gargotiers* beyond the city limits," the press implicitly asserted that while some cooks certainly did concoct *gibelottes de chat*, others just as clearly did not. Bezoni's trial cast a cloud of suspicion over many eating establishments, but it still left a few others brightly illuminated. Differentiating the two categories would be no easy task, but then again, nothing about restaurant life was easy. The cat/rabbit scandal revealed (and reveled in) the confusions and dangers of modern city life, but it also provoked chroniclers of the city's eateries to ever finer degrees of chromaticism. By demarcating the *gargotes* where "rabbit" always meant "cat" from the grand restaurants where it never did, journalists attempted to control the anxiety of minor differences by turning those differences into major ones. Yet by bringing the two together (in order to tell them apart), such hierarchies could only contribute to establishing the fundamental comparability of all eatinghouses (of every place that we would today term a "restaurant").

A forum for the confusion of appearances (used to such brilliant comic effect in *Les Cabinets particuliers*), the restaurant dining room was a prime arena for the anxious interplay of hierarchy and democratization so characteristic of modern social life. The spectrum of "How Paris Eats" might be read as tribute to the variety of human experience within the bustling city, or as confirmation that social difference expressed itself in every aspect of daily life, but it might also be read as political satire, calling on those who supped on cat-meat stew or lunched on other people's leftovers to rise up and displace the wealthy in the dining rooms of Champeaux, the Café de Paris, and the Grand Véfour.[52] Since identifying who was eating what proved a constantly more complicated task, there was no sure way to use gastronomic hierarchies to affirm social structures. The unsettled and uncertain relationship of the two was largely responsible for restaurant life's insistent presence in the popular press of the Restoration, and even more so during the July Monarchy. For although some voices regularly mentioned restaurants as sites of significant cultural democratization, France in the nineteenth century had not really been miraculously transformed into a land of universalized foie gras, oysters, and epigrammes d'agneau.

Images of France as a Land of Cockaigne—a wondrous "gastronomic map" where bonbons were capable of spontaneous generation, where champagne filled the rivers and pullets dropped, perfectly cooked, from the clear blue sky—recurred during these decades, further intimating that the nation was itself a sort of giant restaurant (where all the hungry person needed to do, according to Brillat-Savarin, was wish).[53] Yet the famously disastrous potato harvest of 1845 and 1846 was only part of a mid-century subsistence crisis that sparked serious unrest and rioting across France and much of Europe. If Paris restaurant patrons of the mid-1840s felt no shortages other than that of ice, they were hardly the national norm.[54] References to France as a land of plenty were common, but they served mainly to highlight gross inequalities, to note—as did the various guides to eating in Paris—that while some were feasting, many more were not (Figure 21). In the caricatures of the republican artist Honoré Daumier, tables set along every roadside and larks falling from the sky "roasted and ready to eat" figured only as one of the extravagant promises made by the wily charlatan, Robert Macaire, as he schemed to sell stock options to innocents and fools.[55]

If the oppositional press routinely made use of, and thereby further contributed to the ubiquity of, gastronomic references and examples, it was primarily in order to protest against the increasingly dominant vision of France as nothing but one giant dining room. Ambivalence, not endorsement, motivated their reports on Paris's new oyster market or their

Figure 21. A rare polemical illustration of "how Paris eats" that juxtaposes the "too much" found in a grand restaurant (notice the man vomiting from the balcony) with the "too little" of an open-air soup kitchen below.

accounts of meaty smells emanating from hidden restaurant kitchens.[56] Much as it had been in the 1790s, culinary language in the 1830s and 1840s—saturated with references to truffles, game fowl, and other icons of privilege—could be as critical as it was celebratory. The caricature of Louis Philippe as Gargantua devouring France—surely the most well-known, public, and memorable attempt to revive the language of fat and lean—was suppressed, but other imagery and anecdotes participating in the same rhetoric continued to circulate freely.[57] In the tightly policed world created by the July Monarchy's press laws of September 1835, gastronomy's insistence on the table as a nonpolitical topic made it, paradoxically, an ideal setting for sarcasm and slander. When journalists writing in *Le Corsaire* or *Le Charivari* parroted the triumphalist pronouncements of the *Physiology of Taste,* they threw down the gauntlet within an arena that was already marked as festive, burlesque, or mildly ridiculous. For the censors to react to such provocation would have been tantamount to admitting, openly and awkwardly, that they could not take a joke, that they really were venally preoccupied with tasty (and expensive) morsels.[58]

With almost daily regularity, the satirical press of the July Monarchy remarked on the banquets, feasts, and other celebrations hosted by government officials at home and by French ambassadors abroad.[59] "The muse of history has put down her burin, and picked up her fork," suggested one writer in the pages of *Le Charivari*.[60] Yet what was repeatedly being emphasized in these reports was not so much the blossoming of French culinary genius as it was the waning of French military and diplomatic glory.[61] To the minds of bellicose republicans and monarchists alike, the possibility that valiant military commanders would be remembered as garnishes—or that fifteen years of fighting in North Africa had produced no more substantial gains than couscous—was hardly flattering. "Under the Republic and the Empire, our victories enlarged the maps [*cartes*] of France, but today they have no influence except on the menus [*cartes*] of restaurateurs," worried one author as he sighed for France's lost honor.[62] A writer for the entertainment biweekly, *L'Aspic* (so titled because its pages were like a gelatinous medium in which many tasty morsels could be suspended), intoned a typical tribute to French culinary genius—"From the Palace of the Tuileries to the last sub-prefecture of France, gastronomy unites, sustains, softens, and reconciles the most intractable of men"—but was he praising the peace-making qualities of a good meal or commenting wryly on the number of official dinners hosted by administrators who had few other obvious responsibilities?[63] Bemoaning the obsessive concern with cuisine as a pastime suited to domestic servants and greedy notaries, voices opposed to making France into a center of culinary excellence asked whether it was taste, or simply greed, that manifested itself in restaurants. "Our system easily swallows both dinners and insults," noted another author bitterly.[64]

Oppositional political culture in France of this period was overwhelmingly dominated by the image of complaisant officials who willingly compromised their personal or national honor in exchange for material luxuries. Béranger's 1818 song, "Le Ventru," gave a new and enduring title to the elected officials who "represent us even when they are eating"[65] (Figures 22 and 23). Though he derived his name from the word *ventre*, meaning "stomach," the *ventru* was much more than a plump prefect or a chubby councilman. In opposition lore and popular caricature, he was a member of that rapidly expanding group of Center deputies—*centre* rhyming, obviously, with *ventre*—motivated only by the desire for personal gain and happy to pay with votes for dinner invitations. To his mind, the best argument was a "truffled beefsteak," and the few hours between the end of a long lunch and the beginning of an early dinner were the only time for debate.[66] Since the *ventre* sold his soul for truffles, pheasants, and oysters (and not for just any old mess of porridge), the gastronomic murmurings and rumors of the 1820s and 1830s need also to be understood as an insistent string of political commentaries, each noting the exaggerated importance attached to such goods within a system that was fundamentally corrupt.[67] "When will we be finished with these gorging parliamentarians?" asked *Le Charivari*. "Will there ever come a time when chickens no longer fall roasted onto the plates of our legislators?"[68]

Against this flood of ridicule and mockery, the famous reform banquets of 1840 and 1847–1848 gain new meaning, for if the table was figuratively available for innuendo and appropriation, it was literally available as well. Although the July Monarchy's restrictive 1834 law governing associations effectively prohibited any club, society, or political organization that met on a regular basis, it specifically did not apply to chance gatherings, occasional meetings, or private parties. During the legislative debate, peers and deputies supportive of the new measures all emphasized that "pleasure" meetings would be in no way regulated; dinners, in particular, remained outside the law's jurisdiction, no matter how numerous the guests.[69] Opponents of the law jested that meals were fast becoming a Frenchman's only freedom: the liberal *Courrier français* and the legitimist *Gazette de France,* though rarely in sympathy on other issues, concurred in

Figure 22. The "Ventre," or centrist "Belly" of the legislative assembly, became a favorite target after Béranger's song of 1818, in which a deputy chirped to his constituents about the dinners he had been fed in Paris.

finding "dinner with one's friends, and attendance at a scheduled ball" rather paltry liberties.[70]

Faced with fifteen years' worth of relentless satire (much of which had been directed against the now ousted Bourbon regime), the Orleanist July Monarchy needed to establish that its own ministers were not really truffled, that a dinner was, and would always be, "just a dinner." Banquets, as long as they gave the appearance of being impromptu, private events, therefore remained legal, even when several hundred "guests" were invited and a dozen speakers proposed toasts to legislative reform. In practice, it was logistically daunting to send so many invitations (say, to the thousands who attended the September 1840 banquet held outside Paris) and often difficult to find a sufficiently large "private" locale; in theory, these meetings were all nothing but dinner parties.[71] And if the July Monarchy had continued to treat them as such, then dinner parties they might

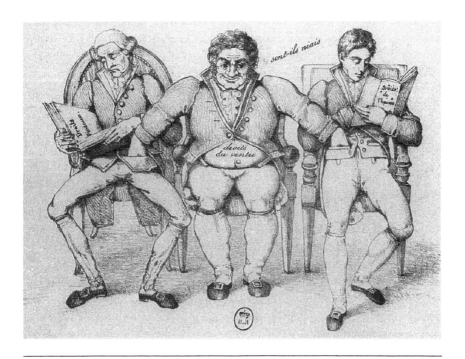

Figure 23. Twice the size of the aristocratic right (who reads about "Feudal Rights") or the republican left (who studies "The Rights of Man"), the "Belly" steals from both.

well have remained. For while the dozens of banquets held across France during the summer and autumn of 1847 are often said to have caused the February Revolution of 1848, it was the regime's attempt to ban them that more immediately triggered its downfall.

Perhaps neither the banquets' organizers, nor the King himself, had taken into account how fully France's print and political culture had been marked by the delineation of the table as a realm of private pleasures. "Festivity" was foisted on all who would organize banquets; "despotism" could be the only name for a regime that would prohibit them.

In the public, shared, and open spaces of modern life, that is where things can best be hidden (as Poe told us in his "Purloined Letter"). Thus, in the "public" space of restaurants, mistresses, political actions, and slaughtered cats were all concealed. Precisely because restaurants had come to be seen as the physical manifestation of gastronomy and, hence, as distinct from other urban sites, they could be used to many ends. Paradoxically, it was thanks to the very specific ways in which they were marginalized that restaurants could play such an important and varied role in urban life. In the privacy of a restaurant, it was possible to host banquets calling for legislative reform; in the obscurity of a long, drawn-out series of associations and satires, it was possible to treat the July Monarchy as a cheap restaurant and the king as a portly grocer. Public and private were not features of physical spaces, but of how people used those spaces. One often shielded the other: gastronomy, the public face of restaurant culture, might conceal (and maybe eventually contaminate) fraternally equitable meals.

In little more than fifty years, the restaurant was transformed from a semi-public space into a semi-private one. The difference may seem minor, or merely semantic, but it identifies a key shift. For while the cabinets of a nineteenth-century restaurant afforded a "private" retreat that was widely known and acknowledged, eighteenth-century sensitivity was an expression of personal feeling that could not help spilling over into "public" life. In the eighteenth-century restaurant, the weak-chested could stage their private ailments, thereby giving proof of a sentiment that had public significance. The restaurant's style of service responded to the imperatives of medicalized sensibility, but that sensibility, like the aristocratic, refined "taste" it claimed to challenge, itself required display. While the definition of "good taste" would change with the decades, the logic of its demonstration remained the same. Whether a sensitive bouillon sipper or a ragoût-savoring gourmet, the ideal restaurant customer distinguished himself or herself from the realm of simple appetite, leaving mere eaters and vulgar gluttons far behind.

Yet the broad structural similarity between weak-chested individuals and epicurean gourmets masks an important shift in the sociopolitical significance given to the restaurant's realms of taste. In the last decades of the Old Regime, lawyers could convincingly argue that the customers in any restaurant, simply by the delicacy of appetite that brought them there in the first place, necessarily formed part of "good society." Later, during the reign of the revolutionary police state known as the Terror, the restaurateur's complicity with systems of social and cultural hierarchy was still obvious to all concerned, but far more menacing and negative in its repercussions. In the aftermath of the Revolution, as the restaurant became a depoliticized space, the use of taste as a marker of specifically social distinction would become more muted, hidden in the promise and the conceit of gustatory universals.

Epilogue:
Restaurants and Reverie

In a restaurant one is both observed and unobserved.

DAVID MAMET, *WRITING IN RESTAURANTS*

You can get anything you want . . .

ARLO GUTHRIE, "ALICE'S RESTAURANT"

Writing of the sumptuous decor typical of Palais-Royal restaurants, authors often invoked the palaces of *The Thousand and One Nights,* as if Oriental despotic splendor reigned unquestioned in a few square acres of central Paris.[1] References to Aladdin's palace might have suggested that the work in restaurants was done by magical spirits and that the ordinary mortal had nothing to do except wish, but mention of that marvelous structure—built by the Genie, conjured from thin air, never fully finished—also highlighted the restaurant's ephemeral and phantasmatic qualities. A tissue of lies and illusions, a fabulous home that sprang up overnight, one gained not by honest hard work but by dealing with the Djin: this was what Isaac Appleton Jewett implied when he compared restaurants to Aladdin's palace.[2]

To write of restaurant culture in terms of tales told, retold, and rewritten is not to belittle or downplay the place of restaurants in nineteenth-century France. Instead, it is to identify something central to their functioning—for as surely as restaurants relied on fish and fresh vegetables, silverware and champagne, they depended on legend. Fame (*Renommée*) was the first of a restaurant's household gods; Venus, the second; and Comus, only the third.[3] Restaurants required rumors and lore; their mystique resided in the suspicion that somebody else was having a better dinner, a more titillating dalliance, a more exotic bottle of wine. Every time a restaurant was mentioned, another layer of excitement and mystery accrued to it; unlike Barère's "fraternity" or Roze de Chantoiseau's Cheshire-cat-like credit notes, a restaurant's reputation grew as it was passed along. As the fame of the city's restaurants spread, so the myth was

234

disseminated of Paris as the nation's *grand couvert*. Like myths, restaurants used whatever materials were at hand to cobble together, over and over, the same, strangely repetitive stories of desire and hunger. Their tale was not about completion or satiety or closure, but about desires never quite fully satisfied and inevitably aroused again on the morrow.

The grand restaurants of the nineteenth century mattered as objects of reverie; they were known as odors that wafted from kitchens, as names that recurred in literature and journalism, as palaces glimpsed from the street. Restaurants were places of daydream and fantasy, places to tell tales of who the other patrons were and of who one was oneself. But not everyone was allowed to dream. Restaurants, according to an editorialist for the ultra-conservative *La France,* were not really friends of all the world. Rather, by placing the pleasures of the wealthy before the eyes of the poor, restaurants aroused insatiable and dangerous desires. Once restaurant life had lulled him into a false sense of his own prosperity, an ordinary worker or clerk would soon grow to hate his own humble home. He would spurn day-to-day reality and live in a world of illusion, enjoying a restaurant's "gilded woodwork and luxurious mirrors . . . just as if these things belonged to him." Abandoning any effort to make the best of his lot, the modern Parisian worker—so *La France* feared—would sacrifice wife and children for the specious pleasures of restaurant life. Driven by the desire to surround himself with all the comforts of nobody's home, the Parisian would first pawn his possessions and then turn to a life of crime in order to support his habit of luxury. "When our good King Henri IV promised a chicken in every pot," concluded the article ominously, "he meant for his peasants to eat their chickens at home."[4]

La France missed the point. For even in the era of "beef, dressed in eleven different ways" and "poultry, under thirty-two various forms," restaurant culture had little to do with the putting of chickens into pots. Restaurants were cornucopic in theory, but in practice their full bounty was never seen: the complete harvest—"all that sea, land, and air provide for human sustenance"[5]—remained concealed in the kitchen, the pantry, and the storeroom, allowed to emerge only in individual portions. Lest it overwhelm, the restaurant provided pleasure already prepared and fully dressed, in plate-size synecdoches of plenty; in the restaurant, the invisible hands of dozens of unseen workers transformed the dirty, hairy, slimy, or feathered products of the market into neatly balanced pyramids of fruit and tidy columns of minuscule print. The restaurant represented cornucopia, and alluded to it, but between the bulk produce of the marketplace and the brilliant scene in a restaurateur's dining room intervened, necessarily, a dark and steam-filled kitchen. Thus the restaurant kept modernity's bounty from overwhelming the individual; every customer believed he could have anything he desired (the gender-specific pronoun is intentional), but he needed to confront only his own small portion of the Land of Cockaigne. The partridge may not have fallen from the sky fully roasted, but it emerged from the kitchen ready-carved.

The practices of restaurant going and the conventions of gastronomic sensibility demarcated the meal, setting it apart and framing it, requiring a quite literal move into a space other than that of preparation. The kitchen nearly vanished—in all these accounts, it would seem to have disappeared in a puff of roast-scented smoke. While numerous works promised to reveal the varied mysteries of Paris, and while the idealistic artist's disappointment at the realities of the literary market was a common enough nineteenth-century plot device, descriptions of the restaurant's backstage regions remained extraordinarily rare. For, throughout this period, the whole purpose of a restaurant (unlike that of a *gargote* or a *traiteur*'s establishment) was to eclipse the kitchen, to pull a curtain of illusion across the real conditions of production, to aestheticize and tidy. From the kitchen, often located in the basement, steam was said to bellow as from the mouths of Hell; there, filth-spattered cooks sweltered in the life-threatening heat of pitched battle.[6] But the restaurant's customers never witnessed the cooking of food, the chopping of ingredients, the plucking of feathers, or the draining of blood; instead they waited, drinking wine and swallowing oysters (Figure 24), until the waiter, a Charon-figure passing between worlds, appeared with a paradisiacal bounty of flavors, smells, textures, and sights.

Descriptions of restaurants often emphasized their specular—and spectacular—functions. Like a theater, a restaurant was a stable frame around an ever-changing performance, a stage where fantasies might be brought to life.[7] Restaurant reviews gave an illusory permanence to culinary accomplishments and printed menus hinted that the "same" dish might every night make its eternal return, but the restaurant's performance could not be reproduced exactly. The restaurant, like the theater, was a privileged locus of ephemerality. But the parallel of restaurant and theater always skirted around the question of separating players from audience. The patrons all took turns as audience, watching each other carefully, but rarely did they acknowledge that they, too, might be under surveillance. In a restaurant, everybody observed from polite obscurity, and performed with blithe indifference. If, in some senses, the world of the grand Paris restaurants generalized the behaviors of the courtly *grand couvert*—attendants followed an elaborate code of etiquette, being seen was as important as being satiated, a definite dress code determined who was admitted and who left at the door—in another key respect, it did not. For whereas the king's public meal—during which he *ate*, and others *watched*—had been part of a

Figure 24. Boilly, "The Oyster Eaters" (1825). Raw oysters, consumed in vast quantities, were a key part of any restaurant dinner.

calculated performance of monarchial power, a restaurant meal could not derive its significance from any comparable center. Each "prince" in a dining room might feel royal and important, but how was he to maintain that sensation when all the members of his audience were eating as well? The Old Regime court-society calculus of position had been far easier to map: the monarch functioned as a sort of gold standard (the assumption that so fatally haunted Roze de Chantoiseau's debt reduction scheme). But what was the source of value in a restaurant, where every wall was hung with mirrors but all the diners remained unknown?

In September 1839, a former infantry officer, Alphonse Robert by name, ran up a modest twelve-franc dinner bill at the restaurant Véfour, at that time one of the best known of the Palais Royal's still famous establishments. As he finished his meal and discovered his pockets empty, he asked the *restauratrice* for credit, suggesting that she send a waiter with him to his hotel where, he claimed, he had the money. She refused, and in "a strange act of violence" that prompted doubts about his sanity and earned him instant notoriety, he angrily threw a bottle at a mirror, causing 1400 francs' worth of damage. At the moment of reckoning, when the restaurant's pleasures took their place in the modern economy, Alphonse Robert literally shattered the illusion of hospitality, sending glass shards flying across the room.[8] The veneer splintered, the mirror broke, and the hierarchies of taste were threatened by violence no longer limited to the witty retorts of a clever *garçon*.

The Paris press covered his trial in considerable detail, relishing the story of the madman who had struck fear into the hearts of restaurateurs.[9] Much more than the bill for the Véfour's mirror (originally reported as the astronomical sum of 5000 francs) was at stake. For if Alphonse Robert could throw a bottle, what was to prevent other restaurant customers from behaving in an equally erratic fashion, and bringing the whole menu-monde crashing down in a shower of sharp and shiny fragments?[10] During his trial, Robert dwelt bitterly on the refusal of credit, on Madame Hamel's distrust. "This *gargotière* insulted me," he said. "She said they would not give credit to people like me [*gens de mon espèce*] and so I got angry." For the unemployed former soldier, recently arrived in Paris with little to his name but a manuscript (suspiciously entitled "Constitution for a Republican Government"), Madame Hamel's refusal had been not a sensible business policy, but a class-based snub directed at "people like him." She first, he implied, had broken the restaurant's illusion—had shown herself, by refusing him and people like him credit, to be nobody's friend. In reply, Madame Hamel asserted that all she had meant was that she did not grant credit to people with whom she was not personally acquainted: a category far broader, and surely more innocuous, than Robert's reading of *gens de mon espèce*.

Discussion at the trial and in the press, however, turned not on the question of whether the restauratrice had unfairly insulted Robert, but on the epithet, *gargotière,* which he hurled at her with the same force and vehemence he put behind the mirror-splintering bottle. The presiding judge, Pinondel, and the restaurateur's lawyer, Wollis, both seized on his use of the disrespectful slang term. Wollis explained at length that the proprietors of the restaurant Véfour, far from being the owners of some crude eatery, were known for their genteel manners and "urbanity," while Pinondel reprimanded Robert: "Your first error was to treat the restaurant Véfour as a *gargote*."[11] When Alphonse Robert threw the bottle and then called Madame Hamel a *gargotière,* he broke both a mirror and the image in the mirror. He shattered the reflected picture of what a restaurant was and should be, while at the same time literally fracturing an important part of the restaurant's furnishings. Calling the Véfour a *gargote* was but another punishable offense to be added to the list of unpaid bills and broken looking-glasses.

Compare Robert's story with the hero of Balzac's *Lost Illusions,* Lucien de Rubempré, who comes to Paris with little but a manuscript entitled "les Marguerites." Dejected when the woman with whom he is infatuated, Madame de Bargeton, refuses to be seen with him, and disturbed that his fine blue suit makes him look every inch the country bumpkin, he seeks solace in a dinner at the restaurant Véry.[12] Throughout dinner he is lost in daydream, imagining his future successes as a poet, his anticipated conquest of beautiful women. The restaurant encourages reverie; seated in a posh salon, enjoying his bottle of Bordeaux, his oysters from Ostende, his partridge and his macaroni, Lucien feels himself to be part of Paris's high society and imagines that nothing will interfere with his rise to fame. He will win friends by his wit and patrons by his intelligence. Cheered by these thoughts, he prepares to leave—and is startled from his dreams by a bill for fifty francs. Lucien pays (though he had counted on spending less than that sum each month) and, upon leaving the restaurant, realizes that his dreams of cerebral success have been nothing but delusions. He runs to buy new clothes.

For the restaurant offered its delights only at a cost (Figure 25); one

Figure 25. "Arrival in Paris," a tale of deception, dreams, and, inevitably, Rabelais's fifteen minutes. The central figure claims that his "new friends" had invited him to dinner, but they are already well out the door when the check arrives.

might postpone the "quart d'heure de Rabelais"—the fatal moment at which the check arrived—by ordering yet another bottle of champagne, another glass of armagnac, another bowl of punch, but further consumption could not delay it indefinitely. A restaurant was called "chez Véry" as if the brothers Jean François and Jean Baptiste had invited a guest into their home, but this was only an illusion, one that lasted long enough to drive up the cost and lead the unwary eater to the brink of despair. Only by running out on the check might his patrons force the restaurateur to some version of true generosity; only by breaking the law was some sort of simple, unmediated interchange established. Nobody invited the restaurateur to dinner—and when one did dine with the restaurateur (remember Rousseau), it was as if all bills came due at once.

And yet the illusion persisted, even after Jean Baptiste and Jean François were dead and gone, and the latter's son had placed classified advertisements and rented the restaurant to the highest-bidding merchant. For the 1843 sale contract made explicit that Joseph Neuhaus was to operate the business "under the name and sign: Restaurant Véry"; to maintain the high standards with which that name had long been associated; and to give the name back to Théodore August Véry when he had finished with it.[13] One restaurant Véry had been torn down to make way for the rue de Rivoli; another would go bankrupt in 1856; yet another, this one on the boulevard Magenta, would be destroyed by the bomb of a fin-de-siècle anarchist.[14] Denounced by sans-culottes and blown up by nihilists' dynamite, the restaurant Véry endured in literature and legend, myth and street sign.

The restaurant, as everybody came to realize, was nobody's home—if one was forced by circumstances to live in a restaurant it was a *vie pénible;* the French, after all, have restaurants "because they have no homes."[15] For a regular restaurant patron like Doctor Louis Véron, a comfortably middle-class Parisian bachelor, theater manager, editor, and physician, the crowded dining rooms of a fashionable restaurant offered the pleasurable sensation of "silence and solitude in the middle of a crowd."[16] Véron's ability to ignore other people and to feel alone because seated at his "own" table without a companion was, however, still relatively uncommon in the mid-nineteenth century; this was a behavior pattern that had to be observed and consciously mastered before a novice could fully exploit it. As widely accessible, publicly open, and yet reserved and private places, where strangers rarely spoke to each other and certainly did not share tables, restaurants unquestionably required some getting used to.

To the well-traveled American author Caroline Stansbury Kirkland, for example, it was not at all self-evident that she would be able to have any peace of mind in the dining room of a Paris restaurant. Though she had edited a newspaper, directed the Detroit Female Seminary, and kept company with Edgar Allan Poe, eating in public demanded of Mrs. Kirkland a new attitude and a sharply changed perspective. "It really requires some practice before one can refrain from casting sly glances around . . . to see whether anyone is looking," she wrote. "Yet nobody looks at you, or seems to know that you are there," she continued, concluding that "one feels at first that it is a transgression; but after a while this subsides into a feeling of agreeable abandon."[17]

Mrs. Kirkland had to sneak glances at the other patrons before she could persuade herself that she was safely ignored, but after some practice she came to appreciate the lightheartedness of restaurant life. She may even have experienced the same giddy freedom she had felt a decade earlier when she wrote her first novel, a scathing satire of American frontier life which she had wisely published under a pseudonym. The people of "Montacute" (Pinckney, Michigan) had not been fooled by this ruse, however, and Mrs. Kirkland had been mortified when her irate provincial neighbors deduced the real identity of the caustic "Mrs. Mary Clavers." Chagrined, she had taken a gentler tone in all her later works and lamented that, with her incognita violated, she would probably never again write anything so successful. "A lady always feels under a certain degree of restraint," she explained to a friend, "when she feels that the world is looking her in the face all the time."[18] Surprised when she lost her anonymity to the busybodies of Pinckney, Mrs. Kirkland was initially just as perplexed when she found it again in the dining rooms of Paris restaurants. Yet a meal at the Trois Frères Provençaux—with its gilt moldings, silver forks, and porcelain fruit baskets, an establishment "fine enough for royalty"—had sufficiently reassured her that "nobody . . . knows you are there."[19] Other, perhaps less trusting, souls might have come to the conclusion that Mrs. Kirkland was no more hidden in the restaurant than she had been behind her pseudonym. But was obscurity really the point of restaurant life?

The proprietor of the Rocher de Cancale (the famous rue-Montorgeuil seafood restaurant so beloved of Grimod de la Reynière) repeatedly went to court to maintain a monopoly on his restaurant's name, defending it successfully against the competing "rocher de Cantale" and the "Petit

Rocher."[20] But when the first Rocher finally closed its doors, the nearby Petit Rocher de Cancale happily inherited its mantle. And as it had been named after another restaurant so, in the logic of quotation and imitation that made the restaurant a genre and an institution of its own, the Petit Rocher was decorated with murals that copied Daumier's, Gavarni's, and Boilly's well-known caricatures of gourmandise. Painted oysters, opened in one panel by Gavarni's smiling young *écaillère,* slid in the next down the throats of Boilly's connoisseurs (see Figure 24). One man relished the first

Figure 26. *Le Charivari*'s "Physiognomatic Gallery" depicted Parisians in a variety of settings, including this restaurant patron intently slicing his meat.

Figure 27. Honoré Daumier, "I have three sous," lithograph from *Le Charivari* (Aug. 11, 1839).

glass of his Bordeaux, another energetically sliced his dinner (Figure 26); all encouraged the diners at the Petit Rocher to enjoyment.[21]

On another wall of the Petit Rocher, Daumier's poor devil stood enviously outside a restaurant's display window, hands in his no doubt empty pockets (Figure 27).[22] A staple of restaurant life, that man outside had often been seen before. Eleven years earlier, in 1830, Auguste Luchet wrote as if he had Daumier's sketch before him, describing the pale and yellowed figures who drifted through the Palais Royal at dinner time: "Sometimes rushing, sometimes slow, they stop from time to time, pausing beside the vents exhaling balsamic odors from the justly famous kitchens of the Véfours and the Vérys." With their hands deep in their pockets, "they stare at the symmetrical arrangements of foie-gras pâtés and galantines, lobsters, partridges, pheasants and who knows what else," sometimes making plaintive little gestures "like a cat who wants something on the other side of the window."[23] Such a situation in 1794 would have required police action; in 1830, Luchet perhaps hoped that his description would provoke a revolution.

But the man outside was a necessary part of restaurant life. Even in the second-floor *(premier étage)* dining room, removed from the crowds and the noise of a street-level salon, the Petit Rocher's customers were watched with hungry eyes. For the nineteenth century's restaurant fantasy implicitly required the presence of somebody outside: some poor devil with his nose pressed to the window, some plotting parasite endeavoring to get a free dinner chez Véry, or some group of young street urchins devouring their bread seasoned only by the savory fumes emanating from a restaurant's hard metal grate.

Notes

Introduction: To Make a Restaurant

1. Master Chiquart Amiczo, *Du fait de cuisine,* ed. Terence Scully, "Du fait de cuisine par Maistre Chiquart 1420 (Ms. S 103 de la bibliothèque Supersaxo, à la Bibliothèque cantonale du Valais, à Sion)," *Vallesia, Bulletin annuel de la Bibliothèque et des Archives cantonales du Valais,* 40 (1985): 101–231, citation from p. 188. Philip Hyman kindly brought this source to my attention. All translations from French are my own, unless otherwise noted.

   As the word "restaurant" is not used in English for a restorative substance, I have italicized it in those cases where it refers exclusively to a bouillon. The attributes of a restaurant and of a *restaurant* often overlapped, however, somewhat falsifying the typographic distinction.

2. *Abrégé du Dictionnaire universel françois et latin, vulgairement appellé Dictionnaire de Trévoux* (Paris: Libraires associés, 1762), vol. 3, p. 508. For Furetière's definition, cited among the epigraphs at the front of the book, see *Dictionnaire universel, contenant généralement tous les mots français,* 3rd ed. (Rotterdam: Leers, 1708), vol. 3, n.p. *Encyclopédie ou dictionnaire raisonné des sciences, des arts et des métiers, par une société des gens de lettres* (Paris: 1751–1772), art. "Restauratif ou restaurant." My reading of the *Encyclopédie* was stimulated, and to some extent guided, by Jean-Claude Bonnet's excellent article, "Le réseau culinaire dans *L'Encyclopédie*," *Annales: ESC,* 31 (1976): 891–914.

3. Most major cookbooks published in France between 1651 and 1780 (a peak period in cookbook production) include a recipe for a *restaurant* or "waterless soup." See, for example, Pierre de Lune, *Le Nouveau cuisinier* (Paris: Pierre David, 1660), p. 16; Pierre de la Varenne, *L'Ecole des ragoûts, ou le chef d'oeuvre du cuisinier,* 11th ed. (Lyon: Canier, 1685), p. 34; Massialot, *Le Cuisinier royal et bourgeois* (Paris: de Sercy, 1691), p. 386; Massialot, *Le Nouveau cuisinier royal et bourgeois* (Paris: Prudhomme, 1712), vol. 2, pp. 118–119; La Chapelle, *Le Cuisinier moderne,* 2nd ed. (La Haye: 1742), vol. 1, p. 62; [Menon] *Traité historique et pratique de la cuisine ou le Cuisinier instruit* (Paris, 1758), vol. 1, p. 9; [Marin], *Les Dons de Comus* (Paris: Prault, 1739), pp. 149–153; *Dictionnaire portatif de cuisine, d'office et de distillation*

(Paris: Vincent, 1767), p. 90. For studies of cookbook publishing and writing in this period, see Barbara Ketchum Wheaton, *Savouring the Past* (Philadelphia: University of Pennsylvania Press, 1983); Stephen Mennell, *All Manners of Food* (Oxford: Basil Blackwell, 1985); Alain Girard, "Le Triomphe de *La Cuisinière bourgeoise*. Livres culinaires, cuisine et société en France aux XVII et XVIII siècles," *Revue d'histoire moderne et contemporaine*, 24 (1977): 497–523.

4. [Marin], *Dons de Comus,* p. 7.

5. A mid-nineteenth century dictionary of French institutions did not hesitate to include an entry for "Restaurant"; see Auguste Chéruel, *Dictionnaire historique des institutions, moeurs, et coutumes de la France* (Paris: Hachette, 1855), vol. 2, pp. 1070–1071.

6. Hezekiah Hartley Wright, *Desultory Reminiscences of a Tour through Germany, Switzerland, and France* (Boston: William Ticknor, 1838), p. 36; Nathaniel H. Carter, *Letters from Europe,* 2nd ed. (New York: Carvill, 1829), vol. 1, p. 418.

7. John P. Durbin, *Observations in Europe* (New York: Harper and Brothers, 1844), vol. 1, p. 37; Jacob Abbott, *Rollo in Paris* (Philadelphia: W. J. Reynolds, 1856), p. 25.

8. Archives Nationales, Paris (hereafter, A.N.) F⁷ 3025 (Census des débitants, 1851–1852). In 1843, an advertisement for a restaurant recently opened at the northern end of the Paris-Rouen railroad stressed that the dishes and prices were "the same as those found in any fine Parisian establishment," *Charivari,* May 5, 1843.

9. A.N. F⁷ 3025.

10. Richard Terdiman, following Pierre Bourdieu, has used this notion very fruitfully in his analysis of nineteenth-century culture and literature. See his *Present Past: Modernity and the Memory Crisis* (Ithaca and London: Cornell University Press, 1993), especially p. 12.

11. For instances of this approach to writing restaurant history, see Robert Baldick, *Dinner at Magny's* (New York: Coward, McCann, 1971); Claude Terrail, *Ma Tour d'Argent* (Paris: Stock, 1974); Raymond Castans, *Parlez-moi du Fouquet's* (Paris: JC Lattès, 1989); Madame Prunier, *Prunier's, The Story of a Great Restaurant* (New York: Knopf, 1957). The three volumes of Robert Courtine, *La Vie parisienne* (Paris: Perrin, 1984–1987) might be termed a compilation of the lives of culinary saints.

12. Thomas Raffles, *Letters During a Tour through Some Parts of France* (Liverpool: Thomas Taylor, 1818), p. 77; J. Jay Smith, *A Summer's Jaunt Across the Water* (Philadelphia: J. W. Moore, 1846); Henry Matthews, *The Diary of an Invalid* (London: John Murray, 1820), p. 480; Caroline M. Kirkland, *Holidays Abroad; or Europe from the West* (New York: Baker and Scribner, 1849), vol. 1, p. 135.

13. Jean-Robert Pitte, *Gastronomie française, histoire et géographie d'une passion* (Paris: Fayard, 1991), p. 155. Another noted scholar makes the invention of

the restaurant into a part of the French revolutionary tradition, stating that the emergence of restaurants "was an unmistakable sign of the crisis in aristocratic culture"; see Pascal Ory, "La Gastronomie," in Pierre Nora, ed., *Les Lieux de mémoire,* vol. 3, part 2, *Traditions* (Paris: Gallimard, 1992), pp. 823–853, quotation from p. 836. See also Theodore Zeldin, *The French* (New York: Pantheon, 1982), chap. 17.

14. As Bourdieu suggests in his critique of Kantian aesthetics, however, the perception of "taste" as removed from social or cultural determinants is, itself, socially and culturally (and historically) determined. See Pierre Bourdieu, *La Distinction* (Paris: Editions de Minuit, 1979), especially the postscript.

15. Alexandre B. L. Grimod de la Reynière, *Almanach des gourmands* (Paris: Chaumerot, 1809), vol. 5, p. 233.

16. *Webster's Third New International Dictionary* (Springfield, Mass.: Merriam, 1961), p. 1936.

17. For the increasingly important notion of France's "culinary heritage," see the articles in the *Revue des deux mondes,* Jan. 1993, which include contributions by government figures, chefs, and educators.

18. Jean-Paul Aron, *Le Mangeur du XIXe siècle* (Paris: Robert Laffont, 1973), p. 80. Another survey of past Paris eateries claims to be "a walk through the streets and through history"; see Beatrice Malki-Thouvenel, *Cabarets, cafés, et bistros de Paris: Promenade dans les rues et dans le temps* (Paris: Hovarth, 1987).

19. An anthology on "the table and sociability" makes no mention of restaurants; see Martin Aurell, Olivier Dumoulin, and Françoise Thelamon, eds., *La Sociabilité à table,* Actes du colloque de Rouen, November 14–17, 1990 (Rouen: Université de Rouen, 1992). The history of food and diet is well on its way to becoming an established subdiscipline but has rarely touched on the restaurant. Indeed, a recent inventory of work in "European food history" does not even consider "restaurants" a topic worth indexing. See Hans J. Teuteberg, ed., *European Food History: A Research Review* (Leicester: Leicester University Press, 1992).

20. Joachim C. Nemeitz, *Séjour de Paris, c'est à dire, Instructions fidèles pour les voiageurs de condition* (Leyden: 1727), p. 58.

21. Ibid., p. 59.

22. Ibid., p. 58.

23. Ibid., p. 60.

24. Tobias Smollett, *Travels through France and Italy,* ed. Frank Felsenstein (Oxford: Oxford University Press, 1979), p. 71; Arthur Young, *Travels during the Years 1787, 1788, and 1789* (Dublin: Cross, 1793), vol. 1, pp. 72, 159; Helen Maria Williams, *Letters Written in France in the Summer 1790 to a Friend in England,* 5th ed. (London: T. Cadell, 1796), p. 100.

25. Philip Thicknesse, *A Year's Journey through France* (London: W. Brown, 1778), vol. 2, p. 175.

26. René de Lespinasse, *Métiers et corporations de la Ville de Paris* (Paris:

Imprimerie Nationale, 1886), vol. 1; Daniel Roche, *The People of Paris*, trans. Marie Evans and Gwynne Lewis (Leamington Spa: Berg, 1987), pp. 247–250.

27. For the statutes of these three corporations, see Lespinasse, *Métiers et corporations*, vol. 1, pp. 259–299, 317–340, 352–366.

28. Most accounts paraphrase Pierre Jean-Baptiste LeGrand d'Aussy, *Histoire de la vie privée des françois* (Paris: Pierres, 1782), vol. 2, pp. 213–214. This tale is repeated unquestioningly, sometimes garbled, never supported. For a few of the many instances, see Jean-François Revel, *Un Festin en paroles* (Paris: J.-J. Pauvert, 1979), pp. 207–208; Mennell, *All Manners*, pp. 138–139; Wheaton, *Savouring*, pp. 73–77; Pitte, *Gastronomie*, pp. 158–160; Esther Aresty, *The Delectable Past* (New York: Simon and Schuster, 1964), p. 107; F. M. Marchant, *Le nouveau conducteur de l'étranger à Paris*, 9th ed. (Paris: Moronval, 1821), pp. 16–17; T. Harmand, *Manuel de l'étranger dans Paris pour 1824* (Paris: Hesse, 1824), p. 224; Chéruel, *Dictionnaire historique des institutions*, vol. 2, pp. 1070–1071. More examples could easily be added.

29. Revel, *Un Festin en paroles*, p. 208. Gustave Isambert included restaurateurs among the "great variety of businessmen" who, "thanks to the liberalizing of trade," were free to satisfy the new needs of a quickly changing society. Gustave Isambert, *La Vie à Paris pendant une année de la Révolution, 1791–1792* (Paris: Félix Alcan, 1896), p. 185. In other words, this common narrative links the restaurant's development to the eventual triumph of enterprising individuals over a corporate monopoly (to the capitalist spirit's defeat of archaic feudal structures). As the Marxist historian Albert Soboul wrote, when the Revolution's d'Allarde Law finally abolished the guilds, the "forces of capitalist production were thus freed from existing fetters, and the right to become a master craftsman was thrown open to all." Albert Soboul, *The French Revolution*, trans. A. Forrest and C. Jones (New York: Vintage, 1975), p. 190.

30. Jacques Revel, "Les corps et communautés," in *The French Revolution and the Origin of Modern Political Culture*, vol. 1, *The Political Culture of the Old Regime*, ed. Keith Baker (Oxford: Pergamon, 1987), pp. 225–242.

31. Ibid. François Oliver-Martin made a similar point many years ago: "If, instead of simply repeating the physiocrats' grievances with the corporate system, we were to take the time to look at these events in detail, I think we would find that the system was far less stagnant than we imagine . . ." See his classic, *L'organisation corporative de la France d'ancien régime* (Paris: Libraire du Recueil Sirey, 1938), p. 169. See also the discussion of taverns, inns, and other drinking establishments in Daniel Roche, *The People of Paris*, pp. 247–251. Michael Sonenscher, in his study of the luxury building and decorating trades, comes to a similar conclusion, arguing that eighteenth-century masters and workers often used guild law in an instrumental fashion: *Work and Wages* (Cambridge: Cambridge University Press, 1989), pp. 217–

218. For an empirical study that offers a nuanced critique of Sonenscher's "revisionism," see Cissie Fairchilds, "The Production and Marketing of Populuxe Goods in Eighteenth-Century Paris," in John Brewer and Roy Porter, eds., *Consumption and the World of Goods* (London: Routledge, 1993), pp. 228–248.

32. The carriage maker example is from *Factum pour Laurent Meunier, Claude Brouard, Jean David, et Guillaume Guibor, jurés en charge de la Communauté des Maîtres Pâtissiers (intimés) contre Maîtres Charcutiers (apellans)* (Paris, 1711), Bibliothèque Nationale, Paris (hereafter, B.N.) mss f.f.a. 21640, fol. 316. Olivier-Martin comments, "It was common for food-trades to be combined, as it was often too difficult to follow strictly the letter of the law"; *L'organisation du travail*, p. 170.

33. Statement of the caterers' guild to the Conseil d'état du Roi (July 16, 1748), cited in *Recueil d'Arrêts, Ordonnances, Statuts, et Réglemens, concernant la communauté des maîtres queulx, cuisiniers-traiteurs de la ville, faubourg, banlieue de Paris* (Paris: Le Breton, 1761), p. 11.

34. From the late seventeenth century, at least, cabaret-keepers (part of the powerful guild of *marchands de vin*) had legally served their patrons bread, meat, and salad. The *marchands de vin* included both retail cabaret-keepers and wholesale wine merchants. For their statutes, see Lespinasse, *Métiers et corporations*, vol. 1, pp. 635–695.

35. *Arrêt de la Cour du parlement*, July 15, 1760, in *Recueil d'Arrêts* (Paris: Le Breton, 1761), p. 66.

36. In 1781, there were 371 masters in the amalgamated guild of Caterers-Roastcooks-Pastrycooks who had become masters before the 1776 combination of the three trades. Of these, 110, or less than one-third, were simple master *traiteurs*. Nearly twenty percent (72) were joint *traiteurs–marchands de vin;* another seventeen percent (63) were *traiteurs-rôtisseurs. Catalogue des Maîtres Queulx-Cuisiniers-Traiteurs* (Paris: L. Jorry, 1781).

37. *L'Avantcoureur*, Mar. 9, 1767, p. 151; A.N. Y 9390 (Aug. 20, 1767).

38. "Les restaurateurs sont-ils sujets aux mêmes règles de police que les autres traiteurs?" in Des Essarts, compiler, *Causes célèbres, curieuses et intéressantes de toutes les cours souveraines du royaume* (Paris: 1786), vol. 143, p. 174.

1. The Friend of All the World

1. Roze de Chantoiseau was termed "the creator of the restaurant" in Louis Petit de Bachaumont, *Mémoires secrets pour servir à l'histoire de la République des lettres en France, depuis 1762 jusqu'à nos jours* (London: John Adamson, 1777–1789), vol. 5, p. 48 (Jan. 3, 1770). Variations on his name do appear in some versions of the "a first restaurateur named Boulanger, who was sued by the caterers" story. See *Vie publique et privée des français* (Paris: Sigault, 1826), vol. 1, p. 353; Jules Cousin, "Les Cafés de Paris en 1772," *Revue de*

Poche, July 15, 1867; Camille La Broue, "Restaurants et restaurés," *Grandgousier,* 4 (1937): 278.

2. Roze de Chantoiseau made his presentation to Louis XVI and the Estates-General on April 29, 1789. See *La Gazette de France,* May 1, 1789.

3. Mathurin Roze de Chantoiseau, *Lettre à Messieurs les députés de l'Assemblée nationale et autres officiers* (Paris: Cailleau, n.d.), p. 5.

4. (Bibliothèque de l'Arsenal) Archives de la Bastille 12357, folio 195 (Sept. 14, 1769).

5. Ibid., folio 192 (Sept. 6, 1769).

6. Roze de Chantoiseau, *Lettre à Messieurs les députés.* The proposal was re-titled to suit each successive regime. Hence the *Trésor public* later became *La Richesse du peuple républicain* (Paris, 1791), and then *Caisse d'union fraternelle, de crédit national* (Paris, n.d.). For his letter to the Committee of Public Safety, see A.N. AB^XIX 3899, piece 107.

7. A.N. Min. Cen. XI-800 (Ventôse 26, Year VII [Mar. 16, 1799]).

8. Archives de la Seine DQ^8 31, folio 246v. Several years earlier, Grimod de la Reynière had suggested that prominent Paris restaurateurs should acknowledge their debt to him, and support him, "much as actors often give benefit performances to help their indigent colleagues." Alexandre B. L. Grimod de la Reynière, *Almanach des gourmands* (Paris, 1803–1812), vol. 1, p. 212.

9. Two entertainers took the name "Comus": one held crowds enraptured with his scientific experiments, the other performed sleight of hand and acrobatics; their choice of stage name perhaps indicates the extent to which eighteenth-century culinary fashion overlapped with science and entertainment. See *L'Avantcoureur,* April 18, 1763, pp. 250–252, and Sept. 9, 1765, p. 563; *Rapport de Messieurs Cosnier, Maloet . . . Sur les avantages reconnus de la nouvelle méthode d'administrer l'électricité* (Paris: Pierres, 1783); Emile Campardon, *Les Spectacles de la foire,* reprint (Geneva: Slatkine, 1970), vol. 1, pp. 214–215. Comus, in Classical lore the frightening son of Circe and Bacchus, was the subject of a masque by Milton; his frequent invocation in the French context can probably be traced to the 1739 *Les Dons de Comus (The Gifts of Comus),* an index to dish titles and recipes that played a major role in launching the eighteenth century's "nouvelle cuisine": [Marin], *Les Dons de Comus* (Paris: Prault, 1739).

10. *Gazetin de comestible,* Feb. 1, 1778, p. 355.

11. Claude Fleury, *Collection des opuscules de Monsieur l'abbé Claude Fleury,* vol. 1, *Moeurs des israelites; Moeurs des chrétiens* (Nîmes: Beaume, 1780); on Foncemagne, see Peter-Eckhard Knabe, "Esthétique et art culinaire," *Dix-huitième siècle,* 15 (1983): 125–136.

12. *Encyclopédie ou dictionnaire raisonné des sciences, des arts et des métiers, par une société des gens de lettres* (Paris: 1751–1772), arts. "Cuisine" and "Frugalité."

13. Thémiseul de Saint-Hyacinthe (Hyacinthe Cordonnier), "Des Causes de la corruption du goût," *Journal littéraire* (de la Haye), vol. 7 (1715), pp. 323–

343. On the popularity of this now quite obscure author see Robert Darnton, *The Literary Underground of the Old Regime* (Cambridge, Mass.: Harvard University Press, 1982), p. 167. On Du Bos and culinary parallels, see Knabe, "Esthétique et art culinaire." On Madame Dacier's famous "Greek" dinner, see Alfred Gottschalk, *Histoire de l'alimentation* (Paris: Hippocrate, 1948), vol. 2, p. 141. François Marie Arouet de Voltaire, art. "Goût," in Voltaire, *Oeuvres complètes*, vol. 19, *Dictionnaire philosophique* (Paris: Garnier, 1879), p. 270.

14. On mesmerism, clandestine literature, and the underside of the Enlightenment, see the work of Robert Darnton.

15. I thank Jim Livesey for suggesting the comparison with Cerutti. Ray was prolific in his self-promotion; see *Affiches, annonces, avis divers* (hereafter, *AAAD*), Feb. 12, 1770, pp. 142–144. On Claude-Mammès Pahin de la Blancherie, see the very interesting discussion in Dena Goodman, *Republic of Letters* (Ithaca: Cornell University Press, 1994), pp. 242–280. Beaumarchais is obviously the best known of these figures today; for recent discussions of his significance see Simon Schama, *Citizens* (New York: Knopf, 1989), pp. 138–146, and Sarah Maza, *Private Lives and Public Affairs* (Berkeley: University of California Press, 1993), especially pp. 120–140.

16. On the eighteenth century's nouvelle cuisine, see Chapter 2. The period 1651–1790 witnessed the steady publication of cookbooks, a genre that had barely existed in the first 150 years of printing; see Alain Girard, "Le Triomphe de *La Cuisinière bourgeoise*. Livres culinaires, cuisine et société en France aux XVIIe et XVIIIe siècles," *Revue d'histoire moderne et contemporaine*, 24 (1977): 497–523; Daniel Alcouffe, "La Naissance de la table à manger au 18e siècle," in Ecole de Louvre, ed., *La Table et le partage* (Paris: Documentations françaises, 1986), pp. 57–65; pastry-making was described as a pastime for "ladies and gentlemen" by Jourdan Lecointe, *La Pâtisserie de la santé* (Paris: Briand, 1792), pp. 18–22, 219.

17. "I eat so little at these great dinners that I am often obliged to drink a third glass of water to appease my hunger. I owe to the severity of this diet my good health. I will be faithful to it until I die." Geoffrin's letter to her daughter, July 8, 1766, in a private collection, cited in Goodman, *The Republic of Letters*, p. 79.

18. Mathurin Roze de Chantoiseau's sister-in-law, the wife of his brother Armand, was the sister of Anne Eulalie Fessard, who was married to Jean Baptiste Henneveu. Jean Baptiste Henneveu inherited the Cadran Bleu from his father, Pierre, and passed it on to his son, Jean Baptiste. For the changes involved in converting it from a cabaret to a restaurant, see Chapter 3. For genealogical information, see Félix Herbert, *L'Ancien Fontainebleau* (Fontainebleau: M. Bourges, 1912), p. 106; A.N. Min. Cen. LXI-536 (July 26, 1772), XIV-446 (May 18, 1775), and XXII-86 (Oct. 23, 1792).

19. *Gazetin de comestible*, January 1767.

20. Petit de Bachaumont, *Mémoires secrets*, vol. 5, p. 40.

21. Chantoiseau (sometimes, "Chamoisaut"), a section of Thomery village, does not appear on all maps of the Fontainebleau area. See Claude François Denecourt, *Guide du voyageur dans le palais et la forêt du Fontainebleau* (Fontainebleau: Lhuillier, 1840), map; and Felix Herbert, *Dictionnaire historique et artistique de la Forêt du Fontainebleau* (Fontainebleau: M. Bourges, 1903), p. 88.

22. A.N. Min. Cen. LIV-973 (March 2, 1778). Armand Roze died in Chantoiseau in September 1774, but his estate was divided in Paris years later. His houses were worth over 10,000 livres, and his entire estate was valued at 25,370 livres. In very rough terms, his fortune was fifteen times that of the average Parisian wage earner; see Daniel Roche, *The People of Paris,* trans. Marie Evans and Gwynne Lewis (Leamington Spa: Berg, 1987), p. 75.

23. Petit de Bachaumont, *Mémoires secrets,* vol. 2, p. 40 (April 3, 1764). For a modern economic historian's analysis of the debt's significance in this period, see James C. Riley, *The Seven Years' War and the Old Regime in France: The Economic and Financial Toll* (Princeton: Princeton University Press, 1986), chap. 6.

24. Mathurin Roze de Chantoiseau, *L'Ami de tout le monde, ou Précis d'un plan de banque générale de crédit public* (Arsenal, Archives de la Bastille 12357, fol. 204–209), p. 8.

25. On Law see Edgar Faure, *La Banqueroute de Law* (Paris: Gallimard, 1977); Thomas Kavanagh, *Enlightenment and the Shadows of Chance* (Baltimore: Johns Hopkins University Press, 1993), chap. 3; John Law, *Oeuvres complètes,* ed. Paul Harsin (Paris: Libraire du Recueil Sirey, 1934); Herbert Lüthy, *La Banque protestante en France de la révocation de l'édit de Nantes à la Révolution* (Paris: SEVPEN, 1959).

26. *L'Ami de tout le monde,* p. 6.

27. John Law, *Money and Trade Considered,* in *Oeuvres complètes,* vol. 1, p. 2.

28. Any such plan would have to depend on the (metaphorical) short-sightedness of the note's possessors, on their failure to look forward to its end. At the end of the chain of creditors, after all, nobody would accept the letter of credit since, "completely depleted," it could no longer be passed along. The individual above this point on the chain would also realize that nobody below him would accept it, so he too would refuse it. All the way along, in fact, if people recognized that this piece of paper would eventually have no value, they would treat it as worthless in the present and refuse to accept it. I thank Ben Polak for his very helpful thoughts on this subject.

29. On consumerism and consumption in eighteenth-century Paris, see Cissie Fairchilds, "The Production and Meaning of Populuxe Goods in Eighteenth-Century Paris," in John Brewer and Roy Porter, eds., *Consumption and the World of Goods* (London: Routledge, 1993), pp. 228–248; Roche, *The People of Paris,* part 2; Annik Pardailhé-Galabrun, *La Naissance de l'intime* (Paris: Presses Universitaires de France, 1988); Colin Jones and Rebecca Spang, "Sans-culottes, *sans tabac, sans sucre:* Shifting Realms of

Necessity and Luxury in Eighteenth-Century France," in Maxine Berg and Helen Clifford, eds., *Consumers and Luxury: Consumer Culture in Europe, 1650–1850* (Manchester: Manchester University Press, 1999), pp. 37–62.

30. For the marriage contract see A.N. Min. Cen. XVII-1068 (Nov. 5, 1791). Marie Prost's cosmetic concoctions, approved by the Academy of Science, were touted in [Mathurin Roze de Chantoiseau], *Tablettes de renommée des Musiciens* (Paris: 1785), n.p.

31. M. Rouxel, avis des éditeurs, *L'Ami des hommes*, by Victor Riquetti Mirabeau (1757; Paris: Guillaumin, 1883), p. vi; Henri Ripert, *Le Marquis de Mirabeau, ses théories politiques et économiques* (Paris: A. Rousseau, 1901), pp. 129–130.

32. Though there is some evidence that Roze had business dealings with the Marquis's family. In 1790, a piece of property was supposed to pass from Roze to Mirabeau's widow, but they nullified the transfer a week later. A.N. Min. Cen. XXVII-501 (July 5 and 11, 1790).

33. Mirabeau had argued that French agriculture (and hence, population) was in decline because gold did not circulate throughout the country, but accumulated in Paris. Resorting often to the metaphor of the social body, he defined increased circulation as the basis of national "vivification." Wealth, like blood, was equally necessary to all parts of the body. As long as the luxurious living of a few funneled gold and agricultural products into the bloated capital, the French countryside would be neglected, production of food would lessen, and the population would diminish. *L'Ami des hommes*, pp. 201, 208–209.

34. Roze de Chantoiseau, *Ami de tout le monde*, p. 6.

35. The *Almanach* was the print version of the Bureau général d'Indication, a private information clearing-house that Roze had managed in the mid-1760s. (And which, incidentally, was located in the Hôtel d'Aligre, where Roze later opened his restaurant.) The Bureau was abolished by the state in December 1766, when it established its own monopoly on such businesses. B.N. mss, f.f.a. 22084, folios 19–27; Henri Sée, "La Création d'un Bureau de correspondance générale en 1766," *Revue d'histoire moderne*, 2 (1927): 51–55. Dena Goodman sees the monarchy's establishment of this bureau as an attempt "to invade [the] public space" of the Republic of Letters. Goodman, *The Republic of Letters*, p. 31.

36. [Mathurin Roze de Chantoiseau], *Essai sur l'Almanach général d'indication d'adresse personnelle et domicile fixe, des Six Corps, Arts et Métiers* (Paris: Duchesne, 1769), title page, original emphasis.

37. Mathurin Roze de Chantoiseau, *Almanach dauphin d'adresses et d'indications générales des six-corps marchands, artistes et fabriquants ou Tablettes de renommée* (Paris: Cailleau, 1784), p. 2.

38. On the alphabet as an organizing principle in this period see Cynthia J. Koepp, "The Alphabetical Order: Work in Diderot's *Encyclopédie*," in

Cynthia Koepp and Steven Kaplan, eds., *Work in France* (Ithaca: Cornell University Press, 1986), pp. 229–257.

39. [Roze de Chantoiseau], *Essai sur l'Almanach général,* n.p.

40. Ibid., n.p.

41. Roze de Chantoiseau, *Almanach dauphin d'adresses et d'indications,* p. 3.

42. More than a century later, it was still earning praises; see Alfred B. Benard ("Bing"), *Les Annuaires parisiens* (Le Havre: Lemale, 1897), p. 24.

43. The *Gazette de France* reported his presentation of the 1777 almanac to the royal family. See *Gazette de France,* Jan. 10, 1777, p. 13.

44. *Tablettes de renommée, ou Almanach général d'Indication* (1773), n.p.

45. The Bureau was modeled on the first Bureau d'Adresse, established in 1630 by Théophraste Renaudot. On Renaudot, whose enormous range of business and scientific ventures makes him a worthy predecessor of Roze de Chantoiseau, see Howard M. Solomon, *Public Welfare, Science, and Propaganda in Seventeenth-Century France* (Princeton: Princeton University Press, 1972). On the luxury debate in eighteenth-century France, see Ellen Ross, "Mandeville, Melon and Voltaire: the Origins of the Luxury Controversy in France," *Studies on Voltaire and the Eighteenth Century,* 155 (1976): 1897–1912.

46. Colin Jones, "Bourgeois Revolution Revivified," in Colin Lucas, ed., *Rewriting the French Revolution* (Oxford: Clarendon Press, 1991), pp. 69–118, especially p. 88.

47. It is notoriously difficult and misleading to estimate equivalent values across centuries, and even today, one hundred dollars means one thing to an eight-year-old and something else to an investment banker. Still, it may be helpful to consider that the "fair" price for a four-pound loaf of bread was, throughout the eighteenth century, said to be approximately 8 sous (20 sous = 1 livre). Roze's meals, then, sold for the price of 7–15 heavy loaves of bread. On bread prices see, most recently, Judith Miller, *Mastering the Market* (Cambridge: Cambridge University Press, 1999).

48. Though the astute reader might have noticed that both the *Almanach's* office and the restaurateur's business were located in the Hôtel d'Aligre.

49. Jean-Jacques Rousseau, *Rousseau juge de Jean Jacques,* in *Oeuvres complètes* (Paris: Gallimard Bibliothèque de la Pléiade, 1959), vol. 1, pp. 657–992.

50. Jean Starobinski, *Jean-Jacques Rousseau: La transparence et l'obstacle* (Paris: Plon, 1957), p. 290.

51. Roze de Chantoiseau, *Almanach général* (1769), n.p.

52. *AAAD,* Jan. 12, 1767, pp. 39–40; Jan. 23, 1777, p. 107.

53. A.N. V³ 193 (Jan. 26, 1768).

54. On the privileged merchants and artisans who nominally "followed the Court," see Emma Delpeuch, "Les marchands et artisans suivant la cour," *Revue historique de droit français et étranger,* 4e série, vol. 52 (1974): 379–413; Roland Mousnier, *Les Institutions de la France sous la monarchie absolue* (Paris: Presses universitaires de France, 1980), vol. 2, p. 12; Leora Auslander,

Taste and Power: Furnishing Modern France (Berkeley: University of California Press, 1996), pp. 89–92. Delpeuch compares the cost of being received a master with that of purchasing a privilege, p. 393.

55. A.N. V³ 193 (June 24, 1767; Mar. 16, 1772; Feb. 2, 1773); A.N. Y 11408 (May 13, 1778).

56. Michael Sonenscher, *Work and Wages* (Cambridge: Cambridge University Press, 1989); Colin Jones, "The Great Chain of Buying: Medical Advertisement, the Bourgeois Public Sphere, and the Origins of the French Revolution," *American Historical Review,* 101 (1996): 13–40.

57. For customers see Vacossin's account book, Archives de la Seine D⁵B⁶ 5057. At the wedding of Vacossin's daughter, Henriette Sophie, to Jacques Simon Antoine Thevenin, a minor judicial officer, the witnesses included: the Marquis de Charras; Joseph Charles Roettiers de la Breteche, "squire"; and the officials of the Jersey abbey where Henriette Sophie had lodged for the previous six months. See A.N. Min. Cen. X-649 (July 8 and 10, 1775). See also Berger's wedding contract, A.N. Min. Cen. LXXVI 410 (Mar. 27, 1760) and Naudet's, A.N. Min. Cen. XXVIII-467 (Jan. 29, 1778).

58. Berger's wife's family, the Sansons, consisted largely of wine merchants; A.N. Min. Cen. LXXVI-410 (Mar. 27, 1768). For the restaurateurs who joined in his lawsuit, see the discussion in Chapter 3.

59. Jones, "The Great Chain of Buying"; Colin Jones and Laurence Brockliss, *The Medical World of Early Modern France* (Oxford: Oxford University Press, 1997).

60. In addition to Jones and Brockliss, see Peter Gay, *The Enlightenment: An Interpretation,* vol. 2, *The Science of Freedom* (1969; New York: Norton, 1977), pp. 12–23; Robert Mauzi, *L'Idée du bonheur dans la littérature et la pensée françaises au XVIIIe siècle* (1960; Geneva: Slatkine, 1979), pp. 293–329; Jean Ehrard, *L'Idée de la nature en France* (Paris: S.E.V.P.E.N., 1963), vol. 2, pp. 575–577; Robert Muchembled, *L'Invention de l'homme moderne* (Paris: Fayard, 1988), pp. 275–289; William Coleman, "Health and Hygiene in the *Encyclopédie:* A Medical Doctrine for the Bourgeoisie," *Journal of the History of Medicine,* 29 (1974): 399–421.

61. Many of these letters are preserved in the archives of the Ecole de médecine; see also Paul Delaunay, *Le Monde médical parisien au XVIIIe siècle* (Paris: J. Rousset, 1906), pp. 35–36, and Lindsay Wilson, *Women and Medicine in the French Enlightenment* (Baltimore and London: Johns Hopkins University Press, 1993), p. 7. Each issue of the *Recueil périodique d'observation de Médecine, de Chirurgie et de Pharmacie* contains numerous examples of these epistolary consultations, almost all of which condemn "ragoûts." See the recommendations for cases of suppressed menstruation and for "phthisis with scurvy," Sept. 1754, pp. 205, 207. For the popularity of legal mémoires see Maza, *Private Lives and Public Affairs,* especially the introduction.

62. Physicians claimed that unqualified persons, in reading about diseases, would start to see all the symptoms in themselves. The *Gazette de santé* decried inex-

pensive medical dictionaries as "just so many swords in the hands of fools" and reported a case of "cholera induced by reading popular medical books," *Gazette de santé* (1776), pp. 211–212; (1777), 111–112. See also the review of Le Begue de Presle, *Le Conservateur de la santé*, in *Journal de Trevoux*, 63 (1763), art. lxxiv.

63. Louis Jean Levesque de Pouilly, *Théorie des sentimens agréables*, 5th ed. (1736; Paris: Debure, 1774), pp. 95–96.

64. William I. Beveridge, *Influenza: The Last Great Plague* (New York: Prodist, 1978), pp. 28–29; Delaunay, *Monde médical*.

65. Robert Darnton, *Mesmerism and the End of the Enlightenment in France* (Cambridge, Mass.: Harvard University Press, 1968).

66. Menon, *Cuisine et office de santé* (Paris: Leclerc, 1758); Menon, *La Cuisinière bourgeoise* (Paris: Guillyn, 1744); Menon, *Les Soupers de la Cour* (Paris: Guillyn, 1755).

67. My interpretation of the social construction of health here runs counter to Alain Girard's. In his comparatively early and often cited study, he equated nouvelle cuisine (defined as healthy) with "cuisine bourgeoise." He claimed that scientifized manners and the myth of "our frugal forefathers" contributed to the creation of a "cuisine bourgeoise," which enabled the bourgeoisie to excuse itself from the too expensive complications of aristocratic cookery. Girard thus failed to recognize that the search for "simplicity" in cookery extended to the aristocracy as well. His account merely shifted the (once standard) account of eighteenth-century France as a land of nascent class conflicts into the kitchen. Girard, "Le Triomphe de *La Cuisinière bourgeoise*."

68. Advertisements for "health chocolate" are ubiquitous. See *AAAD,* Dec. 20, 1770, p. 1179; April 29, 1773, p. 383; and *l'Avantcoureur,* April 13, 1772, pp. 228–231. More rare is the listing of a "café de santé," fabricated from a roasted and ground mixture of rice, barley, rye, almonds, and sugar, *AAAD,* Jan. 22, 1785, p. 214. The best-known purveyor of "beautiful tortoises of all varieties and the necessary quality to make medicinal bouillons, good for purifying the blood, and efficacious in cases of chest illnesses" was Morel, hôtel d'Auvergne, rue St. Honoré; see *AAAD,* Dec. 21, 1766, p. 926. On medical advertising more generally see Jones, "The Great Chain of Buying."

69. Maille's mustard giveaway is first announced in the *AAAD,* Dec. 24, 1770, p. 1195. See also *Année littéraire,* 7 (1777): 211–213; *Journal de Politique et de Littérature* (Brussels, 1776), pp. 137–138.

70. Petit de Bachaumont, *Mémoires secrets,* vol. 9, pp. 11–12.

71. *Tablettes de renommée ou Almanac géneral d'Indication* (Paris: Desnos, Dessain, Lacombe, 1776), n. pag. This term was also used for semi-private hospitals administered by Dehorne, a former army physician, and De Caubotte, a surgeon, both of whom specialized in the treatment of sexually transmitted diseases; see Delaunay, *Monde médical*, pp. 273–275; Nicolas-Edme Restif de la Bretonne, *Les Nuits de Paris,* part 9, 210th night, most readily available in a recent compilation of Mercier and Restif de la Bretonne,

Michel Delon and Daniel Baruche, eds., *Paris le jour, Paris la nuit* (Paris: Robert Laffont, 1990), p. 940.

72. ". . . et ego vos restaurabos," *L'Avantcoureur,* July 6, 1767, p. 421. By most accounts this would make Vacossin's restaurant the first, for guidebook authors, tourists, and culinary historians all cite versions of this as the slogan of the first restaurant.

73. *L'Avantcoureur,* March 9, 1767, p. 151; July 6, 1767, pp. 421–424; *AAAD,* Oct. 19, 1769, p. 918.

74. Michel Jeanneret, *Des Mets et des mots* (Paris: José Corti, 1987), pp. 70–83; Bruno Laurioux, "Entre savoir et pratique: le livre de cuisine à la fin du moyen âge," *Médiévales* (1988): 68–71; Jean Céard, "La diététique dans la médecine de la Renaissance," in Jean-Claude Margolin and Robert Sauzet, eds., *Pratiques et discours alimentaires à la Renaissance* (Paris: G.-P. Maisonneuve et Larose, 1982), pp. 20–36; Jean-Louis Flandrin, "Médecine et habitudes alimentaires anciennes," in ibid., pp. 85–95. For a very brief overview of the delineation of cuisine and dietetics, see Claude Fischler, "Diaforus et Lustucru," in Fabrice Piault, ed., *Nourritures* (Paris: Autrement, September 1989), pp. 127–133.

75. Toby Gelfand, *Professionalizing Modern Medicine* (Westport, Conn.: Greenwood Press, 1980), especially chap. 4. Londa Schiebinger sees the barring of cooks from medicine as a gendered development paralleling the replacement of midwives by male gynecologists; see *The Mind Has No Sex?* (Cambridge, Mass.: Harvard University Press, 1989), pp. 112–116. While her argument may be partially valid, she fails to take into account the fact that "professional" cooks, outside the realm of domestic service, were overwhelmingly male.

76. Abbé Pierre-François Guyot Desfontaines, *Le Nouveau Gulliver, ou voyage de Jeune Gulliver, fils du capitain Gulliver* (Paris: Clouzier et Breton, 1730), vol. 2, pp. 61–72.

77. *Encyclopédie,* art. "Assaisonnemens." One 1742 cookbook preface queried: "They are making war on us in our homes; must we yield without firing back?" *Suites des dons de Comus,* reprinted in Stephen Mennell, *Lettre d'un pâtissier anglais, et autres contributions à une polémique gastronomique du XVIIIe siècle* (Exeter: Exeter University Press, 1981), p. 49.

78. Cissie Fairchilds, *Domestic Enemies* (Baltimore: Johns Hopkins University Press, 1984), chaps. 1–2.

79. Des Essarts (Nicolas-Toussaint Le Moyne), *Dictionnaire universel de police* (Paris: Moutard, 1786–1790), vol. 1, p. 252. In her memoirs, an Old-Regime duchess describes sending the kitchen staff one hour ahead, "to avoid the bad dinners served in inns"; Henriette de la Tour du Pin, *Mémoires d'une femme de cinquante ans* (Paris: Chapelot, 1914), vol. 1, p. 46.

80. See Meusnier's advertisements for bouillon cubes that would never spoil, *AAAD,* June 30, 1766, p. 526; Feb. 2, 1767, p. 106; June 7, 1770, p. 571. In the 1759 play *L'Ancienne et nouvelle cuisine,* the character Extract (close friend of the protagonist, Restaurant) has just come from making bouillon

cubes. He explains, "They are for a financier who is going to do his rounds through the provinces. Can a man of his importance put up with the horrible soups they serve in inns?" B.N. mss n.a.f. 2862, fol. 32.

81. *Recueil périodique d'observations de médecine, de chirurgie et de pharmacie,* March 1755, pp. 147–149; April 1755, pp. 283–302; Oct. 1755, pp. 260–265; Nov. 1757, pp. 340–354.

82. Ami (avocat en Parlement), "Réfutation d'une Lettre de maîtres Euler et Formey, qui tend à prouver que l'on peut se servir avec sécurité des vaisseaux de cuivre dans les Cuisines et les Pharmacies," *Recueil périodique d'observations de médecine, de chirurgie et de pharmacie,* Nov. 1757, p. 341. The dangers of copper cookware were a popular subject for this periodical: vol. 2 (March 1755), pp. 147–149; and vol. 3 (Oct. 1755). The Swedish monarch was often praised for his sagacity in outlawing copper cookware. See also, among many other sources: *Gazette de santé,* May 1776, pp. 75–76; *L'Avantcoureur,* Dec. 7, 1772, pp. 771–772; Le Begue de Presle, *Le Conservateur de la santé, ou avis sur les dangers qu'il importe à chacun d'éviter* (Paris: Didot, 1763), pp. 170–171; and d'Holbach's *Encyclopédie,* art. "Cuivre."

83. *AAAD,* Oct. 19, 1769, pp. 918–919.

84. A.N. Y 13790 (June 8, 1775). See also the statement by an engraver who returned "from eating dinner at his inn, as is his custom" to find the door of his residence forced open, and his possessions stolen, A.N. Y 13700 (July 2, 1785).

85. A.N. Y 13125 (Feb. 22, 1773), Y 15680 (June 3, 1786).

86. "No supper for Monsieur Doricourt," noted a Place Maubert traiteur. Archives de la Seine, D⁵B⁶ 4088 (account book of Pierre Porcebeuf), Sept. 2, 1766; similar notation, Sept. 7, 1766. Police reports, like account books, present an image of regular patrons. In reporting stolen silverware, Grapin said five of the six eaters were regulars, A.N. Y 13125 (Feb. 22, 1772). For cases of "selling" the regular clientele, see A.N. Min. Cen. X-672 (Oct. 14, 1778) and XCVI-528 (Oct. 18, 1783). The idea of transferring the customers who constituted a "practice" was also common among barber-wigmakers; see, for example, A.N. Min. Cen. VII-491 (May 25, 1789).

87. A.N. Y 12800 (Sept. 24, 1779); Y 13127 (Oct. 29, 1775).

88. Many *traiteurs* also kept *hôtels garnis.* The 1769 *Almanach général* combined *traiteurs,* innkeepers, and hostelers into one category. A historian of Paris interiors notes that the division of private household from business in these trades was fluid throughout the eighteenth century, so a room sometimes used for family might at some other point be rented to a guest; Pardailhé-Galabrun, *La Naissance de l'intime,* p. 243.

89. The police archives are full of cases of customers stealing silverware, e.g., A.N. Y 15682 (Jan. 1, 1788), yet the practice of sending it along with the food continued.

90. See, for example, Porcebeuf's account book, Archives de la Seine D⁵B⁶ 4088,

entry for Oct. 5, 1766: "Today M. de Villiers' month came to term. He owes 41 livres, 13 sous, 4 deniers, of which he paid me 18 livres."

91. For the nine-months bill, see A.N. Y 14304 (June 27, 1780); and for the customer's parrot, A.N. Y 7554 (April 19, 1769). On the other hand, the circumstances under which Jacques Thomas Trianon, a member of a family very prominent in all the food trades, lent approximately 1400 livres to Julie de Villeneuve-Vence, wife of a Président à mortier of the Parlement of Aix, are admittedly rather extraordinary; see *Mémoire pour le sieur Jacques-Thomas Trianon, Maître Traiteur à Paris . . . contre Dame Julie de Villeneuve-Vence* (Paris: Valleyre, 1777) and Maza, *Private Lives and Public Affairs,* pp. 140–166.

92. Louis Sébastien Mercier, *Tableau de Paris* (Amsterdam: 1783–1788), vol. 4, pp. 65–72. Dictionaries agreed that *traiteurs* were distinguished by the preparation of wedding banquets; Jean-Louis Féraud, *Dictionnaire critique de la langue française* (Marseille: Mossy, 1787), vol. 3, p. 722; Pierre Jaubert, *Dictionnaire raisonné des arts et métiers* (Paris: Libraires Associés, 1793), vol. 4, pp. 296–297.

93. David Garrioch, *Neighborhood and Community in Paris* (Cambridge: Cambridge University Press, 1987), pp. 26, 93; Thomas Brennan, *Public Drinking and Popular Culture in Eighteenth-Century France* (Princeton: Princeton University Press, 1988); Daniel Roche, "Cuisine et alimentation populaire à Paris," *Dix-huitième siècle,* 15 (1983): 7–18. *Traiteurs* continued to host wedding feasts; see Paul de Kock, "Les Restaurans," in *Nouveau Tableau de Paris au XIX siècle* (Paris: Charles Béchet, 1834), vol. 4, p. 78.

94. A police ordinance of February 20, 1782, banned ornamental glass beads that might "mix with foods . . . and cause the most deadly accidents," *AAAD,* Feb. 25, 1782, p. 445.

95. De Jaucourt's article "Hospitalité" reiterates an argument made by Montesquieu. See *De l'esprit des lois,* book 20, chap. 2, in which he asserts that commerce tends to stamp out both vices, such as brigandage, and certain moral virtues, such as hospitality.

96. *Tablettes de renommée,* 1773, n.p.

2. The Nouvelle Cuisine of Rousseauian Sensibility

1. *L'Avantcoureur,* March 9, 1767, p. 150.

2. Barbara Ketchum Wheaton, *Savouring the Past* (Philadelphia: University of Pennsylvania Press, 1983), pp. 77, 205; Stephen Mennell, *All Manners of Food* (Oxford: Basil Blackwell, 1985), pp. 138–139.

3. "Hic sapidè titillant juscula blanda palatum; Hic datur effaetis, pectoribusque salus." *L'Avantcoureur,* March 9, 1767, p. 151.

4. Peter Burke, "*Res et verba:* Conspicuous Consumption in the Early Modern World," in John Brewer and Roy Porter, eds., *Consumption and the World of Goods* (London: Routledge, 1993), pp. 148–161.

5. "Par privilège du Roi, au vrai Restaurateur," *L'Avantcoureur,* July 6, 1767, pp. 421–424.

6. Barbara Stafford, *Body Criticism* (Cambridge, Mass.: MIT Press, 1992), pp. 423–431; Alain Corbin, *The Foul and the Fragrant* (Cambridge, Mass.: Harvard University Press, 1986), quotation from p. 13; and Jocelyne Livi, *Vapeurs de femmes* (Paris: Navarin, 1984). For the revolution wrought in chemistry by the discovery that "air" consisted of chemicals in vaporous states, see Thomas Hankins, *Science and the Enlightenment* (Cambridge: Cambridge University Press, 1985), pp. 85–106.

7. Denis Diderot, *Entretien entre D'Alembert et Diderot* (1769; Paris: Garnier-Flammarion, 1965), pp. 38–43.

8. Samuel Tissot, *De la santé des gens de lettres* (1767; Paris: J. Ballière, 1822), p. 44.

9. *L'Avantcoureur,* Oct. 10, 1763, p. 642; Simeon Prosper Hardy, *Mes loisirs,* ed. Maurice Tourneux and Maurice Vitrac (Paris: Picard, 1912), vol. 1, p. 80.

10. The basic physiology was explained in numerous texts. For example, see Louis Lémery, *Traité des alimens,* ed. Jacques Jean Bruhier (Paris: Durand, 1755), vol. 1, p. lxi.

11. Rozière de la Chassagne, *Manuel des pulmoniques, ou traité complet des maladies de la poitrine* (Paris: Humaire, 1770), p. 236. On Rozière de la Chassagne's contribution to nineteenth-century tuberculosis treatment, see Pierre Guillaume, *Du désespoir au salut: les Tuberculeux aux XIXe et XXe siècles* (Paris: Aubier, 1986).

12. Coste, *Traité des maladies du poumon* (Paris: Herrisant, 1767), p. 35; Joseph Raulin, *Traité de la phthisie pulmonaire* (Paris: Valade, 1782), p. 213; Jacquin, *De la santé, ouvrage utile à tout le monde* (Paris: Durand, 1762), p. 163.

13. Coste, *Traité des maladies du poumon,* p. 35.

14. Domergue, *Moyens faciles et assurés pour conserver la santé* (Paris: LeGras, 1706), p. 4; Charles Auguste Vandermonde, *Dictionnaire portatif de santé* (Paris: Vincent, 1759), vol. 1, p. 531.

15. Claude Nicolas LeCat, *Traité des sensations et des passions en générale et des sens en particulier* (1740; Paris: Vallat-la-Chapelle, 1767), vol. 1, pp. 218–220.

16. George S. Rousseau, "Towards a Semiotics of the Nerve: The Social History of Language in a New Key," in Peter Burke and Roy Porter, eds., *Language, Self, and Society* (Oxford: Polity, 1991), pp. 213–275.

17. Elizabeth L. Haigh, "Vitalism, the Soul and Sensibility: The Physiology of Théophile Bordeu," *Journal of the History of Medicine,* 31 (1976): 30–41; Sergio Moravia, "From *Homme Machine* to *Homme Sensible:* Changing Eighteenth-Century Models of Man's Image," *Journal of the History of Ideas,* 39 (Jan. 1978): 45–60.

18. Livi, *Vapeurs de femmes;* for the argument that vapors are a disease of eighteenth-century individualism, see Maret, *Mémoire dans lequel on cherche à*

déterminer quelle influence les moeurs des français ont sur la santé (Amiens: Godard, 1772), pp. 53–55.

19. Anne Vincent-Buffault, *The History of Tears*, trans. Teresa Bridgeman (Basingstoke: Macmillan, 1991); G. J. Barker-Benfield, *The Culture of Sensibility* (Chicago: University of Chicago Press, 1992) focuses almost exclusively on British examples, but much of his discussion is relevant.

20. *Tableau du nouveau Palais Royal* (Paris: Maradan, 1788), pp. 65–66. In the 1769 play *Arlequin, restaurateur aux Porcherons*, Harlequin has just opened a restaurant, and receives constant business advice from a knowledgeable friend. His friend counsels him to serve only tiny portions, because many of his customers will feel that "one does not show proper upbringing if one can eat in the evening." B.N. mss., n.a.f. 2866, fol. 57.

21. Jacques Albert Hazon, "La diète nécessaire à tout le monde, l'est-elle davantage aux Habitans de la Ville de Paris?" defended May 27, 1755. See the account in the *Recueil périodique de médecine, chirurgie et pharmacie*, vol. 3 (1755), p. 250.

22. Medical texts, cookery books, and the *Encyclopédie* all described certain foods—potatoes, ham, dark bread—as suited only to rugged peasants and manual laborers. Novelists, as well, knew that diet distinguished "les honnêtes gens" from servants, artisans, and countryfolk: see Jean-Claude Bonnet, "Le Système de la cuisine et du repas chez Rousseau," in Serge A. Thériault, ed., *Jean-Jacques Rousseau et la médicine naturelle* (Montreal: Editions univers, 1979); Roseann Runte, "Nature and Culture: Jean-Jacques Rousseau and the *Confessions*," *Eighteenth Century Life*, 4 (May 1978): 70; Henri Lafon, "Du Thème alimentaire dans le roman," *Dix-Huitième Siècle*, 15 (1983): 171–173.

23. "To remain seated too long causes the humors to stagnate; the body's corridors clog, causing headaches, upsetting the stomach . . ." Mauvelain to the Société typographique de Neuchâtel (June 5, 1781) quoted in Robert Darnton, *The Literary Underground of the Old Regime* (Cambridge, Mass.: Harvard University Press, 1982), p. 123.

24. Ann Thomson, *Materialism and Society in the Mid-eighteenth Century: La Mettrie's "Discours préliminaire"* (Geneva: Droz, 1981); Pierre Naville, *D'Holbach et la philosophie scientifique au XVIIIe siècle* (Paris: Gallimard, 1967), pp. 143–145, 277–278.

25. *Encyclopédie ou dictionnaire raisonné des sciences, des arts et des métiers, par une société des gens de lettres* (Paris: 1751–1772), art. "Régime."

26. Tissot, *De la santé des gens de lettres*, pp. 46–61; for an earlier, very similar, set of recommendations see [La Mettrie], *Lettres de M. d. l. M., docteur en médecine, sur l'art de conserver la santé et prolonger la vie* (Paris: Prault, 1738), pp. 19–25.

27. Anne-Charles Lorry, *Essai sur les alimens, pour servir de commentaire aux livres diététiques d'Hippocrate* (Paris: Vincent, 1757), vol. 2, pp. 234–242. See also Tissot, *De la santé des gens de lettres*.

28. Darnton, *The Literary Underground*, chaps. 1–2.

29. Lorry, *Essai sur les alimens,* vol. 2, p. 232.

30. Coste, *Traité des maladies de poumon,* p. 110; Vandermonde, *Dictionnaire portatif de santé,* p. 303.

31. *L'Avantcoureur,* July 6, 1767, pp. 423–424; *Encyclopédie,* art. "Bain marie."

32. Etienne Laureault de Foncemagne, "Dissertation préliminaire," in [Menon], *Science du maître d'hôtel cuisinier,* nouvelle édition (1749; Paris: les Libraires associés, 1789), pp. xix–xx, reprinted (Paris: Corlet, 1982). The attribution of the text to Menon and the preface to Foncemagne are both by Antoine Barbier, *Dictionnaire des ouvrages anonymes* (Paris: Barrois, 1822–1827).

33. Bonnet, "Le Système de la cuisine et du repas chez Rousseau." See also Michel Onfray, *Le Ventre des philosophes* (Paris: Grasset, 1989), pp. 59–79.

34. [Menon], *Nouveau traité de la cuisine,* vol. 3, *La Nouvelle Cuisine* (Paris: M. E. David, 1742), pp. 37–42; *L'Ancienne et nouvelle cuisine,* B.N. mss n.a.f. 2862; Alexandre Louis Bertrand Robineau, dit de Beaunoir, *Blanquette et Restaurant,* B.N. mss n.a.f. 2875.

35. Jacques-Elie Gastelier, who sent weekly reports of intellectual, social, and political gossip to Héricart de Thury, a high-ranking official, immediately noted the publication of the key texts in the ancienne- and nouvelle-cuisine debate. Jacques-Elie Gastelier, *Lettres sur les affaires du temps,* ed. Henri Duranton (Paris: Champion Slatkine, 1993), pp. 341, 359–360.

36. *Essai sur la préparation des alimens, dont le but est la Santé, l'Economie et la perfection de la Théorie* (London and Paris: Onfroy, 1782), p. 4.

37. On the Grands-Danseurs' audience, see Michèle Root-Bernstein, *Boulevard Theatre and Revolution in Eighteenth-Century Paris* (Ann Arbor, Mich.: UMI Research Press, 1984), pp. 79–81; Robert M. Isherwood, *Farce and Fantasy: Popular Entertainment in Eighteenth-Century Paris* (New York: Oxford University Press, 1986), pp. 167–180. Though now unknown, Beaunoir was an extraordinarily popular playwright, described by some critics as more talented than Beaumarchais. Of the 191 plays performed by Nicolet's troupe between 1762 and 1780, Beaunoir wrote 114. See E.-Béatrice Abbott, "Robineau, dit de Beaunoir et les petits théâtres du XVIIIe siècle," *Revue d'histoire littéraire de la France,* 43 (1936): 20–54, 161–180.

    Under a variety of titles, *Blanquette et Restaurant* remained in the repertory for twelve years, being performed regularly through the 1780s (the *AAAD* listed performances for July 1777; July and September 1779; February 1780; May, June, July 1784; May, June, December 1787; April 1788; and July 1789) and a steady 30 times between the fall of the Bastille and the declaration of the Republic. See André Tissier, *Les Spectacles à Paris pendant la révolution* (Geneva: Droz, 1992), p. 156. Restif de la Bretonne evokes one performance in his account of Nicolet's; see *Les Nuits de Paris,* part 6, night 122, most readily available in Michel Delon and Daniel Baruche, eds., *Paris le jour, Paris la nuit* (Paris: Robert Laffont, 1990), pp. 841–842.

38. *AAAD,* Jan. 22, 1785, p. 207 (the same day on which the Théâtre Français

was performing Voltaire's *Sémiramis*); with the Fricassee, April 14, 1779, p. 1559; Aug. 29, 1788, p. 2439.

39. For other discussions of eighteenth-century nouvelle cuisine see Philip and Mary Hyman, "La Chapelle and Massialot: An 18th-Century Feud," *Petits Propos Culinaire*, 2 (Aug. 1979): 44–54; Jean-François Revel, *Un Festin en paroles* (Paris: J.-J. Pauvert, 1979), pp. 173–212; Stephen Mennell, *All Manners of Food*, pp. 78–83. Mennell also has edited four key texts of the nouvelle-cuisine controversy as: *Lettre d'un pâtissier anglais et autres contributions à une polémique gastronomique du XVIIIe siècle* (Exeter: University of Exeter Press, 1981).

40. Jean Ehrard, *L'Idée de la nature en France* (Paris: S.E.V.P.E.N., 1963), vol. 1, p. 256.

41. On efforts to define "simplicity" in other, primarily English, contexts see Raymond Havens, "Simplicity, A Changing Concept," in *Journal of the History of Ideas*, 14 (1953): 3–32.

42. [Marin], *Suite des Dons de Comus* (Paris: Pissot, 1742), pp. 42–43.

43. Alfred Gottschalk, *Histoire de l'alimentation* (Paris: Hippocrate, 1948), vol. 2, p. 141; Elisabeth Vigée Lebrun, *The Memoirs of Elisabeth Vigée Lebrun*, trans. Siân Evans (London: Camden Press, 1989), pp. 43–45; Monique Mosser, "Le Souper grec de Madame Vigée Lebrun," *Dix-huitième siècle*, 15 (1983): 155–168. In 1751, the English novelist Tobias Smollett satirized the vogue for "ancient" dinner parties; see his *The Adventures of Peregrine Pickle*, chap. 48.

44. François Marie Arouet de Voltaire, letter of September 6, 1765, in Voltaire, *The Complete Works of Voltaire*, ed. Theodore Besterman (Banbury, Oxfordshire: Voltaire Foundation, 1973), vol. 113, pp. 287–288.

45. "Petit dictionnaire des arts et métiers avant 1789, Cuisinier," *Magasin pittoresque*, 1881, p. 223. Barbara Ketchum Wheaton offers a number of Voltaire-at-table anecdotes in *Savouring the Past*, pp. 212–219.

46. Mennell, *All Manners of Food*, p. 82.

47. Voltaire, *Complete Works of Voltaire*, ed. Besterman, vol. 113, p. 288; Voltaire, *Oeuvres de Voltaire*, ed. Beuchot (Paris: Firmin Didot, 1832), vol. 62, pp. 428–430.

48. Michel Jeanneret, *Des mets et des mots* (Paris: José Corti, 1987).

49. On the importance of this genre in Antiquity, see Florence Dupont, *Le Plaisir et la loi* (Paris: François Maspero, 1977).

50. Jeanneret, *Des mets et des mots*, pp. 195–197.

51. The classic works on the Quarrel in France remain Hubert Gillot, *La Querelle des Anciens et des Modernes en France* (Nancy: Crépin-Leblond, 1914) and Hippolyte Rigault, *Histoire de la Querelle des Anciens et des Modernes* (Paris: Hachette, 1856). For a very concise description of the Quarrel's high points, see Robert J. Nelson, "The Quarrel of the Ancients and the Moderns," in Denis Hollier, ed., *A New History of French Literature* (Cambridge, Mass.: Harvard University Press, 1989), pp. 364–369. Annie Becq's lengthy *Genèse*

de l'esthétique française moderne (Pisa: Pacini, 1984) begins with a useful overview of the Quarrel.

52. Joseph Rykwert, *On Adam's House in Paradise* (Cambridge, Mass.: MIT Press, 1981); Ken Alder, *Engineering the Revolution* (Princeton: Princeton University Press, 1997), especially chapters 1–2.

53. Marquise de Créquy, *Souvenirs,* vol. 3, p. 127.

54. François Marin, *Les Dons de Comus* (Paris: Prault, 1739) and François Marin, *Suites des Dons de Comus* (Paris: Pissot, Didot, Brunet, 1742) reproduced in Mennell, *Lettre d'un pâtissier anglais,* pp. 6, 50.

55. *Journal de Trévoux,* 49 (1749), article 114.

56. Foncemagne, "Dissertation préliminaire," in [Menon], *Science du maître-d'hôtel cuisinier,* p. ix. See also Peter-Eckhard Knabe, "Esthétique et art culinaire," *Dix-huitième siècle,* 15 (1983): 125–136.

57. Discussion of matters culinary and gustatory here approached the key point in the rediscovery of Epicurus. Seventeenth- and eighteenth-century neo-epicureanism hinged on the notion that individual pleasure performed a social good. See Marcy Powell, "Epicureanism in French Literature" (Ph.D. diss., Harvard University, 1948). On the debate over luxury, see Ellen Ross, "Mandeville, Melon and Voltaire: The Origins of the Luxury Controversy in France," *Studies on Voltaire and the Eighteenth Century,* 155 (1976): 1897–1912; Christopher Berry, *The Idea of Luxury* (Cambridge: Cambridge University Press, 1994).

58. *Encyclopédie,* art. "Cuisine." De Jaucourt, author of this article, cites Homeric heroes as dietary role models in his article "Gourmandise."

59. Brumoy and Bougeant, "Preface," *Les Dons de Comus,* reproduced in Mennell, *Lettre d'un pâtissier anglais,* p. 7.

60. There are actually three articles on "Goût." Montesquieu contributed an unfinished piece, and De Jaucourt wrote a briefer article about the physiology of the tongue and palate. Barbara Stafford, *Body Criticism,* attributes the article here discussed to D'Alembert, as does Raymond Naves, *Le Goût de Voltaire* (Paris: Garnier, 1938). However, Beuchot's edition of Voltaire (vol. 19, p. 270) gives Voltaire as its author, because it appears in the 1771 edition of the *Dictionnaire philosophique.* See also Charles Jacques Beyer, introduction, *Essai sur le goût,* by Montesquieu (Geneva: Droz, 1967).

61. *Encyclopédie,* art. "Goût."

62. Jean Ehrard remarks that eighteenth-century thought dichotomized education and nature; *L'Idée de la nature en France,* vol. 2, pp. 760–765.

63. On de Jaucourt's many contributions to the *Encyclopédie,* see Madeleine Morris, *Le Chevalier de Jaucourt, un ami de la terre* (Geneva: Droz, 1979).

64. *Encyclopédie,* art. "Cuisine." The exact same paragraph can be found in François Alexandre Aubert de la Chesnaye des Bois, *Dictionnaire historique des moeurs, usages, et coutumes des français* (Paris: Vincent, 1767), vol. 1, p. 652.

65. Ibid.

66. Raulin, *Traité de la phthisie pulmonaire* (Paris: Valade, 1782), p. vi.

67. *Encyclopédie,* arts. "Frugalité" and "Gourmandise." Supporters of the nouvelle cuisine offered similar chronologies of cookery's development, but they argued that modern techniques would purify dishes of "foreign" aberrations. The introduction of Eastern luxury into Rome had indeed "disfigured foods in hundreds of ways, producing a multitude of over-refined dishes that had lost their natural goodness," but degeneration was reversible. The creation of the "simpler, cleaner, more intelligent" nouvelle cuisine would provide a happy resolution to this tale of Asian debauchery. "Earthy essences" or Persian influences, the nouvelle cuisine removed them both from French cookery. See, for example, [Briand], *Dictionnaire des alimens* (Paris: Gissey Bordelet, 1750), pp. xii–xiii.

68. Jean-Jacques Rousseau, *Emile,* trans. Allan Bloom (New York: Basic Books, 1979), pp. 151–153.

69. *Journal de Trévoux,* 49 (1749), art. 114

70. Dupré de Lisle, *Traité des maladies de la poitrine, connues sous le nom de Phthisie pulmonaire* (Paris: Costard, 1769), p. vi. In a similar vein, see Jacquin, *De la santé,* p. 167; Lémery, *Traité des alimens,* vol. 1, pp. lii, lxviii.

71. Pluquet, *Traité philosophique et politique sur le luxe* (Paris: Barrois, 1786), vol. 2, p. 330.

72. Ibid., vol. 2, p. 399.

73. *AAAD,* Oct. 19, 1769, pp. 918–919.

74. *AAAD,* Dec. 12, 1778, p. 69.

75. *L'Avantcoureur,* July 6, 1767, pp. 421–424.

76. Restaurateurs Aubry and Duclos both advertised rice creams (Aubry's selling for 10 sous), *AAAD,* Oct. 19, 1769, pp. 918–919; *AAAD,* Jan. 28, 1768, pp. 78–79; Rozière de la Chassagne, *Manuel des pulmoniques,* p. 101; Vandermonde, *Dictionnaire portatif de santé,* vol. 1, p. 367, and vol. 2, p. 103; Raulin, *Traité de la phthisie pulmonaire,* p. 212; Rousseau, *Emile,* p. 70.

77. Bonnet, "Système du repas et de la cuisine."

78. In moments of desperation, Diderot put himself on strict milk diets. Arthur M. Wilson, *Diderot, The Testing Years* (Oxford: Oxford University Press, 1957), p. 232. Dupré de Lisle recommended ass's milk as the single most reliable cure for the early stages of chest ailments; *Traité des maladies de la poitrine,* p. 223.

79. Jean-Jacques Rousseau, *La Nouvelle Héloïse,* quoted by Bonnet, "Le Système du repas," p. 126. Milk, honey and fruit are the foods of innocence and simplicity in Bernardin de Saint Pierre's *Paul et Virginie* (1788), as well. See James W. Brown, "The Ideological and Aesthetic Function of Food in *Paul et Virginie,*" *Eighteenth-Century Life* 4:3 (May 1978): 61–67.

80. Werner Sombart's classic *Luxury and Capitalism* (1913; Ann Arbor: University of Michigan Press, 1967) linked sugar to women and ornament, pp. 98–100. For a more specific study of sugar, which concentrates on the case of

Great Britain, see Sidney Mintz, *Sweetness and Power* (New York: Viking Penguin, 1985).

81. See *Emile* for Rousseau's comparison of a lavish meal, prepared from a wide range of foodstuffs and requiring the labor of unseen thousands, with a country meal of brown bread and local wine, where "no hands but theirs [those of the peasant hosts] have touched the food," pp. 190–191.

82. *L'Avantcoureur,* July 6, 1767, p. 422.

83. "Eau du Roi, de la fontaine de Villedavray" had been available in Paris since Jan. 5, 1767; see the long notices, *AAAD,* Jan. 12, 1767, pp. 39–40; Feb. 16, 1767, p. 140. In the very influential neoclassical scholarship of Johann Joachim Winckelmann, Greek art was praised for being flavorless and natural, much like spring water; see Stafford, *Body Criticism,* pp. 156–158.

84. See the recipe in *Dictionnaire portatif du cuisine* (Paris: Vincent, 1767), p. 81. The author commented that such pastries were "easily digested and very healthful, the ideal food for delicate and convalescent individuals," p. 83.

85. By the mid-eighteenth century, the majority of households had at least one mirror, but few in such great numbers as a restaurant or café. See Annik Pardailhé-Galabrun, *La Naissance de l'intime* (Paris: Presses universitaires de France, 1988), pp. 340–342.

86. *Arlequin, restaurateur,* fol. 56.

87. A.N. Min. Cen. LVIII-498 (June 7, 1779). The clock, by Causard, was worth 160 livres, while the mirrors were worth the considerable sum of 760 livres. For a very suggestive interpretation of the thermometer's popularity in this period, see Terry Castle, "The Female Thermometer," *Representations,* 17 (Winter 1987): 1–27.

88. *L'Avantcoureur,* July 6, 1767, p. 422.

89. Jean-Jacques Rousseau, *Discours sur l'origine de l'inégalité* (Paris: Garnier-Flammarion, 1971), p. 168.

90. Rousseau, *Emile,* p. 191.

91. Robert Darnton, "Readers Respond to Rousseau," in Darnton, *The Great Cat Massacre and Other Episodes in French Cultural History* (New York: Vintage, 1984), pp. 215–256.

92. On the cult of Rousseau's grave, see Simon Schama, *Citizens* (New York: Knopf, 1989), pp. 156–161.

93. Jean-Jacques Rousseau, *Oeuvres complètes* (Paris: Gallimard, Bibliothèque de la Pléiade, 1959–1969), vol. 1, p. 1034; for a more extended analysis of this episode, see my "Rousseau in the Restaurant," *Common Knowledge,* 5 (Spring 1996): 92–108.

94. Rousseau's account refers only to "the elder daughter"; Henriette Sophie, the eldest of the three Vacossin daughters, was married and pregnant at the probable time of the incident. For Henriette Sophie's wedding see her marriage contract, A.N. Min. Cen. X-649 (July 8 and 10, 1775). Her husband, Jacques Simon Antoine Thevenin, was a *huissier à cheval* at the Châtelet.

95. Rousseau, *Oeuvres complètes,* vol. 1, p. 1034.
96. Ibid.
97. Jean-Jacques Rousseau, *The Confessions,* trans. J. M. Cohen (Harmondsworth: Penguin, 1953), p. 320.
98. Ibid., p. 321.
99. On Rousseau's efforts to avoid circuits of exchange and payment, see Michel Serres, *The Parasite,* trans. Lawrence Schehr (Baltimore: Johns Hopkins University Press, 1982), especially pp. 103–138.

3. Private Appetites in a Public Space

1. Numerous cafés advertised that they had expanded their standard offerings to include "rice au lait"; see *Affiches, annonces, avis divers* (hereafter, *AAAD*) April 13, 1784, p. 957; Dec. 22, 1784, p. 3380; Oct. 10, 1786, p. 2684; Oct. 20, 1786, p. 2765.
2. For promotions of the "Dutch dairy" near the Jardin des Plantes, which served entire meals of dairy products, see *AAAD,* Thermidor 4, Year VI [July 22, 1798], p. 5960.
3. *AAAD,* Floréal 25, Year VII [May 14, 1799], p. 4328. The Véfour's menu is reproduced in Gérard Oberlé, *Les Fastes de Bacchus et de Comus* (Paris: Belfond, 1989), p. 875. The narrator orders "a *restaurant*" for the fainting allegorical figure of Morality in a song from 1798, *Dîners du vaudeville,* 26 (Brumaire VII [Oct.–Nov. 1798]), p. 42.
4. Honoré Blanc, *Le Guide des dîneurs* (1815; Paris: L'Etincelle, 1985); Fiacre's and Yardin's menus both note a different price for "just soup," pp. 85, 203. In 1826, Brillat-Savarin's *Physiologie du goût* (Paris: Flammarion, 1982) included several recipes for "powerful restoratives," pp. 334–337.
5. [Mathurin Roze de Chantoiseau], *Tablettes de renommée ou Almanach général d'Indication* (Paris: 1773), n. pag.
6. Archives de la Seine, $D^5 B^6$ 5057.
7. Ibid.
8. *AAAD,* Mar. 10, 1781, p. 562; Oct. 28, 1781, p. 2492; April 1, 1782, p. 765; Jan. 29, 1783, p. 236.
9. *AAAD,* Pluviôse 6, Year II [Jan. 25, 1794], p. 5867; Floréal 9, Year VIII [April 28, 1800], p. 3933.
10. *AAAD,* April 3, 1793, p. 1595.
11. Denis Diderot, *Correspondance,* ed. Georges Roth (Paris: Editions du minuit, 1962), vol. 7, p. 152 (letter to Sophie Volland, Sept. 28, 1767).
12. [Mathurin Roze de Chantoiseau], *Supplément aux tablettes royales* (Paris, 1777), p. 65.
13. A.N. Min. Cen. LVIII-498 (June 7, 1779).
14. On the most famous such *marmite,* see Louis Sébastien Mercier, *Tableau de Paris* (1783–1788), chap. 384, most readily available in Michel Delon and Daniel Baruche, eds., *Paris le jour, Paris la nuit* (Paris: Robert Laffont,

1990), pp. 183–184; Alexandre B. L. Grimod de la Reynière, *Almanach des Gourmands* (Paris, 1803–1812), vol. 1, p. 282.

15. Mercier, *Tableau de Paris,* chap. 70 in Delon and Baruche, eds., *Paris le jour, Paris la nuit,* pp. 68–69.

16. Johann J. Volkmann, *Neueste Reise durch Frankreich* (Leipzig: Gaspar Fritsch, 1787), vol. 1, p. 152.

17. Arthur Young, *Travels during the Years 1787, 1788, and 1789* (Dublin: Cross, 1793), vol. 1, pp. 72, 159.

18. Ibid., vol. 1, p. 82.

19. "English conversation at Dinner and thea [*sic*] Table," offered by citizen-interpreter Daix, *AAAD,* April 3, 1793, p. 1423. Not surprisingly, a year later he diplomatically changed his advertisement to highlight the benefits of dining at a table where the "American" language was spoken; *AAAD,* Prairial 9, Year II [May 28, 1794], p. 7820. See also the advertisement, "Wanted to Breakfort [*sic*] three or four persons in a family where is spoken nothing but English," *AAAD,* Vendémiaire 27, Year VII [Oct. 18, 1798], p. 479. Louis Tronchet, *Picture of Paris,* 6th ed. (London: Sherwood, Nealy, and Jones, 1817), pp. xix–xx, recommended the conversational opportunities at the capital's tables d'hôte.

20. Antoine de Caraccioli, *Dictionnaire critique, pittoresque, et sentencieux, propre à faire connaître les usages du siècle, ainsi que ses bisarreries* (Lyon: Duplain, 1768), vol. 1, p. 108.

21. The ordinance is dated to May 21, but took effect from the judgment of April 11, 1784.

22. A.N. Min. Cen. IX-808 (Dec. 5, 1786).

23. A.N. Y 9487a (April 23, 1784).

24. "Les restaurateurs sont-ils sujets aux mêmes règles de police que les autres traiteurs?" in Des Essarts, compiler, *Causes célèbres, curieuses et intéressantes de toutes les cours souveraines du royaume* (Paris: 1786), vol. 143, pp. 147–186, citation from pp. 147–148. I thank Sophia Rosenfeld and Stuart Semmel for bringing this source to my attention.

25. The following discussion of judicial mémoires is indebted to Sarah Maza's excellent *Private Lives, Public Affairs* (Berkeley: University of California Press, 1993).

26. Maza, *Private Lives,* pp. 2, 122–124.

27. While the original mémoire does not seem to have survived, it was reproduced, minus some of the legal precedents, in Des Essarts, ed., *Causes célèbres.* As far as I know, this, and Roze de Chantoiseau's stint in jail for his credit reform pamphlet, are the only major legal issues surrounding the invention of the restaurant. The man named Boulanger (with his incriminating sheeps' feet) simply never appears in the sources I have examined. The historian's knowledge is always partial, and I readily concede that Boulanger's dispute with the *traiteurs* might, conceivably, have occurred. I am, however, more interested in noting that that is the story that has been re-

peated again and again, while this case, or Roze's other business ventures, has never been mentioned. Restaurants, even in the way they are historicized, seem to be of interest for what they serve, and not for where they fit in society.

28. "Des restaurateurs," in Des Essarts, ed., *Causes célèbres*, vol. 143, p. 163.

29. Ibid., p. 162.

30. "If restaurateurs' establishments could be considered as simple luxuries, their case would be far less strong. But given that they serve a real need, the rules should be bent"; ibid., p. 159.

31. Ibid., pp. 159–160.

32. Ibid., p. 159.

33. Ibid., pp. 148–150.

34. Ibid., pp. 150, 155.

35. *Arlequin, restaurateur*, B.N. mss. n.a.f. 2866, fol. 50.

36. "Des restaurateurs," in Des Essarts, ed., *Causes célèbres*, vol. 143, p. 160.

37. Ibid., pp. 160–161.

38. Ibid., p. 165.

39. Ibid., p. 166.

40. Ibid., p. 172.

41. A.N. Y 9487a (April 11 and 12, 1784).

42. A.N. Y 9487a (April 22 and May 14, 1784).

43. *Arrêt de la cour de Parlement, qui entre autres dispositions, permet aux Traiteurs-Restaurateurs de recevoir du monde dans les Salles, et y donne à manger jusqu'à 11h hiver, minuit été, et ce, sous la condition de ne donner à manger que dans les Salles et de la manière usitée*, June 28, 1786. (B.N. Recueil Z le Senne 200(1)).

44. Diderot, *Correspondance*, vol. 7, p. 152 (letter of Sept. 28, 1767, to Sophie Volland).

45. For examples of *traiteurs*-restaurateurs advertising the uses to which their many different-sized rooms might be put, see *AAAD*, Pluviôse 30, Year II [Feb. 18, 1794], p. 6223; Pluviôse 6, Year II [Jan. 25, 1794], p. 5867; Floréal 9, Year VIII [April 28, 1800], p. 3933.

46. *L'Avantcoureur*, March 9, 1767, p. 150.

47. *AAAD*, Germinal 8, Year V [Mar. 28, 1797], p. 3131.

48. The caricatured picture of a table d'hôte's offerings comes from J. C. Nemeitz, *Séjour de Paris* (Leyden: 1727), p. 58.

49. Barbara Stafford, *Voyage into Substance* (Cambridge, Mass.: MIT Press, 1984), p. 42.

50. Already in 1769, the play *Arlequin, Restaurateur* included a scene of reading aloud from a menu that began with soups and *restaurants* and continued with *chapons au gros sel* and spinach; B.N. mss. n.a.f. 2866, fol. 57.

51. *AAAD*, Pluviôse 18, Year II [Feb. 6, 1794], p. 6029.

52. See the Beauvilliers menu reproduced in Francis Blagdon, *Paris as it Was and as it Is, Illustrative of the Effects of the Revolution* (London: C. & R. Baldwin,

1803), vol. 1, p. 444, and the Véry menu in Daniel Morcrette, catalogue no. 131 (1975), item 203, p. 34.

53. Philip Thicknesse, *A Year's Journey through France* (London: W. Brown, 1778), vol. 2, p. 251.

54. "Des restaurateurs," in Des Essarts, ed., *Causes célèbres,* p. 162.

55. The French text includes an interesting typographical error. It actually reads: "Le prix de chaque place est modique, de façon que chacun pourra regler sa depense sur ses facultés . . ." (i.e., "the price of each place [*place,* rather than *plat,* meaning "dish") is modest, so that one can calculate expenses within one's budget"). Since nobody in a restaurant (or at a table d'hôte, for that matter) needs more than one seat, this is a telling substitution of *place* for *plat* and suggests just how extraordinary it was for an eatery to charge by the dish, and not by the place at table. *AAAD,* Oct. 19, 1769, pp. 918–919.

56. A.N. Min. Cen. XIV-446 (May 18, 1775).

57. A.N. Min. Cen. XXII-86 (Oct. 23, 1792).

58. *AAAD,* Oct. 19, 1769, pp. 918–919; Brumaire 20, Year V [Nov. 10, 1796], p. 771.

59. Diderot, *Correspondance,* vol. 7, p. 152.

60. *AAAD,* Sept. 19, 1789, pp. 2681–2682. The "Cirque," which was heated in winter and cooled in summer, also had stalls where thirty-six merchants displayed their goods, exhibition space for artists, and two billiard rooms. It offered free classes to its members (membership was 36 livres for 3 months, or 72 livres for a year), and sponsored nightly concerts. Admission for a single day cost 36 sous, and entitled one to a free refreshment either in the café (a cup of coffee or glass of liqueur) or in the restaurant (a small carafe of wine and a roll).

61. *L'Avantcoureur,* July 6, 1767, p. 422.

62. A.N. Min. Cen. LXXXIII-527 (Nov. 4, 1767). On wallpaper, see Annik Pardailhé-Galabrun, *La Naissance de l'intime* (Paris: Presses universitaires de France, 1988), pp. 372–374.

63. D., *Traité du fouet et de ses effets sur la physique de l'amour ou aphrodisiaque externe,* quoted in Guy Richard, *Histoire de l'amour en France* (Paris: J. Clattès, 1985), p. 226.

64. Emmanuel Bocher, *Les Gravures françaises du XVIIIe siècle,* part one, *Nicolas Lavreince* (Paris: Librairie des Bibliophiles, 1875), p. 42; Pierre Lespinasse, *Lavreince* (Paris: les Beaux-Arts, Edition d'études et de documents, 1928).

65. *Mercure de France,* August 17, 1782. The print was listed as selling for 3 livres, *AAAD,* April 30, 1782, p. 1019. It was also advertised in the *Journal de Paris,* April 26, 1782.

66. Sandra Lipshultz, ed., *Regency to Empire: French Printmaking 1715–1814* (Minneapolis: Minneapolis Institute of Arts, 1984), p. 279.

67. Samuel Tissot, *L'Onanisme* (Lausanne: A. Chapuis, 1760). The work went through numerous editions, and was reprinted well into the nineteenth century. On Tissot's importance see Théodor Tarczylo, *Sexe et liberté au siècle des*

Lumières (Paris: Presses de la Renaissance, 1983). An article in the *Encyclopédie* also made it clear that semen had to be directly replaced with nourishment; see *Encyclopédie ou dictionnaire raisonné des sciences, des arts et des métiers, par une société des gens de lettres* (Paris: 1751–1772), art. "Nutrition."

68. Plato, *Gorgias,* trans. Walter Hamilton (Harmondsworth: Penguin, 1960), pp. 43–47, 105–110. For eighteenth-century versions of this metaphor, see Cartaud de la Villate, *Essai historique et philosophique sur le goût* (1736; Slatkine Reprint: Geneva, 1970), pp. 30, 107; and Brumoy, *Pensées sur la décadence de la poésie latine,* in Brumoy, *Recueil de divers ouvrages* (Paris: Coignard, 1741), vol. 1, p. 32.

69. [Menon], *Cuisine et office de santé* (Paris: Leclerc, 1758). p. x. Compare "an assassin's art that disguises subtle poisons with pleasant sensations," *Journal de Trévoux,* XLIX (1749), art. CXIV.

70. *Tableau du nouveau Palais Royal* (Paris: Maradan, 1788), p. 64; Jean-François Blanvillain, *Le Pariséum, ou tableau actuel de Paris* (Paris: n.p., 1803), p. xxx.

71. *Discours de M. le premier Président de la Chambre du caffé de Dubuisson* (Paris: n.p., n.d.) B.N. Lb^{38} 1080.

72. Jürgen Habermas, *The Structural Transformation of the Public Sphere,* trans. Thomas Burger (Cambridge, Mass.: MIT Press, 1989), chap. 2; Roger Chartier, *The Cultural Origins of the French Revolution,* trans. Lydia Cochrane (Durham, N.C.: Duke University Press, 1991), pp. 20–37, 154–168; Thomas Crow, *Painters and Public Life in Eighteenth-Century Paris* (New Haven: Yale University Press, 1985); Daniel Roche, *Le Siècle des lumières en province* (Paris: Mouton, 1978); Daniel Roche, *Les Républicains des lettres* (Paris: Fayard, 1988); Ran Halèvi, *Les Loges maçonniques dans la France d'ancien régime* (Paris: Armand Colin, 1984).

73. Habermas, *Structural Transformation.* Habermas's work first appeared in German in 1960 and was translated into French in 1978. For reviews of recent historical works based on Habermas, see Benjamin Nathans, "Habermas's 'Public Sphere' in the Era of the French Revolution," *French Historical Studies,* 16 (Spring 1990): 621–644; and Anthony La Vopa, "Conceiving a Public: Ideas and Society in Eighteenth-Century Europe," *Journal of Modern History,* 64 (March 1992): 79–116. See also Craig Calhoun, ed., *Habermas and the Public Sphere* (Cambridge, Mass.: MIT Press, 1992).

74. I borrow this particularly clear and straightforward formulation from Craig Calhoun, "Introduction: Habermas and the Public Sphere," in Calhoun, ed., *Habermas and the Public Sphere,* p. 21.

75. As Sarah Maza has demonstrated in her work on the *causes célèbres,* the print attention given to personal scandals at the end of the Old Regime was instrumental in giving readers a sense of shared experience, the groundwork for a belief in political communality. The "public sphere" was, she writes, preoccu-

pied with "matters common to the scattered 'subjectivities' of its inhabitants and which we would call 'private' . . . love, marriage, child-rearing, and family life." Maza, *Private Lives,* p. 13.

76. In addition to the works mentioned in notes 72–75, Thomas Brennan, *Public Drinking and Popular Culture in Eighteenth-Century Paris* (Princeton: Princeton University Press, 1988) deals specifically with "popular" sociability and its representation, by social elites, as dangerous. See also Jeffrey Ravel, "Seating the Public: Spheres and Loathing in the Paris Theaters, 1777–1788," *French Historical Studies,* 18 (1993): 173–210.

77. For studies of the emergence of modern "political culture," see *The French Revolution and the Creation of Modern Political Culture,* vol. 1, *The Political Culture of the Old Regime,* ed. Keith Baker (Oxford: Pergamon, 1987), and vol. 2, *The Political Culture of the French Revolution,* ed. Colin Lucas (Oxford: Pergamon, 1988); Lynn Hunt, *Politics, Culture, and Class in the French Revolution* (Berkeley: University of California Press, 1984); Mona Ozouf, *La Fête révolutionnaire* (Paris: Gallimard, 1976); Daniel Gordon, *Citizens without Sovereignty: Equality and Sociability in French Thought, 1670–1789* (Princeton: Princeton University Press, 1994).

78. While Habermas has been interpreted to argue that one replaces the other, I would emphasize, rather, the ways in which the theatrical and the judicial continue to play with and work off each other: to host his critical *grand couvert* (see Chapter 4), Grimod de la Reynière needed an audience. In this, he was not unlike other great performers of the late eighteenth century, such as Linguet or Beaumarchais, and, somewhat earlier, Voltaire.

79. Dena Goodman, *The Republic of Letters* (Ithaca: Cornell University Press, 1994).

80. Michelle Perrot, Introduction, in Philippe Ariès and Georges Duby, eds., *A History of Private Life,* vol. 4, *From the Fires of Revolution,* ed. Michelle Perrot, trans. Arthur Goldhammer (Cambridge, Mass.: Harvard University Press, 1989), p. 4; the volume discusses only at-home "bourgeois" meals, pp. 271–277. Omitted from the work on the public sphere, restaurants receive no more attention in the highly touted *History of Private Life* series than they do in a standard political or social history textbook.

81. A.N. Y 11008 (Jan. 5, 1767). Fights might erupt over other tastes as well; for one over salad dressing, see A.N. Y 15869A (April 12, 1764).

82. *L'Avantcoureur,* Mar. 9, 1767, p. 150; *AAAD,* Oct. 19, 1769, p. 918.

4. Morality, Equality, Hospitality!

1. I base my account on Friedrich Melchior Grimm, *Correspondance littéraire, philosophique, et critique de Grimm et de Diderot* (Paris: Furne, 1830), vol. 11, pp. 363–365; Louis Petit de Bachaumont, *Mémoires secrets pour servir à l'histoire de la République des lettres en France, depuis 1762* (London: John Adamson, 1784), vol. 22, pp. 72–78; Nicolas-Edme Restif de la Bretonne,

Les Nuits de Paris, part 12, night 345, and part 13, nights 346 and 351, most readily available in Michel Delon and Daniel Baruche, eds., *Paris le jour, Paris la nuit* (Paris: Robert Laffont, 1990), pp. 1052–1054, 1062–1064. Grimod's supper was mentioned, though not described, by Métra, *Correspondance secrète, politique, et littéraire ou Mémoires pour servir à l'histoire des cours, des sociétés, et de la littérateur en France depuis la mort de Louis XV* (London: John Adamson, 1788), vol. 14, p. 178. It was described, but the host not named, in Jean Baptiste Nougaret, *Spectacle et tableau mouvant de Paris* (Paris: Duchesne, 1787), vol. 2, pp. 22–24.

2. The nineteenth-century press, as well, sometimes told the tale of Grimod's funereal supper, as if it were still a worthy topic of gossip. See the feuilleton of *La Presse,* Sept. 10, 1839.

3. On the practices of freemasonry, see Margaret Jacob, *Living the Enlightenment* (Oxford: Oxford University Press, 1991).

4. Paul Lacroix, *Histoire des mystificateurs et des mystifiés* (Brussels: Schnée, 1858), vol. 1, pp. 111–118; Ned Rival, *Grimod de la Reynière, le gourmand gentilhomme* (Paris: Pré aux clercs, 1983), p. 52; Charles Monselet, *Les Oubliés et les dédaignés, figures littéraires de la fin du XVIIIe siècle* (Alençon: Poulet, Malassis, et deBroise, 1857), vol. 2, pp. 203–206.

5. Aron notes that the dinner was a scandal precisely because of the audience, but he does not elaborate further on this point. Instead, he argues that Grimod's supper marked the beginning of a culinary discourse and prefigured the intimate link between literature and the table that "will so profoundly mark French civilization of the nineteenth century"; Jean-Paul Aron, *Le Mangeur du XIXe siècle* (Paris: Robert Laffont, 1793), pp. 13–14.

6. Petit de Bachaumont, *Mémoires secrets,* vol. 22, p. 78.

7. Siméon Prosper Hardy, *Mes loisirs,* published by Maurice Tourneux and Maurice Vitrac (Paris: Picard, 1912), p. 408.

8. For an extensive description of the Saint Roch's Day Feast, see A.N. H*² 1872.

9. Simon Schama, *Citizens* (New York: Knopf, 1989), pp. 378–379.

10. Though much discussed in the manuscript news and scandal sheets of the day, both have since been utterly forgotten. On the first, staged as Marriage's triumphant defeat of Love and Pleasure, see Petit de Bachaumont, *Mémoires secrets,* vol. 4, p. 242. The Marquis de Brunoy famously squandered his inheritance on tinting a river black and dressing his gardeners, cooks, and other servants in lavish, gold-braid-festooned costumes, while he himself dressed in rags; see *Les Folies du Marquis de Brunoy, ou ses mille et une extravagances* (Paris: Lerouge, 1804).

11. Grimm, *Correspondance littéraire,* vol. 11, p. 363.

12. For the little old lady who followed the First Consul everywhere in the hope of inviting him to dinner, see A.N. F⁷ 3832 (Floréal 9, Year XII [April 28, 1804]).

13. Aron, *Le Mangeur,* pp. 13–35; Stephen Mennell, *All Manners of Food* (Ox-

ford: Basil Blackwell, 1985), chap. 6; Jean-François Revel, *Un Festin en paroles* (Paris: J-J. Pauvert, 1979), pp. 207–208; Maguelonne Toussaint-Samat, *A History of Food*, trans. Anthea Bell (1987; Oxford: Basil Blackwell, 1992), pp. 731–734; Barbara Ketchum Wheaton, *Savouring the Past* (Philadelphia: University of Pennsylvania Press, 1983), p. 73; Joanne Finkelstein, *Dining Out* (Oxford: Polity, 1989), pp. 144–145; Claudine Marenco, *Manières de table, modèles de moeurs* (E.N.S.-Cachan, 1992), pp. 164–169; Jean-Robert Pitte, *Gastronomie française, histoire et géographie d'une passion* (Paris: Fayard, 1991), pp. 161–169; Marcel Le Clère, *Paris de la Préhistoire à nos jours* (St.-Jean-d'Angély: Bordessoules, 1985), p. 503; Edmond and Jules Goncourt, *Histoire de la société française pendant la Révolution* (Paris: Dentu, 1854), pp. 116–121; Edmond and Jules Goncourt, *Histoire de la société française pendant le Directoire*, 2nd ed. (Paris: Dentu, 1855), pp. 76–81; *Le Palais Royal*, catalogue of Musée Carnavelet exhibit, May-Sept. 1988, pp. 200–201; and, no doubt reaching the largest readership, Alice Furlaud, "What do you do Après Revolution? Go Out to Eat," *New York Times*, July 12, 1989, p. C1. For Hobsbawm's offhand discussion of the restaurant as obvious evidence of nineteenth-century France's "bourgeois" nature, see *The Age of Revolution* (New York: Signet, 1962), p. 220.

14. Félicité Stéphanie de Genlis, *Dictionnaire critique et raisonné des étiquettes de la cour* (Paris: P. Mangie, 1818), vol. 1, p. 242; Louis Sébastien Mercier, *Le Nouveau Paris* (Paris: Fuchs, 1798), vol. 3, p. 174. For a note of succinct dismay in assessing the joint effects of the Revolution and the restaurant, little could rival one writer's conclusion that "all was overturned"; see Paul Vermond, "Les Restaurants de Paris," *Revue de Paris*, ser. 2, no. 15 (1835), pp. 109–121. According to Balzac and his collaborator Horace Raisson, the restaurant "is, like so many other institutions, the product of the Enlightenment." [A. B. de Périgord], *Nouvel almanach des gourmands*, vol. 3 (Paris: Baouduin, 1827), p. 47.

15. Pierre Jouhard, *Paris dans le XIXme siècle, ou Réflexions d'un observateur* (Paris: Dentu, 1810), pp. viii–ix, 137.

16. For studies of Jacobin insistence on new times and spaces, see *L'Espace et le temps réconstruits*, Marseilles colloque, Feb. 22–24, 1989 (Aix en Provence: Publications de l'Université de Provence, 1990); Lynn Hunt, *Politics, Culture, and Class in the French Revolution* (Berkeley: University of California Press, 1984), pp. 26–32; Mona Ozouf, *La Fête révolutionnaire* (Paris: Gallimard, 1976); and François Furet, *Penser la révolution française* (Paris: Gallimard, 1978), chap. 1.

17. "Images of illness and of degeneration flowed from writers' pens," argues one historian of the pamphlet literature of 1788 and 1789; see Antoine de Baecque, *Le Corps de l'histoire* (Paris: Calmann-Lévy, 1993), p. 103.

18. *Margot, la vieille bonne femme de 102 ans, soeur de curé de 97 ans, à messieurs des états généraux* (1789), cited in de Baecque, *Le Corps de l'histoire*, p. 130.

19. Mona Ozouf, "Fraternity," in François Furet and Mona Ozouf, eds., *A Crit-

ical Dictionary of the French Revolution, trans. Arthur Goldhammer (Cambridge, Mass.: Harvard University Press, 1989), pp. 694–703; Hunt, *Politics, Culture, and Class in the French Revolution,* p. 86; "Since the Revolution, there has not been a political event in France that was not both organized at, and celebrated with, a banquet," Armand Lebault, *La Table et le repas à travers les siècles* (Paris: Laveur, n.d.), p. 683.

20. B.N. Cabinet des estampes, coll. DeVinck, vol. 3, numbers 430, 478, 631; B.N. Cabinet des medailles, Med. Revol. 200.

21. Report of municipal officers of Amboise (Messidor 11, Year II [June 29, 1794]) in *Archives parlementaires* (Paris: CNRS, 1980), ser. 1, vol. 92, p. 261. See also A.N. C 289, report of Société républicaine du Rochefort (Brumaire 30, Year II [Nov. 20, 1793]).

22. For many analyses of the Revolution in these terms, see Furet and Ozouf, eds., *Critical Dictionary of the French Revolution.*

23. George Rudé, *The Crowd in the French Revolution* (1959; Oxford: Oxford University Press, 1973).

24. Similar points have been made with particular elegance by William Reddy, *Money and Liberty in Modern Europe* (Cambridge: Cambridge University Press, 1987), especially chap. 2, and William Sewell, *Work and Revolution in France* (Cambridge: Cambridge University Press, 1980).

25. The literature on the Revolution's uses of antiquity is considerable; see H. T. Parker, *The Cult of Antiquity and the French Revolutionaries* (Chicago, 1937); Claude Mossé, *L'Antiquité dans la Révolution française* (Paris: Albin Michel, 1989); R. Chevallier, ed., *L'Antiquité gréco-romaine vue par le siècle des Lumières* (Tours: Centre de Recherches A. Piganiol, 1987); R. Chevallier, ed., *La Révolution française et l'Antiquité* (Tours: Centre de Recherches A. Piganiol, 1991).

26. M. Hano, "*L'Encyclopédie* et l'archéologie au XVIIIe siècle: l'article 'Herculaneum,'" in Chevallier, ed., *L'Antiquité vue par le siècle des lumières,* pp. 229–246; J. J. Barthélemy, *Voyage du jeune Anacharsis en Grèce* (Paris: 1788), chaps. 25 and 48; Pierre Jean Baptiste LeGrand d'Aussy, *Histoire de la vie privée des françois* (Paris: Pierres, 1782); [Athénée], *Le Banquet des savants,* trans. LeFebvre de Villebrune (Paris: Lamy, 1789–1791); Elisabeth Vigée Lebrun, *The Memoirs of Elisabeth Vigée Lebrun,* trans. Siân Evans (London: Camden Press, 1989), pp. 43–45. See also Monique Mosser, "Le Souper grec de Madame Vigée Le Brun," *Dix-huitième siècle,* 15 (1983): 155–168.

27. *Révolutions de France et de Brabant,* 30: 290; 35: 520.

28. Homer, *L'Illiade,* trans. Anne Dacier, new ed. (Paris: Martin, 1756), vol. 1, pp. ix, 90–91.

29. *Chronique de Paris,* July 18, 1789, reprinted in Charles Villette, *Lettres choisies* (Paris: Marchands de nouveauté, 1792), pp. 6–7.

30. Ozouf, *La Fête,* p. 59. Starobinski distinguishes the republican festival, which is a moment of foundation, from the deliberately ephemeral, aristocratic cele-

bration. Jean Starobinski, *1789, les emblèmes de la raison* (Paris: Flammarion, 1979), p. 65.

31. Norbert Elias, *The Court Society*, trans. E. Jephcott (New York: Pantheon, 1983) does not explicitly discuss the *grand couvert*, but his comments about the *levée* are germane; see pp. 83–90. See also *Affiches, annonces, avis divers* (hereafter, *AAAD*), Jan. 9, 1782, p. 71, for an announcement of ticket availability for the *grand couvert*.

32. Arthur Young, *Travels during the Years 1787, 1788, and 1789* (Dublin: Cross, 1793), vol. 1, p. 20; *Considérations philosophiques* (Paris, 1787), p. 155.

33. For more on the popularity of this work, see Robert Darnton, *The Forbidden Best-Sellers of Pre-Revolutionary France* (London and New York: Harper-Collins, 1996).

34. Louis Sébastien Mercier, *L'An 2440, rêve s'il en fut jamais*, vol. 1, p. 132.

35. Daniel Roche, *Histoire des choses banales* (Paris: Fayard, 1997), p. 254; Steven Kaplan, *Bread, Politics, and Political Economy in the Reign of Louis XV* (The Hague: Martinus Nijhoff, 1976), pp. 3–6, 32–33, 614–676.

36. For Rousseau's distinction of virtuous festival from corrupting theater, see his *Lettre à M. D'Alembert sur les spectacles*.

37. Villette may well have known the work of the early eighteenth-century police administrator and theorist, Nicolas Delamare, who wrote that "shared meals are among the best ways to ensure peace and sincere friendship between men"; *Traité de la police* (Paris: S. & P. Cot, 1705), vol. 1, p. 427.

38. Maximilien Isnard, writing to one of the weekly newspapers, similarly described the May 1790 confederation of Draguignan and Fréjus as "liberty's wedding" and proclaimed "I see them [600 representatives from the two towns] at the same table, because they form but a single family." *Révolutions de France et de Brabant*, 30: 264.

39. For more extended discussions of this celebration, see Ozouf, *La Fête*, pp. 59–101; and Marie-Louise Biver, *Fêtes révolutionnaires à Paris* (Paris: Presses universitaires de France, 1979), pp. 11–31.

40. Tributes to the Federation often stressed that the words were on everybody's lips simultaneously; for example, see *Archives parlementaires* (Paris: 1879–), vol. 17, p. 323.

41. There is not space here to offer an exhaustive inventory of tributes to the Federation. For a representative sampling, see *Chronique de Paris*, July 10, 1790, p. 763; René Levasseur, *Mémoires* (Paris: Rapilly, 1829), vol. 1, pp. 28–30; John G. Millengen, *Recollections of Republican France, 1790–1801* (London: Henry Colburn, 1848), p. 59. For a less euphoric account, see the memoirs of the royalist Georges Duval, *Souvenirs de la Terreur* (Paris: Werdet, n.d.), vol. 1, p. 167.

42. *Repas dans tous les districts de Paris* (Paris: Joliot, 1790).

43. *Chronique de Paris*, July 19, 1790, p. 798. According to this account, the patriotic banquet replaced Old Regime "cold etiquette" with "masculine military music," garlands of natural flowers, and a centerpiece representing the natural beauty of an English garden.

44. *Chronique de Paris,* July 17, 1790, p. 787. By one estimate, only one-fifth the number of expected official guests arrived; *Révolutions de France et de Brabant,* 35: 519–522. Ozouf discusses the exclusion of "le peuple" from provincial federations; see *La Fête,* pp. 99–100. Christian Jouhaud, *Mazarinades: la Fronde des mots* (Paris: Aubier, 1985), pp. 127–137, considers the role of "the people" as spectators, and as grateful recipients of leftovers, in mid-seventeenth-century civic feasts.

45. *Le Patriote français,* June 23, 1790, p. 4.

46. Charles Philippe Ronsin, *La Fête de la liberté ou le dîner des patriotes* (Paris: de Cussac, 1790); *Chronique de Paris,* July 14, 1790, p. 779.

47. Jean-Marie Collot d'Herbois, *La Famille patriote ou la fédération* (Paris: Duchesne, 1790).

48. *Mémoires de Madame la duchesse de Tourzel* (Paris: Plon, 1883), cited in Ozouf, *La Fête,* p. 61.

49. For a polemical account of their confusion upon reaching the great city, see *Révolutions de Paris,* July 3–10, 1790, pp. 726–727.

50. *Archives parlementaires,* vol. 17, pp. 84–85; Schama, *Citizens,* pp. 500–513.

51. For images of the work on the Champs de Mars see B.N. Cabinet des Estampes, coll. DeVinck, vol. 22, 3719–3731.

52. *Archives parlementaires,* vol. 16, p. 137.

53. Ibid., vol. 16, pp. 138–140.

54. B.N. mss n.a.f. 2666 (section Butte des Moulins, July 7, 1790). Velloni organized the banquet for the Paris "electors," as well as the festival that followed; fireworks, a ball, and a tournament "featuring combats with live horses" were a few of the delights he promised; *AAAD,* July 3, 1790, p. 1929. At the end of the month, he advertised dinners for 12 livres per head: "for groups of fifty or more, military music will be provided free of charge"; *AAAD,* July 31, 1790, p. 2266. See also *Chronique de Paris,* July 5, 1790, p. 744.

55. *Chronique de Paris,* July 12, 1790, p. 772. LeSage, "pastrycook to Mesdames [the King's aunts]," had previously marketed the same products for winter holidays; *AAAD,* Dec. 25, 1789, p. 3649.

56. B.N. mss n.a.f. 2666, section Butte des Moulins, July 9, 1790. The Marquis de Ferrières, a delegate to the National Assembly, wrote to his wife that "the provincial deputies are well pleased with Parisian hospitality. Most of them are fed in the homes where they are lodged"; Charles E. de Ferrières, *Correspondance inédite* (Paris: Armand Colin, 1932), p. 242.

57. *Révolutions de Paris,* June 26–July 3, 1790, p. 703.

58. Helen Maria Williams, *Letters Written in France in the Summer 1790 to a Friend in England,* 5th ed. (London: T. Cadell, 1796), pp. 5, 18.

59. *Révolutions de Paris,* July 3–10, 1790, p. 726.

60. *Révolutions de France et de Brabant,* 30: 290. Desmoulins printed excerpts from Villette's proposal earlier in this same issue; see p. 280.

61. Ibid., 35: 520.

62. *Détails circonstanciés des fêtes patriotiques, illuminations, banquets civiques,*

services, etcetera qui ont eu lieu depuis dimanche 18 juillet 1790 (Paris, 1790) (Bibliothèque de l'Arsenal Ra⁴ 719); Prudhomme, *Révolutions de Paris*, July 3–10, 1790, p. 726.

63. Later songs written for republican repasts often contrasted the frank and simple gaiety of the sans-culottes with the austere good manners of Old-Regime banquets. See "Couplets patriotiques, chantés au repas fraternel," *AAAD*, Messidor 29, Year II [July 17, 1794], p. 8511.

64. Montesquieu, *Esprit des lois*, book 20, Jean-Jacques Rousseau, *Emile*, trans. Allan Bloom (New York: Basic Books, 1979), pp. 224, 413.

65. Sarah Maza, *Servants and Masters in Eighteenth-Century France* (Princeton: Princeton University Press, 1983), pp. 100–102; Cissie Fairchilds, *Domestic Enemies* (Baltimore: Johns Hopkins University Press, 1984), pp. 71–74, 129–130, 156–157.

66. *Archives parlementaires*, first series, vol. 27, pp. 611–615 (debates of July 1, 1791); Armand Dalloz, *Répertoire méthodique et alphabétique de législation, de doctrine, et de jurisprudence* (Paris: Bureau de la jurisprudence générale, 1847), vol. 44, part 2, pp. 1168–1169.

67. *Gazette des nouveaux tribunaux* (Paris: Perlet, c. 1790–1795), vol. 12, p. 120; vol. 13, pp. 35–41.

68. *Encyclopédie ou dictionnaire raisonné des sciences, des arts et des métiers, par une société des gens de lettres* (Paris: 1751–1772), art. "Hospitalité."

69. Claude Fleury, *Collection des opuscules de M. l'abbé Claude Fleury*, vol. 1, *Moeurs des chrétiens* (1682; Nimes: Beaume, 1780), p. 188; Montesquieu, *Esprit des lois*, book 20; *Révolutions de Paris*, Oct. 6–13, 1792, pp. 97–102.

70. Montesquieu, *Esprit des lois*, book 20; *Encyclopédie*, art. "Hospitalité."

71. Gérard-Antoine de Halem, *Paris en 1790*, ed. Arthur Chuquet (Paris: Léon Chailley, 1896), p. 195. The Englishman Millengen witnessed one of the actual *grands couverts* that included Lafayette; *Recollections of Republican France*, p. 29.

72. *Révolutions de Paris*, Feb. 9–16, 1793, reprinted in Christoph Cave, Denis Reynaud, and Danièle Willemart, eds., *1793, l'esprit des journaux* (Saint-Etienne: Publications de l'Université de Saint-Etienne, 1993), pp. 65–66.

73. Jean-Pierre Gross, *Fair Shares for All: Jacobin Egalitarianism in Practice* (Cambridge: Cambridge University Press, 1997), p. 88.

74. William H. Sewell, Jr., "The Sans-Culotte Rhetoric of Subsistence," in *The French Revolution and the Creation of Modern Political Culture*, vol. 4, *The Terror*, ed. Keith Baker (Oxford: Pergamon, 1994), pp. 249–269.

75. The grain maximum, established in May 1793, is the most famous of these regulations, but prices were set for a host of other articles. Colin Jones and I have argued that the eighteenth century witnessed a considerable expansion in the definition of "necessity"; see our "Sans-culottes, *sans café, sans tabac*: Shifting Realms of Necessity and Luxury in Eighteenth-Century France," in Maxine Berg and Helen Clifford, eds., *Consumers and Luxury: Consumption and Culture in Europe, 1650–1850* (Manchester: Manchester University Press, 1999), pp. 37–62.

76. *Gazette des nouveaux tribunaux,* vol. 8, pp. 345–351.

77. Railing against merchants and hoarders who did not abide by the maximum, the père Duchesne, a popular journalistic character, explicitly exempted bakers and concentrated on wine merchants, butchers, and grocers; *Le Père Duchesne,* numbers 341 and 345.

78. *Journal de la montagne,* Ventôse 6, Year II [Feb. 24, 1794], p. 821; Priscilla Parkhurst Ferguson, *Paris as Revolution* (Berkeley: University of California Press, 1994), p. 27.

79. See the Bibliothèque Nationale's microfilmed copy of Ronsin, *La Fête de la liberté.*

80. *Révolutions de Paris,* Frimaire 10–18, Year II [Nov. 30–Dec. 8, 1793], reprinted in Cave, Reynaud, and Willemart, eds., *1793, l'esprit des journaux,* p. 316. For more on revolutionary statues of Hercules, see Hunt, *Politics, Culture, and Class,* pp. 94–119; on David, see David L. Dowd, *J.-L. David: Pageant-Master of the Republic* (Lincoln: University of Nebraska Press, 1948); Warren Roberts, *Jacques-Louis David, Revolutionary Artist: Art, Politics, and the French Revolution* (Chapel Hill: University of North Carolina Press, 1989); Ronald Paulson, *Representations of Revolution* (New Haven: Yale University Press, 1983), chap. 1.

81. For the difficulty in enforcing the Maximum on goods other than those transported in large quantities, such as grain and wine, see Richard Cobb, *The People's Armies,* trans. Marianne Elliott (New Haven: Yale University Press, 1987), pp. 308–309.

82. A.N. F^7 4774^{94} (dossier Robert; Ventôse 14, Year II [Mar. 4, 1794]); A.N. W 112, reproduced in Pierre Caron, ed., *Paris pendant la Terreur: Rapports des agents secrets du Ministre de l'Intérieur* (Paris: Alphonse Picard, 1910–), vol. 4, p. 217.

83. *Gazette nationale ou le Moniteur universel,* Messidor 5, Year II [June 23, 1794], vol. 21, p. 36. Some months earlier, a speaker in the radical Cordeliers section had denounced restaurants for harboring "suspicious types" and claimed that if the police were doing its job properly, it would find "in these houses, the emigrés they cannot find anywhere else." *L'Abbréviateur universel,* Oct. 28, 1793, p. 1203.

84. A.N. F^7 4775^{44}.

85. Ibid.

86. It is difficult to get a sense of how many "fraternal meals" actually occurred, but see Marcel David, *Fraternité et révolution française* (Paris: Aubier, 1987), pp. 157–159.

87. *Suite du Journal de Perlet,* Messidor 23, Year II [July 11, 1794], p. 318. Pierre-François Palloy, the entrepreneur responsible for the dispersal of Bastille memorabilia across France, wrote in similar terms of the shared meal's effectiveness. Proposing a patriotic repast to take place on the site of the Bastille in July 1792 (as it had in July 1790), he wrote that the "imminent danger demands the most intimate union"—that is, the unity forged by a meal; *Affiches du soir,* July 25, 1792, p. 759, and *Avis au 48 sections de la capitale, à*

l'occasion d'un banquet civique (Paris: n.d.). During the Empire, Palloy wrote a song celebrating Napoleon's Tilsit banquet with the Russian and Prussian monarchs as a "family fête"; *Le Banquet de famille* (Paris, 1807).

88. Raymond Aubert, ed., *Journal de Célestin Guittard de Floriban, bourgeois de Paris sous la Révolution* (Paris: Editions France-Empire, 1974), pp. 411–412.

89. *Journal de la Montagne,* Messidor 29, Year II [July 17, 1794], p. 658.

90. We might take a royalist's claim that he was forced to drink directly from a wine pitcher (see Auguste François Frénilly, *Mémoires 1768–1828, Souvenirs d'un ultraroyaliste* [Paris: Perrin, 1987], p. 131) with a grain of salt, but see also Duval, *Souvenirs de la Terreur,* vol. 4, pp. 246, 248; Aubert, ed., *Journal de Célestin Guittard de Floriban,* p. 411.

91. Millengen, *Recollections,* pp. 251–252.

92. "The people, left to themselves, showed their true side, as good as they always are; the national character reappeared in all its honest gaiety," F.-Emmanuel Toulongeon, *Histoire de France, depuis la révolution de 1789* (Paris: Didot jeune, 1803), vol. 4, p. 368; Dulaure, *Esquisses historiques des principaux événemens de la révolution française* (Paris: Baudouin, 1824), vol. 3, p. 240; Duplessi-Bertaux, *Tableaux historiques de la révolution française* (Paris, 1817), vol. 2, p. 67; *Vie publique et privée des français* (Paris: Signault, 1826), vol. 1, pp. 387–390.

93. François-Alphonse Aulard, ed., *La Société des Jacobins: Recueil des documents* (Paris: Jouast, 1889–1897), vol. 6, p. 224.

94. Séance of Messidor 28, Year II [16 July 1794], cited in *Le Moniteur,* Messidor 29, Year II (reimp.; Paris: Plon, 1854), vol. 21, pp. 233–235. The civic meals, he said, "are multiplying at an unnatural rate."

95. For the critique of cookery in general (and the nouvelle cuisine in particular) as deceptive, see Chapter 2. On Barère see Jean-Pierre Thomas, *Bertrand Barère: la voix de la Révolution* (Paris: Desjonquères, 1989). Many of Barère's points are also found in a speech by Payan to the Paris Commune. Though Payan gave his report before Barère did (on Messidor 27, Year II), the *Moniteur* printed it after Barère's. See *Le Moniteur,* Thermidor 2, Year II [July 20, 1794], vol. 21, pp. 253–254.

96. Barère sounds paranoid, but the royalist Baron Frénilly claimed to have survived the winter of 1794 in Paris thanks to weekly pâtés sent to him from Reims and the vestiges of his wine cellar; see Frénilly, *Mémoires, 1768–1828,* p. 143. It is of course more than possible that the Baron "remembered" this diet only years after Barère's speech.

97. *Moniteur,* vol. 21, p. 233.

98. Ibid., p. 233.

99. Barère underlined this danger by describing tables set in the dark shadows of the Palais Royal, long famous as the haunt of prostitutes.

100. *AAAD,* Messidor 29, Year II [July 17, 1794], p. 8511. I thank Michael Cooperson for his metrical translation.

101. Mercier complained that the Feast of Reason, organized by the Conven-

tion, had strayed from this model: "The Church of Saint Eustache looked like a huge cabaret . . . Around the altar, people had set tables loaded with bottles of wine, and piled high with sausages, pâtés, and other meats." Louis Sébastien Mercier, *Le Nouveau Paris* (Paris: Fuchs, 1798), vol. 3, p. 141.

102. *Le Moniteur universel*, Ventôse 5, Year II [February 23, 1794], reprint vol. 19, pp. 535–536. As he would with the "repas fraternel," Barère stopped short of asking the Convention to actually pass a law banning the consumption of meat, even though others called for the institution of a "civic Lent."

103. According to the angry diatribes of the Père Duchesne, the honest Frenchman required little food—"a glass of wine and a crust, that's all that true sans-culottes need"—but his enemies were all hoarders and gluttons. *Père Duchesne*, n. 351, p. 2. See also Richard Cobb, *The Police and the People* (Oxford: Oxford University Press, 1970), pp. 246–324.

104. Villette and Desmoulins both cited the American revolutionaries as exemplars of austerity. In *Le Dîner des peuples*, another instructive play, Nature invites all her "children" for a frugal meal, but only France and America attend. For a review and plot summary, see *AAAD*, Floréal 18, Year II [May 7, 1794], pp. 7519–7520.

105. At Chazay d'Azergues, a festival celebrating the capture of Toulon began with songs and speeches, then ended in a shared meal to which the people of the commune brought "simple dishes without preparation," *Journal de la Montagne*, Pluviôse 16, Year II [Feb. 4, 1794], p. 662; the Jacobins of Fontainebleau also enjoyed a "frugal and fraternal snack," *Précis historique de la fête de la raison et de l'inauguration du buste de Michel LePelletier à Fontainebleau, le 20 frimaire* (Melun: Tarbé and Lefevre, 1794), p. 6.

106. *Moniteur*, vol. 21, p. 234.

107. Ozouf, "Fraternity," in Furet and Ozouf, eds., *Critical Dictionary*, p. 697.

108. When the period's didactic theater presented a meal, it was meant to teach a similar point. In Piis's *Plaisirs de l'Hospitalité* (Paris, 1794), a hard-working lumberjack and his son invite a modest widow and her daughter to share their spartan fare. In their forest clearing, hospitality, "the daughter of fraternity," brings all true sans-culottes together. The play further stresses that this table is not open to all: the woodsman's lazy, gluttonous apprentice, a former monk, is not allowed to share the "ravishing apples, beautiful nuts, and succulent pears" but is instead sent into the woods to look for a missing donkey. "Vigorous applause" greeted the play's "fraternal moral"; *Journal des théâtres et des fêtes nationales*, Brumaire 25, Year III [Nov. 15, 1794], pp. 721–723. See also Rézicourt, *Les Vrais sans-culottes, ou l'hospitalité républicaine* (Paris: Huet, 1794).

109. Compare De Jaucourt's *Encyclopédie* article, "Hospitalité."

110. On related questions, see Michel Serres, *The Parasite*, trans. Lawrence Schehr (Baltimore: Johns Hopkins University Press, 1982), especially pp. 116–124.

111. Jean-Jacques Rousseau, *The Confessions,* trans. J. M. Cohen (Harmondsworth: Penguin, 1953), p. 108.
112. Villette, *Lettres choisies,* pp. 6–7.
113. *Moniteur,* vol. 21, p. 233.
114. Ibid., p. 235.
115. A.N. AB^XIX 3899, piece 107.
116. Aileen Ribeiro, *Fashion in the French Revolution* (London: B. T. Batsford, 1988).

5. Fixed Prices: Gluttony and the French Revolution

1. For versions of this scene, see B.N. Cabinet des Estampes, collection DeVinck, vol. 17, nos. 2814–2815, and the Histoire de France series, Qb¹ 1790 (June), M99968. In the latter, "chacun son écot" appears as one of a number of medallions representing important moments in the first year of the Revolution.
2. L. Alexandre DeVérité, *Le Dîner des députés* (1789), Bibliothèque de l'Arsenal Rf 9108.
3. Ibid., p. 89.
4. Ibid., p. 91.
5. Daniel Roche, *The People of Paris,* trans. Marie Evans and Gwynne Lewis (Leamington Spa: Berg, 1987), pp. 83–89.
6. For an effort to estimate the amount of credit extended in Paris even in the first half of the century, see Philip Hoffman, Gilles Postel-Vinay, and Jean-Laurent Rosenthal, "Redistribution and Long-Term Private Debt in Paris, 1660–1726," *Journal of Economic History,* 55 (1995): 256–284. They comment that the credit market expanded considerably in the latter part of the century (p. 274).
7. *Grand détail de la révolte arrivée hier et les jours derniers au Palais Royal, occassionnée par les Marchands d'argent qui ont été chassés et assomés par le Peuple, et la punition exemplaire d'un Restaurateur qui n'a pas voulu recevoir en payement un Assignat* (Paris: Tremblay, 1791), p. 7.
8. *Le Père Duchesne,* no. 352, p. 5.
9. *Archives parlementaires,* ser. 1, vol. 92 (Paris: CNRS, 1980), pp. 37–38 (Messidor 2, Year II [June 20, 1794]), p. 376 (Messidor 16, Year II [July 4, 1794]); *Père Duchesne,* no. 352.
10. A.N. F⁷ 4775⁴, dossier Rose.
11. On the terms "cannibal" and "blood-drinker" as ways of identifying and expelling former terrorists, see Bronislaw Baczko, *Ending the Terror,* trans. Michel Petheram (Cambridge: Cambridge University Press, 1994), especially pp. 210–216.
12. The satire substitutes *courtille* (beer garden) for *patrie* (fatherland) and *boire* (drinking) for *gloire* (glory) in the first two lines of the *Marseillaise.* M. de L. . ., *Portefeuille d'un émigré* (Paris: marchands de nouveauté, n.d.), p. 36.

13. On the prevalence of gastro-culinary insults, see also William Sewell, Jr., "The Sans-Culottes Rhetoric of Subsistence," in *The French Revolution and the Origin of Modern Political Culture*, vol. 4, *The Terror*, ed. Keith Baker (Oxford: Pergamon, 1994), pp. 249–270.

14. A considerable literature has recently addressed the accusations of libertinage directed against Marie Antoinette; see Chantal Thomas, *La Reine scélérate: Marie-Antoinette dans les pamphlets* (Paris: Seuil, 1989); Lynn Hunt, *The Family Romance of the French Revolution* (Berkeley: University of California Press, 1992), pp. 89–123.

15. Ernst Kantorowicz, *The King's Two Bodies: A Study in Mediaeval Political Theology* (Princeton, N.J.: Princeton University Press, 1957).

16. "Varennes made the First Republic certain," Crane Brinton, *A Decade of Revolution* (New York: Harper and Row, 1963), p. 52. The author of a recent survey text on European history since the Renaissance begins his chapter on the French Revolution with an account of the Flight to Varennes: John Merriman, *A History of Modern Europe: from the Renaissance to the Present* (New York: W. W. Norton, 1996), p. 495.

17. A tradition beginning with the governess's diary: Jean Chalon, ed., *Mémoires de Madame la duchesse de Tourzel* (Paris: Mercure de France, 1969), p. 199. See also Noelle Destremau, *Varennes en Argonne* (Paris: NEL, 1987), p. 55.

18. Albert Soboul, *The French Revolution*, trans. Alan Forrest and Colin Jones (New York: Vintage, 1975), p. 223; Jules Michelet, *Histoire de la révolution française*, chap. 13.

19. Michel Winock, *L'Echec au roi* (Paris: Olivier Orban, 1991), p. 79; Marcel Reinhard, *La Fuite du roi* (Paris: Centre du Documentation Universitaire, 195?), vol. 1, pp. 50–53; vol. 2, pp. 128–129.

20. In addition to the examples discussed in the text, note the following: Bertha M. Gardiner, *The French Revolution*, 7th ed. (London: Longmans, 1893), p. 90; "Demands refreshment, as is written," says Thomas Carlyle, *The French Revolution* (New York: A. L. Burt, n.d.), vol. 1, p. 419.

21. *Révolutions de Paris*, June 18–25, 1791, p. 542; compare *La Feuille villageoise*, June 30, 1791, p. 244.

22. *Lettres de deux habitans des frontières* (Paris, 1791), p. 5; *Procès-verbal de ce qui s'est passé en la Ville de Varennes* (Paris: Imprimerie nationale, 1791), p. 9; *Nouveaux détails sur ce qui est arrivé à Louis XVI à Varennes et à Chalons* (Paris: Toussaint, 1791), p. 7.

23. Claude Antoine Gabriel Choiseul, *Relation du départ de Louis XVI*, Collection des mémoires relatifs à la Révolution française 14 (Paris: Baudouin frères, 1822), p. 92; Charles Nicolas Gabriel, *Louis XVI, le Marquis de Bouillé et Varennes* (Paris: Verdun, 1874), p. 245; François Victor Fournel, *L'Evénement de Varennes* (Paris: Champion, 1890), p. 173.

24. Larousse, *Grand dictionnaire universel du XIXe siècle* (Paris: Larousse, 1864–1890), vol. 15, pp. 782–783.

25. His scene presents the arrest at Varennes not as Rabelais's fifteen minutes

but, set up like a courtroom viewed from the judge's perspective, as the judgment of History; B.N. Cabinet des estampes, M100704.

26. B.N. Cabinet des estampes, Qb¹ 1791, M100674; *Courrier français,* June 22, 1791, p. 422.

27. *Révolutions de France et de Brabant,* 82, p. 187.

28. Ibid., p. 179. For discussions of the pig motif, see Hunt, *The Family Romance of the French Revolution,* pp. 49–51; Antoine de Baecque, *Le Corps de l'histoire* (Paris: Calmann-Lévy, 1993), pp. 85–98.

29. *Révolutions de Paris,* June 18–25, 1791, pp. 526–532.

30. Ibid., June 25–July 2, 1791, p. 583.

31. *Courrier français,* June 24, 1791, p. 439.

32. B.N. Cabinet des estampes, collection De Vinck vol. 23, no. 3944. The image was the frontispiece for *Révolutions de France et de Brabant,* no. 82.

33. André Castelot, *Le Rendez-vous de Varennes, ou les occasions manquées* (Paris: Perrin, 1971), pp. 249–250; *Révolutions de Paris,* June 25–July 2, 1791, p. 579; *Révolutions de France et de Brabant,* 82, p. 189.

34. *Révolutions de France et de Brabant,* 82, p. 193.

35. Ibid, p. 193; *Révolutions de Paris,* June 25–July 2, 1791, p. 587.

36. See Donna M. Hunter, "Swordplay: Jacques Louis David's painting of Le Peletier de Saint-Fargeau on His Deathbed," in James Heffernan, ed., *Representing the French Revolution* (Hanover, N.H.: University of New England Press, 1992), pp. 169–191.

37. A.N. F⁷ 4774⁶³.

38. Ibid.

39. On the David painting, see Hunter, "Swordplay." Simon Schama juxtaposes a drawing of the memorably ugly Le Peletier with David's sketch for the portrait in *Citizens* (New York: Knopf, 1989), p. 671.

40. On January 22, the deputy Delacroix moved that Le Peletier's inspirational dying words (about spilling blood for his country) should appear on his tomb; *Archives parlementaires,* vol. 57, p. 542.

41. Félix Le Peletier, *Vie de Michel LePeletier* (Paris: Imprimerie des Sans culottes [1793]).

42. *Archives parlementaires,* vol. 57, p. 516.

43. Ibid., p. 527.

44. In some contexts, the move either happened very quickly or signaled competing versions of the story. For example, on the front page of one newspaper, Le Peletier was seated alone in a Palais Egalité grotto (according to the Convention), but by page 6 (and the minutes of the local section), "Saint Fargeau was paying for his dinner." *L'Auditeur national,* 123 (January 22, 1793).

45. "To each his own taste" depends on each pays his own way.

46. A. V. Arnault, *Souvenirs d'un sexagénaire* (Paris: Dufey, 1833), vol. 2, p. 270; Jean Pierre Fabre de l'Aude, *Histoire secrète du Directoire* (Paris: Ménard, 1832), vol. 2, pp. 166–167; John G. Millengen, *Recollections of Republican*

France (London: Henry Colburn, 1848), p. 361; Armand F. d'Allonville, *Mémoires secrets de 1770–1830* (Brussels: Société typographique belge, 1845), vol. 4, pp. 74–83; Louis Sébastien Mercier, *Le Nouveau Paris* (Paris: Fuchs, 1798), vol. 4, pp. 196–198, and vol. 5, p. 195.

47. For an overview of the historiography, see Martin Lyons, *France Under the Directory* (Cambridge: Cambridge University Press, 1975), pp. 1–4. For all his efforts to reject the caricature, Lyons goes on to endorse the equation of Directory and pleasure, writing, "After the puritan régime of the Terror, society now set out to enjoy itself," p. 64. See also Adolphe Granier de Cassagnac, *Histoire du Directoire* (Paris: Furne, 1851), vol. 1, p. 381; Jean-Paul Aron, *Mangeur du XIXe siècle* (Paris: Laffont, 1973), p. 25; Jules Bertaud, *Les Parisiens sous la Révolution* (Paris: Amiot-Dumont, 1952), p. 219.

48. Carlyle, *The French Revolution*, book 9, chaps. 1–2 (vol. 2, p. 363); Edmond and Jules Goncourt, *Histoire de la société française pendant le Directoire* (Paris: A. Taride, 1854), p. 77; Richard Sennett, *The Fall of Public Man* (1977; London: Faber and Faber, 1986), pp. 184–187. See also the references to "hideous saturnalias" and "political impotence" in Amédée Gabourd, *Histoire de Paris depuis les temps les plus reculés jusqu'à nos jours* (Paris: Gaume frères, 1865), vol. 4, p. 477; and to the regime's "incredible ineptitude" and "most shameful spectacle" in Philippe Ludovic Sciout, *Le Directoire* (Paris: Firmin-Didot, 1895–1897), vol. 1, p. 489.

49. Jean Robiquet, *La Vie quotidienne au temps de la Révolution* (Paris: Hachette, 1938), p. 249.

50. Jacques Chabannes, *Amours sous la Révolution* (Paris: Perrin, 1967), p. 303. For other twentieth-century variations, in addition to those works already cited, see Albert Soboul, *The French Revolution*, trans. Alan Forrest and Colin Jones (New York: Vintage, 1975), pp. 429–330; Alfred Cobban, *A History of Modern France* (Harmondsworth: Penguin, 1957), vol. 1, pp. 251–252.

51. Lyons, *France Under the Directory*, pp. 1–4.

52. Albert Mathiez, *After Robespierre*, trans. C. A. Phillips (New York: Knopf, 1931), pp. 5, 260; R. R. Palmer, *The Age of the Democratic Revolution* (Princeton: Princeton University Press, 1964), vol. 2, p. 216.

53. One historian attributes the era's conspicuous consumption to the "inflationary" mentality produced by the assignat. Since money was not worth saving, he suggests, it made more sense to spend it; Denis Woronoff, *La République bourgeoise* (Paris: Seuil, 1972), p. 135.

54. Pierre Vinçard, *Les Ouvriers de Paris: Alimentation* (Paris: Gosselin, 1863), pp. 256–257; Eugen Weber, "The Nineteenth-Century Fallout," in Geoffrey Best, ed., *The Permanent Revolution: The French Revolution and Its Legacy, 1789–1989* (London: Fontana, 1989), p. 173.

55. Edmond and Jules Goncourt, *Histoire de la société française pendant le Directoire*, p. 78.

56. *Paris-Restaurant* (Paris: A. Taride, 1854), p. 22; Aron, *Mangeur*, p. 17. Numerous twentieth-century historians have delighted in this idea, one writing that "the men who had been cooks in the old families had become eating-house keepers; Vatel's name was Véry now, or Beauvilliers or Méot"; Louis Madelin, *The National History of France* (Paris, 1916), vol. 6, p. 551. See also Jacqueline Munck's contribution in *Palais Royal,* Musée Carnavalet catalogue (Paris: Editions Musées Carnavalet, 1988), pp. 200–203; *Paris, capitale de la gastronomie,* catalogue of a 1984 exhibit sponsored by the Paris mayor's office, pp. 5–6; Stephen Mennell, *All Manners of Food* (Oxford: Basil Blackwell, 1983), p. 141; Jean-François Revel, *Un festin en paroles* (Paris: J-J Pauvert, 1979), p. 210; Joanne Finkelstein, *Dining Out* (Oxford: Polity, 1989), pp. 37–38. Finkelstein offers Carême as an example, but this most famous of early nineteenth-century French chefs, notorious for claiming that pastry is the most important branch of architecture, in fact never worked in a restaurant. See Audiguier, *Coup d'oeil sur l'influence de la cuisine et sur les ouvrages de M. Carême* (Paris: Levasseur, 1830); Frédéric Fayot, "La Mort de Carême," in *Paris, ou le Livre des Cent-et-un* (Paris: Ladvocat, 1833), vol. 12, pp. 291–313; Georges Bernier, *Antonin Carême* (Paris: Grasset, 1989).

57. Jean Anthelme Brillat-Savarin, *Physiologie du goût* (1826; Paris: Flammarion, 1982), pp. 233–234; paraphrased later by Eugène Briffault, *Paris à table* (1846; Geneva: Slatkine, 1980), pp. 147–148; Eric Hobsbawm, *The Age of Revolution, 1789–1848* (New York: Mentor, 1962), p. 220. Beauvilliers's notoriety owes much to his authoring of *L'Art de la cuisine* (Paris: Pillet, 1816). In Paris today, Edouard Carlier presides over the well-known restaurant "A. Beauvilliers" (52, rue Lamarck).

58. A.N. Y 15680 (Sept. 25, 1786); A.N. R⁴ 286.

59. In 1782, Paulo, of the café de Genie, and "formerly confectioner to the late Prince de Conty" advertised that he would "teach how to make all sorts of ices and creams," *AAAD,* Jan. 25, 1782, p. 197. In 1786, an unknown party advertised that he would like to hire an "excellent cook, trained in a princely household," *AAAD,* Oct. 15, 1786, p. 2733.

60. *Catalogue des Maîtres-Queux-Cuisiniers-Traiteurs-Rôtisseurs-Pâtissiers de la Ville, Faubourgs, et Banlieux de Paris* (Paris: L. Jorry, 1781), n. pag. The 1773 baptismal certificate of his daughter calls LaBarrière by the vague title of "bourgeois de Paris," but the 1777 certificate of his next daughter indicates a change of address and calls him "officier de maison." (An "officier" worked in the "office," the area of the kitchen where desserts and entremets were prepared.) Archives de la Seine, *Fichier des baptêmes, mariages . . . de Parois St. Eustache,* vol. 84, pp. 165–166.

61. A.N. R⁴ 821; *Tableau du nouveau Palais Royal* (Paris: Maradan, 1788), p. 68.

62. A.N. R⁴ 285; A.N. Y 15680 (May 2, 1786); A.N. Min. Cen. IX-836 (May 16, 1788); *AAAD,* Jan. 1788, p. 84.

63. A.N. W 369; see also W 387 (dossier Brâlon) and W 399 (dossier Nottaire).

Female cooks of aristocrats were somewhat more likely to escape with their lives; see A.N. W 441 (Dume), W 381 (Fleury), W 278 (Lavoignac). During the Thermidorean Reaction, a similar logic pursued the former employees of Terrorists: Saint-Just's cook was jailed for fourteen months, A.N. F⁷ 4775[47].

64. Dominique Filet was denounced as Talleyrand's former chef, A.N. F⁷ 4707; see also A.N. F⁷ 4774[28] (dossier Machet).

65. Auguste François Frénilly, *Mémoires, 1768–1828, Souvenirs d'un ultra-royaliste* (Paris: Perrin, 1987), p. 128.

66. Brillat-Savarin, *Physiologie*, p. 279.

67. Louis Sébastien Mercier, *Le Nouveau Paris* (Paris: Fuchs, 1798), vol. 4, pp. 196–197.

68. Ibid., vol. 3, pp. 109–110, 174; vol. 5, p. 76.

69. See Chapter 4.

70. Mercier, *Le Nouveau Paris*, vol. 3, p. 109

71. See also Marant, *Tout Paris en vaudevilles* (Paris: Barba, 1801), p. 166.

72. Jean-Baptiste Pujoulx, *Paris à la fin du XVIIIe siècle*, 2nd ed. (Paris: Librairie économique, 1800), p. 143; *Almanach parisien ou Guide de l'Etranger* (Paris: Barba, 1800), p. 25.

73. *Tableau de Paris en l'an VIII* (Paris: Laran, 1800), p. 4.

74. Police reports of Fructidor 6, Year II [Aug. 23, 1794]; Nivôse 18, Year III [Jan. 7, 1795]; Pluviôse 14, Year III [Feb. 2, 1795]; all reproduced in François-Alphonse Aulard, ed., *Paris pendant la réaction thermidorienne et sous le Directoire* (Paris: L. Cerf, 1898–1902), vol. 1, pp. 57, 370, 443. On popular unrest in Paris in spring 1795, see George Rudé, *The Crowd in the French Revolution* (London: Oxford University Press, 1959), chap. 10.

75. On dancing, another emblematic activity of this period, see Gabriel Vauthier, "Les Bals d'hiver et les jardins d'été sous le Directoire," *Annales révolutionnaires*, 15 (1923): 146–155; Ronald Schechter, "The *Bals des victimes*, the Fantastic, and the Production of Historical Knowledge in Post-Terror France," *Representations*, 61 (1998): 78–94.

76. Police spies interviewed restaurant waiters who reported they "had never seen such excesses," cited in Aulard, *Paris pendant la réaction thermidorienne*, vol. 1, p. 445; see also pp. 623, 654.

77. One journalist assumed that cheese sat in shops because there was no bread with which to eat it; see *La Quotidienne ou Tableau de Paris*, Floréal 18, Year III [May 17, 1795], p. 4.

78. François Gendron, *La Jeunesse dorée* (Sillery, Quebec: Presses de l'Université du Québec, 1979).

79. On the importance of dress as a way of marking political allegiance in this period, see Lynn Hunt, *Politics, Culture, and Class in the French Revolution* (Berkeley: University of California Press, 1984), chap. 2; Lynn Hunt, "Freedom of Dress in Revolutionary France," in Sara Melzer and Kathryn Norberg, eds., *From the Royal to the Republican Body* (Berkeley: University of California Press, 1998); Aileen Ribeiro, *Fashion in the French Revolution*

(London: B. T. Batsford, 1988). As Albert Soboul noted, the category "sans-culottes" was itself an explicitly vestiary mode of political definition; Albert Soboul, *Les Sans-culottes parisiens en l'an II* (Paris: Seuil, 1968), pp. 22–23.

80. "In society, we talked only of what we had eaten during the day," *Journal de la duchesse de Duras,* quoted in P. Bessand-Massenet, *La France après la Terreur* (Paris: Plon, 1946), p. 53.

81. Aulard, *Paris pendant la réaction thermidorienne,* vol. 2, p. 431.

82. On the pineapples, see *Le Narrateur impartial,* Pluviôse 28, Year III [Feb. 16, 1795], cited in Aulard, *Paris pendant la réaction thermidorienne,* vol. 1, p. 467. Compare the image of an East German joyously brandishing a pine-apple, which was repeatedly broadcast in November 1989 immediately after the fall of the Berlin Wall.

83. Quite literally; songs on those topics (and on noses, dances, and beds) were among the dozen included in one month's *Dîners du Vaudeville* (Paris: Huet, 1797), Nivôse, Year V [Jan. 1797]. Founded by Piis, Barré, Radet, and Desfontaines, the singing society's statutes specified that everyone was to pay his own share of the dinner bill and that songs on political and religious top-ics were not allowed; *Dîners du Vaudeville* (Paris: Huet, 1796), Vendémiaire, Year V [Sept. 1796], pp. 5–6.

84. Jean-Pierre Gross, *Fair Shares for All: Jacobin Egalitarianism in Practice* (Cambridge: Cambridge University Press, 1997), p. 91; François Brunel and S. Goujon, eds., *Les Martyrs de prairial: textes et documents inédits* (Geneva: Georg, 1992).

85. A.N. F[1] cIII, Seine 17, cited in Aulard, *Paris pendant la réaction thermidorienne,* vol. 2, p. 404.

6. From Gastromania to Gastronomy

1. A.N. F[7] 3829 (Pluviôse 24, Year IX [Feb. 12, 1801]); see also A.N. F[7] 3830 (Prairial 3, Year X [May 22, 1802]).

2. *Journal des débats,* Ventôse 27, Year VIII [Mar. 17, 1800],reproduced in François-Alphonse Aulard, ed., *Paris sous le Consulat* (Paris: Cerf, 1903–1909), vol. 1, p. 212.

3. Ibid.

4. Ibid.

5. Henri Welschinger, *La Censure sous le Premier Empire* (Paris: Charavay frères, 1882), p. 215.

6. Consulate police officials were pleased to report that although the first anni-versary of Bonaparte's coup had not been declared a state holiday, it had nonetheless been spontaneously celebrated by "the fatherland's real friends" with a civic banquet in the rue de Rohan. This attitude contrasts sharply with Barère's denunciation of the "spontaneous" frittering away of hospitality; see A.N. F[7] 3702 (Brumaire 18, Year IX [Nov. 9, 1800]), cited in Aulard, *Paris sous le Consulat,* vol. 1, p. 798.

7. One historian introduces her discussion of revolutionary songs by citing Piis's "Hymn to the Printing Press"; see Laura Mason, "Songs: Mixing Media," in Robert Darnton and Daniel Roche, eds., *Revolution in Print* (Berkeley: University of California Press, 1989), pp. 252–269; Laura Mason, *Singing the French Revolution* (Ithaca: Cornell University Press, 1996), pp. 86–89, 118. For more on Piis, see Lanzac de Laborie, *Paris sous Napoleon: La Cour et la ville, la vie et la mort* (Paris: Plon, 1906), vol. 1, pp. 57–59, and Jean Tulard, Jean François Fayard, and Alfred Fierro, *Histoire et dictionnaire de la révolution française* (Paris: Laffont, 1987), pp. 1031–1032.

8. *Affiches, annonces, avis divers* (hereafter, *AAAD*), Pluviôse 12, Year II [Jan. 31, 1794], pp. 5946–5947. Piis's productions were also compiled in A. A. Piis, *Chansons patriotiques* (Paris, 1794).

9. Piis and Barré ran the Théâtre de Vaudeville when it first opened in 1792; see Mason, *Singing*, pp. 86–89, and John McCormick, *Popular Theatres of Nineteenth-Century France* (London: Routledge, 1993), p. 115. For an account of Piis's largely ceremonial police duties, see Jean Tulard, *Paris et son administration, 1800–1830* (Paris: Ville de Paris Commission des Travaux Historique, 1976), p. 129.

10. *Journal des hommes libres*, Frimaire 28, Year VIII [Dec. 19, 1799], reproduced in Aulard, *Paris sous le Consulat*, vol. 1, p. 59; *Le Citoyen français*, Vendémiaire 19, Year IX [Oct. 10, 1800], in Aulard, *Paris sous le Consulat*, vol. 1, p. 667.

11. *Journal des gourmands et des belles*, 4 (1807), p. 120.

12. *Gazette de France*, Jan. 25, 1813, p. 98.

13. A.N. F^7 3833 (Germinal 25, Year XIII [April 14, 1805]). The police also kept Napoleon up to date on conditions in the fan industry (declining in July 1802), the wine-export business (booming in November 1801), and the embroidery trades (suddenly suffering in February 1802), among others. See the daily police reports dated Messidor 23, Brumaire 28, and Pluviôse 28, Year X, A.N. F^7 3830.

14. A.N. F^7 3830 (Ventôse 17, Year X [Mar. 7, 1802]), F^7 3833 (Brumaire 20, Year XIII [Nov. 10, 1804]).

15. A.N. F^7 4706; *Moniteur: Réimpression de l'ancien Moniteur* (Paris, 1858–1863), May 25, 1793, vol. 16, p. 463.

16. Commission des Inspecteurs de la Salle du Conseil des Cinq Cents, Thermidor 11, Year V [July 29, 1797], cited in the papers of René Farge, Bibliothèque Historique de la Ville de Paris.

17. André Cabanis, *La Presse sous le consulat et l'Empire* (Paris: Société des études robespierristes, 1975); Welschinger, *La Censure*; Alfred Cobban, *A History of Modern France*, vol. 2 (Harmondsworth: Penguin, 1961), p. 35. See also the distinction Fouché drew between "administration," which he called "visible to all," and "police," which he said should "almost never let itself be seen." A.N. F^7 4343, cited in Tulard, *Paris et son administration, 1800–1830*, p. 75.

In a letter naming a government censor to supervise the *Journal des débats* (later renamed the *Journal de l'Empire*), Napoleon ordered that censorship "must not extend so far as the feuilleton or any literary articles"; see his letter to Fouché, quoted in Gustave LePoittevin, *La Liberté de la presse depuis la Révolution, 1789–1815* (Geneva: Slatkine, 1975), pp. 136–137. See also Claude Bellanger et al., eds., *Histoire générale de la presse française* (Paris: Presses Universitaires de France, 1969), vol. 1, p. 553.

18. A.N. F[7] 3491, dossier 1 (May 25, 1812). Lemontey continued to advocate this sort of diversion, later recommending Eugène Scribe's 1823 play about Rossini's trip to Paris, *Le Grand dîner ou la subscription*, in similar terms: "The performance of this play cannot fail to excite debate in the newspapers, which will do much to distract malicious chatterers from politics," A.N. F[21] 972 (Nov. 28, 1823). As early as 1802, one English visitor reported on the rumor that the Consulate encouraged the "decadent" amusements of the Palais Royal in order to "distract consideration from public affairs," Henry Redhead Yorke, *France in 1802*, ed. J. A. C. Sykes (London: Heinemann, 1906), p. 75.

19. Alexandre B. L. Grimod de la Reynière, *Almanach des gourmands* (Paris, 1803–1812), vol. 4, p. 240.

20. Grimod de la Reynière, *Almanach*, vol. 1, pp. 61, 133; vol. 2, p. 80; vol. 7, p. 300.

21. Alfred Fierro, André Palluel-Guillard, and Jean Tulard, *Histoire et dictionnaire du consulat et de l'empire* (Paris: Robert Laffont, 1995), p. 797; Jean-Claude Bonnet, introduction to Grimod de la Reynière, *Ecrits gastronomiques* (Paris: Union des Editions générales, 1978), p. 72; Stephen Mennell, *All Manners of Food* (Oxford: Basil Blackwell, 1985), p. 268; Ned Rival, *Grimod de la Reynière, Le Gourmand gentilhomme* (Paris: Le Pré aux clercs, 1983); Giles MacDonogh, *A Palate in Revolution* (London: Robin Clark, 1987).

22. Grimod de la Reynière, *Almanach*, vol. 2, p. 34.

23. Ibid., vol. 6, p. xi.

24. Chazet, Lafortelle, and Francis, *Ecole des gourmands* (Paris: Cavanagh, 1804), performed first at the théâtre Montansier, Thermidor 30–Fructidor 6, Year XII [Aug. 17–23, 1804]. Grimod was also the model for the eponymous character of Barré, Radet, and Desfontaine's never-printed *Arlequin gastronome, ou Monsieur de la Gourmandière;* see Rival, *Le Gourmand gentilhomme*, chap. 10, and MacDonogh, *Palate in Revolution*, pp. 72–73.

25. *Journal des dames et des modes*, Jan. 20, 1805, cited in Aulard, *Paris sous le Premier Empire*, vol. 1, p. 545.

26. Immediately after the almanac appeared, guidebook writers began deferring to its expertise. See L. Prudhomme, *Miroir de l'ancien et de nouveau Paris... Ouvrage indispensable aux Etrangers et même aux Parisiens* (Paris, 1804), vol. 2, p. 220; L***, *Paris et ses modes* (Paris: Michelet, 1803), p. 203. Debauve, manufacturer of *chocolats analeptiques* or "restorative chocolates,"

used Grimod's endorsement (*Almanach*, vol. 1, pp. 296–297) in his advertising; see *Le Journal de Paris*, Dec. 15, 1808, p. 2535. For travelers' accounts that depend heavily on Grimod, see John Pinkerton, *Recollections of Paris, 1802–1805* (London: Longman, Hurst, Rees, and Orme, 1806), vol. 2, pp. 195–216; Augustus von Kotzebue, *Travels from Berlin, through Switzerland to Paris* (London: Richard Phillips, 1804), vol. 2, pp. 76–93; C. C. de Berkheim, *Lettres sur Paris* (Heidelberg: Mohr and Zimmer, 1809), p. 431.

27. Grimod de la Reynière, *Almanach*, vol. 8, pp. 27–29; vol. 5, pp. 163–171.

28. Ibid., vol. 8, p. 56; vol. 7, p. 298.

29. Madame de Sévigné, *Correspondances* (Paris: Bibliothèque de la Pléiade, 1972), vol. 1, p. 234 (letter dated April 24, 1671). See also the hagiography, Jean Moura and Paul Louvet, *La Vie de Vatel* (Paris: Gallimard, 1929).

30. Charles Colnet de Ravel, *L'Hermite du faubourg Saint Germain* (Paris: Pillet, 1825), vol. 1, pp. 17–18.

31. Grimod de la Reynière, *Almanach*, vol. 1, p. 224.

32. On other ways in which the Paris of this era became more walkable, see Susan Siegfried, *The Art of Louis-Léopold Boilly: Modern Life in Napoleonic France* (New Haven and London: Yale University Press, 1995), pp. 135–136.

33. Grimod de la Reynière, *Almanach*, vol. 4, p. 139; vol. 5, p. 366; vol. 6, p. 220.

34. *Le Gastronome à Paris* (Paris: Suret, 1803), pp. 42–43.

35. Grimod de la Reynière, *Almanach*, vol. 1, p. 206; vol. 8, pp. 40–43.

36. Alexandre B. L. Grimod de la Reynière, *Manuel des Amphitryons* (1808; Paris: A. M. Métailié, 1983), p. 9; Grimod de la Reynière, *Almanach*, vol. 1, pp. 28–29.

37. Grimod de la Reynière, *Almanach*, vol. 1, p. 208.

38. A restaurant, the Veau qui tette, was famous for its sheeps' feet "that run everywhere they are wanted"; ibid., vol. 4, p. 150.

39. Ibid., vol. 1, pp. xv–xvi.

40. Ibid., vol. 4, pp. 47–50. Another of the *Almanach*'s rare ventures in recipe publishing concluded: "one would eat one's own father if he were prepared with this sauce," vol. 1, p. 156.

41. Ibid., vol. 3, p. 179.

42. Ibid., vol. 2, p. 70.

43. Ibid., vol. 4, p. 5; vol. 6, p. 145.

44. Ibid., vol. 3, pp. 164–166, 191. In honor of the Opéra's production of *Cinderella*, Rouget created a puff pastry "cushion" on which sat a large pastry "slipper"; the cushion could be opened to reveal small slippers in several different flavors, vol. 8, p. 162.

45. Ibid., vol. 3, p. 314. Once again, many thanks to Michael Cooperson for the lyrical translation.

46. Rouget's company was delightful and his conversation educated; Balaine "would have governed a realm as well as he does a restaurant, if Heaven

had blessed him with birth near the throne instead of in the shadow of a stewpot," ibid., vol. 7, p. 220.

47. *L'Epicurien lyonnais* (Lyons: Yvernault et Cabin, 1810), pp. 53–55; *Gazette de France,* April 19, 1813, p. 451.

48. At least one of the Russian apprentices, Yvan Costay, felt so badly mistreated at the Rocher that he threatened to kill the owner; *Gazette des tribunaux,* Oct. 12, 1837, pp. 1209–1210. For comments on the restaurant's drawn-out demise, see *Le Corsaire,* April 27, 1843; *Le Charivari,* April 22, 1843; *La Presse,* May 1, 1843, p. 2; *Satan,* April 23, 1843.

49. *Le Gastronome,* a twice weekly tabloid-format journal, published in 1830–1831, used "to legitimate" as a synonym for "to taste," April 15, 1830, p. 2.

50. Grimod de la Reynière, *Almanach,* vol. 2, pp. 128–134; vol. 1, p. 65; vol. 5, pp. 338–339.

51. "We have left *hunger* for the common people, because it is satisfied by anything and is therefore bad for Art. We have kept appetite for ourselves, because it must appeal to science to stimulate it," ibid., vol. 8, pp. 60–61. The title page to vol. 3 cites Horace: "The fasting stomach is satisfied with the most common dishes." On women's appetites, see ibid., vol. 2, p. 53.

52. Ibid., vol. 3, p. 1.

53. Ibid., vol. 5, p. 232.

54. Ibid., vol. 4, pp. 142–143.

55. Ibid., vol 8, p. 219.

56. Ibid., vol. 8, pp. 77–78; vol. 2, p. 91.

57. Rival mentions that funeral announcements were not censored, *Le Gourmand gentilhomme,* p. 57; on legal memoirs, see Sarah Maza, "Le tribunal de la nation: les mémoires judiciaires et l'opinion publique à la fin de l'Ancien Régime," *Annales: E.S.C.* (1987), pp. 73–90. Numerous textual and iconographic details further linked the *Almanach* to these earlier productions. The legal memoir's first-page engraving featured the cat who appears in many of the *Almanach* frontispieces, as well as the jester's rattle which is Grimod's emblem in the "gastronomic map of France." Alexandre B. L. Grimod de la Reynière, *Mémoire à consulter et consultation pour M. Marie-Emile-Guillaume Duchosal* (Paris: Simon, 1786).

58. Grimod de la Reynière, *Almanach,* vol. 1, p. xii.

59. Ibid., vol. 7, p. 220.

60. The analogy between Grimod's work and that of the First Empire could be extended much further. Napoleon's continental blockade, though primarily intended to prevent Great Britain from trading with other European countries, had as a secondary goal the making of Paris into the central market of all of Europe (Tulard, *Paris et son administration,* p. 231). At the beginning of the Empire, the new Minister of the Interior made a tour of all the capital's poorhouses, where he "gave particular attention to the foods, tasting bread, bouillon and wine." *Courrier français,* Feb. 26, 1805, cited in Aulard, *Paris sous le Premier Empire,* vol. 1, p. 608.

61. *Annales de l'inanition, pour servir de pendant à l'"Almanach des gourmands"* (Paris: Frechet, 1808); *Almanach perpétuel des pauvres diables* (Paris: Caillot, 1803). Even after his retirement, Grimod continued to be the avatar of nineteenth-century gastronomy until Brillat-Savarin's *Physiologie du goût* was published in 1826. See the critique of Grimod for having made one of the seven deadly sins into a cult: Gallais, *Moeurs et caractères du dix-neuvième siècle* (Paris: Belin-le-Prieur, 1817), vol. 1, pp. 254–260.

62. *Journal des arts,* April 20, 1807, pp. 130–133; May 20, 1807, p. 334.

63. Ibid., May 20, 1807, p. 336.

64. J. Dusaulchoy, *Histoire du couronnement ou relation des cérémonies religieuses, politiques et militaires* (Paris: Dubray, 1805).

65. *Nouvelle biographie générale* (Paris: Firmin Didot, 1856–1866), vol. 15, col. 485–486.

66. *Journal des arts,* March 8, 1808, p. 87.

67. Grimod de la Reynière, *Almanach,* vol. 1, pp. 60–61.

68. Wanting to insist that the bookseller Desenne was the very soul of gullibility, the *Journal de Paris* said that to deny him that quality would be like "refusing to call Monsieur Grimod de la Reynière a gourmand," *Journal de Paris,* March 4, 1807, in Aulard, *Paris sous le Premier Empire,* vol. 3, p. 75.

69. Dusaulchoy occasionally conceded that "some" might think the *Almanach* a work of satire, but he rejected that reading as too indulgent of a vice that threatened to corrupt France as it had Imperial Rome; *Journal des arts,* April 20, 1807, p. 132.

70. *Journal des arts,* April 20, 1807, pp. 132–133.

71. Grimod de la Reynière, *Almanach,* vol. 2, p. 124.

72. Ibid., vol. 4, p. 47.

73. Ibid., vol. 4, p. vii.

74. Ibid., vol. 7, p. 106.

75. Ibid., vol. 5, p. 315.

76. Ibid., vol. 2, pp. xviii–xxi.

77. Ibid., vol. 2, p. xx; vol. 6, pp. 165, 189; vol. 8, p. 114.

78. Ibid., vol. 5, p. 83.

79. Ibid., vol. 8, p. 119.

80. See Bruno Latour, *The Pasteurization of France,* trans. Alan Sheridan and John Law (Cambridge, Mass.: Harvard University Press, 1988).

81. The Jury's findings were "in their final form, only the echo of public opinion"; Grimod de la Reynière, *Almanach,* vol. 7, p. 196.

82. One rumored associate, Grimod's longtime friend and distant cousin, the Provençal nobleman and infamous practical joker Alphonse Toussaint Fortia de Piles, claimed that the Jury had several hundred members who served on a rotating basis, but Grimod referred only to a dozen or so distinguished full members, and a number of non-voting affiliates. Alphonse Toussaint Fortia de Piles, *A bas les masques* (Paris: Delaunay, 1813), p. 38. For a chatty biography of Fortia de Piles, see Jean Vartier, *Alphonse de Fortia et l'âge d'or de la mystification* (Paris: France-Empire, 1985).

83. Grimod de la Reynière, *Almanach,* vol. 2, pp. 118–119; vol. 5, pp. 177–178; vol. 7, p. 195.

84. Pierre Béarn, *Grimod de la Reynière* (Paris, 1930), pp. 198–201; Paul Lacroix, *Histoire des mystificateurs et mystifiés* (Brussels: Schnée, 1858), vol. 1, pp. 143–145; Rival, *Le Gourmand gentilhomme,* pp. 199–203.

85. Grimod de la Reynière, *Almanach,* vol. 1, p. 184.

86. Louis Petit de Bachaumont, *Mémoires secrets pour servir à l'histoire de la République des lettres en France, depuis 1762 jusqu'à nos jours* (London: John Adamson, 1777–1789), vol. 22, p. 72; Rival, *Le Gourmand gentilhomme,* p. 18; Lacroix, *Histoire des mystificateurs et mystifiés,* vol. 1, pp. 94–98.

87. Charles Louis Cadet de Gassicourt, *Cours gastronomique* (Paris: Capelle and Renand, 1809), frontispiece; see the negative review in *Gazette de santé,* Aug. 1, 1808, pp. 193–197, and compare the maps in Prosper Montagné, *Larousse gastronomique.*

88. Articles by chefs, government officials, and educators about France's "culinary patrimony" can be found in *Revue des deux mondes,* Jan. 1993.

7. Putting Paris on the Menu

1. Isaac Appleton Jewett, *Passages in Foreign Travel* (Boston: Little and Brown, 1838), vol. 2, p. 23.

2. [Francis Blagdon], *Paris as it Was and as it Is, Illustrative of the Effects of the Revolution* (London: C. & R. Baldwin, 1803), vol. 1, p. 443. See also Augustus von Kotzebue, *Travels from Berlin, through Switzerland to Paris* (London: Richard Phillips, 1804), vol. 2, pp. 98–100; *Englishman's Vade Mecum at Paris* (Paris: J. Smith, 1814), p. 38; and *Memorandums of a Residence in France, in the Winter of 1814–15* (London: Longman, Hurst, and Rees, 1816), p. 179. Thirty years later, an American also felt the urge to count: "Fifty-six forms of vegetable,—twenty of eggs,—ten of coquillages,—fourteen of salads," etc.; Jewett, *Passages in Foreign Travel,* vol. 2, p. 15. The trope eventually found its way into dictionary definitions as well; Larousse defined "Restaurant" with reference to "a dozen soups, twenty appetizers, thirty beef dishes, and another thirty of veal . . ." *Grand dictionnaire universel du XIXe siècle* (Paris: Larousse, 1864–1890), vol. 13, p. 1049.

3. John Sanderson, *The American in Paris* (Philadelphia: Carey and Hart, 1839), vol. 1, p. 87.

4. *Guide dans le choix des étrennes* (Paris: Delaunay, 1824), p. 203; Jean Anthelme Brillat-Savarin, *Physiologie du goût* (1826; Paris: Flammarion, 1982), p. 278. Further references are to this edition unless otherwise noted.

5. Historians often reproduce the enthusiastic tones of foreign travelers; see Ernest Lavisse, ed., *Histoire de France contemporaine,* vol. 3, G. Pariset, *Le Consulat et l'Empire* (Paris: Hachette, 1921), p. 154; Gwynne Lewis, *Life in Revolutionary France* (London: Basford, 1972), p. 85; Alfred Fierro, André Palluel-Guillard, and Jean Tulard, *Histoire et dictionnaire du consulat*

et de l'empire (Paris: Robert Laffont, 1995), pp. 797, 1053. For other versions see, among others, "Mangenville," *L'Art de ne jamais déjeuner chez soi* (Paris: Librairie universelle, 1827), p. 94; *Le Pariséum moderne* (Paris: J. Moronval, 1816), p. 146; F. M. Marchant, *Le Nouveau conducteur de l'étranger à Paris,* 9th ed. (Paris: Moronval, 1821), pp. 16–22.

6. John Scott, *A Visit to Paris in 1814* (Philadelphia: Edward Parker, 1815), p. 114; *Promenade gastronomique dans Paris, par un Amateur* (Paris: Librairie Orientale de Dondey Dupré, 1833), p. 58.

7. *Affiches, annonces, avis divers* (hereafter, *AAAD*), Feb. 15, 1792, p. 619; emphasis added.

8. Brillat-Savarin, *Physiologie,* p. 276; Jules Besset, *L'Art culinaire* (Albi: G.-M. Nouguiès, 1895), p. 25, unattributed. Larousse's *Grand dictionnaire du XIXe siècle* says that, in restaurants, "desire is unlimited"; vol. 13, p. 1049.

9. Jean-Paul Aron, *Le Mangeur du XIXe siècle* (Paris: Robert Laffont, 1973); Edmond and Jules Goncourt, *Histoire de la société française pendant le Directoire* (Paris: Didier, 1864); René Héron de Villefosse, *Histoire et géographie gourmande de Paris* (Paris: Editions de Paris, 1956); Beatrice Malki-Thouvenel, *Cabarets, cafés, et bistros de Paris: Promenade dans les rues et dans le temps* (Paris: Hovarth, 1987). A particularly inept manifestation of the tour-giving impulse, which asserts that Brillat-Savarin was the "most famous cuisinier [*sic*] in Europe," can be found in Frederick Artz, *France Under the Bourbon Restoration* (Cambridge, Mass.: Harvard University Press, 1931), pp. 243–244.

10. *Almanach du commerce* (Paris: de la Tynna, 1815), p. 618.

11. A.N. F^7 3025 (Census des débitants, 1851–1852). The Ministry recorded figures for 83 departments; of these, 53 reported no restaurants. The prefect of the Vosges reported that Epinal, Remiremont, and St. Die each had a single restaurateur, but that he had recorded them under different categories because the first was also a café-keeper, the second a bar-keeper, and the third an innkeeper (letter, Jan. 17, 1852).

12. "Restaurants: . . . Establishments that for many years were specific to Paris, and that even today one finds only in large cities. Everywhere else, the man suffering hunger pangs has no other recourse than the common inn or even the hotel and its table d'hôte"; W. Duckett, ed., *Dictionnaire de la conversation et de la lecture,* 2nd ed. (Paris: Firmin Didot, 1875), vol. 15, p. 378.

13. Louis Prudhomme, *Miroir historique, politique et critique de l'ancien et de nouveau Paris* (Paris, 1804), p. 222.

14. For the claim that comestibles sold better than learning and literature, see Prudhomme, *Miroir,* p. 221; *A Practical Guide During a Journey from London to Paris* (London: R. Phillips, 1802), p. 106. On this period as that of the restaurant's birth see, most recently, Jean-Robert Pitte, "Naissance et expansion des restaurants," in Jean-Louis Flandrin and Massimo Montanari, eds., *Histoire de l'alimentation* (Paris: Fayard, 1996), pp. 767–778.

15. *Tableau du nouveau Palais Royal* (Paris: Maradan, 1788), vol. 1, p. 62.

16. A traiteur-restaurateur on the rue de Bondy advertised private dining rooms, billiard tables, and a garden, *AAAD*, Aug. 10, 1793, p. 3354; Piat, restaurateur in the Palais Royal, promised an orchestra playing "overtures and symphonies, mixed with songs," *AAAD*, supplement, Thermidor 11, Year VII [July 29, 1799], p. 2.

17. A.N. F⁷ 4610.

18. *AAAD*, April 13, 1791, p. 1374.

19. Duverneuil and La Tynna, eds., *Almanach du commerce de Paris* (Paris, 1799), p. 307; *Almanach du commerce de Paris* (Paris, 1809), p. 265.

20. *AAAD*, Germinal 2, Year IV [March 22, 1796], p. 3676.

21. *AAAD*, Thermidor 18, Year VI [Aug. 5, 1798], p. 6240; *AAAD*, Pluviôse 23, Year VII [Feb. 11, 1799], p. 2471.

22. For comparable examples drawn from a variety of trades, see Richard Cobb, *The Police and the People* (Oxford: Clarendon, 1970), pp. 63–65.

23. *Gazette de France*, Frimaire 1, Year XIII [Nov. 22, 1804], quoted in François-Alphonse Aulard, ed., *Paris sous le Premier Empire* (Paris: L. Cerf, 1912–1923), vol. 1, p. 400.

24. *A Trip to Paris in July and August 1792* (London: Minerva Press, 1793), p. 114; *A Practical Guide During a Journey from London to Paris*, p. 104; J. G. Lemaistre, *A Rough Sketch of Modern Paris* (London: J. Johnson, 1803), p. 278. "*Restaurateur* is now universally used instead of *traiteur*," John Carr, *The Stranger in France* (London, 1803), p. 77.

25. See, for example, *A Short Excursion in France, 1814* (London: J. J. Stockdale, 1814), p. 34; *A Practical Guide*, p. 104; Louis Tronchet, *Picture of Paris*, 6th ed. (London: Sherwood, Nealy, and Jones, 1817), p. 49; Lemaistre, *Rough Sketch*, p. 278; Edward Planta, *A New Picture of Paris*, 15th ed. (London: Samuel Leigh, 1827), p. 104; Edward Planta, *A New Picture of Paris*, 16th ed. (London: Samuel Leigh, 1831), p. 98.

26. Blagdon, *Paris as it Was and as it Is*, vol. 1, pp. xvi, 443.

27. Stephen Weston, *A Slight Sketch of Paris* (London: R. Baldwin, 1814), p. 31; Caroline W. Cushing, *Letters Descriptive of Public Monuments, Scenery, and Manners in France and Spain* (Newburyport: E. W. Allan, 1832), vol. 1, p. 8. Another Anglo-American traveler wrote that it was "by way of curiosity" (rather than hunger) that she and her friends entered one of the Palais Royal's restaurants; see *Letters from a Lady to her Sister, During a Tour of Paris in the Months of April and May, 1814* (London: Longman, Hurst, Rees, Orme, and Brown, 1814), p. 31.

28. Edward Planta, *A New Picture of Paris, or the Stranger's Guide to the French Metropolis*, 12th ed. (London: Samuel Leigh, 1820), p. 114.

29. A mid-century American traveler made a similar point: "Families that intend to make a lengthened stay in Paris, if they would consult comfort and convenience should proceed at once to housekeeping, but, for a short period, the restaurant-life is preferable, as affording an insight into French manners and

cookery to be obtained in no other way"; *Parisian Sights and French Principles Seen Through American Spectacles* (New York: Harper, 1852), p. 16. I thank Jann Matlock for this reference.

30. Sir Francis Head worried that his "fixed regimen" would be disturbed by restaurant meals, but nonetheless he ate at the Café de Paris in order to witness "the process of dining at a restaurateur's at Paris"; *A Faggot of French Sticks; or, Paris in 1851* (New York: George Putnam, 1852), p. 49.

31. Sydney Owenson, later Lady Morgan, *France*, 4th ed. (London: Henry Colburn, 1818); *London Magazine* (1824), quoted in Paul Gerbod, *Voyages au pays des mangeurs de grenouilles* (Paris: Albin Michel, 1991), p. 219; Thomas Raffles, *Letters During a Tour through Some Parts of France* (Liverpool: Thomas Taylor, 1818), pp. 62, 67.

32. By the mid-1820s, 20,000 Britons entered through Calais every year, and if not all of them went to Paris, many did, as did many of those who entered through other ports; Gerbod, *Voyages*, p. 89. Guillaume de Bertier de Sauvigny, *La France et les français vus par les voyageurs américains* (Paris: Flammarion, 1982), vol. 1, pp. 17–19.

33. John Barnes, *A Tour Throughout the Whole of France* (London: William Darton, 1815), p. 97.

34. The literary scholar Christopher Prendergast has commented that the restaurant in nineteenth-century French novels is "a scene of considerable narrative and descriptive attention"; *Paris and the Nineteenth Century* (Oxford: Basil Blackwell, 1992), p. 19.

35. François Victor Fournel, *Ce qu'on voit dans les rues de Paris* (Paris: Adolphe Delahays, 1858), p. 369.

36. Alexandre B. L. Grimod de la Reynière, *L'Almanach des gourmands* (Paris, 1803–1812), vol. 1, pp. 207–208.

37. Honoré de Balzac, *Une fille d'Eve;* Stendhal, *Lucien Leuwen*, trans. H. L. R. Edwards (Harmondsworth: Penguin, 1991), p. 43.

38. The paper referred to Véry's as "that famous establishment, known to all"; *Gazette des tribunaux*, April 3, 1840, p. 535.

39. Prendergast refers to "the ubiquitous Rocher de Cancale," *Paris and the Nineteenth Century*, p. 20; on Balzac and restaurants, see Patrice Boussel, *Les Restaurants dans la "Comédie humaine"* (Paris: Editions de la Tournelle, 1950); Fernand Lotte, "Balzac et la table dans *La Comédie humaine*," *L'Année balzacienne* (1962): 119–179.

40. Flicoteau's is memorably described in Honoré de Balzac, *Illusions perdues* (1837–1842; Paris: Gallimard, 1972), pp. 207–211, 251.

41. Theodore Lyman, *A Few Weeks in Paris, during the Residence of the Allied Sovereigns in that Metropolis* (Boston: Cummings and Hilliard, 1814), was especially impressed by the new king's proportions, p. 62; similar remarks can be found in William Shepherd, *Paris in 1802 and 1814* (London: Longman, Hurst, 1814), p. 209. Even a recent, generally friendly, biographer writes of Louis's "huge size which, if nothing else, was to make him

such a remarkable king"; Philip Mansel, *Louis XVIII* (London: Blond and Briggs, 1981), p. 147.

42. Some restaurateurs' invoices for army feedings can be found in the Bibliothèque Historique de la Ville de Paris, ms. 1014 (folios 52–78); see also Eugène Briffault, *Paris à Table* (1846; Geneva: Slatkine, 1980), pp. 153–154. When one author in 1816 wrote of "roasting, boiling, frying, and stewing all going on at the same time . . . fowls, turkeys, hares, partridges, beef, mutton, and veal, with everything else that has ever been or is the food of man," he was referring not to the Palais Royal's restaurants, but to the camp kitchens set up to feed 95,000 occupying soldiers; see *Memorandums of a Residence in France, in the Winter of 1814–15*, p. 50.

43. Charles Rousset, *Code parisien* (Paris: Denain, 1829), pp. 280–284. The invasions of 1814–1815 had been "disastrous from the perspective of glory" but nonetheless very profitable; *Nouvel Almanach des gourmands* (1827), p. 162.

44. Later described by the American John Griscom, *A Year in Europe* (New York: Collins, 1823), vol. 1, p. 286, these were common enough images to be referred to in a song written for the vaudeville theater; see Ymbert and Varner, *Le Dîner de garçons* (Paris: Huet, 1820), p. 7.

45. Lady Morgan, *France*, vol. 2, pp. 80–81.

46. Edward Fitzsimons, *Letters from France and the Netherlands in the Summers of 1820 and 1821* (Dublin: William Underwood, 1821), pp. 14, 102, 112, 119.

47. A partial inventory of pre-1820 printed accounts of chez Véry would include Blagdon, *Paris as It Was and as It Is*, vol. 1, pp. 119–120; Raffles, *Letters During a Tour*, pp. 77–79; Carr, *The Stranger in France*, pp. 80–81; Benjamin Brevity, *Winter Evenings in Paris* (Paris: Galignani's, 1815), p. 68; William Fellowes, *Paris During the Interesting Month of July 1815* (London: Gale and Fenner, 1815), p. 35; Stephen Weston, *The Praise of Paris* (London: Baldwin, 1803), p. 155; Edmund J. Eyre, *Observations Made at Paris During the Peace* (Bath: W. Meyler, 1803), pp. 114–127. Véry's owed its ubiquity, at least in part, to the fact that there were two restaurants by that name: one in the splendid Tuileries Gardens and the other in the equally impressive Palais Royal.

48. Fitzsimons, *Letters from France*, p. 116; Raffles, *Letters during a Tour*, pp. 67–68. Compare, too, ". . .—combinations inconceivable,—compositions indescribable—names unintelligible," Thomas Jessop, *Journal d'un voyage à Paris*, ed. F. C. Whiley (Paris: Champion, 1928), p. 75. One guidebook referred to the Jardin des Plantes, much like a restaurant menu, as the site of a great "profusion of labels unintelligible," Hervé, *How to Enjoy Paris*, p. 65.

49. These sights were all suggested by John Barnes, *A Tour Throughout the Whole of France*, pp. 98–102.

50. See the definition cited at the beginning of the Introduction in *Dictionnaire de l'Académie française*, 6th ed. (Paris: Firmin-Didot, 1835), vol. 2, p. 645.

51. Thomas Jessop, *Journal d'un voyage à Paris*, p. 75; *Memorandums of a Residence in France, in the winter of 1814–1815*, p. 179; James Simpson, *Paris After Waterloo, Notes Taken at the Time and Hitherto Unpublished* (Edinburgh: Blackwoods, 1853), p. 136. Simpson's *A Visit to Flanders and the Field of Waterloo* went through nine editions in the ten years after its publication.

52. Blagdon, author of *Paris as it Was and as It Is*, entered into dialogue with his reader: "Fudge! Fudge! you cry—Pardon me, my good friend, 'tis no fudge. Take the tremendous bill of fare into your own hand . . . As we are in no particular hurry, travel article by article through the whole enumeration," vol. 1, p. 443. For other reproductions of a menu in the text, see Eyre, *Observations Made at Paris During the Peace*, pp. 114–127; Planta, *A New Picture of Paris*, 15th ed., pp. 105–109.

53. One study has suggested that cheap editions of Menon's mid-eighteenth-century classic, *La Cuisinière bourgeoise*, circulated widely through the provinces and may have been read almost novelistically, providing a range of vicarious pleasures (think of some famished Emma Bovary eating bread crusts as she loses herself in the imagined pleasures of "Entrées de poisson"); but we have no indication that city dwellers, and certainly not bachelors or tourists, sat down to peruse cookbooks—until, perhaps, after they had read a menu. Lise Andries, "Cuisine et littérature populaire," *Dix-huitième siècle* 15, (1983): 33–52.

54. For examples, see Léon Maillard, *Menus et programmes illustrés* (Paris: Librarie artistique, 1898); Gérard Oberlé, *Les Fastes de Bacchus et de Comus* (Paris: Belfond, 1989).

55. Blagdon, *Paris as it Was and as it Is*, vol. 1, p. 443. Augustus von Kotzebue, the German dramatist, similarly began his description of the menu at Véry's by noting, in surprise, that it was *"imprimis"; Travels from Berlin*, vol. 2, p. 97.

56. *Voyage autour du Palais Egalité* (Paris: Moller, 1800), p. 75.

57. On cafés in the nineteenth century, see W. Scott Haine, *The World of the Paris Café* (Baltimore: Johns Hopkins University Press, 1996).

58. Sanderson, *The American in Paris*, vol. 1, pp. 88–89.

59. Honoré Blanc, *Le Guide des dîneurs, ou statistique des principaux restaurans de Paris* (1815; Paris: L'Etincelle, 1985), pp. 54, 65, 73, 97, 118, 141, 160.

60. Véfour menu in Oberlé, *Les Fastes*, p. 875. In 1838, in the midst of the July Monarchy's recuperation of Napoleonic legend, another author mentioned a *"vol-au-vent de turbot à la Marengo"*; Jewett, *Passages in Foreign Travel*, vol. 1, p. 312.

61. Ivan S. Jirkévitch, *Mémoires*, in A. Smirnov, ed., *Les Russes découvrent la France*, trans. C. Lambert, H. Guterman, H. Mongault, M. Orlov, and G. Struve (Paris: Editions du Progrès, 1990), p. 144.

62. Blanc, *Guide des dîneurs*, p. 15.

63. Ibid.

64. Tronchet, *Picture of Paris*, 6th ed., p. 50.

65. On booklet-style menus, see Paul de Kock, "Les Restaurans et les cartes de

restaurateurs," in *Nouveau tableau de Paris au XIXe siècle* (Paris: Charles Bechet, 1834), vol. 4, p. 85; James Grant, *Paris and its People* (London: Saunders and Otley, 1844), vol. 2, p. 179; J. Jay Smith, *A Summer's Jaunt Across the Water* (Philadelphia: J. W. Moore, 1846), vol. 1, p. 150. John Sanderson told his readers that the menu at Véry's was "as big as your prayer book," *The American in Paris*, vol. 1, p. 88; Isaac Appleton Jewett, also describing Véry's, reported that "the carte is not only bound into a handsome volume, but also fortified with brass," *Passages in Foreign Travel*, vol. 2, p. 12; one French author said it looked like the supplement to a dictionary, "Mangenville," *L'Art de ne jamais déjeûner chez soi*, p. 92. Several booklet menus can be found in B.N. Recueil W² 861 folio.

66. Armand Dalloz, *Répertoire méthodique et alphabétique de législation, de doctrine, et de jurisprudence* (Paris: Bureau de la jurisprudence générale, 1847), "Patentes," vol. 35, pp. 41–144; Armand Husson, *Consommations de Paris*, 2nd ed. (Paris: Hachette, 1875), p. 112.

67. For a basic account of technological developments in printing, see James Smith Allen, *In the Public Eye: A History of Reading in Modern France* (Princeton: Princeton University Press, 1991), pp. 30–32, 43.

68. See the "Nourishing Calendar" in Grimod de la Reynière, *Almanach*, vol. 1. A gastronomic publication from the 1830s referred to "September, our own private springtime"; *Flâneries du culinophile* (extract from *Cabinet de lecture*), Sept. 17, 1833, p. 2.

69. Cookbooks of this era also began to bring together recipes from many places; see *Le Cuisinier étranger, pour faire suite au Parfait cuisinier* (Paris: Delacour, 1811).

70. *Promenade gastronomique dans Paris, par un amateur*, p. 59; Frédéric de Courcy, Hyppolite Lasagne, and Gustave Valpion, *Le Restaurant ou le quart d'heure de Rabelais* (Paris: Barba, 1828), p. 4.

71. *Le Charivari*, Feb. 21, 1843.

72. His patent reads, in part: "Until now, we have had only imperfect menus . . . voluminous notebooks or newspapers that list an infinite variety of foods, most of which do not exist." Imperfect they may have been, but they were also enticing. Patent of September 27, 1843 (Ministry of Agriculture and Commerce), reproduced in Colin Lucas, dir., French Revolution Research Collection microfiches (Pergamon), 10.3/131, fiche 2.

73. *Gazette des tribunaux*, Nov. 26, 1830, p. 86; see also Louis-Gabriel Montigny, *Le Provincial à Paris* (Paris: Ladvocat, 1825), vol. 2, pp. 203–204.

74. Benedict Anderson, *Imagined Communities*, revised ed. (London: Verso, 1991), pp. 170–178.

75. Pierre Jouhard, *Paris dans le XIXe siècle, ou Réflexions d'un observateur* (Paris: Dentu, 1809), pp. 137–138.

76. Ibid., pp. 137–138.

77. Derek Jarrett, *England in the Age of Hogarth* (London: Granada, 1976),

pp. 20–23; Harriet Ritvo, *The Animal Estate* (Cambridge, Mass.: Harvard University Press, 1987), pp. 46–47; Roy Porter, *English Society in the Eighteenth Century* (Harmondsworth: Penguin, 1982), p. 381; Ronald Paulson, *Representations of Revolution* (New Haven: Yale University Press, 1983), pp. 200–205.

78. Dupré de Lisle, *Traité des maladies de la poitrine* (Paris: Costard, 1769), p. 48; Coste, *Traité des maladies du poumon* (Paris: Herrisant, 1767), p. 35; Maret, *Mémoire dans lequel on cherche à déterminer quelle influence les moeurs des français ont sur la Santé* (Amiens: Godard, 1772), p. 53; P. Gallet, *Voyage d'un habitant de la lune à Paris* (Paris: Levrault, 1803), p. 156.

79. *A Collection of Modern and Contemporary Voyages* (London: Richard Phillips, 1805), vol. 1, p. 32.

80. Pinkerton, *Recollections of Paris, 1802–1805* (London: Longman, Hurst, Rees, and Orme, 1806), vol. 1, p. vii.

81. Ibid., vol. 2, p. 213.

82. Ibid., vol. 1, p. 266.

83. Pinkerton cited Grimod's hyperbolic injunction to householders, "Purge your chefs!" to support his otherwise unsubstantiated claim that "the French" had carried "luxury" so far "that their cooks regularly take medicines, in order to preserve the fineness of their palate, and of their sauces," ibid., vol. 2, pp. 207, 209. He cribbed his comments from *Almanach des gourmands*, vol. 2, pp. 216–222, 265–272; vol. 3, p. 126; vol. 4, pp. vi–vii.

84. Kotzebue in *A Collection of Modern and Contemporary Voyages and Travels*, vol. 1, pp. 35, 47; compare *Almanach des gourmands*, vol. 2, pp. 56–70.

85. Francis Kinloch, *Letters from Geneva and France* (Boston: Wells and Lilly, 1819), vol. 1, p. 472; vol. 2, p. 14.

86. *A Practical Guide*, p. 104; P. Villiers, *Manuel du voyageur à Paris* (Paris: Favre, 1801).

87. *Englishman's Vade Mecum at Paris*, p. 51; *A Few Days in Paris* (London: Hatchard, 1802), p. 58; *A Practical Guide*, p. 32; compare Planta, *A New Picture of Paris* (1814), p. 24.

88. Henry Redhead Yorke, *Letters from France* (London: Sherwood, Neely, and Jones, 1814), vol. 1, pp. 169–170.

89. Louis Sébastien Mercier, *Le Nouveau Paris* (Paris: Fuchs, 1798), vol. 3, p. 110. When Yorke's letters were edited and published again in 1906, the editor simply omitted any reference to Mercier; Henry Redhead Yorke, *France in Eighteen Hundred and Two*, ed. J. A. C. Sykes (London: William Heineman, 1906), pp. 73–74. The Goncourt brothers, writing in the 1850s, also incorporated Mercier's description of Méot's ceiling; their account was then recycled by Jean-Paul Aron, *Le Mangeur du XIXe siècle*, p. 20.

90. Scott, *A Visit to Paris in 1814*, p. 114; Raffles, *Letters During a Tour*, p. 77; Jewett, *Passages in Foreign Travel*, vol. 2, pp. 22–27.

91. Cushing, *Letters Descriptive of Public Monuments*, p. 10, asserted that Paris restaurants were kept in business by foreigners. For examples of the many

British people who commented on how cheap Paris was, see *A Practical Guide During a Journey from London to Paris,* p. 26; Fitzsimons, *Letters from France and the Netherlands,* p. 30; Charles Maclean, *An Excursion in France and other Parts of the Continent of Europe* (London: Longman and Rees, 1804), pp. 247–248; *A Short Excursion in France, 1814,* p. 10; James Paul Cobbett, *A Ride of Eight Hundred Miles in France* (London: John Dean, 1827), paragraph 189. One French author asserted that the English in France were all there to economize· Defauconpret, *Observations sur l'ouvrage intitulé 'La France' par Lady Morgan* (Paris: Nicolle, 1817), pp. 4–5. As the number of American travelers increased throughout the century, they too came to appreciate the cheapness of life in Paris; see N. Parker Willis, *Pencillings by the Way* (New York: Charles Scribner, 1852), pp. 61–62.

92. Grimod de la Reynière, *Almanach,* vol. 3, p. 98.

93. Smith, *A Summer's Jaunt Across the Water,* vol. 1, pp. 150–151.

94. Sir Francis Head, *A Faggot of French Sticks,* p. 47.

95. Samuel Topliff, *Letters from Abroad in the Years 1828–1829* (Boston: Athenaeum, 1906), pp. 200–201.

96. Charlotte Bronson, *The Letters of Charlotte Brinckerhoff Bronson, Written during her Wedding Journey in Europe in 1838* (Cambridge, Mass., privately printed, 1928), vol. 1, pp. 35, 44, 46, 51, 61, 76. See also Fanny W. Hall, *Rambles in Europe* (New York: E. French, 1839), vol. 1, p. 45; Marianne Baillie, *First Impressions on a Tour Upon the Continent* (London: John Murray, 1819), pp. 41–42.

97. Emma Willard, *Journal and Letters from France and Great Britain* (Troy, N.Y.: N. Tuttle, 1833), p. 82. On the other hand, her friends allowed her to attend a debate in the House of Deputies and introduced her to Lafayette.

98. Barnes, *A Tour Throughout the Whole of France,* p. 112; for someone willing to entertain the thought that women might belong in restaurants, see Scott, *A Visit to Paris in 1814,* p. 115.

99. John Durbin, *Observations in Europe* (New York: Harper and Brothers, 1844), vol. 1, p. 39; John M. Cobbett, *Letters from France* (London: Mills, Jowett, and Mills, 1825), pp. 105–106; William Playfair, *France as it is, Not Lady Morgan's France* (London: C. Chapple, 1819), vol. 1, p. 110; Henry Matthews, *Diary of an Invalid,* 2nd ed. (London: John Murray, 1820), p. 480; *Impressions and Observations of a Young Person during a Residence in Paris* (Paris: Galignani, 1845), p. 132; Planta, *A New Picture of Paris* (1827), p. 104; Jewett, *Passages in Foreign Travel,* vol. 2, pp. 23–24; Scott, *A Visit to Paris in 1814,* p. 113; Tronchet, *A Picture of Paris,* pp. 79–80.

100. Griscom, *A Year in Europe,* vol. 1, p. 284; James Freeman Clarke, *Eleven Weeks in Europe and What May be Seen There* (Boston: Ticknor Reed, 1852), p. 107.

101. J. W. Cunningham, *Cautions to Continental Travellers* (London: Hatchard, 1818), p. 45.

102. Jewett, *Passages in Foreign Travel,* vol. 2, p. 23. He went on to suggest that a happy medium between English exclusivity and French promiscuity could only arise in a "young and flexible nation" such as his native United States.

103. Hall, *Rambles in Europe,* vol. 1, p. 45; Sanderson, *The American in Paris,* vol. 1, p. 90; Grant, *Paris and its People,* p. 181; Smith, *A Summer's Jaunt,* vol. 1, p. 151.

104. *The Wedding Journey of Charles and Martha Babcock Amory* (Boston, privately printed, 1922), pp. 19–20. For another account emphasizing the "enchanting" effect produced by groups of people reflected in "looking glass plates of very large dimensions," see Topliff, *Letters from Abroad in the Years 1828–1829,* p. 200.

105. Raffles, *Letters During a Tour,* p. 79.

106. Brillat-Savarin, *Physiologie,* p. 63.

107. Ibid., pp. 163–168.

108. Ibid., pp. 38, 146.

109. Alphonse Karr, introduction to Brillat-Savarin, *Physiologie du goût* (Paris: Gabriel de Gonet, 1852), pp. ii–iii.

110. Brillat-Savarin, *Physiologie,* pp. 141–142, 147. Fourier wanted to make all of the passions into positive social forces. For a selection of his writings on gourmandise, see Jonathan Beecher and Richard Bienvenu, eds., *The Utopian Vision of Charles Fourier* (London: Jonathan Cape, 1971).

111. Brillat-Savarin, *Physiologie,* p. 149.

112. Ibid., pp. 278–279.

113. Several years before Brillat-Savarin, a guidebook author had claimed that while Paris had always been a land of plenty for the rich and titled, it was now so for anyone with a little money to spare in the city's "numerous temples"; Marchant, *Nouveau conducteur,* 9th ed., p. 15.

114. *L'Officier de bouche,* March 17, 1836, p. 2.

115. I thank Jann Matlock for a reference to the Countess of Blessington, who found restaurant dinners humorous since they meant "two or three ill-dressed garçons humming about, instead of half a dozen sedate servants in rich liveries"; *The Idler in France* (Paris: Baudry's European Library, 1841), p. 221. James Fenimore Cooper, during his travels, made it a point to ascertain whether French people really did live in restaurants as they were rumored to do and concluded, based on his interviews with several duchesses, that they did not; see James Fenimore Cooper, *Gleanings in Europe, France,* ed. Thomas Philbrick and Constance Ayers Denne (Albany: State University of New York Press, 1983), pp. 76–77.

116. *Promenade gastronomique dans Paris, par un Amateur,* pp. 70–71; see also Hezekiah Wright, *Desultory Reminiscences* (Boston: Ticknor, 1838), p. 293.

117. N. H. Carter, *Letters from Europe* (New York: Carvill, 1829), vol. 1, pp. 418–419; Sanderson, *The American in Paris,* vol. 1, p. 88.

118. Caroline Kirkland, *Holidays Abroad or Europe from the West* (New York:

Baker and Scribner), vol. 1, p. 134; Zachariah Allen, *The Practical Tourist, or Sketches of the State of the Useful Arts and of Society* (Providence: A. Beckwith, 1832), vol. 2, p. 81.

119. Jewett, *Passages in Foreign Travel,* vol. 2, pp. 7–35; *L'Entr'acte,* March 21, 1836, p. 1; Eugène Scribe and Mazères, *Vatel, ou le petit-fils d'un grand homme* (Paris: Pollet, 1825).

120. Blanc, *Le Guide des dîneurs de Paris; Promenade gastronomique dans Paris par un Amateur.* Other examples include De Kock, "Les Restaurans et les cartes de restaurateurs"; Eugène Briffault, *Paris à table* (1846; Geneva: Slatkine, 1980); I. D. Derville, "Les Tables d'hôte parisiens," in *Paris, ou le Livre de Cent-et-un* (Paris: Ladvocat, 1832–1834), vol. 6, pp. 289–317; Paul Vermond, "Les Restaurants de Paris," *Revue de Paris,* 2nd series, 15 (1835): 109–121; César Gardeton, *Nouveau guide des dîneurs* (Paris: Breauté, 1828); Jacques Arago, *Comme on dîne à Paris* (Paris: Berquet and Pétion, 1842); Victor Bouton, *La Table à Paris, mystères des restaurants, cafés et comestibles* (Paris, 1845). For later decades, see *Paris-Restaurant* (Paris: A. Taride, 1854) and Eugène Chavette, *Restaurateurs et restaurés* (Paris: Le Chevalier, 1867).

121. On the physiologies and the *tableaux,* two closely related genres, see Nathalie Basset, "Les Physiologies au XIXe siècle et la mode," *L'Année balzacienne,* n.s. 5 (1984): 157–172; Priscilla Ferguson, *Paris as Revolution* (Berkeley: University of California Press, 1994), chaps. 2 and 3; Judith Wechsler, *A Human Comedy: Physiognomy and Caricature in Nineteenth-Century Paris* (Chicago: University of Chicago Press, 1982), pp. 13–41; Richard Terdiman, *Discourse/Counter-Discourse* (Ithaca: Cornell University Press, 1985), pp. 93–197, 163–168.

122. See Boussel, *Les Restaurants,* and Lotte, "Balzac et la table." The series "How people in Paris dine" appeared in *Le Charivari* throughout the autumn and early winter of 1845; the journal had touched on the same topic a decade earlier, see *Le Charivari,* Nov. 21, 1836. See also *La Mode,* Dec. 21, 1839; *La Caricature provisoire,* June 23, 1839.

123. Arago, *Comme on dîne à Paris; La France,* May 16, 1843.

124. Charles Dupeuty and Cormon, *Les Cuisines parisiennes* (Paris: Tresse, 1843); for reviews, see *Le Charivari,* May 18, 1843, and *Le Journal des Débats,* May 22, 1843, p. 4.

125. Antoine Caillot, *Mémoires pour servir à l'histoire des moeurs et usages des français* (Paris: Dauvin, 1827), vol. 1, p. 357.

126. Arago, *Comme on dîne à Paris,* pp. 34, 66–72.

127. In the two eighteenth-century plays that have protagonists named "Restaurant," an older male figure, husband to the female embodiment of the "old cuisine," is named "Gargotin." See *L'Ancienne et nouvelle cuisine,* B.N. mss n.a.f. 2862, and *Arlequin, restaurateur aux Porcherons,* B.N. mss n.a.f. 2866. François Gasnault, *Guinguettes et lorettes* (Paris: Aubier, 1986).

128. The case concerned a property in the Palais Royal, where one tenant's lease

granted him the right to operate only a café, and the neighboring tenant had the exclusive right to run a restaurant. The latter brought suit against the former, claiming that his neighbor's expanded lunch menu violated the definition of a café. In court, the restaurateur's lawyer brandished the café's menu, declaiming, "Here, Gentlemen of the jury, is the menu! I have counted the dishes: there are 120 of them!" *Gazette des tribunaux,* Nov. 26, 1830, pp. 85–86. For discussions of the café-restaurant, see Merville, "La Vie de café," in *Paris, ou le Livre de Cent-et-un,* vol. 9, p. 216; *Nouveaux tableaux de Paris* (Paris: Pillet, 1828), vol. 1, p. 63; *Vie publique et privée des français* (Paris: Sigault, 1826), vol. 1, p. 366; De Kock, "Les Restaurans et les cartes de restaurateurs," pp. 63–65.

129. *Physiologie des cafés de Paris* (Paris: Desloges, 1841), pp. 50–57; see also James Rousseau, "Les Cafés et les estaminets," *Nouveau tableau de Paris,* vol. 4, p. 53. For the decision in the case of the café-restaurant illegally turned *estaminet,* see *Gazette des tribunaux,* Dec. 29, 1837, p. 222. The courts also decided on a case concerning the different ways of serving coffee (a *régal* was officially defined as a full demi-tasse, four pieces of sugar and a shot of brandy, while a *gloria* was slightly less than a full demi-tasse, only two pieces of sugar, and a shot of brandy); see *Gazette des tribunaux,* July 20, 1844, p. 927.

130. Jewett, *Passages,* vol. 1, p. 297; Charles de Forster, *Quinze ans à Paris* (Paris: Firmin Didot, 1848), vol. 1, p. 97; *L'Eclaireur des barrières* (Paris: Dépôt générale, 1841), p. 34; *Le Constitutionnel,* Feb. 20, 1835 (advertisement for "le nouveau restaurant du petit Véry à 18 sous par tête"). The owner of the original, rue-Montorgeuil, Rocher de Cancale went to court several times in the 1830s and 1840s to defend his monopoly of the name, see *Gazette des tribunaux,* Dec. 2, 1836, p. 105; Feb. 14, 1840, p. 369; Aug. 30, 1841, p. 1153. A wedding gala was described as taking place "at Lesce's, the Véfour of one of the city barriers," *Le Droit,* Mar. 15, 1838, p. 2979; theft was a problem at "some Véry's in the suburbs," *Gazette des tribunaux,* Feb. 3, 1839, p. 343.

131. *L'Entr'acte,* April 6, 1838; *Journal de Paris,* May 5, 1818, p. 1.

132. Pascal Ory, "La Gastronomie," in Pierre Nora, ed., *Les Lieux de mémoire,* part 3, vol. 2, *Les France: Traditions* (Paris: Gallimard, 1992), pp. 823–853, quotation from p. 824. For the definition of a "dominant discourse" as that which "goes without saying," see Terdiman, *Discourse/Counter-discourse,* p. 61.

8. Hiding in Restaurants

1. Xavier and Duvert, *Les Cabinets particuliers* (Paris: Barba, 1832); *Journal des Débats,* Oct. 29, 1832, p. 1. According to *Le Corsaire's* theater listings, *Les Cabinets particuliers* opened on October 23, 1832, and stayed in the repertory through mid-February, though daily performances ended in January.

According to that newspaper, *Les Cabinets* was a "necessary" part of the Vaudeville's holiday-season offerings (*Le Corsaire*, Dec. 14, 1832, p. 3).

2. *Le Corsaire*, Oct. 24, 1832, p. 2. Another reviewer wondered whether the audience was laughing at the play, or vice versa; *Le National*, Oct. 29, 1832, p. 2.

3. Louis Sébastien Mercier, *Le Nouveau Paris* (Paris: Fuchs, 1798), vol. 3, p. 173.

4. A 1832 decision of the Cour Royal reminded café-keepers, caterers *(traiteurs)*, and tavern-keepers that they were not allowed to have private rooms; see *Gazette des tribunaux*, March 25, 1832, p. 540.

5. Martha Amory, *The Wedding Journey of Charles and Martha Babcock Amory* (Boston, privately printed, 1922), pp. 19–20.

6. F. Hervé, *How to Enjoy Paris in 1842* (Paris: Amyot, 1842), pp. 105–106.

7. A.N. Min. Cen. XXII-86 (Oct. 23, 1792), VII-535 (Frimaire 22, Year V [Dec. 12, 1796]).

8. A.N. Min. Cen. XLVI-693 (May 25, 1811), XVI-981 (Dec. 3, 1810).

9. Robert's Palais-Royal restaurant had a billiard room on the same floor as the cabinets; A.N. Min. Cen. VII-535 (Frimaire 22, Year V [Dec. 12, 1796]). The Restaurant Dagneaux advertised the separate entrance to its cabinets; see *Le Corsaire*, Dec. 13, 1829, p. 4.

10. For cases of suicide in a restaurant cabinet, see A.N. F⁷ 3830 (Nivôse 15, Year X [Jan. 4, 1802]); *Cabinet de lecteur*, Oct. 29, 1834, p. 8; Frances Trollope, *Paris and the Parisians* (New York: Harper, 1836), pp. 196–197. It is unclear whether the murder of a lingerie merchant by her lover, a Russian servant, happened in a cabinet or in the restaurant's main salon; A.N. F⁷ 3835 (Feb. 3, 1811).

11. *Scènes de jour et de nuit au Palais Royal* (Paris: Mien, 1830), p. 68. Similar references to restaurant cabinets are commonplace in this era; see, for example, H. Chaussier, *Le Gros lot, ou une journée de Jocrisse au Palais Egalité* (Paris: Roux, 1801), pp. 127–128; Marant, *Tout Paris en vaudevilles* (Paris: Barba, 1801), pp. 166–168; L***, *Paris et ses modes, ou les soirées parisiennes* (Paris: Michelet, 1803), p. 175; Horace Raisson, *Code gourmand* (Paris: A. Dupont, 1827), p. 121.

12. One recent analysis argues that Mayeux, though a "deformed dwarf," was a "hero of the people"; see Elizabeth Menon, "The Image that Speaks: The Sign of M. Mayeux in the Art and Literature of the July Monarchy," in Petra ten-Doesschate Chu and Gabriel Weisberg, eds., *The Popularization of Images: Visual Culture under the July Monarchy* (Princeton: Princeton University Press, 1994), pp. 37–57; Gabriel Weisberg, "The Coded Image: Agitation in Aspects of Political and Social Caricature," in exhibition catalogue, *The Art of the July Monarchy* (Columbia: University of Missouri Press, 1990), pp. 148–191, especially pp. 186–189.

13. Gavarni's "Do not do unto others as you would not want done unto you," for example, depicted the interior of unlucky cabinet "number thirteen,"

where a woman hides behind an overturned table and a middle-aged man (presumably her husband or father) beats a Romantically-coiffed young man (presumably her lover); *Charivari*, Sept. 27, 1843. Gavarni's many scenes of cross-dressed Carnival festivities further reinforced the association of restaurant private rooms with scenes of transgression.

14. Eugène Scribe, *Philibert marié*, in *Oeuvres complètes d'Eugène Scribe* (Paris: Furne, 1841), vol. 3; Frédéric de Courcy, Gustave Valpion, and Hyppolite Lassagne, *Le Restaurant ou le quart d'heure de Rabelais* (Paris: Bara, 1828); Paul de Kock, Duvert, and Varin, *Les Soupers de Carnaval* (1843); Eugène Labiche, *Un Garçon de chez Véry*, in Labiche, *Théâtre complet* (Paris: Calmann Levy, 1878), vol. 4.

15. This period is particularly well served by historians of prostitution. See Alain Corbin, *Women for Hire*, trans. Alan Sheridan (Cambridge, Mass.: Harvard University Press, 1990); Charles Berkheimer, *Figures of Ill Repute: Representing Prostitution in Nineteenth Century France* (Cambridge, Mass.: Harvard University Press, 1989); Jann Matlock, *Scenes of Seduction* (New York: Columbia University Press, 1994).

16. On the importance of the family dining room as a public reception room, see William Reddy, *The Invisible Code* (Berkeley: University of California Press, 1997), pp. 122–129, and Leora Auslander, *Taste and Power* (Berkeley: University of California Press, 1996), pp. 280–281; for the text of the law defining adultery, see Armand Dalloz, *Répertoire méthodique et alphabétique de législation, de doctrine, et de jurisprudence* (Paris: Bureau de la jurisprudence générale, 1847), "Adultère," vol. 3, pp. 336–364, especially p. 353.

17. A.N. AF IV 1470 (Mar. 7, 1793).

18. Both police reports are cited in François-Alphonse Aulard, ed., *Paris pendant la réaction thermidorienne et sous le Directoire* (Paris: L. Cerf, 1898–1902), vol. 1, p. 322, and vol. 2, pp. 182–183.

19. *Le Dîner du restaurateur, dialogue patriotique* (Paris: n.p., n.d.); A.N. AF IV 1470 (April 29, 1793).

20. The numerous turn-of-the-century singing societies have yet to find their historian, but see Arthur Dinaux, *Les Sociétés badines, bachiques littéraires et chantantes* (Paris: Bachelin, 1867); Nicolas Brazier, *Histoire des petits théâtres de Paris* (Paris: Allardin, 1838); Marie-Véronique Gauthier, "Les Sociétés chantantes au XIXe siècle" (diss., Université de Paris I, 1989).

21. *Dîners du vaudeville*, Thermidor Year VI [July-August 1798].

22. For example, see *Journal des arts, de littérature et de commerce*, Brumaire 30, Year VIII [Nov. 21, 1799], pp. 7–8; *Journal des arts*, Nov. 8, 1808, pp. 60–62; *Journal des arts*, Jan. 20, 1809, pp. 152–155; *Gazette de France*, Nov. 15, 1811, p. 1268; *Gazette de France*, Dec. 24, 1813, pp. 217–219. A selection of songs might simply be reprinted in other papers, thus further disseminating them; see *Paris, pendant l'année 1799* (London), July 31, 1799, pp. 7–14; August 8, 1799, pp. 137–152; Sept. 30, 1799, pp. 563–576. The "joy-

ous conviviality" of restaurant-based singing societies was also celebrated by *L'Arlequin, ou tableau des modes et des goûts* (Paris: Deferrière, 1799), pp. 21–22; Jean Baptiste Cuchet and Alexandre de Lagarencière, *Almanach des plaisirs de Paris* (Paris: 1815), p. 79; Pierre Jouhard, *Paris dans le XIXe siècle* (Paris: J. G. Dentu, 1809), pp. 262–265; Jean Baptiste Salgues, *De Paris, des moeurs, de la littérature, et de la philosophie* (Paris: Dentu, 1813), pp. 285–287.

23. Louis Philippe de Ségur, "Le Carnaval en carême," in his *Oeuvres complètes* (Paris: Emery, 1824–1827), vol. ?, pp. 224–231; *Le Gastronome*, April 15, 1830, p. 2; *Promenade gastronomique*, p. 66.

24. A.N. F²¹ 987, censor's report on Dartois and Gabriel, *M. Pique-assiette* (Paris: Barba, 1824).

25. In addition to the references on prostitution in note 15, see John McCormick, *Popular Theatres of Nineteenth-Century France* (London: Routledge, 1993), chap. 7; Odile Krakovitch, *Les Pièces de théâtre soumises à la censure, 1800–1830* (Paris: Archives nationales, 1982); François Gasnault, *Guinguettes et lorettes* (Paris: Aubier, 1986).

26. A.N. F⁷ 3890 (Feb. 13, 1839).

27. *Le Charivari*, Jan. 1, 1833. The seesaw was a staple of post-revolutionary French political imagery. It was especially common in depictions of the physically slight Napoleon and the bulky Louis XVIII; see B.N. Cabinet des Estampes, Tf 23. For discussion of how the pear came to represent the King, see James Cuno, "Charles Philipon and the Maison Aubert: The Business, Politics and Public of Caricature in Paris, 1820–1840" (Ph.D. diss., Harvard University, 1985); Robert J. Goldstein, *Censorship of Political Caricature in Nineteenth-Century France* (Kent, Ohio: Kent State University Press, 1989), pp. 138–145; Sandy Petrey, "Pears in History," *Representations*, 35 (1991): 52–71.

28. Accounts describing the trickery and ruses of restaurant life are ubiquitous in this period; see, among others, [J. B. Auguste d'Aldeguier], *Le Flâneur, galerie pittoresque, philosophique et morale* (Paris: Marchands de nouveauté, 1826), pp. 61–73; Auguste Luchet, *Paris, Esquisses* (Paris, 1830), pp. 300–318; Paul de Kock, "Les Restaurans et les cartes de restaurateurs," in *Nouveau tableau de Paris au XIXe siècle* (Paris: Charles Bechet, 1834), vol. 4, pp. 73–86; Frédéric Soulié, "Restaurants et gargotes," in Paul de Kock et al., *La Grande ville* (Paris, 1842), vol. 2, chap. 1.

29. De Kock, "Les Restaurans et les cartes de restaurateurs," p. 81.

30. [A. B. de Périgord], *Nouvel almanach des gourmands* (Paris: Baudouin, 1825–1829), vol. 3, pp. 20–21.

31. *Cabinet de lecture*, Dec. 20, 1839, pp. 535–536.

32. Alexandre B. L. Grimod de la Reynière, *Almanach des gourmands* (Paris, 1803–1812), vol. 2, pp. 85, 91, 281; vol. 5, p. 123. See also Joseph Berchoux, *La Gastronomie, ou l'homme des champs à table* (Paris: Giguet, 1801), p. 235.

33. *Nouvel almanach des gourmands*, vol. 3, p. 3.

34. *Caricature provisoire*, June 23, 1839, p. 2; for more references to this literature, see Chapter 7, notes 120–122.

35. *Nouvel almanach des gourmands*, vol. 3, p. 21.

36. Jacques Arago, *Comme on dîne partout* (Paris: à la librairie curieuse, 1842).

37. For these particular landmarks see, among other sources, Paul Vermond, "Les Restaurans de Paris," *Revue de Paris* (1835).

38. John Durbin, *Observations in Europe* (New York: Harpers, 1844), vol. 1, p. 38.

39. *Gazette des tribunaux*, Jan. 23, 1833, p. 283; Jan. 22, 1835, p. 280; March 21, 1836, p. 501; Oct. 11, 1837, p. 1208; Oct. 12, 1837, p. 1212; April 19, 1838, p. 611; *La France*, Mar. 21, 1838, p. 3; April 20, 1838, p. 4; *La Presse*, Sept. 21, 1839, p. 3; *Cabinet de lecture*, Sept. 15, 1939, p. 238. Robert Macaire, that arch con man of the July Monarchy, was no stranger to such ruses; see Daumier's "Robert Macaire au restaurant," *Le Charivari*, Dec. 28, 1836.

40. *Gazette des tribunaux*, Sept. 8, 1839, p. 1135.

41. For more general commentary on the anxiety of social mapping in the physiologies of this period, see Christopher Prendergast, *The Order of Mimesis* (Cambridge: Cambridge University Press, 1986), p. 93; Nicholas Green, *The Spectacle of Nature* (Manchester: Manchester University Press, 1990), pp. 28–43.

42. *Promenade gastronomique*, p. 40. Other authors also mentioned this feature of waiters' parlance; see C. Verdot, *Historiographie de la table* (Paris: Delaunay, 1833), p. 294; César Gardeton, *La Gastronomie pour rire* (Paris: Dentu, 1827), p. 113; Eugène Briffault, *Paris à table* (1846; Geneva: Slatkine, 1980), p. 181; *L'Epicurien français*, 55 (July 1810), p. 209. Another text described a novice restaurant customer who suffered "an attack of nerves" upon hearing her neighbor request that his feet be grilled and his brains, sautéed. See *La Silhouette* (1830), vol. 4, p. 24.

43. "An Englishman, in France, is surprised at never seeing a joint of meat brought to table," *Monthly Magazine, or, British Register* 38:6 (London: Richard Phillips, 1815), p. 517. I thank Stuart Semmel for this reference.

44. "Tell me what you eat, and I will tell you who you are." Versions of this, Brillat-Savarin's fourth aphorism, appeared all over the place. For example, it was: the epigraph for a report on a restaurateur's substitution of donkey meat for beef, *Le Droit*, April 14, 1838, p. 3028; the retort of a sly waiter, in De Courcy, Gustave, and Hyppolite, *Le Restaurant*, p. 12; and probably the inspiration for Grandville's wonderful "Carte vivante de restaurateur" ("The restaurant menu brought to life"). The first three of Brillat-Savarin's aphorisms ("I. The Universe would be nothing without life and everything that lives must eat. II. Animals feed; man eats; only a man of intelligence knows *how* to eat. III. The fate of nations depends on their diet.") were less commonly cited.

45. [Mangenville], *L'Art de ne jamais déjeûner chez soi* (Paris: Librairie universelle, 1827), p. 89.

46. Xavier and Duvert, *Les Cabinets particuliers*, pp. 3–5.

47. D***, *Les Numéros parisiens* (Paris: l'Imprimerie de la Vérité, 1788), p. 12; [Francis Blagdon], *Paris As it Was and As it Is* (London: C. & R. Baldwin, 1803), vol. 1, p. 453.

48. Mercier, *Le Nouveau Paris*, vol. 5, p. 75.

49. *Le Charivari*, Feb. 3, 1843.

50. *Le Constitutionnel*, May 28, 1838, p. 3; *Gazette des tribunaux*, April 9, 1838, p. 679, and May 27, 1838, p. 755; *La Quotidienne*, April 11, 1838, p. 3; *Le Temps*, April 11, 1838, p. 4921; *Le National*, April 11, 1838, p. 2; *La Presse*, April 11, 1838, p. 3. See also *Gazette des tribunaux*, July 24, 1833. There are plenty of references to this practice that predate this scandal; see, for instance, Brazier, *Histoire des petits théâtres*, vol. 2, p. 218.

51. *Le Constitutionnel*, May 28, 1838, p. 3.

52. The leftover trade has been an enduring source of fascination; see *Le Charivari*, Sept. 23, 1845; John Durbin, *Observations in Europe* (New York: Harper, 1844), vol. 1, p. 38; Charles de Forster, *Quinze ans à Paris: Paris et les parisiens* (Paris: Firmin Didot, 1848), vol. 1, p. 93; Jean-Paul Aron, "Sur les consommations avariées à Paris dans la deuxième moitié du dix-neuvième siècle," *Annales E.S.C.*, 30: 2–3 (March–June 1975), 553–562.

53. The utopian socialist Charles Fourier had offered a "scientific" perspective on this ideal, arguing that when humanity progressed from the state of "Civilization" to that of "Harmony," the polar icecaps would melt and fill the oceans with lemonade.

54. On the agricultural crisis, see Ernst Labrousse, *Aspects de la crise et de la dépression de l'économie française, 1846–1852* (La Roche-sur-Yonne: Imprimerie centrale de l'Ouest, 1956). Several prominent restaurateurs sued their ice merchant for failing to deliver during the hot summer of 1846; see *Gazette des tribunaux*, Sept. 24, 1846, p. 1457; Oct. 1, 1846, p. 1475.

55. "Robert Macaire, Restaurateur," *Le Charivari*, Nov. 13, 1836.

56. *Le Charivari*, Jan. 13, 1845; July 23, 1845; *La France*, Jan. 23, 1838, p. 3.

57. Elizabeth Childs, "Big Trouble: Daumier, Gargantua, and the Censorship of Political Caricature," *Art Journal*, 51 (Spring 1992): 26–37.

58. On the press laws and journalistic strategies for coping with them, see H. A. C. Collingham, *The July Monarchy* (London: Longman, 1988), chaps. 13–14; Reddy, *The Invisible Code*, chap. 5; Richard Terdiman, *Discourse/Counter-Discourse* (Ithaca: Cornell University Press, 1985).

59. *Le Corsaire*, Jan. 17, 1835; *Le Satan*, April 9, 1843; *Le Charivari*, April 4, 1843.

60. *Le Charivari*, March 18, 1845; a year earlier, Guizot had been "quoted" swearing that he would put down France's sword and pick up a larding-needle, *Le Charivari*, April 12, 1844.

61. Robert Gildea has claimed that the French cult of glory is a matter of salvaging stories of narrow victory from episodes of obvious defeat; see *The Past in French History* (New Haven: Yale University Press, 1994), pp. 112–165. I am

hardly persuaded that this is a peculiarly Gallic way of coping with the past, but it does at least partially describe the process by which cookery became central to definitions of French national genius.

62. *Le Charivari,* Feb. 8, 1844; *Le Charivari,* Mar. 10–13, 1845.

63. *L'Aspic,* January 1837, p. 12.

64. *Le Charivari,* Dec. 22, 1837.

65. For an early instance of this character, see the *Courrier républicain,* Prairial 1, Year V [May 18, 1797], cited in François-Alphonse Aulard, ed., *Paris pendant la réaction thermidorienne,* vol. 4, p. 122; compare Viennet, "La Vie d'un député," in *Paris ou le Livre de cent-et-un* (Paris: Ladvocat, 1831–1834), vol. 6, p. 195. Béranger's "Ventru" was sufficiently popular to provoke a sequel the following year, "Le Ventru aux élections de 1819"; see Pierre Jean de Béranger, *Oeuvres complètes* (Paris: Perrotin, 1852), vol. 1, pp. 290–293, 306–309. The literature on Béranger is extensive; on the success enjoyed by *les ventrus,* see Joseph Bernard, *Béranger et ses chansons* (Paris: Dentu, 1858), pp. 149–150; Léon Fours, *La Vie en chansons de Béranger* (Paris: Lemerre, 1930), pp. 103–104; Jean Touchard, *La Gloire de Béranger* (Paris: Armand Colin, 1968), vol. 1, pp. 216–217. See also François de Comberousse, *Le Ministériel, ou la manie des dîners* (Paris: Ladvocat, 1819), the lead characters of which are a deputy named "Ventru" and his friend, "Bascule."

66. Léon Thiessé and Eugène Balland, eds., *Lettres normandes ou correspondance politique et littéraire* (1819), pp. 58, 188.

67. Wisecracks about truffled representatives are omnipresent in these decades; see *Le Corsaire,* Jan. 23, 1826, p. 3; Mar. 1, 1827, p. 3; *La Pandore,* Jan. 21, 1826, p. 4; Mar. 15, 1827, p. 4; *Revue de Paris,* 47 (1833), p. 219; *Le Charivari,* Feb. 22, 1833; Jan. 24, 1843; Du Bouchet, *La Truffe, anecdote ministerielle de l'année 1826* (B.N. Ye 5889).

68. *Le Charivari,* Aug. 13, 1845.

69. Collingham, *The July Monarchy,* pp. 147–148; Dalloz, *Répertoire méthodique et alphabétique,* vol. 5, pp. 279–310.

70. *Le Courrier français,* Feb. 27, 1834, p. 2; *Gazette de France,* Mar. 21, 1834, p. 1.

71. The *Gazette de France* (Sept. 2, 1840, pp. 1–3) claimed that several thousand invitations were sent for the banquet at Châtillon; in Metz, reformers unable to find a single, sufficiently large, banquet hall, split among several hotel dining rooms, *Le National,* Aug. 5, 1840, p. 3. For more on the banquets of 1848 see my "A Confusion of Appetites: The Emergence of Paris Restaurant Culture, 1740–1848" (Ph.D. diss., Cornell University, 1993), pp. 279–282, 305–319.

Epilogue: Restaurants and Reverie

1. Jean-Baptiste Nougaret, *Paris metamorphosé* (Paris: Desenne, 1799), vol. 1, p. 6; *Caricature provisoire,* July 19, 1840; Frédéric Soulié, "Restaurants

et gargotes," in Paul de Kock et al., *La Grande Ville* (Paris, 1842), vol. 2, p. 21.

2. Isaac Appleton Jewett, *Passages in Foreign Travel* (Boston: Little and Brown, 1838), vol. 2, p. 12; N. Parker Willis, *Pencillings by the Way* (New York: Charles Scribner, 1852), p. 39.

3. *Promenade gastronomique dans Paris, par un Amateur* (Paris: Dondey Dupré, 1833), p. 69.

4. *La France,* Sept. 23, 1839, p. 4. Compare the story of two contented male restaurant patrons whose meal is interrupted by the arrival of the haggard, obviously impoverished wife of one of them; *Le Parisien,* Oct. 27, 1842, p. 2.

5. Pierre Jouhard, *Paris dans le XIXe siècle* (Paris: Dentu, 1809), p. 57.

6. *Promenade gastronomique dans Paris,* pp. 74–75. Carême, by far the most famous chef and cookbook author of the first half of the nineteenth century, prefaced his books with calls for martyrdom; no sacrifice was too great for the chef's art and to die famous, as well as young, was the best for which a cook could hope. See Marie-Antonin Carême, *L'Art de la cuisine française au dix-neuvième siècle* (Paris: Comptoir des Imprimeurs-Unis, 1847), vol. 2, p. vii.

7. *Le Gastronome,* April 15, 1830, p. 2. Several periodicals were jointly devoted to restaurants and theaters, or were theater programs meant to be inserted into booklet-style menus; see *L'Entremets* (1838), *Le Moniteur des restaurans* (1843), *L'Entr'acte du gastronome* (1851).

8. For accounts of this "most peculiar incident," see *Le Journal des Débats,* Sept. 15, 1839, p. 2; *Le Constitutionnel,* Sept. 15, 1839, p. 3; *Le National,* Sept. 15, 1839, p. 3; *Gazette des tribunaux,* Sept. 15, 1839, pp. 1158–1159; and Gaetan Niépovié, *Etudes physiologiques sur les grands métropoles de l'Europe occidental: Paris* (Paris: Charles Gosselin, 1840), p. 77.

9. *La France,* Oct. 30, 1839, p. 4; *La Quotidienne,* Oct. 30, 1839, p. 3; *Le Constitutionnel,* Oct. 30, 1839, p. 4; *Journal des débats,* Oct. 30, 1839, p. 4; *Gazette des tribunaux,* Oct. 30, 1839, p. 1310.

10. Reportedly, Paris restaurants saw a spate of "copycat" mirror-threatening acts in the days that followed Robert's arrest; see *Gazette des tribunaux,* Sept. 20, 1839, p. 1175.

11. *Gazette des tribunaux,* Oct. 30, 1839, p. 1310.

12. Honoré de Balzac, *Illusions perdues* (1837–1843; Paris: Gallimard, 1972), pp. 179–185.

13. A.N. Min. Cen. XIV-800 (April 8, 1843); *Journal des débats,* Jan. 2, 1843. For an account of the legal conflict that arose over advertising the name, see *Gazette des tribunaux,* June 29, 1842, p. 1003.

14. *Journal de Paris,* Aug. 11, 1817, p. 1; A.N. Min. Cen. XIV (Oct. 28, 1856); *Le Petit parisien,* April 27–29, 1892, p. 1.

15. "Restaurants are tedious if one lives in them from necessity, but they are not without their delights for those who are not in the habit"; Etienne de Jouy, *L'Hermite de la Chaussée d'Antin,* no. 66 (*Gazette de France,* June 28, 1812), reprinted in *Oeuvres complètes d'Etienne Jouy* (Paris: Jules Didot,

1823), vol. 2, p. 256. Anglo-American travelers often remarked that Parisians did not have "homes," see John Durbin, *Observations in Europe* (New York: Harper and Brothers, 1844), vol. 1, p. 39; Henry Matthews, *Diary of an Invalid,* 2nd ed. (London: John Murray, 1820), p. 480; further references in Chapter 7.

16. Louis Véron, *Mémoires d'un bourgeois de Paris* (Paris: de Gonet, 1853), vol. 2, p. 2.

17. Caroline M. Kirkland, *Holidays Abroad; or Europe from the West* (New York: Baker and Scribner, 1849), vol. 1, p. 133.

18. Letter to Rufus Griswold (Jan. 21, 1843), Detroit Public Library, quoted in Sandra Zagarell, "Introduction," in Caroline Kirkland, *A New Home, Who'll Follow? Or Glimpses of Western Life* (New Brunswick, N.J.: Rutgers University Press, 1990), p. xvii.

19. Kirkland, *Holidays Abroad,* vol. 1, p. 134.

20. *Gazette des tribunaux,* Dec 2, 1836, p. 105; Feb. 14, 1840, p. 369; Aug. 30, 1841, p. 1153.

21. M. Vimont, "Le Rocher de Cancale, notes artistiques," in *Le Centre de Paris* (bulletin de la société historique des 1re et 2me arrondissements), 1921, pp. 211–213.

22. Daumier's oeuvre included numerous "men outside restaurants," several of whom were featured in *Le Charivari*'s series, "How Paris Eats." See the wedding "guest" parasite, *Le Charivari,* Dec. 25, 1841, and the "Imperial prefect" who decides to change ruses and claim to be a banker who has forgotten his wallet, *Le Charivari,* Dec. 28, 1841.

23. Auguste Luchet, *Paris esquisses* (Paris: Barbezat, 1830), pp. 269–270. There is a strikingly similar description in Lanfranchi (Lamothe-Lagnon), *Voyage à Paris* (Paris: Lepetit, 1830), pp. 182–183.

Acknowledgments

Versions of this book have been with me for rather a long time now, and so it is not surprising that many people and institutions have become involved with it. I owe them much. I am especially indebted to Simon Schama, the supervisor of my Ph.D. dissertation. Since it was his interest in my undergraduate work that prompted me to become a historian, I have more than fifteen years' of ebullient support and inspiration for which to thank him. Dominick LaCapra has also been unfailingly supportive of this project, and James Boon deserves many thanks for his exuberance and generosity. Alison Casarett, Hilary Ford, and Miranda Massie also played major roles in making my graduate career a pleasant one.

Many friends and colleagues have read parts of this work or have offered help in other ways. Robert Darnton, Caroline Ford, Raymond Grew, Patrice Higonnet, Colin Jones, Jann Matlock, and several anonymous readers have all read sections of the text, providing helpful comments and useful references. Pushing the project in myriad directions, their comments have helped me to realize fully that a book about restaurants could be a book about nearly everything. Many friends from graduate school have also read drafts; I especially thank Ron Schechter for his cheery enthusiasm and Jim Livesey for his measured criticism. Michael Cooperson has distinguished himself by his rare talent for the translation of doggerel. John Rabinowitz and Tony Coretto have had less academic, but no less helpful, responses to this manuscript. Special thanks, for their more than generous hospitality, go to Tom and Martha Sieniewicz in Cambridge, and to Mary and Philip Hyman in Paris.

While I was conducting my dissertation research, Jean-Louis Flandrin and Jean-Robert Pitte both gave me opportunities to air my early thoughts about restaurants. Since then, I have presented sections of this work at numerous conferences, seminars, and workshops, always gaining from the experience. The Voltaire Foundation/International Society for Eighteenth-Century Studies East-West symposium on "the public" was an especially valuable week, for which I would again like to thank Robert Darnton. I am also grateful to all those who responded with questions, criticisms, and comments when I presented sections of this material to the Society for French Historical Studies, the Conference on Nineteenth-Century

317

French Studies, the Group for Early Modern Cultural Studies, the Cornell University graduate history seminar, the Harvard Center for European Studies, the Modern France seminar at the Institute for Historical Research, the social history seminar at the University of Warwick, and the Enlightenment seminar at Oxford. These presentations all grew from research conducted in numerous archives and libraries. I would especially like to thank the helpful staff members at the Bibliothèque Nationale, the Bibliothèque Historique de la Ville de Paris, the Archives Nationales, the Archives de la Seine, the British Library, and the Harvard University Libraries. The breadth of this book's topic required many papers and much research, but they would not have been possible without generous material support as well. For financial assistance I would like to thank Cornell University, the Olin Foundation, the Cultural Services branch of the French Embassy, the Voltaire Foundation, the History Department of University College London, the Michigan Society of Fellows, the University of Michigan Department of Romance Languages and Literatures, the Paris branch of the American Institute of Wine and Food, and the Society for French Historical Studies.

The British Library and the Bibliothèque Nationale have generously allowed me to reproduce images in their collections. Portions of Chapters 2 and 3 appeared in an earlier form in my "Rousseau in the Restaurant," *Common Knowledge,* Spring 1996, pp. 92–108; I thank Oxford University Press for permission to reuse that material here. To Lindsay Waters and Mary Ellen Geer, my editors at Harvard University Press, I owe much indeed.

A few trusted individuals have read this manuscript almost as often as I have written it; "thank you" seems inadequate recompense for their efforts, but it (and this finished book) will have to suffice. Stuart Semmel read many early versions and was unfailingly cheerful, observant, and astute—a rare combination. Elizabeth Ezra responded to multiple drafts with intelligence, energy, wit, and good measures of common sense and stubborn faith. David Polly has patiently endured countless conversations about Rousseau, restaurants, or Roze de Chantoiseau; our marriage is many, many other things as well, but for this book it has been an especially happy demonstration of the virtues of interdisciplinary dialogue. My parents, siblings, and nephews have been with me even longer than this project has been, and have always been sources of comfort, sustenance, and good humor. This book is dedicated to them.

Index